BIBLIOTHERAPY

and

Its Widening Applications

by

Eleanor Frances Brown

The Scarecrow Press, Inc.

Metuchen, N.J.   1975

Library of Congress Cataloging in Publication Data

Brown, Eleanor Frances, 1908-
    Bibliotherapy and its widening applications.

    Bibliography: p.
    Includes index.
    1. Bibliotherapy. I. Title. [DNLM 1. Bib-
liotherapy. WM450 B787b]
RC489. B48B76   615'. 8516   74-28187
ISBN 0-8108-0782-3

FOR SYLVIA FOSTER
WHOSE UNDERSTANDING OF PEOPLE AND BOOKS
WOULD MAKE HER A SPLENDID BIBLIOTHERAPIST
IF SHE WERE SO MINDED

PREFACE

This book, like those I have written on other subjects, attempts to bring together into one volume a synthesis of opinions, developmental steps, basic considerations, and techniques--in this case, of the science and art of bibliotherapy. It is an overview, an effort to include the history, the changing status, and the practical applications.

While much has been written on the subject, most of it has been in periodicals, and some of it highly technical. Other material has appeared in individual chapters of books on librarianship or psychiatry, in symposia, proceedings of conferences, dissertations, or manuals on specialized aspects of the subject.

Since bibliotherapy is comparatively young in its development, certain aspects are highly controversial. It is still too early for final pronouncements. Such a time may indeed never arrive, for research and development in this field, as in many others, should continue as long as man exists.

The only area in which I have veered from reporting to personal opinion is in stating that according to definition and practice, bibliotherapy in this modern period seems to fall into two distinct types: the medical and the non-medical. I have chosen to designate these as the science of bibliotherapy and the art of bibliotherapy. Others may disagree. Many still do not acknowledge the status of bibliotherapy as a science, but I believe it has reached a stage where the medical aspect is legitimately so-called. Typifying non-medical bibliotherapy as an art is merely a way of distinguishing it from the medical or clinical practice associated with hospitals and the medical profession. As I have indicated in the final chapter, however, the exact terms used do not seem as important as proper training and the use of skillful and effective techniques in practice. To achieve these there must be recognition, and there is no doubt that bibliotherapy needs wider acceptance, despite the giant strides which have been taken in the last thirty years.

Standard terminology is highly to be desired, and it is one of the goals of those working actively in the field.

Although much of the literature has been anecdotal, relating case histories--a fact which has been criticized often-- the volume of case histories showing the therapeutic effects of reading under controlled conditions where the effects of the accompanying forms of treatment were known, has now grown to such proportions that their value in proving the efficacy of bibliotherapy cannot be minimized. Library Literature and Index Medicus will lead the reader to so many such case studies that only a representative group covering a variety of problems has been included in this volume.

This work attempts to reach the non-technical worker, counselor, parole officer, juvenile officer, social case worker, nurse, teacher, guidance director; librarians and officials of correctional institutions, recreational directors in nursing and rest homes for the elderly, Outreach library staff, Vista volunteers--anyone, in fact, who would like to know more about the subject of bibliotherapy but does not want to become bogged down in psychiatric and other medical terminology.

This author makes no pretense of being an authority on the subject. Her job has been to gather together related material, quote opinions, organize, and generally provide an overview of the material, to save the time and effort of those who would otherwise have to search through countless books, periodicals, and theses to gain the same knowledge. This volume is a product of the reportorial approach, with little or no attempt to criticize or evaluate. For those who wish to read widely, appropriate reading lists are provided for the bibliotherapist, and references are given to all sources not otherwise identified.

Constant reference is made in the literature and among bibliotherapists to the lack of scientific research in bibliotherapy. The very people who are in institutional libraries or other positions of advantage where bibliotherapy is being used seem to be the most concerned in this regard, so the question arises: Why do not these practitioners or experts in the field conduct such research? If time and money are the problems, these are the people who should be approaching foundations and philanthropists to initiate such studies. Perhaps we are all expecting too much too soon. The cooperation of many more physicians, psychiatrists, and institutional boards and directors may be necessary before a considerable volume of research can be undertaken.

In 1969 Margaret E. Monroe, Head of the Library School at the University of Wisconsin said, in an article in the ALA Bulletin, "The door is just beginning to open on the potential of bibliotherapy. The climate is right to undertake an elaboration of the field."[1]

Doctoral and advanced master's degree library science students could find research experiments a fruitful and fascinating field.

---

1. Monroe, Margaret E. "Services in Hospital and Institution Libraries." ALA Bulletin, v. 63, no. 8, Oct. 1969, p. 1282.

CONTENTS

ix

CHAPTER 1

DEFINITIONS:
THE TWO ASPECTS OF BIBLIOTHERAPY

In spite of marked progress in the last decade, the value of bibliotherapy is still not as widely recognized as the practical results of its use would justify.

The special application of reading to medical and non-medical personal problems requires techniques and approaches which are different from the usual type of reader guidance provided by school, public, and special librarians. It also requires a background of training which is not being emphasized in most of the nation's schools of librarianship.

Exactly what is this discipline that has such great potentiality and requires such skill in its application? Webster's Third defines it as "the use of selected reading materials as therapeutic adjuvants in medicine and in psychiatry; guidance in the solution of personal problems through directed reading."

Actually this definition places bibliotherapy upon two levels. The first is reading associated with medicine and psychiatry; the second or non-medical aspect suggests that reading guidance as given by public librarians, school librarians, social workers, juvenile officers, counselors, the clergy, and other interested individuals in an effort to help others solve personal problems may also, under certain conditions, be regarded as bibliotherapy, even though there is no physical or mental disorder requiring medical or psychiatric help.

If we accept this broader definition, bibliotherapy has a much wider application to human life, and the non-medical aspects may well outweigh the medical in extent and total value. Let us examine a few more definitions:

David C. Chambers, M.D., Director of Physical

1

Medicine, Queen of Angels Hospital, Los Angeles, gave this definition from the medical standpoint: "Supportive or specific treatment utilizing reading material."

Sister M. Bridget, CST, on the other hand, says, "Bibliotherapy is the non-medical use of books as therapeutic aids in the emotional stabilization of unhappy and worried children in a normal classroom environment, providing the child with books which concern problems similar to his own and letting him abreact to them." In this definition we have the non-medical or guidance approach as teachers and librarians apply it to children.

In "The Library as a Therapeutic Experience," an article in the Bulletin of the Medical Library Association, July, 1959, Ruth Darrin, editor, characterizes bibliotherapy as "a treatment of illness by the use of books and other reading materials."[1]

Margaret C. Hannigan, librarian of the Patients' Library, National Institute of Health, Bethesda, Maryland, comments, "To me, it seems appropriate that bibliotherapy has become the accepted term for describing the help and guidance which librarians in institutions are in a position to give their patrons.... It is our ordinary technique in giving library service to our charges, a technique acquired through training and experience which provides an ever-increasing knowledge of books on the one hand and an ever-growing understanding of people on the other. In a stricter sense bibliotherapy refers to the use of books as prescribed reading in the treatment of patients."[2]

Dorlands Illustrated Medical Dictionary contained its first definition of the term in 1941. It was short and quite limited: "The employment of books and the reading of them in the treatment of nervous diseases."

The 1966 Random House Dictionary contains a very general and somewhat ambiguous meaning: "The use of reading as an ameliorative adjunct to therapy." To be more specific it is necessary to determine how "therapy" is defined. We find it to be "treatment of illness or a disability." Thus a more recent definition than Webster's tends again to restrict the term bibliotherapy to an association with medical science.

Dr. Lore Hirsch has said that friendship, love, a

good meal, some extra money, or what not, might be called therapy. These may be therapeutic, but if they come about spontaneously without prescription, or without deliberate intention to improve the patient's health, they would not be called therapy.

Thus a definite book or books recommended by a specific person, and the presence of a physical, mental, or emotional problem are the basic ingredients which distinguish bibliotherapy from random reading which may have a good effect but does not involve a suggestion or prescription of such reading by another individual.

An important precept is that the reading material must be carefully selected. A casual recommendation of a book to a friend, with no problem apparent and no motive other than to further the friend's enjoyment, does not constitute bibliotherapy.

In "Bibliotherapy: A Critique of the Literature,"[3] Armando R. Favazza, Sr., then a medical student, says, "Most of the literature on bibliotherapy has been non-scientific because of the too broad use of the term." Mr. Favazza proposed that for the sake of clarification, bibliotherapy be defined as "a program of selected activity involving reading materials, which is planned, conducted, and controlled under the guidance of a physician as treatment for psychiatric patients, and which uses, if needed, the assistance of a trained librarian."

This, of course, constitutes the purely medical viewpoint. It limits bibliotherapy in one sense but broadens it in another, in that "selected activity" can fall into three categories: books prescribed for a patient, books selected by a patient, and group discussion of books.

Interestingly, Mr. Favazza goes on to state a very relevant fact: the librarian states his pre-eminence in bibliotherapy, the social worker his, the psychologist his, the physician his, the nurse hers, according to which journal one happens to read. How much more satisfactory it would be, and undoubtedly more effective, if each could recognize that all share in the process and all work together rather than each emphasizing his own importance.

The prescription of reading in the treatment of actual mental or physical illness may well be regarded as the science of bibliotherapy; whereas the attempt to remedy personality defects or help an individual solve personal problems through the proper reading suggestions given by a librarian, teacher, guidance counselor, or other individual outside the medical field, can be regarded as the art of bibliotherapy. The latter is not based upon clinical diagnosis, but upon sensitive discernment on the part of librarians, teachers, or counselors, which enables them to detect an individual's emotional or psychological need; and upon a broad enough knowledge of books to be able to suggest the kind of reading or the specific books or articles that will be of the most help to a particular individual.

The science of bibliotherapy requires cooperative effort on the part of doctors, nurses, and librarians. The doctors and nurses are not reading specialists and their knowledge of books is usually not as broad as that of the practicing librarian. The art of bibliotherapy, on the other hand, can be practiced by a single individual who understands people thoroughly, has a wide knowledge of books, and is very sympathetic to human needs. This could be a librarian, teacher, guidance counselor, welfare worker--almost anyone who possesses these attributes, plus another highly important requirement: the ability to suggest the right reading material tactfully and without being too obvious. There is no question but that these are special skills, not possessed by everyone. Practicing bibliotherapy cannot be made to appear too simple, or it is possible to do more harm than good.

To clarify the distinction between the art and science of bibliotherapy, concrete examples of each may be in order.

A public librarian knows that a certain patron is facing with dread the thought of retirement from active work. The patron likes the librarian and has talked to her about his problem a number of times. The almost morbid fear that he has of the day he must leave the company where he has worked for some thirty years has made him lose sleep and lose weight; he has become depressed and generally a problem to his wife and the rest of his family. He complains of not feeling well and is seeing a doctor frequently, but the doctor cannot find any physical illness to account for the insomnia and weight loss.

The librarian knows of several books in the library collection which may help the reader make a better psychological adjustment to retirement, both before and after. She also knows, from his conversations with her, that this patron will never be happy unless he is engaged in some sort of challenging activity. He lives on a busy road near a fishing stream and is an avid fisherman. He tells her he will fish to his heart's content when he retires, but even that can become monotonous and is not exactly a creative activity. He prefers fly fishing, although he is good at all kinds.

The librarian suggests a book on fly-tying, one on raising earthworms, and a booklet on repairing fishing poles, especially the rewinding of ferrules, innocently suggesting that since he will have so much time to fish he may want to do some of these things for himself.

After reading the suggested books there is a decided change in the man's attitude. He tells the librarian in cheerful tones that he may just build a little shop down by the road where the fishermen pass, and start a small business mending rods, selling lures and other tackle, tying flies, and repairing reels. He is very mechanical and has a wide knowledge of the area in which he lives and its fishing potentialities. "And, " he tells the librarian, with an added gleam in his eye, "I might even offer fishing guide service for strangers or tourists. This retirement idea had me really bugged. I could just see myself doing nothing but fishing or sitting in a rocking chair. Thanks for the books and for listening to my troubles and ideas. "

The man held to his new plans and created a lucrative business which he thoroughly enjoyed. Here is a clear case where a man was helped mentally and physically by books and by a librarian who knew her people as well as her books. The prescription was books, but it was not given by a doctor in his office, in a hospital, nor in a retirement or nursing home. It was simply given by a good librarian in her role as reader's advisor. Yet it was not the usual casual reader-advisor relationship. It involved a greater acquaintance with the patron as an individual, a knowledge of his interests, and a special effort to find just the right books to recommend. This case may be considered an example of the practice of the art of bibliotherapy.

By contrast, the following would be regarded as a case, though somewhat extreme, of the science of bibliotherapy. This case study was reported by John S. Pearson in his article, "Bibliotherapy and the Clinical Psychologist, " in Library Trends. [4]

A man whom we shall call Richard X, aged 23
years, was a patient in a psychiatric hospital for
help in overcoming an addiction to drugs originally
prescribed for pain in his leg.   The physical problem arose after an accidental injury which involved
litigation and compensation.   Although doctors could
find no organic causes for the pain, he had had
several operations and had become disabled. Eventually he gave up his work as a salesman.

Richard X seemed charming and intelligent. He
usually selected Life or Look and occasionally a
comic book, but he accepted other books suggested
by the hospital librarian on her visits to the psychiatric unit, and later remarked upon their value
or lack of it in helping him to understand his own
problems.

However, when the first formal psychological
examination was given some days after admittance,
it was discovered to everyone's surprise that the
patient could not read or write, except to recognize
and sign his own name.   He had set up a chain of
remarkable deceptions to conceal this fact for many
years from his friends, business associates, employers, even his wife.   As a child of unstable
itinerant parents, he had never had the opportunity
to obtain even an elementary education.

When Richard X became cognizant of the importance of 'book learning, ' pride and habit kept him
from confessing his deficiency and doing something
about it.   He carried a broken pair of glasses as
an excuse to get others to read necessary information to him; he complained of eyestrain, or had any
one of a dozen other plausible excuses for getting
someone else to do whatever reading was essential.
He was very clever in fitting the cause to the immediate situation and so had managed to fool everyone completely.

Once the problem was uncovered, the hospital
behavior of Richard X changed markedly.   At first
he begged that his secret be kept from all but the
examining doctor, but when he was made to see
that this 'deficiency' was the root of his entire
problem he began to compulsively confess his inability to read to anyone who would listen.   When
he found that others were really sympathetic and
accepted him as a worthwhile person even though
he could not read, he gradually became more re-

laxed and matter of fact about the matter.

Since the psychological testing had shown that Richard X had better-than-average general intelligence and there were no physical visual obstacles for learning reading, a program of tutored reading instruction was begun, and the patient entered the world of books with great enthusiasm.

A follow-up program after Richard X left the hospital indicated that the experience of unburdening his secret and becoming a genuine reader had caused a dramatic change in his life. He found a new job, and both his leg pain and his dependence upon drugs ceased to be a problem, at least as far as follow-up checkups indicated.

Here is a case where psychiatrist and hospital librarian working together, with an opportunity to study the patient and his behavior, to communicate back and forth between medical staff and librarian, and having the instructional tools needed, as well as the right books to offer when reading was established, worked a definite change in the life of an individual, in a hospital setting and with clinical and medical aid.

Evalene P. Jackson in her article, "Reading Guidance: a Tentative Approach to Theory,"[5] chooses to distinguish the two types of bibliotherapy as "explicit" and "implicit." The explicit type is administered by a psychotherapist, with the hospital librarian frequently involved. The implicit type she characterizes as "a resource of the culture, present under some circumstances for those who can find and make use of it. The reader's adviser may provide guidance in the implicit sense." Thus the distinction between the two types of bibliotherapy has already been made, but this writer finds it more satisfactory to use "science" and "art" as distinguishing terms, since medicine is so definitely a science, whereas the ability to practice the art of bibliotherapy does not have definite medical connection and is a general art or skill.

The ideal situation would be, in the case of those who require institutional care for mental or physical illness, to have available the science of bibliotherapy while the patient is under treatment by the medical profession, with a follow-up of the reader and guidance art of bibliotherapy when the patient returns to a normal social environment. This would mean cooperation between doctors and public librarians or whatever other non-medical individuals were involved. In

short, the most effective bibliotherapy is a combination of
both types when hospitalization or medical treatment is the
starting point.   The medical profession can provide the public
or school librarian with the background information and understanding of the patient's problems needed so that she can
do an effective job.   The librarian supplies the wide general
knowledge about books which most doctors have not had the
time to acquire.   While we have seen many successful team
efforts toward rehabilitation through the science of bibliotherapy, with doctors, nurses, and hospital librarians working together, we have seen too few examples of a continuing
post-hospital program of bibliotherapy accomplished by voluntary cooperation between the medical profession, public librarians, school librarians, social workers, parole officers,
the clergy, or other counselors.

As an example of this problem, when the writer was
head of a public library in a town where one of the state
mental hospitals was located, it was customary to bring
groups of patients ready to be released to their own communities for a tour of the library, with the emphasis on the
various services and materials likely to be available in their
own home towns.   This was a regular part of their reorien-
tation to society, and it was to the credit of this particular
institution that it arranged for such tours.   However--and
this is the big problem--unless the local libraries involved
are alerted to the patient's return, what has been done in his
reading program previously, and what his general problem
has been, they cannot do a proper job of reading guidance.
If the community is a small one the returned patient may be
a former patron or someone the librarian already knows.   In
that case, persuading him to become a regular library user
may not be difficult.   Since returned patients usually require
a period of readjustment, employment is often not immediate.
The library may help to fill otherwise lonely hours and to
avoid periods of depression.

One school of thought insists on restricting bibliotherapy to "a program of selected activity involving reading
materials, planned, conducted, and controlled as treatment
under the guidance of the physician for emotional and other
problems.   It must be administered by a skilled, professionally trained librarian within the prescribed purposes and
goals."   The dynamic factors in this program are the relationships between doctor and patient, librarian and doctor,
and librarian and patient; the patient's reactions to the reading program, and the librarian's reporting back to the doctor

on these reactions and responses. [6] The doctor can then interpret, evaluate, and issue directions for further steps in the program. Obviously this is the scientific aspect. To put it more simply: a medical staff member requests a specific title or type of reading for a patient; the librarian fills the request, observes the patient, reports back to the medical staff any reactions, comments, or changes in attitude associated with the reading.

Sadie P. Delaney, one of the early American practitioners of bibliotherapy, was at first a public librarian, but she defined the term in 1938 as "The treatment of a patient through selected reading, " one of the most concise and apt definitions to be found anywhere, if one interprets "patient" as being anyone with a physical, mental, or emotional problem, and not necessarily hospitalized, institutionalized or under medical treatment. Mrs. Delaney's use of the word "patient" arose from the fact that she found her greatest opportunity to use bibliotherapy after she became hospital librarian at Tuskegee, Alabama.

It was not until 1961 that a definition of the term appeared in a general standard dictionary. At that time Webster's Third New International Dictionary included the twofold definition stated at the beginning of this chapter. This definition was later officially accepted by the Association of Hospital and Institution Libraries. At that same time the association also accepted the definition of "therapy" as "treatment of the maladjusted to further their restoration to society, a force to relieve social tension. "

Reading used to help children has been variously called "bibliotherapy, " "therapeutic reading, " and "biblioprophylaxis. "

In summary, then, the "science" of bibliotherapy requires:

1. Personnel involved as follows: Patient; Member or members of the medical profession; Librarian.

2. Thorough analysis of patient's condition and needs by the medical personnel.

3. Reading prescription by the medical personnel.

4. An adequate and varied collection of books,

periodicals, and other library materials housed
in a library room or building.

5. Establishment of the proper rapport between librarian and medical staff so that doctors will
use bibliotherapy in their treatment programs.

6. Establishment of rapport between librarian and
patient so that patient has confidence in the librarian and will use the library.

7. The writing of reports on the patient's reaction
by the librarian and delivery of them to the
medical personnel.

If we accept the concept that bibliotherapy as an art
may be practiced by those who know books and people excep-
tionally well, the following will be required.

1. Personnel involved as follows: A reader with a
mental or physical problem; a sympathetic and
unusually perceptive individual with a broad
knowledge of human psychology and books.

2. A collection of books varied enough to provide
help with most problems likely to be encountered.

3. Establishment of a good rapport between reader
and librarian in order that his or her reading
advice may be sought and followed.

The art of bibliotherapy is clearly less complicated
than the science.   There are those who will maintain that including the "art" aspect broadens the definition to cover almost all reader advisor activity.   However, the last part of
the word itself, "therapy, " limits the field.   It means, as
indicated earlier, "the treatment of an illness or disability. "
Thus the librarian or readers' advisor who finds a good book
on carpentry for a man who wants to build a house is not
engaged in bibliotherapy.   Only those reader problems which
involve mental or physical illness or disability, including
emotional problems not severe enough to be characterized as
mental illness, would involve bibliotherapy in its broader definition.   The average librarian or reader's advisor in a
public library or the typical school librarian will receive far
more regular reference or reader-advisory questions than
questions deserving the designation of bibliotherapy.   Yet it

is highly desirable that when these special opportunities arise, the librarian be prepared to handle them, since it has been proved that the right book to the right person at the right time is of inestimable value in helping to solve important personal problems.

The basic question seems to be whether bibliotherapy must be restricted to its use in the medical field, or whether it may also include skillful reading guidance by a librarian or other non-medical person with the necessary background of book knowledge, psychology, and sensitivity awareness or perception. It boils down to a difference of opinion as to who has the proper qualifications and right to prescribe specific materials.

It does not seem essential that everyone agree upon an exact definition of bibliotherapy, for a careful scrutiny of the various definitions reveals that they include the same three essential factors: 1) An individual or group with physical, mental, or emotional problems; 2) An interested person who knows books and people and will "prescribe" reading; 3) Available materials in sufficient quantity to fill the needs likely to arise.

Margaret Monroe, in a 1968 address before an Institute on Serving Readers through Hospital and Institution Libraries held at the University of Wisconsin Library School, said, "Is there a correct definition? Obviously none is agreed upon. Let me suggest that the essence of help through books is more important than the term 'bibliotherapy.' We must not let our uneasiness and insecurity about our proper function mislead us into irrelevant bickering on terminology. Let us spend our energies exploring what books can do for people and how we as librarians can help."[7]

Notes

1. Darrin, Ruth, ed. "The Library as a Therapeutic Experience." Bulletin of the Medical Library Association, v. 47, July 1959, p. 305-311.

2. Hannigan, Margaret C. "Bibliotherapy: Its Part in Library Service." The Bookmark (New York State Library), v. 15, March 1956, p. 127.

3. Favazza, Armando R., Sr. "Bibliotherapy: A Critique

of the Literature. " Bulletin of the Medical Library Association, v. 54, April 1966, p. 138-141.

4. Pearson, John S. "Bibliotherapy and the Clinical Psychologist. " Library Trends, v. 11, October 1962, p. 178-180.

5. Jackson, Evalene P. "Reading Guidance: A Tentative Approach to Theory. " Library Trends, v. 11, October 1962, p. 122.

6. Tews, Ruth M. Introduction: "Bibliotherapy, " Library Trends, v. 11, October 1962, p. 99.

7. Monroe, Margaret E. "Reader Services and Bibliotherapy. " In: Reading Guidance and Bibliotherapy in Public, Hospital and Institution Libraries. Edited by Margaret E. Monroe. Madison: University of Wisconsin, Library School, 1971. p. 42.

CHAPTER 2

ORIGINS AND PIONEERS

The basic idea of bibliotherapy goes back to antiquity. The early Greeks recognized the healing value of reading by placing an inscription over their library entrances which, translated, meant "Place of Healing for the Soul, " or "Medicine for the Soul. "

The Romans also associated medicine and reading. Aulus Cornelius Celsus, an encyclopedist, suggested that the works of great orators be read by patients in order to improve their judgment. An appreciable number of early historical writings emphasized the curative properties of books, particularly for those who were emotionally disturbed.

The practice of bibliotherapy, although not commonly known by that term, flourished in Europe before 1900. It was an important method of psychotherapy and was generally considered secondary only to outdoor exercise in its curative efficacy. Libraries were established in most of the better mental hospitals of Europe by the end of the 18th century and in America by the middle of the 19th.

Pinal in France, Chiarugi in Italy, and Tuke in England, among others, advocated more humane treatment of the insane in the latter part of the 18th century and included reading as an important part of the recreational program. This seems to be the earliest general mention of the use of books in the care and treatment of the mentally handicapped.

Sometimes, however, the reading of novels was not looked upon with favor. Some even regarded such reading as a cause of insanity rather than a curative agent. Nevertheless, one of the early American pioneers in the use of bibliotherapy with mental patients, Dr. Benjamin Rush, wrote in his Medical Inquiries and Observations Upon the Diseases of the Mind, published in 1812 and reprinted in 1962, "when there is no relish for the simple and interesting stories contained in the Bible, the reading of novels should be recommended to our patients. "[1]

13

John Minson Galt II, according to the literature of bibliotherapy, was the first American to write about it, in the early 1850's.   By that time every major mental hospital had a patients' library.   Many were quite large, containing many periodicals and newspapers together with the books. The works of Sir Walter Scott were said to be especially popular.

Dr. Benjamin Rush first recommended the Bible as therapeutic reading in 1815.   By 1850 some basic principles in book selection had been established that are still followed today:

1.   Meet the specific needs of each individual;

2.   The range of materials may extend from newspapers to the scholarly or scientific book;

3.   Choice of books is based on medical considerations, the patient's education, and his mental state.

Dr. Rush was influenced by the procedures at the York Retreat in England, a Quaker institution administered by members of the Tuke family for several generations.   Samuel Tuke, in his "description of the Retreat," recommended that works of imagination and books in any degree connected with the peculiar notions of the patient were to be avoided.   He encouraged the patients to follow one subject, particularly one with which they had been previously acquainted, in order that they might understand it more easily.   Some branch of mathematics or the natural sciences were his favorite subjects.

These same principles were adopted by several American asylums, including the Hartford Retreat, the Bloomingdale Asylum, the McLean Hospital and the Asylum for the Relief of Persons Deprived of the Use of Their Reason (later called The Friends Asylum).

Rush's 1812 book on the diseases of the mind, which went through five American editions, had a tremendous influence upon the practice of psychiatry in the United States. Dr. Rush looked with much more favor than Tuke upon fiction, and his book relates several cases where reading novels was beneficial.   Many of Rush's recommendations concerning bibliotherapy were, in fact, carried out by many American insane asylums.

John Minson Galt's writings were the first to give an overall view of libraries in American insane asylums. He treated the theory and practice of bibliotherapy in considerable detail in his annual reports of the Eastern Lunatic Asylum of Virginia, of which he was head, in his book The Treatment of Insanity and in an essay "On Reading, Recreation, and Amusements for the Insane, " published in 1853 after being given as a lecture in 1848. Galt expanded the asylum's small collection of books and newspapers and emphasized the value of books and reading for mental patients. He made it a point to procure books to fit the special needs of patients as carefully as he would purchase additional medicine to treat some rare physical symptom. He thought of a library as a kind of intellectual pharmacy stocked with remedies for every kind of emotional disorder and he stressed the importance of proper guidance and supervision. Since Galt was a doctor he made it clear that the choice of books for the individual patient must always be based upon medical considerations, upon the patient's exact mental state, and whether or not he was morbid. Another and basic consideration, he insisted, was that the collection of books be large enough to satisfy the requirements of any case. Thus the requirements for the science of bibliotherapy in the mid 1800s did not differ materially from the requirements today. John Minson Galt was a forward-looking pioneer in the field of scientific or medical bibliotherapy.

The Crichton Asylum in Scotland was said to practice most thoroughly the prescription of books for patients. Dr. W. A. F. Browne was the guiding light there. Collections of books were contemporary with the laboratory; and the medical personnel invariably carried a catalog, along with a prescription book, in their daily visits to every patient.

American asylum libraries tended to contain large numbers of newspapers, considered ideal for patients because they contained something for everyone; the articles were short, and they were light reading. However, librarians were urged to "avoid all papers that are filled with horrible suicides and murders. " It is hard to see how one could avoid such papers today, with crime on the increase and newspapers saturated with such stories. One current exception is the Christian Science Monitor, which excludes accounts of crime and violence.

The staple stock of American asylum libraries of the 1800s, according to Galt, included history, biography, travel,

reviews, and such standard fiction writers as Maria Edge-
worth, Sir Walter Scott, and Mary Martha Sherwood. The
Bible, however, was often stressed for reading by mental
patients. In some hospitals a patient acted as librarian; in
others, perhaps a "teacher." Library service to mental patients in the 19th century was surprisingly extensive and sophisticated, in some cases surpassing that in comparable
institutional libraries today.

As far back as 1912 the McLean Hospital at Waverly,
Massachusetts was described by E. K. Jones[2] as having
learned through its seventy-five years of service that: 1) The
inclusion of an organized library under a professional librarian
was important; 2) The administration should be as free of red
tape as possible; 3) Mental patients were no more careless
with books than general readers; 4) The value of a well-se-
lected library can hardly be over-estimated as a therapeutic
agent.

Bibliotherapy was first accepted as an aspect of librarianship in 1904 when a trained librarian became administrator of libraries at McLean and assumed a leading role in
the use of books as therapy. [3] Although the program flourished
for many years, it finally had to be discontinued for lack of
money and trained personnel.

Samuel McChord Crothers was one of the first to use
the term "bibliotherapy." In an article in Atlantic Monthly in
August, 1916, he described a "bibliopathic Institute" of a
friend, Bagster. Bagster stated, "Bibliotherapy is such a new
science it is no wonder there are many erroneous opinions as
to the actual effect which any particular book can have."[4]

A figure who stands out in the history of 20th century
bibliotherapy in America is Sadie P. Delaney. As librarian
of the Veterans' Hospital in Tuskegee, Alabama, she achieved
state, national, and international fame as a librarian and bibliotherapist. Born in 1889, Dr. Delaney received her professional library training in the New York Public Library.
When assigned to the 135th Street Branch in 1920 she provided
service to Negroes, Chinese, Jews, Italians and many other
nationalities and races. Her work with delinquent boys and
girls and the foreign-born earned her world-wide recognition.
Here at the 135th Street Branch a beginning was made in helping delinquents through the use of bibliotherapy, and among
her many other interests, Sadie Delaney became interested in
work with the blind to the extent that she learned both Braille

and Moon Point. In 1923 she was asked to organize the Veteran's Administration Hospital Library at Tuskegee, Alabama, and went on to earn a reputation far beyond the boundaries of the United States. [5] Of Mrs. Delaney's work, Gladys Oppenheim said in "Bibliotherapy--a New Word for Your Vocabulary," "one can see bibliotherapy in practice at its very best ... and its success in this hospital is entirely due to the gifted and devoted librarian, Mrs. Sadie Peterson Delaney. "[6]

Mrs. Delaney increased monthly circulation from 275 to 10,000 during her regime; the collection at the end of the first year had grown from 200 volumes to 4,000 for the patients, with 85 in the medical library. So successful was this pioneer bibliotherapist that library schools in Illinois, North Carolina, and Georgia sent students to study her programs and methods. Her work became a model for other Veterans' Administration hospital librarians. She was acclaimed by such outstanding librarians and educators as Dr. Keyes D. Metcalf, Dr. Luther Evans, Dr. E. W. McDiarmid, and Dr. Virginia Lacy Jones. Her life and work has been discussed in more than fifty publications. The United States Information Service sent information on Mrs. Delaney to one hundred USIS units in seventy-five countries, giving her life and work as an example of what is great and good in "The American Way of Life."

Dr. Karl Menninger wrote a series of articles for the New York Herald Tribune, starting in 1927, on "Why Men Fail." The paper received many compliments on the series. Menninger then collected some of the lectures he was giving to Washburn College students on abnormal psychology, together with other papers, in his book The Human Mind, published in 1930. Many people wrote to him saying it had a therapeutic effect. Karl Menninger also prepared "A Guide to Psychiatric Books" for the benefit of librarians. "We had a long struggle over the problem of how to list the self-help books, "[7] he noted.

Although librarians have been concerned since 1923 about the practical applications of reading as therapy, most of the voluminous literature for several decades reflected librarians working alone, unaided by scientific data and hypotheses.

In 1937 William Menninger read a paper on bibliotherapy before the American Psychiatric Association in Pitts-

burgh. It covered ideas gained from five years of using bibliotherapy at the Menninger Clinic in Topeka, Kansas. The
Menninger brothers, Karl and William, were both proponents
of the young discipline, and hospital librarians are deeply in-
debted to them for their experimentation and writings. Many
believe that research in bibliotherapy started with the Menninger studies.

The Menningers believed that the physician was responsible for the contents of the library and the approval of
the books before purchase; for approving any reading assignments given to a patient; for weekly conferences with the librarian regarding results and problems; for communicating
historical information and the psychological status of each new
patient, along with that patient's particular reading habits and
interests, to the librarian for her aid and guidance; and for
expressing a personal interest in the patient by frequent discussions regarding his therapeutic reading. [8]

This was the modus operandi in the medical world at
the time as far as bibliotherapy was concerned, and it reflected the attitude of most doctors. Since reading was a
treatment method it must be directed by a physician. The
librarian was simply the tool to perform the mechanics and
report the observations. Psychiatry was not yet accepted
wholeheartedly by general physicians.

In 1939 in an article in Library Journal, Alice Bryan
asked, "Can there be a science of bibliotherapy?" She answered her own question by stating the prerequisites for its
emergence as an established science. She believed that bibliotherapy would require the close cooperation of physicians
and specially-trained hospital librarians who would: establish
a broad and provable definition for the term; accumulate experimental data to establish basic principles; and carry on
basic research along scientific lines. [9]   Thirty-five years
later it is apparent that the scientific or medical aspect of
bibliotherapy has come close to achieving these goals. But
bibliotherapy as an art still needs to gain wider recognition.
Counseling and guidance are old techniques. Using books as
effective tools in other fields than medicine and librarianship
is comparatively new.

In the same year, 1939, the Hospital Division of the
American Library Association established a Bibliotherapy
Committee to explore the possibility of using books as a treat-
ment to reshape attitudes. After several years of study it

became apparent that answers to some basic questions on the
effect of reading in general were necessary before the use of
books as a method of treatment could be investigated. It also
became obvious that help was needed from other fields.   The
Bibliotherapy Committee proposed to the Association of Hospital and Institution Libraries in 1957 at the ALA Kansas City
conference that an interdisciplinary committee be organized
to outline basic questions and identify responsible areas with
regard to the effect of reading in hospitals and institutions.
This committee, when formed, included librarians, psychiatrists, psychologists, educators and sociologists.

A meeting of Canadian and British physicians, librarians and writers was held in 1945 in London on "Reading as a
Restorative. " A paper by Sir Drummond Shiels, M. D. on the
therapeutic value of reading was considered so practical and
helpful that it was quoted almost in its entirety in Canadian
Hospital in November, 1945.

In the January, 1956 issue of Library Journal there
appeared one of the first advertisements in a library periodical seeking the services of a bibliotherapist.   Few have
appeared since.

In 1957 M. J. Ryan, writing in Special Libraries,
stated her opinion that bibliotherapy was not yet a science;
she considered it an art.   Ruth M. Tews, librarian at the
Mayo Clinic in Rochester and chairman of the AHIL Bibliotherapy Committee, commented in 1958 that "librarians stand
now on the threshold of new opportunities in the development
of the profession. "[10]   Support for the concept of bibliotherapy
as an art was provided in 1957 by a statement by C. R.
Rogers that, in the main, diagnostic skill is not needed for
therapeutic interaction. [11]

In 1958 Floch investigated the influence and potential
of specific books upon drug addicts in correctional institutions, reflecting a broadening trend in the application of bibliotherapy. [12]   Earlier in the '50s group reading programs
were introduced in Veterans' Administration hospitals; thus
remedial reading was linked with group therapy:

An early (1952) experiment in group reading combined
with psychotherapy was performed by a psychiatrist, philoso-
pher, and psychiatric social worker, J. W. Powell, A. R.
Stone, and J. D. Frank, respectively. [13]   A research study
by M. Roman, entitled Reaching Delinquents through Reading,

was published in book form in 1957. The Roman study demonstrated that the combination of group reading and psychotherapy was far more successful in reaching children than either method by itself. [14]

Group reading was also applied to the treatment of alcoholism. During the 1950s as a whole, however, bibliotherapy was still in the experimental stage.

A small invitational bibliotherapy workshop sponsored by the Association of Hospital and Institution Libraries was held in connection with ALA's annual conference in June, 1964. The theme was "What is Bibliotherapy and What Can It Do for Mental Health?" Financing was provided by the U. S. Public Health Service through the National Institute of Mental Health. The workshop brought together librarians, physicians, psychologists, social scientists, chaplains, and educators with a broad spectrum of views and theories. A program of development was outlined in three major areas: education, research, and a standard terminology. Twelve consultants were each asked to prepare a brief statement of their concern for bibliotherapy as it related to their fields. They were to base their comments on a symposium on bibliotherapy which appeared in Library Trends in October, 1962. This excellent 1962 survey included papers from the fields of nursing, occupational therapy, psychology, psychiatry, and librarianship in the hospital and medical fields.

A group of thirty-one observers from a wide variety of interests was invited to attend and to take part in the question and discussion sessions. The moderator was Dr. Marion Bunch, Head of the Psychology Department of Washington University in St. Louis. The keynote address was by Dr. Howard P. Rome, a psychiatrist with the Mayo Clinic. Orrilla T. Blackshear, Assistant Director of the Madison Public Library, represented the public library interests. [15]

This workshop was especially noteworthy for its invigorating exchange of views and because bringing together representatives of so many different fields emphasized the spreading usefulness of bibliotherapy, both as a science and as an art. A sub-committee for research design was proposed, and in 1965 it was made a standing committee for continuing research. The symposium upon which the participants based their comments was another landmark in the progress of bibliotherapy. Edited by Ruth M. Tews, Hospital Librarian, Mayo Clinic, Rochester, Minnesota, this work gave greater

definition to several aspects of bibliotherapy and furthered the
view that it is not confined to the medical field.   It also
proved a worthy prologue to the 1964 workshop.

Ruth M. Tews has been a leader in bibliotherapy in
the last several decades.   Her position at the Mayo Institute
has given her a splendid opportunity to participate in and observe bibliotherapy in a modern clinic among physicians who
are themselves leaders in the field of medicine.   She has
contributed a number of articles to periodicals, written a
chapter in Thomas E. Keys' Applied Medical Library Practice (1958), chaired the AHIL Bibliotherapy Committee of the
American Library Association, and supplied an important
chapter entitled "Progress in Bibliotherapy" in the 1970 volume of Advances in Librarianship.

During the latter part of the 1950s there was also a
greater sharing of responsibility in the medical application of
bibliotherapy.   Since about 1957 the psychiatrist has been regarded as the captain of a treatment team which included
specialists in the behavioral sciences, group techniques, and
research methods.   Many functions formerly reserved for the
physician have gradually been delegated to members of the
treatment team.   These include the choice of therapeutic
materials for purchase; weekly conferences with the librarian
regarding group and individual reading programs; providing
historical, psychological, and sociological data regarding patients to the librarian for guidance; designing, measuring,
and evaluating group bibliotherapy activity; selecting, recommending, and motivating patients for individual and group
reading; inspiring, encouraging and counseling the librarian
in her role as bibliotherapist; and taking an important part in
conducting group bibliotherapy sessions with the librarian.
However, the psychiatrist, as captain of the team, plays a
major role, for without his support and guidance hospital librarians could not conduct such programs adequately. [16]

At the time of the workshop there also emerged the
concept of a name for a worker in the professional specialty
of bibliotherapy: "the clinical librarian. "   Such a person
would have broad training in psychology and other factors of
human relationships.   With graduate training, seminars and
field work, a "clinical librarian" should be able to work
effectively in a hospital, institution, school or public library,
or as a case worker in the social field.

After the 1964 workshop the various committees of

AHIL concerned with bibliotherapy worked with renewed vigor. A special committee of children's librarians worked on the problems of the troubled child. Annotated bibliographies of books for specific situations were compiled and published for the benefit of librarians, social workers, counselors, or parole officers.

During the two decades, 1950 to 1970, a resurgence of interest and activity occurred. W. J. Coville noted in 1960 that in the previous decade, 1950-1960, two-thirds of the papers on bibliotherapy appeared in journals outside the library field, and more than 80 percent of the authors were in fields outside medicine. Bibliotherapy was no longer confined to the traditional clinical setting in hospitals and institutions. Basic concepts were being defined and analyzed. The development of the social and behavioral sciences between 1950 and 1960 helped to give greater significance to the use of reading as a means of changing behavior.

During the 1960-1970 period bibliotherapy as an art was more formally accepted. E. T. Gendlin wrote in 1967 that persons not experienced in or exposed to therapeutic pursuits can be trained to relate and to establish empathy with people. This comment was made in connection with a study of psychotherapy with schizophrenics. It is a long step toward the concept that non-professionals might even be used in a medically-related bibliotherapy program. [17]

Noticeable but inadequate progress has been made by library schools in developing courses for those wishing to work in hospital or institutional libraries. The same period saw greater progress toward the realization that the public library, with its varied resources, can be effective in helping to solve mental health problems in the community as well as in a hospital or institutional setting.

Others whose work and writings gave bibliotherapy impetus in the last few decades include Dr. Josephine A. Jackson, whose book Outwitting Our Nerves had a potent therapeutic effect; Elizabeth Pomeroy, a frequent contributor to periodicals, who wrote one paper discussing 1,538 case reports; Dr. Magnus C. Petersen, who outlined some of the possibilities for future research in bibliotherapy; Dr. Gordon R. Kamman, who stressed the importance of records of reading; Eleanor Mascarino, a librarian, and Dr. Delmar Goode, a physician, who reported one of the first attempts to use bibliotherapy in shock treatment for a specific disease; Dr.

Salomon Gagnon, Chief Executive Officer at the Boston Psy-
copathic Hospital, one of whose articles summarized data
taken from the reading records of 529 patients; Ilse Bry, who
defined the bases upon which bibliotherapy rests; Perrie
Jones, who reviewed the present and future of hospital libraries in 1944 and stressed the need for better training of
bibliotherapists, more scientific studies, and accurate records; and Sofie Lazarsfeld, one of the first to use the "fiction
test. " By studying reactions of patients to what was in the
text and between the lines she drew many helpful conclu-
sions. [18]

Yet others included Dr. William Sadler, whose book
Modern Psychiatry devoted a whole chapter to "Therapeutic
Reading and Study"; Caroline Shrodes, whose Ph. D. dissertation in 1949 was a major effort to put the subject into the
proper perspective; Esther A. Hartman, whose doctoral thesis
laid a more solid foundation for the "science" of bibliotherapy;
Suzanne Connell, who challenged the assumption that librarians are readers and prescribed bibliotherapy for herself and
others; and Dorothy Long, who pointed out a possible danger
--librarians should not be seen as "ministering angels to the
unfortunate sick, " she said, but as responsible, mature, professional workers doing an important job. One of the best
outlines of bibliotherapy used for children was given by Vera
Flandorf in 1953. Dr. Ralph Ball contributed the thoughts
of a general practitioner in 1954. And Dr. Thomas V. Moore
was one of the few writers to give an early Greek version of
the Theban inscription well known to all bibliotherapists. [18]

Over the years many Veterans' Administration librarians and staff members have written on aspects of bibliotherapy and produced valuable lists of references. Veterans'
Administrative officials have been quick to recognize the significance of bibliotherapy: of importance in establishing the
role of the hospital librarian as a bibliotherapist was the
Veterans' Administration Position-Classification Guide, July
1952, now superseded by new Civil Service standards. The
Guide specifically listed the practice of bibliotherapy as a
distinctive feature of this category of position. Ruth Tews,
in her chapter in Keys' Applied Medical Library Practice,
cited training courses and the planning and completion of research studies as major needs. [18]

Statistics and a sensible outlook are found in a master's thesis by Artemisia J. Junier, A Subject Index to the
Literature of Bibliotherapy, 1900-1958, which analyzes 601

references by date, type of publication, author, and subject.
Maurice Floch described some of his work at the Detroit
House of Correction in 1958, emphasizing that bibliotherapy
can also be useful in prisons. [18]

Others whose work or papers contributed much to the
development of bibliotherapy are: Dr. Jerome M. Schneck,
Margaret M. Kinney, Dr. Edward B. Allen, Minette Condon,
Dr. Melba H. Duncan, Louis A. Gottschalk, Dr. Lore Hirsch,
Isabelle H. Rust, Elizabeth A. Stein, Melvin C. Oathout,
Ruby Hannah, John H. McFarland, W. B. McDaniel II, Mary
Jane Ryan, Ruth Darrin, Richard L. Darling, Pearl G. El-
liott, L. B. and Ella U. Firman, and R. S. Morrow. Of
recent years Margaret C. Hannigan, Hospital Library Con-
sultant with the Library Extension Division of the New York
State Library, has been a leader in the bibliotherapy move-
ment and a prolific contributor to journals. [18]

Two notable contributions to the literature of bibliotherapy appeared in 1971. Bibliotherapy Methods and Materials was produced by two committees of the Association of
Hospital and Institution Libraries of ALA: the committee on
bibliotherapy chaired by Mildred T. Moody, and the sub-committee on the troubled child, with Hilda K. Limper as chairman. This 161-page paperback devotes only 55 pages to
methods and a list of material useful to the bibliotherapist;
the remainder, over 100 pages, is a bibliography of books
for readers, classified by the types of problems the book
might help solve; for example, "Adjusting to Physical Handicaps," "Gangs and Youth Involved with the Law," etc. Each
book is annotated with a one-fourth to one-half-page summary and evaluation. Interest level, reading level, audience,
and a capsule description of the theme is given for each title.
Published by ALA, the book sold for $5.95. Since it contains
only books for the troubled child and adolescent, its primary
value lies in the use by children's librarians and bibliotherapists working with children and adolescents; the general material contained in the first 55 pages, however, has general
application for all ages.

In the same year the Library School of the University
of Wisconsin issued a 76-page mimeographed collection of
papers presented at three Adult Services Institutes held at the
school in 1965, 1966, and 1968. Entitled Reading Guidance
and Bibliotherapy in Public, Hospital and Institution Libraries,
six of its ten papers discuss bibliotherapy quite fully; the
other four discuss it in connection with reading guidance in

general, although the exact term is not always used to describe the bibliotherapeutic approach.   Edited by Margaret E.
Monroe, this is an exceedingly worthwhile publication, available from the University library school for $3.00.   Another
slightly older but excellent volume is Facilitating Human Development through Reading; The Use of Bibliotherapy in Teaching and Counseling.   Although it is primarily devoted to the
educational uses of bibliotherapy, as the title indicates, the
authors, Joseph S. Zaccaria and Harold A. Moses of the
University of Illinois faculty, do include some material on
the adult clinical aspects and the 123 pages of suggested
books for readers are, as in the ALA publication, arranged
by the physical or emotional problems likely to be encountered.   The subject of each book is very briefly explained in
two or three lines and the age appeal is given, but there is
very little evaluation.   Published by Stipes Publishing Company, Champaign, Illinois, this 270-page volume also sold
for $5.95.

As further proof of the growth in importance of bibliotherapy, several lengthy bibliographies of the literature about
it have appeared in recent years.   They are listed in the
appendix of this volume.

The theory and practice of bibliotherapy have progressed far since the publication in 1931 of The Poetry Cure
by R. H. Schauffler, who dedicated his book "to the noble
army of creative librarians, practitioners all--consciously or
unconsciously--of the poetry cure."   He thought of librarians
as bibliotherapists and as the group from which a promise of
better bibliotherapy might arise. [19]

Finally, looking briefly at the beginnings of institutional librarianship, the first person to organize and admin-
ister a hospital library for the benefit of the patients, according to Ruth Hyatt, was E. Kathleen Jones.   Her library
was in the McLean Hospital for the Feeble-Minded at Waverly,
Mass.   In 1904 the first general hospital to establish a library department as part of the therapeutic work was also in
Massachusetts, the Massachusetts General Hospital.   Iowa,
Minnesota, and Nebraska pioneered in institution libraries in
the early 1900s and the army libraries established by the
American Library Association in the First World War stimulated the growth of hospital library work by the federal
government, the states, and the cities. [20]

In 1840 a library was established in Sing Sing Prison

and directed by the prison chaplain.   When the state administration changed, the library was abolished in 1843.   In 1853
the Board of Inspectors recommended it be re-opened, and
in 1855 an appropriation of $200 was made for that purpose.[21]

At the American Library Association meeting in Chicago in 1912, it was strongly recommended that an ALA representative attend the annual meeting of the American Prison
Association to urge the establishment of institution libraries.

The Soviet Union places a great deal of emphasis upon
bibliotherapy, according to A. M. Miller, Hospital Librarian,
Kharkhov, U. S. S. R.   He says that many Russian doctors and
persons in pursuit of culture have, in the course of several
centuries, maintained in their writings that books are as indispensable as drugs.   A great surging forward in the use of
books in the battle for quicker recovery and for the main-
tenance of the best qualities of the human personality followed
the publishing of a book, Idealism as a Psychological Factor,
by A. Jarotsky in 1908.   Miller pointed out, in 1972, that
since the foundation of bibliotherapy 70 years earlier, librarians and doctors have collected extensive and interesting data.
One bibliography on bibliotherapy contains 400 titles. [22]

Notes

1.   Weimerskirsh, Philip J.   "Benjamin Rush and John Min-
       son Galt II, Pioneers of Bibliotherapy in America. "
       Bulletin of the Medical Library Association, v. 53,
       October 1965, p. 510-13.

2.   Jones, E. K.   "Library Work Among the Insane. "
       American Library Association Bulletin, v. 6, July
       1912, p. 310-324.

3.   Tews, Ruth M.   "Progress in Bibliotherapy. "   In: Voigt,
       Melvin.   Advances in Librarianship.   Vol. 1.   N. Y. :
       Academic Press, 1970, p. 173.

4.   Crothers, Samuel McChord.   "A Literary Clinic. "   At-
       lantic Monthly, v. 118, August 1916, p. 291.

5.   Cantrell, Clyde H.   "Sadie P. Delaney: Bibliotherapist
       and Librarian. "   The Southeastern Librarian, v. 6,
       Fall 1956, p. 105-109.

6. Oppenheim, Gladys. "Bibliotherapy--A New Word for
    Your Vocabulary. " Cape Times (Bloemfontein, South
    Africa), January 15, 1938, p. 3.

7. Menninger, Karl, M. D.   "Reading as Therapy. " Ameri-
    can Library Association Bulletin, v. 55, April 1961,
    p. 316.

8. Ryan, Mary Jane.   "Bibliotherapy and Psychiatry--
    Changing Concepts, 1937-1957. " Special Libraries,
    v. 48, May-June 1957, p. 197-99.

9. Bryan, Alice I.   "Can There be a Science of Biblio-
    therapy?" Library Journal, v. 64, Oct. 15, 1939,
    p. 773-76.

10. Tews, Ruth M.   "The Patient's Library. " In: Keys,
    Thomas E. , Applied Medical Library Practice. Spring-
    field, Ill. : Charles C. Thomas, 1958, p. 97-134.

11. Rogers, Carl R.   "The Necessary and Sufficient Condi-
    tions of Therapeutic Personality Change. " Journal of
    Consulting Psychology, v. 21, April 1957, p. 95-103.

12. Floch, M.   "Bibliotherapy and the Library. " The Book-
    mark, v. 18, Dec. 1958, p. 57-59.

13. Powell, J. W. , Stone, A. R. , and Frank, J. D. "Group
    Reading and Group Therapy: A Concurrent Test. "
    Psychiatry, v. 15, Feb. 1952. p. 33-51.

14. Roman, M.   Reaching Delinquents Through Reading.
    Springfield, Ill. : Charles C. Thomas, 1957, p. 109-
    119.

15. Blackshear, Orilla T.   "A Bibliotherapy Workshop. "
    Wisconsin Library Bulletin, v. 60, Sept. -Oct. 1964,
    p. 296-298.

16. Tews, Ruth M.   "Progress in Bibliotherapy. " In: Voigt,
    Melvin, Advances in Librarianship, N. Y. : Academic
    Press, 1970, p. 176.

17. Ibid. , p. 186.

18. Beatty, William K.   "A Historical Review of Biblio-
    therapy. " In: Tews, Ruth M. , ed. , "Bibliotherapy. "

Library Trends, v. 11, October 1962, p. 108-113.

19. McDowell, David J. "Bibliotherapy in a Patients' Library." Bulletin of the Medical Library Association, v. 59, July 1971, p. 457.

20. Hyatt, Ruth. "Book Service in a General Hospital." Library Journal, v. 65, Sept. 1, 1940, p. 684.

21. Chennault, Price. "Correctional Institutions Helping the Functionally Illiterate." American Library Association Bulletin, v. 58, October 1964, p. 804.

22. Miller, A. M. "The Reading Matter of Patients." International Library Review, July 1972, p. 373-77.

CHAPTER 3

THE MEDICAL PROFESSION:
ATTITUDES AND OPINIONS

It is interesting to note the gradual change in attitude toward bibliotherapy on the part of the medical profession. Although there were early pioneers in the medical world who practiced bibliotherapy and even wrote about it, the general attitude was one of skepticism or apathy.

A surprising number of physicians have written about bibliotherapy, mainly of course from the clinical or scientific viewpoint, and to a large extent as a factor in the treatment of mental disorders. But a surprising number of general practitioners, also, have used books in connection with their treatment of patients whose emotional or psychological problems were contributing to their physical problems. This is especially true of the time-honored family physician, often an obscure country doctor, who attempted to treat the whole individual. Unfortunately, the age of specialization has reduced their number. Many of these general doctors in the past suggested books not because they were aware of bibliotherapy as a separate discipline but because they loved books themselves, read widely, and used common sense.

In 1920 we find Admiral C. T. Grayson, M. D. writing in the Bookman on "Books as a Mental Diversion." Dr. Grayson testified to the value of a change of pace in reading as possible therapy in the treatment of certain nervous cases. In this interesting and personal application of bibliotherapy Dr. Grayson includes reading recommendations made in his own treatment of President Woodrow Wilson, for whom he was the personal physician. [1]

Three years later E. P. Bledsoe, a doctor in a neuro-psychiatric Veterans' Administration Hospital, substantiated his belief in the therapeutic value of books for neuropsychiatric patients. However, he stressed that the subjects must relate to the patient and be recommended by a competent li-

brarian who knows books and understands patients as individuals. This doctor firmly recommended that no neuropsychiatric hospital should be without competent librarians as
part of its therapeutic team. [2]

Another neuropsychiatrist in a veterans' hospital, Dr.
G. O. Ireland, saw bibliotherapy as a positive therapeutic
measure in 1930, and supported his thesis with examples and
case histories in Modern Hospital. [3] Dr. J. A. Jackson, in
an article in Modern Hospital in 1925, stressed the relaxation,
tonic and sedative values of a patient's losing himself in a
good book. [4]

A somewhat opposing view was that of Dr. G. A. Ruhberg, who in 1930 in The American Library Association Bulletin maintained that books are solely an adjunct and help to
the doctor, and should be prescribed by him personally.
Though he had had occasional success with neurotics, he
found that books were not of much value as a therapeutic
agent with psychotics. Dr. Ruhberg felt that no general rules
could be applied since each patient is an individual problem
and needs individual personal attention. [5]

Another writer, Dr. G. B. Webb, a year later, pointed
out that the physician is responsible for prescribing the reading matter for the patient's mind as well as for taking care
of his sick body; he emphasized the importance of fitting the
prescription to the patient's exact needs. [6]

Dr. G. R. Kamman in 1934 stated his belief that bibliotherapy is vital to a mental hospital treatment program
and discussed, with specific references, books and patients,
and how and why they can be inter-related and made effective. In 1939 he again strongly endorsed bibliotherapy and
added that close cooperation between the doctor and hospital
librarian is necessary if good results are to be achieved. [7]

Dr. Morris Fishbein, well known for his medical
writing, stressed in 1934, in an article in the American Library Association Bulletin, the need for live, varied collections for patients, and decried assortments of worn discards.
The sick, he said, have the same variety of tastes as those
who are well. [9]

In his book, Essentials of Psychiatry, (3d ed., 1938),
Dr. G. W. Henry recommended "intellectual diversion" as a
treatment in psychiatric disorders and stressed the import-

ance of books and reading as a means toward this end. [8]

These early attitudes reflect the medical profession's growing interest in the possibilities of bibliotherapy. In what we might call a middle period in the changing scene, we find Dr. H. M. Turk, who in 1941 was Superintendent of the Lima State Hospital in Lima, Ohio, stating in Hospitals magazine that since the average mental patient retains many normal interests and reactions, the library and librarian can revive old interests, create new ones, amuse and relax the patient. However, he advocated censorship of the books. [10]

In May and July, 1942, in articles in Diseases of the Nervous System, Dr. Salomon Gagnon stated that carefully selected books, periodicals, and newspapers, an adequate librarian and a central place where patients may come to read and choose books are the three requisites for hospital library service. The article, "Is Reading Therapy?" described an analysis made of the reading of mental patients, and compared them with public library readers. This study showed emphasis on fiction but no specific types of preference related to the various types of mental cases. Quotations from patients regarding the hospital library and its service indicated a favorable attitude toward bibliotherapy. [11]

In 1946 Dr. Maurice Levine, in Psychotherapy in Medical Practice, suggested the values of bibliotherapy in general medical practice, a significant step in the extension of its uses. [12] The same year, Dr. E. B. Allen, in an article in Library Journal, described his own "bibliotherapeutic laboratory" and ways in which the science of bibliotherapy might eventually develop. It is interesting to note that Dr. Allen referred to bibliotherapy as a "science," at a time when few considered it such. He also stressed the idea of discrimination rather than prohibition in the selection of reading materials, [13] a more positive approach to selection than the "censorship" earlier advocated by Dr. Turk.

In 1948 Robert Tyson of Hunter College obtained responses from eight practicing psychiatrists to a specific set of pertinent questions intended to help validate the use of mental hygiene literature. Psychoanalysts were selected because it was felt that their estimate of bibliotherapy would be conservative. Of the eight, none said they used it often, three said occasionally, five said almost never. Five said they felt there was some value in recommending books; three thought it helped very little, and no one replied that it was

very helpful.   Seven felt that in cases where reading did
help, the benefit came from reassurance; five said from information.

Four felt that since there was a shortage of psychiatrists, bibliotherapy could help out in certain selected cases.
The main values the doctors saw were in preventive mental
hygiene (5 responding) and in minor problems of "normals"
(5 responding).   Two thought bibliotherapy of value as an adjunct to psychotherapy, two as an aid to the general practitioner.   Six of the eight made a careful distinction between
an individual requiring deep therapy, who might misuse
mental hygiene literature, and one with minor mental problems who might make good use of it.   It must be pointed out
that in the sense of Mr. Tyson's study, "mental hygiene literature" referred to any reading matter designed to maintain, improve, or restore emotional adjustment. [14]

If this study were repeated today it is doubtful that it
would produce so much skepticism among the respondents,
for bibliotherapy has come to have a more important place
in the treatment of patients in mental hospitals, even those
needing deep therapy.   The intensive work done by conscien-
tious librarians and doctors working together, particularly in
Veteran's Administration Hospitals, has helped bring this
change about.

L. A. Gottschalk is another doctor who considered
prescribed reading a useful tool in psychotherapy, as far
back as 1948.   His beliefs, as expressed in the American
Journal of Psychiatry, are well confirmed by a number of
interesting case histories from his own personal experience. [15]

One of the outstanding proponents of bibliotherapy in
the treatment of psychological problems has been Dr. Lore
Hirsch, a Veteran's Administration Hospital psychiatrist who
has written widely on the subject.   In one article, "How a
Doctor Uses Books," written in 1950, Dr. Hirsch points out
the special value of bibliotherapy to the psychiatrist.   Observation of what the patient reads and how he reacts to it
can be a "hint as to his interests, problems, emotional life,
hopes, dreams, and fantasies," says Dr. Hirsch.   She believes that the healthier the individual is in a mental and
emotional sense, the more benefit he may derive from the
reading of books.   She stresses the need for the patient and
doctor to discuss the books afterwards as an approach to
problems.   Moreover, she makes clear that in order to eval-

uate the patient's reaction, the doctor must also read the
books. She does not feel that reading a book such as How
To Relax, How To Stop Worrying, or How Never To Be Tired
will in itself cure a neurosis or psychosis, but if the patient
then discusses such a book with the doctor it may well provide an opening wedge into discussion of the particular problem involved. [16]

Coming closer to what we might designate as the
modern period, it is of significance that Dr. Hirsch, in spite
of her consistent advocacy of bibliotherapy, says in a 1953
article, "Book Service to Patients, " "It is not one of the
scientific forms of treatment, at least not as yet. It is more
an art of treatment. It belongs in the program of the occupational and educational therapist for the rehabilitation of
chronically ill, physically ill, and mentally ill patients. "

Dr. Hirsch feels that the hospital librarian definitely
becomes a member of the therapeutic team in any hospital
for chronic patients. In the case of psychiatric patients, she
believes the bibliotherapy is done by the psychiatrist himself
and only partly by the librarian; but in the case of physically
ill patients who do not need a psychiatrist, the librarian
alone can give them actual psychological treatment through
books. [17]

The opinion of a Swedish physician, Dr. Hakon Sjogren,
differs from that of others cited because he was not only a
hospital physician and private practitioner for twenty-five
years prior to 1953, but also had long periods in hospital
wards as a patient. Thus he viewed bibliotherapy from both
aspects, and he believed it is important both to those who
are ill and to doctors; and, indeed, to the mutual relations
between patients and doctors. It was his opinion that this
view was in agreement with the opinions of modern psychiatry
as to the scope of psychotherapy. [18]

"Prescription: Books" is the intriguing title of an
article by Dr. Ralph G. Ball in the March, 1954 American
Library Association Bulletin. In this discussion Dr. Ball
reaches out to bring in the public librarian and the value of
her bibliotherapeutic services to both the physician and the
patient. Symptomatic of the changing attitude of the medical
profession is his comment: "In general, doctors realize the
importance of reading for their patients and appreciate hospital library service, yet far too seldom do they prescribe
for their patient. These patients then either receive no

bibliotherapy, that of their own compounding, or that of
the hospital librarian who too seldom knows of the underlying
disease of the patient for whom she finds herself prescribing. "[19]

Dr. Ball's opinions are particularly interesting because
they derive from twenty-one years in the private practice of
medicine in a small Kansas community and are those of the
traditional family doctor.   He says, "I found, as I am sure
many others have, that the prescription of literature is an
extremely valuable addition to the ever increasing therapeutic
equipment of the physician. "   Realizing that many smaller
community hospitals do not have a library, Dr. Ball stresses
cooperation between the doctor and the public librarian and
the use of the community library by the patient, particularly
in the treatment of psychosomatic ailments.

Dr. Hirsch, always explicit, responded to a question
in the Hospital Book Guide of June, 1956.   Her answer was
particularly valuable in that it defined the role of hospital
nurses and aides in carrying out an effective bibliotherapy
program.   She said, "I think every treatment should be presented by the ward doctor.   Every hospital is set up to have
a therapeutic team.   The doctor (a psychiatrist in a mental
hospital) is supposed to be in charge.   He may not know
every patient personally, but the general philosophy of treatment is directed by the doctor in charge of a ward.   If a
doctor gives a list of books for the group bibliotherapy class,
then the patients who attend this meeting should do so by
prescription, and all the nurse or aide has to do is make
sure the patient attends.   Individual bibliotherapy should only
be done between the patient and the therapist.   Many psychiatric patients prefer to discuss their reading rather than
themselves. "   Dr. Hirsch stated that she did not ordinarily
recommend specific books for therapeutic reading. [20]

By 1960 we find Dr. Walter J. Coville, Chief of the
Clinical Psychology Services, St. Vincent's Hospital, New
York City, stating that "the value of bibliotherapy is generally accepted and one wonders why its practice is limited
to so few. "   He believed that interest was keen but that concentrated effort was needed to integrate the techniques more
effectively into the various programs of patient care and
treatment. [21]

The Menninger brothers, Drs. Karl and Will (see
Chapter 2), were among the pioneers in the extensive use of

bibliotherapy in the United States. Writing on "Reading as
Therapy" in 1961, Dr. Karl Menninger said, "Today medical
opinion knows the injunction, 'Treat the patient, not the disease.' This expression has been used loosely and is not always understood." Dr. Karl said, in explanation, "Without
understanding the patient it is difficult to fully understand the
disease. If a doctor thinks only in terms of treating the
disease he thinks only of a library filled with medical reference books. If he is treating the patient he will think of a
library also filled with books to inspire, amuse, comfort,
inform, and in any way help the individual patient." "Perhaps librarians," said Dr. Menninger, "are the only people
in the world able to think of history, biography, religion,
modern painting, mystery stories, and electronics simultaneously, and know just where each one belongs. Most doctors
find it difficult to think of all the pertinent facts about one
individual and his illness at one time. They tend to focus
their attention on one area, keeping other data in their peripheral vision. Sometimes, facts in the peripheral vision
attract their attention and oblige them to change their focus,
at least temporarily."[22]

A possible bad effect of bibliotherapy if not done by a
trained person was pointed out by Dr. Edwin F. Alston, a
psychiatrist at the University of California Medical School in
1961: "Misinterpretation or misunderstanding on the part of
the patient could enhance depressive trends or engender false
hopes which can only be cleared up by discussion with a
trained person." The patient's reactions must be reported
to the physician for his evaluation, Dr. Alston insists. He
believes that, within limits, what is read is of secondary importance to the interest, integrity, authority, and confidence
which the patient sees in the therapist. The personal relationship between patient and librarian or patient and therapist
is, in his opinion, the most important factor.[23]

In this day of far too frequent use of tranquilizing
drugs, the statement made in 1963 by Dr. Bertil Soderling,
"Reading can be as good or better than a tranquilizer," has
special significance. Dr. Soderling goes on to say that books
can be used medicinally in just about the same way as phar-
maceuticals--and, one might add, with far less expense. The
bibliotherapist is an important person in modern hospitals,
says Dr. Soderling, and because books can be medicinal they
must be prescribed as carefully as medicine.[24]

An article by Dr. John D. Walmer, "The Psychology

of Illness and the Use of Reading in the Treatment Plan, " in
the AHIL (Association of Hospital and Institution Libraries)
Quarterly, Spring, 1965, contained this statement addressed
to hospital librarians: "We need you in the treatment program
at our hospitals.   It is my opinion that physicians are not
making optimal use of libraries. "[25]   Dr. Walmer felt that the
librarian has unparalleled opportunities to observe the patients, an immediate advantage in understanding them, and, as
a non-authoritarian person, is likely to be the recipient of
many more confidences.   Many patients are unhappy about
having to be hospitalized.   They resent the doctor for being
unwilling to discharge them, the nurses for requiring them to
submit to various procedures and medicines and restrictions
which they dislike.   The librarian does not require them to
do anything.   A strong point made by Dr. Walmer is that
while medicine can often be effective for only a few hours or
a few days, introducing the patient to reading gives him
something of prolonged and lasting value.

In the same publication, Fall 1965 issue, Dr. Howard
M. Bogard, a leading psychologist, said, "Bibliotherapy so
far has been based on intuitive and personal skills of individuals who have plunged right in.   People in the field, rather
than waiting for definitive research, have, with little hesita-
tion, instituted programs, and the results are not only stimulating but have been of sufficient significance to warrant
meetings and workshops. "   Dr. Bogard believes that we must
rigorously attempt to delineate clinically relevant therapeutic
aspects of bibliotherapy.   In broad terms it lends itself more
to demonstration research than to a classical experimental
design.

Expressing a somewhat conservative view, Dr. Bogard
says,

> Although I feel books can serve an educational pur-
> pose with psychiatric patients I do not regard such
> practices as bibliotherapeutic.   Books can certainly
> be viewed within the light of pleasure, information
> giving, and mental hygiene, but the question re-
> mains--how, when, and where is bibliotherapy thera-
> peutic?   It is potentially therapeutic.   Can books be
> prescribed?   Briggs at the University of Minnesota
> has suggested that bibliotherapy should be prescribed
> as carefully as medication, and vigorously warned
> we must know prior to prescription:

1. Indication for use
2. Contraindications
3. Dose
4. How long to use
5. When to stop
6. What possible adverse effects are to be fore-
   seen.

Bibliotherapy <u>can</u> upset a patient ... If it is to be
regarded as a prescribable therapeutic instrument,
more definitive consideration must be given by the
bibliotherapist to the psychological dynamics of the
patient and to the clinical role of the librarian.
The library work situation wherein the patients
shelve, sort, arrange, check, and assume charge
of the reading room may have more potential value
for their improvement than the actual reading....
Should a bright, depressed, intellectual patient be
permitted to spend his time seated in the library,
his head burrowed in books? Should he be allowed
to withdraw into Proust, Genet, or Alan Gins-
berg? [26]

Although there are still many doctors who accept bibliotherapy with reservations or who are failing to make use
of it, the trend has steadily been toward greater acceptance.
Only a sampling of medical opinions is possible in a volume
of this kind, but the increasing number of physicians who have
written about bibliotherapy in the 1960s and early 1970s
speaks for itself. If all the articles appearing by various
types of authors in medical, psychological, hospital, and library publications, as well as a few of the more popular magazines in this modern period, were to be digested into a short
paragraph each, the total would fill several hundred pages
and provide valid testimony of the increasing interest in this
long-neglected science and art.

Workshops and conferences are proliferating in an attempt to clarify, solidify, and encourage the use of bibliotherapy. The number of controlled experiments, although
still inadequate to supply the needed data, has grown to a
respectable figure. Basic principles have emerged and are
being applied. The need for basic research has been acknowledged and a start has been made in that direction. Thus,
although a purist might still refuse to consider medical bibliotherapy a science, others believe the term is now deserved
and can be used. Dr. Gordon R. Kamman, as far back as

1940, said: "The science of bibliotherapy is still in its infancy, but I believe that it has possibilities for development far beyond the dreams of even its most ardent enthusiasts."[27] Today, Dr. Kammer's prophecy seems well on its way toward fulfillment.

Even earlier, Dr. G. O. Ireland, in 1930 a neuropsychiatrist at the U. S. Veterans' Hospital, American Lake, Washington, said, "As advancement has been made in the study of mental disease; the psychologist has come to realize the value of books as an aid to the proper adjustment of patients. I believe that bibliotherapy can be developed and that it should be accepted as a scientific adjunct to the treatment of mental diseases." If this statement was true in 1930, it is even more so today; both the treatment of mental disease and the applications of bibliotherapy have made significant progress.

Notes

1. Grayson, Dr. C. T. "Books as a Mental Diversion."
    Bookman, v. 52, Dec. 1920, p. 291-295.

2. Bledsoe, Dr. E. P. "The Library as a Therapeutic
    Agent." American Library Association Bulletin, v.
    17, July 1923, p. 238-239.

3. Ireland, Dr. G. O. "Bibliotherapy as an Aid in Treat-
    ing Mental Cases." Modern Hospital, v. 34, June
    1930, p. 87-91.

4. Jackson, Dr. J. A. "The Therapeutic Value of Books."
    Modern Hospital, v. 25, Aug. 1925, p. 50-51.

5. Ruhberg, G. A. "Books as a Therapeutic Agent."
    American Library Association Bulletin, v. 24, Sept.
    1930, p. 422-423.

6. Webb, Dr. G. B. "The Prescription of Literature."
    American Journal of Surgery, v. 12, April 1931, p.
    155-163.

7. Kamman, Dr. G. R. "The Doctor and the Patient's
    Library." Transactions of the American Hospital
    Association, v. 36, 1934, p. 374-384.

8. Henry, Dr. G. W. Essentials of Psychiatry. 3d ed.
    Williams and Wilkins, Baltimore, 1938, p. 291-292.

9. Fishbein, Dr. Morris. "Libraries and the Patient."
    American Library Association Bulletin, v. 28, March
    1934, p. 129-133.

10. Turk, H. M. "The Psychiatrist Evaluates the Library."
    Hospitals, v. 15, Feb. 1941, p. 45-46.

11. Gagnon, Dr. Salomon. "Organization and Physical Set-
    up of the Mental Hospital Library." Diseases of the
    Nervous System, v. 3, May 1942, p. 149-157; and "Is
    Reading Therapy?" v. 3, July 1942, p. 206-212.

12. Levine, Dr. Maurice. Psychotherapy in Medical Prac-
    tice. Macmillan, 1946, p. 107-108.

13. Allen, Dr. E. B. "Books Help Neuropsychiatric Pati-
    ents." Library Journal, v. 71, Dec. 1, 1946, p. 1671-
    75.

14. Tyson, Robert. "The Validation of Mental Hygiene Lit-
    erature." Journal of Clinical Psychology, v. IV, July
    1948, p. 305.

15. Gottschalk, Dr. L. A. "Bibliotherapy as an Adjurant
    in Psychotherapy." American Journal of Psychiatry,
    v. 104, April 1948, p. 632-37.

16. Hirsch, Dr. Lore. "How a Doctor Uses Books."
    Library Journal, v. 75, Dec. 1, 1950, p. 2046-47.

17. Hirsch, Dr. Lore. "Book Service to Patients." Wilson
    Library Bulletin, v. 27, April 1943, p. 634-35.

18. Sjogren, Dr. Hakon. "Patients and Books: Some Per-
    sonal Considerations." Library Association Record,
    v. 59, Sept. 1954, p. 342-46.

19. Ball, Dr. Ralph G. "Prescription: Books." American
    Library Association Bulletin, v. 48, March 1954, p.
    145-46.

20. Hirsch, Dr. Lore. "Bibliotherapy with Neuropsychiatric
    Patients (Individual and Group Therapy)" Hospital
    Book Guide, v. 17, May 1956, p. 87-93; and v. 17,

June 1956, p. 111-117.

21. Coville, Dr. Walter J.   "Bibliotherapy: Some Practical
     Considerations. " Hospital Progress, v. 41, April
     1960, p. 141-42; and v. 41, May 1960, p. 20, 24.

22. Menninger, Karl.   "Reading as Therapy. " American
     Library Association Bulletin, v. 55, April 1961, p. 316.

23. Alston, Dr. Edwin.   "Bibliotherapy and Psychotherapy."
     In: "Bibliotherapy, " Ruth M. Tews, editor.   Library
     Trends, v. 11, Oct. 1962, p. 162.

24. Soderling, Dr. Bertil.   "Bibliotherapeutics. " Medical
     World News, v. 4, Feb. 1963, p. 132.

25. Walmer, Dr. John D.   "The Psychology of Illness and
     the Use of Reading in the Treatment Plan. " Associ-
     ation of Hospital and Institution Libraries Quarterly,
     v. 5, Spring 1965, p. 4-9.

26. Bogard, Dr. Howard M.   "Bibliotherapy--For Whom
     and By Whom?" Association of Hospital and Institution
     Libraries Quarterly, v. 6, Fall 1965, p. 11-17.

27. Kamman, Gordon R.   "Balanced Reading Diet Prescribed
     for Mental Patients. " The Modern Hospital, v. 55,
     Nov. 1940, p. 80.

CHAPTER 4

BIBLIOTHERAPY IN MENTAL HOSPITALS AND WITH
THE MENTALLY DISTURBED OUT-PATIENT

"Multitudes face psychological walls between them and a happy outlook. More than one half of all the hospital beds in the United States are filled with people who suffer from mental disorders."[1]

Making the library experience a therapeutic one for patients in a psychiatric hospital may involve:

Reading aloud to groups of patients in closed wards.

Conducting discussion groups in a ward.

Employment of residents in the library.

Organization of a residents' library committee.

Conduct of trips.

Inclusion of movies, slides, and lectures--the non-book therapeutic part of the program. This could involve the use of tape recordings, both from the point of view of listening to very particular types of taped programs, as well as involving the patient himself in recording on tape.[2]

All activities must be planned with the psychiatrist or treatment team.

Some materials may be harmful to the patient, especially in a mental institution. Thus book selection is all important. Only that which contributes most to the development of the individual should be chosen. In the outside community this practice might be regarded as censorship, but within an institution it may be an important factor in the rehabilitative process and should be considered one of the limits

which have to be set toward helping the individual recover.
Sometimes the wrong identification may lead to a reinforcement of the individual's problems rather than to their elimi-
nation.   Bibliotherapy in the treatment of mental patients has
three main elements:

      1.   Librarian-patient relationship.
      2.   Purposeful use of books and reading as tangible
           evidence of reality.
      3.   The content of the book being communicated as
           experience.

Group therapy is especially helpful with mental patients, particularly those who tend to be withdrawn, depressed
or apathetic.   The objective of motivated group therapy is to
develop communication skills. [2]   Example: short, simple story
or factual material without dialogue is typed on single sheets
with the sentences numbered; members of the group then take
turns reading the sentences.   The discussion leader should
ask questions which require emotional or conceptual answers.
The aim is only to elicit verbal responses when the group
advances to where the members respond easily; discussions
which involve opinions and concepts may be gradually introduced.   The sessions could also be recorded on tape.   Playback of these tape recordings may be useful as the group
progresses.   For an example of beginning group reading material, see Ruthanne Penny's Practical Care of the Mentally
Retarded and Mentally Ill (Springfield, Ill.: Charles C.
Thomas, 1966).

Recently psychiatric counselors have been suggesting
that informal preparation for therapy should be provided by
conducting a "readiness" program.   With the use of general
materials written for a lay audience, and with emphasis on
the informative rather than the therapeutic aspects of the
program, the institution library would be a good location for
such a program.   Participants should be chosen by the psychiatric team (psychiatrist, clinical psychologist, and social
worker).   The material to be used should also be approved
by the team. [2]

Approved films from the Hospital and Community Psychiatry Service Film Catalog, published by the American
Psychiatric Association (1700 18th Street, N.W., Washington,
D.C., 20009), might be used.   Factual magazine articles and
pamphlets written for the general public about mental problems are appropriate.   Suggested readings include:[2]

Diehl, Harold S., et al. <u>Health and Safety for You.</u>
2nd ed. rev. N.Y.: McGraw-Hill, 1964.

Laird, Donald and Eleanor. <u>Psychology: Human Relations and Motivations.</u> 4th ed. N.Y.: McGraw-
Hill, 1967.

An American Heritage discussion group based on
American history, both political and social, was of therapeutic value at the Veterans' Administration Hospital (mental)
at Tomah, Wisconsin, and contributed to desirable changes.
There were remarkably few instances of heated arguments
considering that this group was made up of emotionally disturbed men. [3]

Margaret Hannigan, well-known librarian-bibliotherapist, suggested the following method for developing a group
reading program:

1.   Know the patients' needs and plan an activity
     and select reading material which will be en-
     joyable and beneficial.

2.   Select material you can present well.

3.   Be willing to try anything.   Don't worry about
     how foolish you look.   Neuropsychiatric patients
     especially are quick to recognize a sincere
     effort to help them.

4.   Keep the medical staff informed.   Consult them
     for advice and reassurance frequently.   Written
     reports describing the activity, the materials
     used, the general demeanor and response of the
     group, and individual participation and comment
     by patients are very helpful to doctors and the
     library staff.

5.   Once a program is established <u>keep it up</u>. Have
     it often enough to hold the patients' interest,
     once a week if possible.

6.   Give your program variety by using a wide
     range of subjects and by introducing a new
     procedure occasionally.   For instance, try a
     spelldown or a quiz.   Have the group read in
     in unison; show a film or have free reading now
     and then.

7. Keep your library aim in mind. Even though
    the response may be greater if you entertain,
    provide cigarettes, or feed the patients, these
    are not valid library activities. What you have
    to offer is enough. It can have a lasting effect,
    and it is worth working hard to achieve. [4]

The reading of poetry has been effective with restless
and depressed patients. Programs planned for such patients
should provide social contact and diversion, foster an atmosphere of friendship relating to the individual's needs of belonging, develop interpersonal relationships, encourage relaxation, establish an atmosphere of acceptance, stimulate interest, focus attention on a new idea or experience, project
the patients' feelings, and provide a means of socialization.

The librarian and the activities department can coordi-
nate a program including a reading hour and diversional
activity. Participants might be seated around a large table.
Equipment at the table might consist of water color paints
and brushes, pastel crayons, charcoal, paper, and clay ready
for molding. Participants are told that while they are listening they may paint or color, or work with clay if they wish.
The librarian's materials might include anthologies of poetry
and typed sheets of selected poems, placed so they can be
reached by the patients. The librarian should read poetry
and prose that is descriptive, colorful and evocative of remembered days. A well-remembered poem or psalm may
stimulate a choral recitation by several patients or the telling
of a past incident by a single patient. Any art work produced
should be kept and, if significant, referred to the physician.
Care should be taken that evaluation is kept at a social level;
psychological interpretation is to be left for the physician or
psychologist. [5]

David J. McDowell, [6] patients' librarian at McLean
(mental) Hospital, Belmont, Massachusetts, has broad and
varied experience in interpersonal relationships but is not a
professional librarian. His duties encompass several types
of therapeutic activities not directly related to books, but also
include working with patients and books in the library setting.
He conducts weekly group meetings with five to eight patients
to read and discuss short stories. Stories are chosen by the
group at the end of each session for the next meeting. Selections reflect patients' preferences, although Mr. McDowell
sometimes suggests titles. Stories are chosen that can be
read aloud within forty-five minutes, leaving one-half of the

ninety-minute session for discussion. Each member of the
group in turn reads about a page, after which the stories are
discussed with initial reference to similarities between the
story and the feelings of those present. McDowell, as therapist, includes his own reactions for greater identification with
others in the group.

There is a play-reading group which works in much the
same way. The group of four to eight patients selects short
plays each week for the next session; parts are assigned at
the beginning of the meeting and patients read the play without previous preparation.

A third bibliotherapy activity at McLean is the poetry
reading group which McDowell conducts in the wards rather
than in the library. From three to ten patients usually participate, but this group differs from the others in that Mc-
Dowell, as leader, selects, mimeographs and distributes the
poems at the beginning of the session. He does solicit suggestions for authors and particular poems but takes more responsibility for final selection. Discussion, again, proceeds
from concordances between the poem and the feelings or experiences of the patients.

A writers' group discusses poems by established
writers but emphasis in its meetings is upon the patients' own
work. Problems have been encountered in this group, in that
patients were unable to be objective and were inclined to take
any criticism of their work as criticism of themselves.
McDowell believes that a patient's writing is best explored
individually. Good results in communication and self-insight
have been obtained in all the types of activity, even though
much modern poetry has been included with the poetry group.
Among the authors discussed were Stevens, Aiken, Auden,
Jarrell, Cummings, Rukeyser, Simpson, Plath, Merton, Williams and Frost.

McDowell also holds individual meetings with patients
on an irregular basis, although these are necessarily limited
by the time available. He believes that in such sessions, to
be realistic, the librarian must offer advice, interpretation,
insight or support. Within limits, he says, such contacts
should be encouraged because they represent the best form of
any help: a human relationship. However, he points out that
there are two cautionary principles in regard to the therapist's relationship to the patient in such meetings: first, that
the bibliotherapist is not a psychotherapist; and second, that

patients' poetry must be evaluated as communication, not as
art.   To attempt deep insight therapy may confuse or frighten
a patient and imply a degree and kind of commitment for
which the bibliotherapist is unprepared.   The reason for regarding the poetry as communication rather than art is that
an assessment of patients' writing on aesthetic principles is
too often taken as a judgment of self.   A judgmental attitude,
McDowell believes, is probably the most damaging stance a
therapist could adopt.

The Patients' Library of Agnews State Hospital[7] in San
Jose, California received a grant for a project in bibliotherapy
in June 1968, "to demonstrate that beneficial results could be
achieved through the instrumentality of books in the general
treatment program of a mental hospital. "   A budget of
$4, 650 was allowed for personnel and $350 for equipment and
material.

The techniques used in this experiment were as follows.   A tape recorder was purchased so that group sessions
might be studied in depth from the recordings.   However,
since the landing pattern for the local airport is low and over
the hospital, the resulting tapes were discouraging.   Leah
Ann Griffith, the librarian, felt, nevertheless, that tapes can
have value as an aid in training therapists.

Spoken records were purchased for use as the reading
selections in bibliotherapy sessions.   Although not extensively
used, some recordings of mixed poetry and music introduced
very successful sessions.   These successes encouraged variation in style and aroused interest in further development
along this line.

As the librarian had too many other duties during the
first year of the grant to give the bibliotherapy sessions herself, and no other librarians were available, it was necessary
to find another person having empathy with patients and
knowledge of psychological problems.   This proved a problem
and it took until January to find a bibliotherapist.

The method used was to read aloud, to about eight
patients at a time, a story short enough to be completed in
ten minutes.   Stimulating stories were chosen and discussion
was held concerning the central theme, with no effort made
to steer the discussion.   Staff psychologists and psychiatrists
approved the project and several of them participated inten-
sively.   Ross Alexander, the experimenter, found that pa-

tients gained increased ratings on attitudes, task orientation, interaction capacity, and accessibility.

The first year's success was recognized by a renewed grant supporting the program to June 1970. Play reading was introduced in the second year and some patients who had not been able to follow the short stories, and thus to participate in story groups, were found to enjoy reading their parts in short plays. Bibliotherapy was persuading some participants to read, and a few to write. Sometimes the latter read their work to the group.

The third year of the project, 1971, was one of continued growth and development of the program. The number of sessions nearly doubled over the previous year. Sessions were held in the library, in the wards, and in the high school. Plays, music, stories and poems were used. The interest shown by visitors and others anxious to do bibliotherapy has called attention to the need for training and aids to instruction. The following example shows how a bibliotherapy session was conducted at Agnews:

1. Bibliotherapist and psychologists met in advance and considered the story for the session.

2. The patients came singly and in groups, some being obviously dependent on the good will of another patient for help. Most were greeted by name as they had attended previous sessions.

3. The story, "I'm a Star," was read by the bibliotherapist. In this story Bea and Julia, middle-aged roomates, are arguing. Bea, who is employed, insists that Julia, a faded actress and alcoholic, go to the unemployment office and request benefit payments. Julia feels this step is admitting defeat and will not or cannot do it.

4. After a few comments on Julia, most of the discussion, much to the surprise of the bibliotherapist, centered on the role Bea plays. Points brought out by the patients were Bea's jealousy because she has never had the success Julia has known, and the sly way in which she reveals the hiding place of Julia's liquor. Her "motherly" but non-supportive role was brought out by the patients; they were all against her.

5. The discussion then turned to similar or connotative situations in the lives of the patients. One told about her sister and their interaction. Another thought of her mother and a facet of their relationship which related to the story. Several mentions were made of ways of facing up to dreaded situations. Then another patient explained her difficulties in relating to her family and friends. She told how she had learned to accept what she could not change and gave her rationale for her condition. This narrative brought signs of approval from the psychologists and ended the session.

This was a typical session. The atmosphere of each meeting is relaxed, friendly and non-demanding. Since the patients have attended psychodrama and have had therapy sessions with psychologists and psychiatrists they have enough understanding to look below the surface.

Variations in the sessions occur, of course. At a doctor's request one entire ward of 55 men may meet with the doctor, the ward staff, and the bibliotherapist. Sometimes trips are taken and the sessions are held in some such place as a county park.

At Agnews State Hospital recognition is given to the fact that many people with mental illness are not motivated to read because the illness itself may leave the patient unable to read. Medicines prescribed often affect the eyes of patients so that reading is impossible. Therefore the selections are read by the bibliotherapist so that all present may benefit from them. Also, since the reading selection is presented to the group without its being read beforehand by individuals, the impact is fresh and experiences are more easily shared.

Improvement in socialization is one of the positive results. It may take several meetings before the individual patient trusts the group enough to join the discussion, but eventually he will do so. The librarian and/or bibliotherapist do not lead the discussion; they allow it to move in whatever direction the group desires. No attempt is ever made at probing or psycho-analysis, nor is the author or story studied as a piece of literature. Only the emotional and mental impact of the situation, the characters, and the emotion expressed in the story itself become topics of discussion and means to personal revelation or catharsis.

When bibliotherapy sessions were introduced it was generally felt that any sensitive person with a knowledge of books and empathy with patients would be a competent bibliotherapist. Social workers, technicians, psychologists, chaplains, and college students all organized groups and read stories to induce discussion. Soon, the librarian was called on for stories for older women, for alcoholics, for a mother-son interaction. A librarian's skills are really needed to select the type of stories likely to involve the listeners; and full use must be made of indexes and bibliographies to avoid time-consuming searching and reading. The librarian should also organize the sessions, obtain referrals of patients from the doctors or ward team, set up the rooms, and decide who shall read. Sometimes patients, especially those with any acting experience, like to read the story. The understanding and cooperation of all the hospital staff is desirable and necessary, but the program should be closely allied to the library in philosophy and administration.

G. O. Ireland, then neuropsychiatrist at the Veterans' Administration Hospital at American Lake, Washington, writing more than forty years ago on bibliotherapy as an aid in treating mental cases, gave an interesting list of characteristics which he felt would qualify a librarian to work with mental patients, stressing that it is a very different type of job from that in a public library. [8]

First, says Dr. Ireland, the librarian should be a woman. He does not explain this, but it may well be because there were far fewer male librarians then than now. He does say that the librarian must be intensely sympathetic and must not voice ideas that will antagonize, and may have believed these two traits more common to women that to men. Other points stressed were that the librarian, to do successful bibliotherapy in the setting of a mental hospital, should be in touch with all topics of the day and be prepared to act as friend, adviser, counselor, and guide. She must be interested in sports, ready to investigate any question, willing to give advice, and not be too decided in her opinions. The modern practitioner might well question the matter of the bibliotherapist giving advice. Perhaps, if done discreetly and if medical or highly emotional topics are avoided, a little advice might be permissible, but certainly such a prerogative should be exercised with great caution. It is really not the role of the librarian-bibliotherapist to give advice but rather to provide the materials upon which the patient will base his own decisions.

The ideal library, Dr. Ireland felt, should be as informal and as much like home as possible.   This idea has
been expressed many times, but Dr. Ireland goes on to speci-
fics, citing pictures on the walls, flowers on the table or
desk, curtains at the windows, a rug on the floor, easy
chairs, anything to make the room cozy and inviting.   The
less like an official part of the institution it looks the better.
In such a friendly, homelike environment, a mental patient
especially may find the warmth, peace, and relaxation he so
badly needs.

Sad books obviously should not be given to a mournful
or depressed patient.   A paranoiac--always a potential murderer, Dr. Ireland thinks--should not be given books that
might suggest methods of murder, aggravating his symptoms
and adding fuel to the flame of his delusional system.   Suicidal or nihilistic ideas should also be avoided.

Dr. Ireland proposed a memorandum form to be used
by the librarian in obtaining information from the patient's
doctor.   Understandably, it is brief and thus more likely to
be returned by a busy physician.   Using a 3 x 5 card the
following could be used (adapted with some additions by author):

      Patient's name   Ward   Type

Memo from the librarian to Dr. _____
Kindly suggest the type of books and magazine suitable
for this patient's reading.   Scientific, religious, practical arts (woodworking, gardening), travel, history,
literature (plays, poetry), textbooks (grammars, arithmetic); fiction (exciting or serious), mystery, western,
science fiction, inspirational, nature material, hobbies,
etc.
Types to be avoided_____
Signed_____ Librarian
        _____Psychiatrist or M. D.

For each patient there should be a work sheet for the
librarian-therapist's reference.   It should contain the following information:

Name
Important points in the family history
Home environment
Personal history

Schooling
Opportunities for education
Reasons for leaving school (if a dropout)
Tastes or dislikes
Postwar activities (if in the service during combat)
Postwar adjustment (if in the service during combat)
Short review of event leading up to hospitalization
Present condition and complaint

Hopefully most of this information can be obtained from the admittance file or medical staff. As the therapist becomes better acquainted with the patient, she should add the following items:

Intellectual activity of the patient
Ability to acquire and retain information
Power to outline judiciously what he reads
Is he lazy or active?
What are his sexual ideas and of how much importance are they to him?
What degree of self-reliance does he possess?
Does he feel inferior?
Is he socially inadaptable?
Has he had a love affair?
Is he moody?
Is he inventive?

Brain-damaged Patients

During the academic year 1970-71 Jo Catherine Hynes served as a medical librarian trainee at the Wade Park Veterans' Administration Hospital in Cleveland, Ohio. In her work there Hynes became involved with bibliotherapy with brain-damaged patients. One of the clinical social workers had asked if one of the librarians would read to a group of patients who had been organized into a social club, Club 21, which met each afternoon in the ward dayroom. The social worker had read a few stories which were greatly enjoyed, but she was fast depleting her literary resources. She felt a librarian would be more familiar with a wider range of literature. Jo Hynes volunteered.

Most of the club members were stroke victims and the social worker had chosen those patients with the most brain damage; Ward 21 patients were definitely not readers. Jo Hynes had no previous experience with bibliotherapy or public

library work, and she didn't know what kind of stories to use.
Bibliotherapy literature supplied help: "Know the patient, for
the patient himself is the determining factor in book selection," she read.   Mrs. Hynes studied case histories, including one of a patient who had had two cerebrovascular accidents and was somewhat paralyzed.   He also had a severe
speech impediment and Parkinson's Disease.   This patient
was extremely emotional, cried when disturbed, could not
walk and would eventually go to a nursing home.   Another
case was a chronic alcoholic with accompanying encephalo-
pathy and Wernicke's syndrome.   His memory was defective
and he was confused and disoriented.   Long divorced, he had
no children and lived with his mother who could barely get
around herself.   He was destined to go to a psychiatric hospital.

Stroke, senility, chronic alcoholism, and heart trouble
were the most prevalent ailments of Club 21.   Stroke patients
ranged in age from fifty to ninety.   With all the patients, socialization was badly needed.

Although Margaret Hanningan feels a librarian doing
bibliotherapy should consult with the medical staff for recommendations, this was not possible in Ward 21 as there was
only one doctor to eighty-five patients; he had little time to
prescribe literature.   The majority of the nursing staff were
practical nurses not sufficiently acquainted with literature to
make recommendations.

The major reading for Club 21 had to be reading aloud
because paralysis from strokes prevented some patients from
holding books or turning pages, most of the patients had extremely poor vision because of old age or stroke, and some
patients were not able to read.

Reading materials had to be on an elementary reading
level, as most of the patients had limited vocabularies.
Stories had to be short so as not to exceed brain-damaged
patients' limited attention span.   These stories were mainly
action rather than description.   Brain-damaged patients cannot grasp abstract ideas.

Supplementary reading had to be supplied by establishing a library bookshelf in the ward dayroom.   The books
were large print so that patients with limited vision could
read on their own if they wished.   Picture books were included so that patients who could not read could at least en-

joy the feel of a book.   Magazines provided a link with the
outside world.   The bookshelf collection was constantly
changed.

All reading, both group and individual, was discussed.
Mrs. Hynes had to be re-introduced to the group each week.
She emphasized the connection with the library and the fact
that she would be back in a week.   Refreshments were served.
Hynes walked around helping, and some individuals would talk.
With such patients the regularity of events was important.
The funtime was story time, and the patients wanted it first.
They came to look forward to the visits.   Mrs. Hynes felt,
as a result of her work, that practicing hospital librarians
could work with brain-damaged patients, a group heretofore
considered beyond the realm of bibliotherapy.

Poetry is a natural element of work with such patients.
They appreciate the obvious sounds and rhythms even if they
can't grasp the subtle allusions and metaphors of serious
poetry.   Limericks are a good choice.   Hilarity leads to
conversation.   Two good collections are Good Intentions, by
Ogden Nash, and Out on a Limerick, by Bennett Cerf.   The
most successful poem was "The Prayer of Cyrus Brown, "
by S. W. Foss in A Little Book of American Humorous Verse,
edited by T. A. Daly.   Favorite Poems Old and New by Helen
Ferris (Doubleday, 1957), is a fount of ideas.   It is divided
by subjects--animals, city life, family life, etc. --and provides a way of finding out where a patient's interests lie.
Reflections on a Gift of Watermelon Pickle (Lothrop, 1967)
was indispensable.   Much of the poetry concerns childhood
experiences and may prompt some fine reminiscing, for although brain-damaged patients have faulty memories, it is
usually the most recent events that they forget and the long
past they remember.   In this volume excellent photos accompany almost every poem; it can be used in a variety of ways.

Children's fairy tales and legends are also good fare,
Hynes points out.   Since a future in the real world is bleak
indeed for many, escape into fantasy is enjoyed and is socially acceptable.   Collier's Junior Classics provides an endless supply of these reading materials.   The Elephant's Child
rated extremely high.   An uninhibited librarian can dramatize; this allows a longer story because action and interesting
sounds hold the patients' attention.   Old Woman Who Used Her
Head, also in Collier's series, is good for dramatization;
also, because it is really several short stories put together
in a series, it can be used to help strengthen the brain-

damaged patient's memory. The librarian should read one
segment each week. At first, the main theme of the stories
should be reintroduced but soon this will not be necessary.
With skillful prompting the librarian can help the patients
remember the preceding stories--at first, only the most obvious parts, but gradually becoming more specific. Brain-
damaged patients love stories in which the hero's judgment
is more faulty than their own. This helps explain the immense popularity of Soap, Soap, Soap and Winnie the Pooh,
both also in the Collier Classics. Winnie the Pooh should
be reworded so the story is told directly to the patients
rather than indirectly through Christopher Robin. This is
because such patients have a hard time handling pronouns.

Riddles, jokes and word games are useful, too, if kept
simple; also any type of "what is it?" picture book. About
five pictures are enough for one session. [9]

Empathy (but not sympathy) is important. The librarian must remember it is not easy for these patients to
establish human contacts. Many of her efforts will meet with
frustration. Patients will often be apathetic and uncoopera-
tive. There will be many interruptions, both intentional and
unintentional. The librarian must remain persuasive and enthusiastic and not allow herself to be distracted. Because
the brain-damaged patient is constantly in danger of being a
slave to current stimulation, a disruption by one patient can
turn a reading session into chaos if not immediately checked. [10]

If there is no spontaneous discussion after a reading,
the librarian must start one. Despite her greatest efforts,
there will be days when no ploy seems to work. All she can
do is accept that day as one of her patients' bad days. The
next week she should start on a positive note, as if the last
week's fiasco had never happened. The librarian must interact with her patients individually, asking direct questions.
Sometimes contact must be on a physical basis, the librarian
touching patients, holding their hands, embracing them. This
directs their attention away from their illness and toward
her. [10]

When patients do begin to interact, the librarian must
listen. She must hear the patients' problems and take them
into account in book selection. Attentive listening boosts the
patients' ego: brain-damaged patients do perceive that they
are different. It is easy to ignore this because it is time-
consuming and these patients are often considered hopeless.

But while they may not be able to learn intricate math, they can exercise their minds. To leave them sitting in front of a television with no opportunity for interpersonal communication is no less imprisonment than would be actual incarceration.

Aphasia

Aphasia is a loss or impairment of language caused by brain injury. Special techniques are needed for the practice of bibliotherapy in this field.

The purposes here are to provide a program for improvement of communication skills including understanding, speaking, reading, and writing. Residual skills are employed and those lost or impaired are relearned.

It will then be possible for the patient to adjust to a relaxed environment, to build up a sense of security and belonging; to gain confidence and to foster social interaction. The following steps can be followed:

1. The librarian should consult with the speech therapist or clinician in establishing small groups for sessions lasting about one-half hour.

2. Volunteers may be assigned to individual patients for additional motivation.

3. Patient participation might be encouraged by group or choral reading.

4. Materials and aids needed include low-vocabulary level reading material with adult interest, word cards, colorful pictures, newspapers, magazines, tape recorders, record players and recordings, projectors, and large print books.

Some high-interest, low vocabulary materials are:

Articles from current and back issues of Reader's Digest.

DeWitt, W. A. Illustrated Minute Biographies. rev. ed.
    N.Y.: Grosset, n.d., $3.95.

Publications on travel (Let's Read About ....) and history

(Story of America). Grand Rapids, Mich.: Fideler Publ. Co.

Reader's Digest. New Reading Skill Builders Series. Gr. 1-5. Pleasantville, N.Y.: Reader's Digest Educational Division.

Reading aloud of previously learned poetry and prose aids in recall and also in the use of language. Poems by well-loved poets such as Henry Longfellow, Robert Louis Stevenson, Robert Browning, and James Whitcomb Riley are useful in helping to relate to past events and to establish reality. These sessions can be taped and replayed later for patient discussions. [11]

Group Activity with Adult Mentally Retarded Residents

Purposes: To provide socialization and enrichment and to stimulate reading as a leisure-time activity. [12]

One or two group members should be made responsible for each session of what might be called the "literary club." Each one chooses a topic of general interest for discussion. A topic may be a news item, review of a book, poetry reading, or a display of pictures or objects. This group could also be a "magazine club" in which each member is responsible for reviewing current issues of appropriate magazines. The librarian should recommend specific titles for additional reading on a subject under discussion, and appropriate books should be on display. Some of the classics which have been rewritten in simple language, such as Treasure Island, might be appropriate. Materials must be chosen according to the ability and interests of the individual participant. Light fiction, books for curriculum enrichment and for intermediate grades, and books with mature concepts but written in an easy style and vocabulary are suitable. Current popular magazines and newspapers are satisfactory. Other materials suggested are:

Checkered Flag Series. San Francisco: Field Educational Publications, Inc. (This is a series of eight books written on second to fourth grade level. Filmstrips, records and tapes are also available for use with the series.)

Know Your World. Columbus, Ohio: American Education Publications. Weekly, Sept.-June.

Leedy, Jack J., ed. The Use of Poetry in the Treatment of
   Emotional Disorders. Philadelphia: Lippincott, 1969.
   $7.00.

Scholastic Scope. Englewood, N.J.: Scholastic Press.
   Weekly, Sept. -June.

Speech Development with the Mentally Retarded

      Speech development is a primary need of school-age
mentally retarded children. Library programs can be useful
as supplements to speech therapy.

      Group activities in the library might consist of the use
of records, filmstrips, picture files, and scrapbooks. These
activities can be used to increase verbal response and comprehension of a subject and to correct pronunciation. Games
and stories which incorporate verbal responses are useful.
Suggested readings:[12]

Grossbart, Francine B. Big City. N.Y.: Harper, 1960.
   $3.50. Things to be identified in a big city. Good for
   vocabulary development.

Podendorf, Illa. True Book of Pets. Chicago: Children's
   Press, 1954. $2.50. About 90% of text is written in
   words from "combined word list for primary reading."

      At Central State Griffin Memorial Hospital, Norman,
Oklahoma, [13] children's books have been used successfully
with the more retarded patients, particularly the nonsense
books with large type, simple words, and numerous pictures,
such as the Dr. Seuss books. After a few sessions patients
can begin to take part in the reading of stories and may even
ask to read without any urging. Also useful with these patients are picture books which tell the story without any words.
Patients respond well to large print books. They are able to
see better and therefore gain a greater sense of accomplishment. Large print books, also, are usually titles that have
been popular in regular print or have become classics.

      At Central State the librarian, Preston Gilson, used a
variety of media to help motivate the mentally ill patient. The
majority of the patients at Central State were older people
who were considered long term. They ranged in ability from
those unable to read and concentrate for any length of time to

others who actually selected their own reading materials.

It is interesting to note exactly how patients at the
Veterans' Administration Hospital in Oklahoma City related
to two different books in their group sessions.   Those who
read Wind in the Willows by Kenneth Grahame, with its brilliant analysis of personalities, found themselves comparing
the various characters to personal acquaintances.   This process gradually led the patient to the point where he was able
to identify himself with one or more of the characters. Then,
by talking about his reasons for identifying with a character,
he was better able to understand his own nature.

> When Red Badge of Courage, by Stephen Crane,
> was read the patients got into a very heated dis-
> cussion on the morality of war and the consequences
> of war on the integrity of man.   Because they were
> able to see the inner thoughts of a man struggling
> with self doubts they were better able to look at
> their own thoughts.   They were encouraged by the
> confusion which accompanied Henry's attempts to
> understand himself.

Another book which presents the thoughts of the main
character is Old Yeller, by Fred Gipson.   Two different bibliotherapy groups at Central State read this book.   The first
group, made up of patients with less than a high school education, and who were in a chronic ward, was more interested
in the action and showed little interest in or comprehension
of the mental and emotional development of the hero.   The
second group, patients who were in better contact, was more
aware of the theme of the story and more interested in the
development of the characters than in the action. [13]

The mentally retarded child is, unhappily, represented
in almost every community.   There are in the U.S. more
than five million mildly retarded persons (considered educable)
and nearly half a million moderately retarded (considered
trainable). [14]

Story telling illustrated with colored slides projected
on a screen helps retarded children to follow a simple story
as it is told.   If a large storybook is illustrated with full-
page pictures and the group is small, holding up the pictures
and calling attention to its details may suffice.   However,
some retarded children, especially the trainable group, have
visual problems and the enalrged projected pictures are more

helpful. [14]

As a follow-up the storyteller therapist should, whenever possible, provide book-related activities such as creative dramatics, making simple puppets of the book characters, dioramas, drawing pictures, or retelling the stories in the children's own words. Such activities make the books come alive and serve to stimulate creativity. The elements of bibliotherapy are readily apparent in these activities centering around books: giving the children a sense of achievement, allowing them to participate in an activity common to normal children, bringing happiness to children who sometimes find too little of it in their contacts with their peers or even sometimes with their own families, enlarging their knowledge of the animals, objects, or other subjects of the stories and pictures. [14]

Children in a story telling group should be allowed to express themselves freely, since suppression of words or thoughts is not good from a mental health standpoint. While not always aware of their "differences," such children are often very sensitive and resent suppression. Naturally, the educable group shows more response to a book-related storytelling program than the trainable group. More individual (one-to-one) bibliotherapy is needed with the retarded of all ages. [14]

Experience has shown that in dealing with mental patients in a hospital library, rigid rules are a deterrent. The library and the librarian must seem nonauthoritarian, the library a haven to which the patient may go to relax and escape constant restrictions and routine. It is important for a librarian wishing to do bibliotherapy with a mental patient to know, if possible, what John P. Walmer calls "The Three P's": Predisposing factors, Precipitating factors, and Perpetuating factors. Predisposing factors may be hereditary, stress, an emotional or psychological shock, tragedy, an unresolved conflict, or similar factors. A precipitating factor is one which by its intensity brings on an attack, violence, or other disturbance in the patient's quieter, more normal state; perpetuating factors are those which tend to continue the basic mental problem until it becomes practically irreversible. [15]

Gottschalk points out that the patient who seeks psychotherapeutic help is a better candidate for bibliotherapy than one who does not. If the patient asks the therapist for

reading matter, one would naturally expect that the reading
will be done more enthusiastically and conscientiously and
that the results will be more beneficial.   In general, patients
with mild psychoneurotic disturbances are the most favorable
candidates for supervised reading.   Psychotic or severe psychoneurotic patients are less likely to benefit.   However,
Gottschalk believed that the use of bibliotherapy in severe
illnesses has not been fully exploited by trained therapists
and that the field is fertile for further experimentation. [16]

Some estimates are that from fifty to seventy-five per
cent of all illnesses are complicated by or precipitated by
emotional conflict.   This implies a great need to put emphasis upon what is called psychological therapy, of which
bibliotherapy can be an integral part. [17]

Notes

1.   Porterfield, Austin L.   Mirror for Adjustment: Therapy
      in Home, School, and Society for Seeing Yourself and
      Others in Books.   Leo Potisham Foundation, Texas
      Christian University, c. 1967. p. 4.

2.   Educational Research and Development, Inc.   Institutional
      Library Services: A Plan for the State of Illinois.
      Study authorized by Paul Powell, State Librarian,
      Illinois State Library, Springfield, Ill. , p. 44-45, 76,
      79.

3.   News Item.   Library Journal, v. 82, January 1, 1957,
      p. 36-37.

4.   Hannigan, Margaret C.   "Bibliotherapy: Its Part in Li-
      brary Service." Bookmark, v. 15, March 1956, p.
      127-133.

5.   Educational Research and Development, Inc.   Institutional
      Library Services... op. cit. , p. 75.

6.   McDowell, David J.   "Bibliotherapy in a Patients' Li-
      brary. " Bulletin of the Medical Library Association,
      v. 59, July 1971, p. 450-57.

7.   Griffith, Leah Ann.   "The Agnews State Hospital Biblio-
      therapy Program. " News Notes of California Librar-
      ies, v. 66, Summer 1971, p. 400-04.

8. Ireland, G. O. "Bibliotherapy as an Aid in Treating Mental Cases." The Modern Hospital, v. XXXIV, June 1930, p. 88-90.

9. Hynes, Jo Catherine. "Library Work with Brain-Damaged Patients: A New Mode of Bibliotherapy." Bulletin of the Medical Library Association, v. 60, April 1972, p. 333-339.

10. Edwards, S. L. "Group Work with Brain-Damaged Patients." Hospital Community Psychiatry, v. 18, September 1967, p. 267-270.

11. Educational Research and Development, Inc. Institutional Library Service... op. cit., p. 74-75.

12. Ibid., p. 78-79

13. Gilson, Preston and Al-Salman, Janie. "Bibliotherapy in Oklahoma." Oklahoma Librarian, v. 22, July 1972, p. 12.

14. Limper, Hilda. In: McCrossan, John. Public Library Services for the Handicapped. Unpublished mimeographed publication supplied by Mr. McCrossan.

15. Walmer, John D. "Psychology of Illness and the Use of Reading in the Treatment Plan." Association of Hospital and Institution Libraries Quarterly, v. 5, Spring 1965, p. 5-8.

16. Gottschalk, Louis A. "Bibliotherapy as an Adjunct in Psychotherapy." American Journal of Psychiatry. v. 104, April 1958, p. 633.

17. Coville, Walter J. "Bibliotherapy: Some Practical Considerations. Part 2." Hospital Progress, v. 41, April 1960, p. 138-142, and May 1960, p. 20+.

REFERENCES FOR THE BIBLIOTHERAPIST

Baatz, W. H. "Patients' Library Services and Bibliotherapy." Wilson Library Bulletin, 35:378-379, January 1961.

Discusses briefly the value of a professional library service for hospital patients and how bibliotherapy can be and is being used, principally to help patients in neuropsychiatric hospitals.

Bass, A. H. "Great Books are Good Treatment. " Mental Hospitals, 11:43-44, May 1960.
A Great Books reading group for mentally and emotionally disturbed patients at Mt. Sinai Hospital, New York, has proven to be a valuable therapeutic aid.

Brower, Daniel, M. D. "Bibliotherapy. " In: Brower, Daniel, and Abt, L. E. , Progress in Clinical Psychology. New York, Grune, 1956. v. 2, pp. 212-215.
Dr. Brower discusses some of the problems, advantages and dangers inherent in the reading of psychological books by patients undergoing counseling or psychotherapy, and presents a rationale for the judicious use of bibliotherapy in various aspects of mental hygiene.

Bryan, A. I. "Personality Adjustment through Reading. " Library Journal, 64:573-576, August 1939.
A professor of library education (also trained in psychology) describes how the progressive, interested and trained reader's adviser might guide patrons toward improved mental health through reading recommendations aimed at keeping readers adjusted to their personal problems.

_____. "The Psychology of the Reader. " Library Journal, 64:7-12, January 1, 1939.
The author, a consulting psychologist of the School of Library Science, Columbia University, supports the contention that bibliotherapy as a technique of guidance can be used to give insight and aid in the solution of personal problems. She recommends close interrelation of psychologists and librarians so that the special talents of each may combine to help the reader.

Dreifuss, Henry. "Listening and Viewing: a Group Picture Program for Neuropsychiatric Patients. " Recreation, 55: 43, January 1960.
The use of filmstrips and slides at the Veterans' Administration Hospital in Pittsburgh, Pa. , has led to a considerable increase in the use of library books by neuropsychiatric patients.

Fierman, L. B. , M. D. , and Fierman, E. Y. "Bibliotherapy

in psychiatry. " In: Dunton, W. R. , Jr. , M. D. , and Licht, Sidney, M. D. Occupational Therapy, Principles and Practice. 2nd ed. Springfield, Ill. : Thomas, 1957, pp. 163-176.

A brief historical review of bibliotherapy followed by a discussion on the determinants of reading behavior, the effects of reading on behavior, and the practice of bibliotherapy.

Gallagher, Janet. "Chicago State Hospital Patients' Library. " Illinois Libraries, 40:443-445, May 1958.

Provides an excellent picture of hospital library service in a large psychiatric hospital. Special collections are maintained for the blind and foreign-speaking populations. A Friday Evening Book Club and a Great Books group are two of the bibliotherapeutic projects.

Johnson, N. B. "Group Therapy in a Hospital Library. " Medical Bulletin of the Veterans' Administration, 20: 207- , October 1943.

Results realized from various library programs for closed-ward groups show them to have major therapeutic value for mentally ill patients.

Montagu, Ashley. On Being Human. N. Y. : Hawthorn Books, 1967.

A plan for the reduction of man's tensions and hope for his future.

Rein, D. M. S. Weir Mitchell as a Psychiatric Novelist. N. Y. : International Universities Pr. , 1952, p. 207.

The fiction writings of the great neurologist were analyzed for psychiatric content. Excellent background reading for gaining insight into types of mental disorders and possible reading suggestions for patients.

Seiver, L. M. "A Layman Leads a Great Books Group in a Mental Hospital. " Mental Hygiene, 45:537-542, October 1961.

The impressions of the group and how the author managed the various problems that arose, after a year's experience as group leader.

SUGGESTED BOOKS FOR THE READER WITH
MENTAL, EMOTIONAL, AND PERSONAL PROBLEMS

I.   CHILDREN AND YOUNG ADULTS

General

Cavanna, Betty. Going on Sixteen. Westminster, 1946.
    Personality and the life cycle. Ages 12-16.
Fontaine, Robert. Humorous Monologues for Teen-Agers.
    Plays, 1973. A collection of 25 monologues which pre-
    sent real problems in a humorous manner. Ages 12-16.

Alcoholic Parent

Maddock, Reginald. The Pit. Little, 1968. Ages 12 up.
Norris, Gunilla B. Take My Waking Slow. Atheneum, 1970.
    Ages 8-12.
Sherburne, Zoa. Jennifer. Morrow, 1959. Ages 12 up.

Adolescence

Blume, Judy. Are You There God? It's Me, Margaret.
    Bradbury, 1970. Ages 8-12.
Greene, Constance C. Leo the Lioness. Viking, 1970.
    Ages 8-12.
Wersba, Barbara. The Dream Watcher. Atheneum, 1968.
    Ages 12 up.

Adoption

Arthur, Ruth. Portrait of Margarita. Atheneum, 1968.
    Ages 12 up.
Arthur, Ruth. Requiem ofr a Princess. Atheneum, 1967.
    Ages 12 up.
Clewes, Dorothy. Adopted Daughter. Coward, n. d. Ages 12 up.
Daringer, Helen. Adopted Jane. Harcourt, 1947. Ages 8-12.
Haywood, Carolyn. Here's a Penny. Harcourt, 1944. Ages
    8-12.
Wasson, Valentina. The Chosen Baby. Lippincott, 1950.
    Ages 5-8.

Boy-Girl Relationships

Bruce, Jeanette. The Wallflower Season. Doubleday, 1962.

Four girls get tired of being wallflowers and do something about it.   Ages 12-16.

Calhoun, Mary.   Honestly, Katie John!   Harper & Row, 1963.
Katie learns self-acceptance, improves her relationships with boys, and gains maturity.   Ages 12-16.

Cavanna, Betty.   Accent on April.   Morrow, 1960.   Girl
learns better ways of relating to opposite sex and to
her own brother.   Ages 12-16.

Daly, Sheila.   Questions Teen-Agers Ask.   Dodd, Mead, 1963.
Questions frequently asked by teen-agers are answered
in a direct and sensible manner.   Ages 12 up.

Davies, Nancy.   The American Girl.   Random House, 1963.
Answers to questions girls ask when approaching adolescence.   Ages 12 up.

Felsen, Henry G.   Letters to a Teen-Age Son.   Dodd, Mead,
1962.   A discussion of teen-age problems.   Ages 12 up.

James, Norma.   Bittersweet Year.   McKay, 1961.   Kathy
learns a lot about love and growing up during one short
summer.   Ages 12 up.

Richardson, Frank H.   For Boys Only.   McKay, 1965.   An
M. D. discusses frankly and clearly questions pertaining to the various aspects of adolescent life.   12 up.

Richardson, Frank H.   For Girls Only.   McKay, 1964.   A
book for adolescent girls which explains the physiological aspects of growing up and relates them to the
psychological concomitants.   Ages 12 up.

Stolz, Mary.   To Tell Your Love.   Harper & Row, 1950.
A 17-year-old learns the difference between love and
infatuation.   Ages 13-17.

Brain Injury

Bennett, Eve.   Little Bit.   Messner, 1961.   Girl comes to
a better understanding of herself and others while
caring for her little sister who is brain-damaged.

Conflict of Values

Block, Marie H.   Aunt America.   Atheneum, 1963.   Ages
8-12.

Whitney, Phyllis.   Mystery of the Golden Horn.   Westminster,
1962.   Two girls find something more valuable while
searching for a lost jewel. Ages 10-15.

Courage

Chamberlain, William.   Matt Quarterhill, Rifleman.   John

Day, 1967. A soldier proves himself during World
War II battle in the Pacific. Ages 12 up.

Cotton, Nell. Piney Woods. Vanguard, 1962. Boy learns
courage and self-respect. Ages 8-12.

Dennenborg, H. M. The Talking Tree. Macmillan, 1949.
Jan's love for his crippled pony remains strong in
spite of the taunts from his schoolmates. Ages 5-8.

Detwiler, H. J. How to Stand Up for What You Believe.
Association Press, 1966. A book which tells teen-
agers how to maintain their beliefs and encourages
them to do so, even when under social pressure.
Ages 12 up.

Harnden, Ruth. Golly and the Gulls. Houghton, 1962. Boy
learns the difference between bravery and foolhardi-
ness. Ages 8-12.

Kennedy, John F. Profiles in Courage. Harper & Row,
1961. Story of eight American statesmen who refused
to sacrifice their integrity at the risk of ruining their
careers. Ages 12 up.

MacKellar, William. A Place by the Fire. David McKay,
1966. A boy and a dog prove that spirit and character are more important than age during a crisis.
Ages 8-12.

O'Dell, Scott. Island of the Blue Dolphins. Houghton, 1960.
Story of a young Indian girl who spent 18 years alone
on an island. Ages 8-12.

Singer, Kurt, and Sherrod, Jane. Ernest Hemingway, Man
of Courage. T. S. Denison, 1963. An account of
the struggles, problems, and illnesses faced by the
great writer. Ages 12 up.

Steele, William. The Year of the Bloody Sevens. Harcourt,
1963. A boy learns the real meaning of courage during an Indian siege. Ages 8-12.

Thayer, Jane. A Drink for Little Red Diker. Morrow, 1963.
A small antelope finally learns to be self-confident and
develops his courage. Ages 5-8.

Tibbets, Albert. American Heroes All. Little, Brown, 1966.
Stories about typical American soldiers. Ages 12 up.

Tunis, John R. The Kid Comes Back. Morrow, 1946.
Story of how the bravery of John F. Kennedy saved
the lives of his crew. Ages 12 up.

Death

Buck, Pearl S. The Big Wave. Day, 1948.

Cleaver, Vera and Bill. Grover. Lippincott, 1970. Ages
8-12.

Corbin, William. The Golden Mare. Coward, 1955. Ages
      8-12.
Little, Jean. Home From Far. Little, 1965. Ages 8-12.
Warburg, Sandol. Growing Time. Houghton, 1969. Ages
      8-12.

Divorce

Barnwell, Robinson. Shadow on the Water. David McKay,
      1967. Ages 12 up.
Cleaver, Vera and Bill. Ellen Grae. Lippincott, 1967.
      Ages 8-12.
Cleaver, Vera and Bill. Lady Ellen Grae. Lippincott, 1968.
      Ages 8-12.
Donovan, John. I'll Get There. It Better Be Worth the
      Trip. Harper, 1969. Ages 12 up.
Johnson, Annabel and Edgar. The Grizzly. Harper, 1964.
      Ages 8-12.
Norris, Gunilla B. Lillian. Atheneum, 1968. Ages 8-12.
Platt, Kin. The Boy Who Could Make Himself Disappear.
      Chilton, 1968. Ages 12 up.
Sachs, Marilyn. Veronica Ganz. Doubleday, 1968. Ages
      8-12.

Expression of Self

Stolz, Mary. Belling the Tiger. Harper, 1967. Ages 8-12.
Wojciechowska, Maia. Shadow of a Bull. Atheneum, 1964.
      Ages 12 up.

Family Relationships

Allen, Lorenzo. Fifer for the Union. Morrow, 1964. Boy
      finally realizes that he helped contribute to his prob-
      lems at home. Ages 5-8.
Armer, Alberta. Screwball. World, 1963. Ages 8-12.
Baker, Laura. Cousin Tryg. Lippincott, 1966. A small
      boy learns to accept his father's death and the result-
      ing changes in his life. Ages 8-12.
Ball, Zachary. Kep. Holiday House, 1961. Kep faces a
      difficult time when after his father's death he is sent
      to live with a family whose son has died. Ages 12 up.
Bannon, Laura. The Gift of Hawaii. Albert Whitman, 1961.
      A little Hawaiian boy shows his generosity when he
      buys his mother a birthday present. Ages 5-8.
Bond, Gladys. A Head on Her Shoulders. Abelard-Schuman,

1963.   Girl learns to assume responsibility for younger
siblings.   Ages 8-12.

Bradbury, Bianca.   The Amethyst Summer.   Ives Washburn,
1963.   When her mother must leave to care for an
ill relative, Bayley faces the responsibility of caring
for the family.   Ages 8-12.

Bradbury, Bianca.   Goodness and Mercy Jenkins.   Ives
Washburn, 1963.   A spirited girl revolts against her
Puritan guardians and the marriage they arranged for
her.   Ages 12 up.

Brenner, Barbara.   Nicky's Sister.   Knopf, 1966.   Nicky
finds that his new baby sister needs him.   Ages 5-8.

Brown, Myra.   Ice Cream for Breakfast.   Watts, 1963.   A
little girl and boy show their appreciation for their
mother by serving her breakfast in bed on Mother's
Day.   Ages 5-8.

Brown, Myra.   Pip Camps Out.   Golden Gate, 1966.   Pip is
happy when his father joins him on a camp-out. Ages
5-8.

Buckley, Helen.   Grandmother and I.   Lothrop, Lee and
Shepard, 1961.   Grandmothers serve a special purpose
for young children.   Ages 5-8.

Buckley, Helen.   My Sister and I.   Lothrop, Lee and Shepard, 1963.   An example of a close wholesome relationship between two sisters.   Ages 5-8.

Budd, Lillian.   Larry.   David McKay, 1966.   A little boy
runs away but is happy when he returns to his family.
Ages 5-8.

Cavanna, Betty.   A Breath of Fresh Air.   Morrow, 1966.
A New England family is faced with the problems
created by divorce.   Ages 12 up.

Corcoran, Barbara.   Sam.   Atheneum, 1967.   Ages 12 up.

Dolim, Mary.   The Bishop Pattern.   Morrow, 1963.   The
story of the efforts of a homeless little girl to adjust
to a strange family.   Ages 12 up.

Dubkin, Lois.   Quiet Street.   Abelard-Schuman, 1963.   A
story of the problems faced when a family with an only
child adopts another daughter.   Ages 5-8.

Duncan, Lois.   Giving Away Suzanne.   Dodd, 1963.   Mary
Kay learns that there are more advantages than dis-
advantages to having a smaller sister after she trades
her for a goldfish.   Ages 5-8.

Duncan, Lois.   The Middle Sister.   Dodd, 1960.   A girl has
a difficult time competing with an older and a younger
sister, each of whom is more talented and attractive
than she.   Ages 12 up.

Enright, Elizabeth.   The Saturdays.   Holt, 1941. Ages 8-12.

Estes, Eleanor. A Little Oven. Harcourt, 1955. Ages 5-8.
Falk, Ann. A Place of Her Own. Harcourt, 1964. An
     orphaned girl learns to overcome the problems of liv-
     ing with her married sister. Ages 12 up.
Falk, Ann. Who is Erika? Harcourt, 1963. Erika resents
     her new stepfather but learns to adjust when she takes
     a better look at herself. Ages 12 up.
Fletcher, David. The King's Goblet. Pantheon, 1962. De-
     picts strife created by difference between adolescent
     and family values. Ages 12 up.
George, Jean. Gull Number 737. Crowell, 1964. Ages 12
     up.
Harnden, Ruth. The High Pasture. Houghton Mifflin, 1964.
     Tim faces the difficult adjustment of being separated
     from his ill mother and later of the shock of her death.
     Ages 8-12.
Hartwell, Nancy. Something for Laurie. Holt, Rinehart and
     Winston, 1962. Girl learns to achieve even though she
     is not as capable as the other members of her family.
     Ages 12 up.
Hoban, Russell. A Baby Sister for Frances. Harper & Row,
     1964. A story of how one family convinced their older
     daughter of her importance even if a new baby had
     arrived in the family. Ages 5-8.
Holland, Marion. Casey Jones Rides Vanity. Little, Brown,
     1964. Girl learns that her little sister needs love and
     understanding. Ages 5-8.
Hunt, Irene. Up the Road Slowly. Follett, 1966. Julie is
     forced to live with a stern aunt after her mother's
     death but eventually learns to adjust to her new en-
     vironment and to love her aunt and uncle for what they
     are. Ages 12 up.
Johnston, Johanna. Edie Changes Her Mind. Putnam, 1964.
     Edie learns the value of obedience and of going to bed.
     Ages 5-8.
Klein, Leonore. Huit Enfants et un Bébé (Eight Children and
     One Baby). Schuman, 1966. An amusing tale of an
     overcrowded house. Ages 5-8.
Kraselovsky, Phyllis. The Very Little Boy. Doubleday, 1962.
     A little boy is finally allowed to push his sister's baby
     carriage. Ages 5-8.
Kraselovsky, Phyllis. The Very Little Girl. Doubleday, 1963.
     A little girl learns to accept her new baby brother and
     act as a "big" sister. Ages 5-8.
L'Engle, Madeleine. Meet the Austins. Vanguard, 1960.
     Ages 8-12.
Lenski, Lois. Strawberry Girl. Lippincott, 1945. Ages 8-12.

Lexau, Joan. Benjie. Dial Press, 1963. Benjie learns
self-reliance by helping his grandmother. Ages 5-8.

Lexau, Joan. José's Christmas Secret. Dial Press, 1962.
José, a little Puerto Rican boy, finds a way to earn
money to buy his mother a needed Christmas present.
Ages 5-8.

Lexau, Joan. The Trouble with Terry. Dial Press, 1962.
Terry faces the problems of growing up without adequate attention from her mother and brother. Ages
8-12.

Little, Jean. Spring Begins in March. Little, Brown, 1966.
Meg finds that her grandma can help her solve her
problems. Ages 8-12.

McCloskey, Robert. One Morning in Maine. Viking, 1952.
Ages 5-8.

Marks, Mickey K. What Can I Buy? Dial Press, 1962. A
boy decides to buy something for each member of his
family instead of spending the money on himself.
Ages 5-8.

Martin, Patricia. The Birthday Present. Abingdon Press,
1963. A boy learns valuable lessons while trying to
get a birthday present for his father. Ages 5-8.

Miles, Betty. Feast on Sullivan Street. Knopf, 1963. Boy
proves to his parents that he is capable of accepting
responsibility. Ages 8-12.

Molloy, Anne. Shaun and the Boat: an Irish Story. Hastings House, 1965. Boy who does not like to work
runs away but he returns and uses his initiative to
help his father win the boat race. Ages 8-12.

Neville, Emily. It's Like This, Cat. Harper, 1963. Ages
8-12.

Olson, Gene. Tin Goose. Westminster Press, 1962. Six-
teen-year-old Danny has some problems in getting
along with his grandfather. Ages 12 up.

Piatti, Clastino. The Happy Owls. Atheneum, 1964. The
owls explain to other birds why they are happy even
if they do live in a hole in the tree. Ages 5-8.

Pilgrim, Anne. The First Time I Saw Paris. Abelard-
Schuman, 1961. The death of a girl's father results
in her being able to help others to face loss and new
adjustment. Ages 12 up.

Pliss, Louise. The Trip Down Catfish Creek. Reilly and
Lee, 1962. Boy learns after one day of complete
freedom that rules and parental guidance are necessary. Ages 8-12.

Reese, John. Three Wild Ones. Westminster, 1963. Boy
tries running away as a solution to home problems

with his mother and stepfather.   Ages 12 up.

Schlein, Miriam. Laurie's New Brother. Abelard-Schuman,
1961.   Laura learns to accept a new baby brother.

Sherburne, Zoa. Girl in the Mirror. Morrow, 1966.   A
young girl is faced with the death of her father. Ages
12 up.

Sorensen, Virginia. Miracles on Maple Hill. Harcourt, 1956.
Ages 8-12.

Stanek, Muriel. New in the City. Albert Whitman, 1965. A
farm family is challenged upon moving to the city.
Ages 5-8.

Swanson, Arlene. Dulcy. Reilly and Lee, 1962.   Dulcy begins to grow up after she learns that defiance and rebellion are childish.   Ages 12-16.

Tibbetts, Albert B. A Boy and His Dad. Little, Brown,
1964.   Seven short stories of father-son relationships.
Ages 12 up.

Tolles, Martha. Too Many Boys. Thomas Nelson, 1965.
Katie, who has many brothers and boy neighbors but
no girl playmates, solves her problem in a unique way.
Ages 5-8.

Warnlof, Anna. The Boy Upstairs. Harcourt, Brace &
World, 1963.   Fredrika has a difficult time before
she learns to accept her parents' divorce. Ages 12 up.

White, Florence. My House is the Nicest Place. Golden
Press, 1963.   A book about the joys of home. Ages
5-8.

Wojciechowska, Maia. Shadow of a Bull. Atheneum, 1964.
The problems faced by a boy who is expected to become a great matador like his father. Ages 8-12.

Woolley, Catherine. A Room for Cathy. Morrow, 1956.
Ages 8-12.

Zolotow, Charlotte. Big Brother. Harper, 1960.   Ages 5-8.

Zolotow, Charlotte. Big Sister and Little Sister. Harper &
Row, 1966.   A story of sisterly love. Ages 5-8.

Zolotw, Charlotte. The Quarreling Book. Harper and Row,
1963.   A common problem presented in an amusing
way. Ages 5-8.

Father in Prison

Burch, Robert. Queenie Peavy. Viking, 1965.   Ages 8-12.

Gripe, Maria. Hugo and Josephine. Delacorte, 1969. Ages
8-12.

Fatherless or Motherless Home

Baker, Laura N. Here by the Sea (fatherless).   Lippincott,

1968, Ages 12 up.
Bragdon, Elspeth. There is a Tide (motherless). Viking,
    1964. Ages 12 up.
Ness, Evaline. Sam, Bangs, and Moonshine (motherless).
    Holt, 1966. Ages 5-8.
Phipson, Joan. Peter and Butch (fatherless). Harcourt,
    1969. Ages 12 up.
Ullman, James. Banner in the Sky (fatherless). Lippincott,
    1954. Ages 12 up.

Fears

Bendick, Jeanne. A Fresh Look at Night. Watts, 1963. An
    explanation of the sights and sounds of night helps
    alleviate fear of darkness. Ages 5-8.
Bryngelson, Bryng. Personality Development through Speech.
    T. S. Denison, 1967. This book provides insight into
    why and how of speaking well as self-help for stage
    fright. Ages 12 up.
Clymer, Eleanor. Chipmunk in the Forest. Atheneum, 1965.
    A timid Indian boy overcomes his fears and wins the
    respect of his elders. Ages 5-8.
Kjelgaard, Jim. Two Dogs and a Horse. Dodd, Mead, 1964.
    Three stories illustrating how wise and patient men
    overcame the fear and distrust that three animals had
    toward humans. Ages 5-8.
Lord, Beman. Bats and Balls. Henry Z. Walck, 1964.
    Boy overcomes fear of getting injured while playing
    baseball. Ages 5-8.
Miller, Martha. Timberline Hound. Knopf, 1963. Boy con-
    quers many of his fears as well as losing a lot of
    weight during a summer in the Colorado mountains.
    Ages 8-12.
Nathan, Dorothy. The Shy One. Random House, 1966. Story
    of a shy little Jewish girl. Ages 8-12.
Yashima, Taro. Youngest One. Viking, 1962. Bobby over-
    comes his shyness and makes a friend. Ages 5-8.

Foster Home

Armer, Alberta. Troublemaker. World, 1966. Ages 8-12.

Generation Conflict

Olson, Gene. Tin Goose. Westminster, 1962. Ages 12 up.
Phipson, Joan. Cross Currents. Harcourt, 1966. Ages
    12 up.

Wersba, Barbara. Run Softly, Go Fast. Atheneum, 1970.

Greed

Green, Nancy. Abu Kassim's Slippers. Follett, 1963. The old classic of the miser who is tricked by his own greed. Ages 5-12.

Health and Physical Appearance

Berger, Knute. A Visit to the Doctor. Grosset & Dunlap, 1960. Explanation of what happens to a small boy when he goes to the doctor for a physical check-up. Ages 5-8.

Clymer, Eleanor. Now That You Are Seven. Association Press, 1963. Stories about children of this age which illustrate the satisfactions to be derived from growing and learning. Ages 5-8.

Emberley, Barbara. Night's Nice. Doubleday, 1963. Explanation of the value of night and of sleep. Ages 5-8.

Farb, Peter. The Story of Life. Harvey House, 1962. A well-illustrated story of the development of life. Ages 8-12.

Follett, Robert. Your Wonderful Body. Follett, 1961. The functioning of the human body is described in simple language and elucidated with diagrams and drawings. Ages 5-12.

Frankel, Bernice. Half-As-Big and the Tiger. Watts, 1961. The smallest deer outwits a tiger and wins the name of "Twice-As-Smart." Ages 5-8.

Friedman, Frieda. Now That You Are Ten. Association Press, 1963. Stories about children of this age which illustrate the satisfactions to be derived from growing and learning. Ages 8-12.

Gesell, Arnold. The Miracle of Growth. Univ. of Illinois Press, 1967. An accurate, non-technical description of human development from conception to maturity. Ages 12 up.

Goldsmith, Ilse. Anatomy for Children. Sterling, 1964. An illustrated description of the function and structure of the human body. Ages 8-12.

Greene, Carla. Doctors and Nurses: What Do They Do? Harper & Row, 1963. An attempt to develop more positive attitudes toward doctors and nurses. Ages 5-8.

Nelson, Marg. A Girl Called Chris. Farrar, Straus & Giroux, 1962. Chris, who is too tall, has failed to get a scholarship, is worried about employment, and

has no father, finds that life can be full and exciting.
Ages 12 up.

Neubrath, Marie. Keeping Well. Sterling, 1964. A graphically illustrated book which uses animals to demonstrate the value of good health habits for children.
Ages 5-8.

Priddy, Frances. The Social Swim. Westminster, 1962.
Overweight Gretchen becomes popular due to her pleasant personality. Ages 8-12.

Rand, Ann. So Small. Harcourt, 1962. Adjustment to
small stature is sometimes difficult but is necessary
for self-acceptance. Ages 5-8.

Schlein, Miriam. Billy: the Littlest One. Albert Whitman,
1966. A small boy tells what it is like to be the
smallest. Ages 5-8.

Steiner, Charlotte. Now That You Are Five. Association
Press, 1963. Stories about children of this age which
illustrate the satisfactions to be derived from growing
and learning. Ages 5-8.

Stolz, Mary. The Bully of Barkham Street. Harper & Row,
1963. Overweight boy learns to control his temper
and get along with others. Ages 12 up.

Taylor, Sydney. Now That You Are Eight. Association Press,
1963. Stories about children of this age which illustrate the satisfactions to be derived from growing and
learning. Ages 5-8.

Vinton, Iris. Now That You Are Nine. Association Press,
1963. Stories about children this age which illustrate
the satisfactions to be derived from growing and learning. Ages 8-12.

Honesty

Stuart, Jesse. Andy Finds a Way. McGraw-Hill, 1961.
Andy tries to hide a new-born calf from his father but
learns that honesty pays. Ages 8-12.

Impatience

Smaridge, Norah. Impatient Jonathan. Abingdon, 1964.
Jonathan learns that one must have patience if he is
to have friends or own a pet. Ages 5-8.

Inferiority Complex

Friedman, Frieda. The Janitor's Girl. Morrow, 1956.
Ages 8-12.

Paradis, Marjorie. Flash Flood at Hollow Creek. Westminster, 1963. Cliff learns that failing in school does
not mean that one cannot be successful elsewhere.
Ages 8-12.

Introverted Child

Konigsburg, E. L. George. Atheneum, 1970. Ages 12 up.
Yashima, Taro. Crow Boy. Viking, 1955. Ages 5-8.

Jealousy

Godden, Rumer. Miss Happiness and Miss Flower. Viking
Press, 1961. Belinda learns that we are often jealous
of others when we shouldn't be. Ages 8-12.

Laziness

Collodi, Carlo. The Adventures of Pinocchio. Macmillan,
1962. A lazy marionette is turned into a donkey but
after he changes his evil ways he becomes a real boy.
Ages 5-8.
Seredy, Kate. Lazy Tinka. Viking Press, 1962. Tinka's
laziness is cured by a wise old woman. Ages 5-8.
Watts, Mabel. The Bed of Thistledown. Abelard-Schuman,
1962. When Lazy Paddy is forced to keep his promise, he learns to be a good worker. Ages 5-8.

Lying

Little, Jean. One To Grow On. Little, 1969. Ages 8-12.

Mental Retardation

Baastad, Babbis F. Don't Take Teddy. Scribner, 1967.
Ages 12 up.
Byars, Betsy. The Summer of the Swans. Viking, 1970.
Ages 8-12.
Christopher, Matthew. Long Shot for Paul. Little, Brown,
1966. A retarded boy's family and friends help him
to join a basketball team. Ages 8-12.
Crane, Caroline. A Girl Like Tracy. David McKay, 1966.
Girl helps her retarded sister. Ages 12 up.
Little, Jean. Take Wing. Little, Brown, 1968. Ages 8-12.

Mentally Ill

Burch, Robert. Simon and the Game of Chance. Viking,

1970. Ages 8-12.
Koob, Theodore. The Deep Search. Lippincott, 1969. Ages
        12 up.
Sherburne, Zoa. Stranger in the House. Morrow, 1963.
        Kathy has difficulty in accepting her mother as a well,
        responsible person upon her return from a mental
        hospital. Ages 12-16.
Stolz, Mary. Goodbye, My Shadow. Harper, 1957. Ages
        12 up.
Wojciechowska, Maia. A Kingdom in a Horse. Harper & Row,
        1965. David had withdrawn from relationships with
        others until his love for a horse brought him back.
        Ages 8-12.

Orphan

Benary-Isbert, Margot. The Long Way Home. Harcourt,
        1959. Ages 12 up.
Burch, Robert. Skinny. Viking, 1964. Ages 8-12.
Carlson, Natalie S. "Orpheline" books. Harper, n. d. Ages
        5-8.
Clymer, Eleanor. My Brother Stevie. Holt, 1967. Ages
        8-12.
Cunningham, Julia. Dorp Dead. Pantheon, 1965. Ages 8-
        12.
Eunson, Dale. The Day They Gave Babies Away. Farrar,
        1970. Ages 8-12.
Haugaard, Erik. The Little Fishes. Houghton, 1967. Ages
        8-12.
Haugaard, Erik. Orphans of the Wind. Houghton, 1966.
        Ages 8-12.
North, Joan. The Cloud Forest. Farrar, 1965. Ages 12 up.
Stolz, Mary. Juan. Harper, 1970. Ages 8-12.
Wier, Ester. The Loner. David McKay, 1963. An orphaned
        boy who felt unloved and unwanted learns to trust and
        love others. Ages 10-15.

Persistence

Caldone, Paul. The Hare and the Tortoise. McGraw-Hill,
        1962. The classic fable which demonstrates the su-
        periority of persistence over speed, plus other clas-
        sical tales. Ages 5-8.

Psychological Sex Problems

Hettlinger, Richard. Living with Sex: The Student's Dilemma.

Seabury Press, 1966. An exploration of the sexual
conflicts facing young adults. Ages 12-16.

Levinsohn, Florence. What Teen-Agers Want to Know. Budlong Press Co., 1962. Discusses a variety of personal and physiological aspects of sex and answers
typical questions. Ages 12-18.

Sakol, Jeanne. What about Teen-Age Marriage? Julian
Messner, 1961. A realistic discussion of the various
aspects of teen-age marriage. Ages 16 up.

Rejection

Scott, Ann H. Sam. McGraw-Hill, 1967. Ages 5-8.

Religious Conflict

Fitch, Florence. One God--the Ways We Worship Him.
Lothrop, Lee and Shepard, 1944. Descriptions and
photographs of Protestant, Catholic, and Jewish
methods of worship. Ages 8-12.

Fitch, Florence. Their Search for God. Lothrop, Lee and
Shepard, 1947. A description of the ways that Hindus,
Chinese, Japanese, and Buddhists worship. Ages 10-
14.

Fry, Rosalie. Promise of the Rainbow. Farrar, Straus and
Giroux, 1965. Children from various religious backgrounds develop tolerance and appreciation for each
other while working together to restore an old chapel.
Ages 11-15.

King, Martin L. Strength to Love. Pocket Books, 1965.
A book of sermons written by Dr. King which are
designed to encourage Negroes. Ages 8-16.

Marshall, Catherine. A Man Called Peter. McGraw-Hill,
1951. A biography of the famous chaplain of the
United States Senate. Ages 12-18.

Power-Waters, Alma. The Giving Gift. Farrar, Straus, &
Giroux, 1962. Girl learns that her dancing ability is
a God-given ability which she should use to make
others happy. Ages 12 up.

Responsibility and Maturity

Bannon, Laura. Hawaiian Coffee Picker. Houghton Mifflin,
1962. Tim finally learns the value of time and the
importance of doing his share of the work. Ages 5-8.

Craig, Margaret. Now That I'm Sixteen. Thomas Y.
Crowell, 1959. Girl learns to accept the responsi-

bility for her behavior.   Ages 12-16.

Jordan, Hope. Take Me to My Friend. Lothrop, Lee and
     Shepard, 1962.   Girl grows up fast by being consid-
     erate and accepting responsibility.   Ages 12 up.

Lawrence, Mildred. Girl on Witches' Hill. Harcourt, Brace
     and World, 1963.   A teen-age girl attains maturity.
     Ages 12 up.

Lexau, Joan. Cathy Is Company. Dial, 1961.   Cathy learns
     the responsibilities of being an overnight guest. Ages
     5-8.

MacPherson, Margaret. The Rough Road. Harcourt, Brace
     and World, 1966.   Boy develops maturity during the
     depression days.   Ages 8-12.

Neville, Emily. It's Like This, Cat. Harper & Row, 1963.
     Boy learns that maturity influences his opinion of
     others.   Ages 12-16.

Robinson, Barbara. Across from Indian Shore. Lothrop,
     Lee and Shepard, 1962.   An emergency forces a boy
     to accept responsibility.   Ages 8-12.

Wilson, Hazel. Jerry's Charge Account. Little, Brown, 1960.
     Jerry learns his lesson when he opens a charge account
     without his father's permission.   Ages 8-12.

Self-Acceptance

Borten, Helen. Copy Cat. Abelard-Schuman, 1962.   A cat
     learns that he is happier and better accepted when he
     is himself than when he tries to be like other animals.
     Ages 5-8.

Freeman, Don. Dandelion. Viking Press, 1964.   A lion
     learns that it is better to just be himself.   Ages 5-8.

Gay, Zhenya. I'm Tired of Lions. Viking Press, 1961.   A
     lion cub changes his mind about wanting to be some-
     thing other than a lion.   Ages 5-8.

Uhl, Melvin J. Dexter, a Discontented Dog. Golden Gate
     Junior Books, 1963.   Dexter, after dreaming about
     what it would be like to be some other type of dog,
     finally decides that he wants to remain a bulldog.
     Ages 5-8.

Selfishness

Anglund, Joan. Love Is a Special Way of Feeling. Harcourt,
     1960.   A discussion of the good feelings we experience
     by considering and helping others.   Ages 5-8.

Arora, Shirley. What Then, Raman? Follett, 1960.   Since
     Raman is the only one in his Indian village who gets

to go to school, he has the responsibility of sharing
what he learns with others.   Ages 8-12.

Brown, Eleanor. Wendy Wanted a Pony. Julian Messner,
1951.   Girl struggles against her selfishness and
eventually is rewarded. Ages 8-12.

Gilbert, Nan. The Unchosen. Harper & Row, 1963. Three
high school girls learn that to get the most enjoyment
from life, they must show concern for others. Ages
12 up.

Hill, Elizabeth. Evan's Corner. Holt, 1966. Ages 8-12.

L'Engle, Madeline. A Wrinkle in Time. Farrar, Straus &
Giroux, 1962.   An allegory in which a teen-age girl
rescues her father and a young boy from evil by the
use of love. Ages 12 up.

Matsuno, Masako. Taro and Tofu. World, 1962. A Japanese boy is given too much change but is happier after
he returns it. Ages 5-8.

Piper, Roberta. Little Red. Charles Scribners Sons, 1963.
Nan learns a lesson in generosity and consideration
for others. Ages 8-12.

Sandburg, Helga. Joel and the Wild Goose. Dial, 1963.
Joel who wants a pet very badly finds a wounded goose
which he treats and keeps through the winter but re-
leases in the spring. Ages 5-8.

Shields, Ruth. Mary Kate. McKay, 1963. Katie learns the
difference between selfish and unselfish love when
little Robbie is released from the orphanage. Ages
8-12.

Wibberly, Leonard. The Island of the Angels. Morrow, 1965.
A Mexican fisherman risks his own life to save a
small boy ill with diphtheria. Ages 12 up.

Sex Education and Marriage

Duvall, Evelyn. When You Marry. Heath and Co. , 1967.
Suggestions to help ninth- and tenth-grade students look
at marriage more realistically. Ages 12 up.

Duvall, Evelyn and Sylvanus. Sense and Nonsense about Sex.
Association Press, 1962.   Questions concerning sex,
life, and love are answered in a straight-forward manner. Ages 12 up.

Eyerly, Jeannette. Dropout. Lippincott, 1963. Two adolescents learn that marriage is no solution to an unhappy
home and school situation. Ages 12 up.

Johnson, Eric. Love and Sex in Plain Language. Lippincott, 1965.   An inspiring book to help junior high
school students clarify their attitudes about love and sex.
Ages 12 up.

Komako, Jean, and Rosenthal, Kate. Your Family Tree.
   Parent's Magazine Press, 1963. A heart-warming
   account of family relationships, marriage, babies,
   etc., with colored illustrations. Ages 5-8.
Lerrigo, Marion D., and Southard, Helen. Facts Aren't
   Enough. American Medical Assoc., 1962. Discusses
   the personal aspects of sex education as they relate
   to physical development. Ages 12 up.
Levinsohn, Florence. What Teen-Agers Want To Know. Budlong Press, 1962. Discusses a variety of personal
   and physiological aspects of sex and answers typical
   questions. Ages 12 up.

Social Responsibility

Latham, Jean Lee. Carry On, Mr. Bowditch. Houghton,
   1965. Ages 12 up.

Step-parent

Arthur, Ruth. The Whistling Boy. Atheneum, 1969. Ages
   12 up.
Carlson, Natalie S. Ann Aurelia and Dorothy. Harper, 1968.
   Ages 8-12.
Clapp, Patricia. Constance. Lothrop, Lee and Shepard,
   1968. Ages 12 up.
Corbin, William. Smoke. Coward McCann, 1967. Ages 8-
   12.
Maddock, Reginald. Danny Rowley. Little, Brown, 1970.
   Ages 12 up.
Sherburne, Zoa. Girl in the Mirror. Morrow, 1966. Ages
   12 up.
Strachan, Margaret. Two Families Make One. Washburn,
   1969. Ages 12 up.
Willard, Barbara. Storm from the West. Harcourt, 1964.
   Ages 8-12.

Temper

McGraw, Eloise. Crown Fire. Coward-McCann, 1951. Boy
   learns to control his temper. Ages 12 up.

Too Rich

Ney, John. Ox: the Story of a Kid at the Top. Little,
   Brown, 1970. Ages 12 up.

Urban and Suburban Life

Krumgold, Joseph. Henry 3 (suburban). Atheneum, 1967.
    Ages 8-12.
Stolz, Mary. A Wonderful, Terrible Time (urban). Harper,
    1967. Ages 8-12.

Vocational Problems

Baker, Rachel. The First Woman Doctor. Julian Messner,
    1944. The story of the struggles faced by Dr. Eliza-
    beth Blackwell in her attempts to become an M. D.
    Ages 12 up.
Blassingame, Wyatt. Franklin D. Roosevelt. Garrard Pub-
    lishing Co. , 1966. A sketch of the boyhood and polit-
    ical career of F. D. R. Ages 5-8.
Boynick, David. Pioneers in Petticoats. Thomas Y.
    Crowell, 1959. Brief biographies of famous women.
    Ages 10-15.
Braddon, Russell. Joan Sutherland. St. Martin's Press, 1962.
    Biography of obstacles which were faced and overcome
    by this great soprano. Ages 12 up.
Cavanah, Frances. Adventure in Courage: the Story of The-
    odore Roosevelt. Rand McNally, 1961. The story of
    how a frail boy regained his health and lived a re-
    markably active life. Ages 10-14.
Cook, Fred. Theodore Roosevelt: Rallying a Free People.
    Lippincott, 1961. The account of a sickly boy who
    became one of the world's most famous leaders.
    Ages 12 up.
Daugherty, Sonia. Ten Brave Women. Lippincott, 1953.
    True stories of how ten American women faced crises
    with fortitude and courage. Ages 12 up.
DeMille, Agnes. And Promenade Home. Little, Brown, 1958.
    Story of how Agnes DeMille won fame as a dancer a
    after years of failure. Ages 12 up.
Douglass, Frederick. Life and Times of Frederick Douglass.
    P. F. Collier, 1962. The story of a famous Negro
    abolitionist, statesman, and writer who was once
    slave. Ages 10-14.
Gibson, Althea. I Always Wanted To Be Somebody. Harper
    and Row, 1958. Story of a Negro girl from her slum
    days in Harlem to her life as a famous tennis champ-
    ion. Ages 10-14.
Graham, Alberta. Clara Barton, Red Cross Pioneer. Abing-
    don Press, 1956. Story of the girlhood days of the
    founder of the American Red Cross and of how she

conquered her shyness.   Ages 8-12.
Graham, Shirley. Booker T. Washington: Educator of Hand,
Head and Heart. Julian Messner, 1955. The story
of a man who rose from slavery and founded Tuskegee
Institute. Ages 12 up.
Hennessey, Maurice, and Sauter, Edwin, Jr. A Crown for
Thomas Peters. Ives Washburn, 1964. Story of a
slave who became a fighter for the freedom of his
people. Ages 10-14.
Hickok, Lorena. The Touch of Magic. Dodd, Mead, 1961.
The story of the orphaned and underprivileged Anne
Sullivan who became the famous teacher of Helen
Keller. Ages 12 up.
Splaver, Sarah. Your Career--If You're Not Going to Col-
lege. Julian Messner, 1963. Information to students
who do not plan to attend college. Ages 12-16.
Wylie, Max. Career Girl, Watch Your Step! Dodd, Mead,
1964. The author discusses a number of problems
and safeguards a young girl should consider when going
out on her own. Ages 12-16.

War

Cooper, Susan. Dawn of Fear. Harcourt, 1970. Ages 12
up.
Shemin, Margaretha. The Empty Moat. Coward-McCann,
1969. Ages 12 up.
Walsh, Jill Paton. Fireweed. Farrar, 1970. Ages 8-12.

II. ADULT

Adjustment, General

Hersey, John. Too Far To Walk. Knopf, 1966. The story
of one college student's search for identity and purpose
in life and the various methods he tried to find it.

Brain Injury

Cruickshank, William. The Brain-Injured Child in Home,
School, and Community. Syracuse Univ. Press, 1967.
A guidebook containing practical information for teach-
ers and parents of brain-injured children.
Husing, Ted, and Rice, Cy. My Eyes are in My Heart.
Random House, 1959. Autobiography of a famous

sports broadcaster and disc jockey and his courageous
fight against the effects of a brain tumor.
Lewis, Richard S. The Other Child. Grune and Stratton,
1960. A book for parents and laymen to increase their
understanding of the brain-injured child.
Segel, Marilyn. Run Away, Little Girl. Random House,
1966. An account of one family's attempt to rear a
brain damaged daughter.
Sigel, Ernest. Helping the Brain-Injured Child. New York
Association for Brain-Injured Children, 1961. A
handbook for parents with suggestions on how to provide for the brain-damaged child.

Courage

Hulme, Kathryn. The Wild Place. Little, 1953. Indomit-
ability under stress.

Day Dreaming

Cabell, James Branch. The Cords of Vanity. n. p. , 1927.
Day dreaming as a form of adjustment.
Steinbeck, John. The Wayward Bus. Viking, 1947. Day
dreaming as a form of adjustment.

Death

Frankl, Victor. Man's Search for Meaning. Washington
Square Press, 1963. A personal account of one man's
experience in a World War II prison camp and of the
importance of a why for living.

Egotism

Bromfield, Louis. A Modern Hero. 1932. (Popular Lib. ,
pap.)
Fisher, Dorothy Canfield. Her Son's Wife. 1926.
Hawthorne, Nathaniel. Mosses from an Old Manse. 1845.
Egocentric personality.
Jameson, Storm. The Voyage Home. 1930.
Kipling, Rudyard. The Light that Failed.
Marquand, John Phillips, B. F. 's Daughter. 1946.
Thiess, Frank. The Devil's Shadow. 1927.
Wilde, Oscar. The Picture of Dorian Gray. 1891.

Family Relationships

Anderson, Wayne J. Design for Family Living. T. S.
    Denison, 1964. A candid discussion of how individual
    and family needs can be met within the context of
    family life.
Arnstein, Helene. What To Tell Your Child about Birth, Ill-
    ness, Death, Divorce, and Family Crises. Bobbs-
    Merrill, 1962. Suggestions and answers are provided
    to difficult questions which parents are frequently asked.
Beck, Frances. The Diary of a Widow. Beacon, 1965. A
    young mother faces the adjustment problems caused by
    her husband's death.
Bradbury, Bianca. Goodness and Mercy Jenkins. Ives Wash-
    burn, 1963. A spirited girl revolts against her Puri-
    tan guardians and the marriage they arranged for her.
Buck, Pearl A. A Bridge for Passing. John Day, 1961.
    An account of how the author learned to accept the
    death of a loved one.
Cotton, Dorothy. The Case for the Working Mother. Stein
    & Day, 1965. Suggestions on how the working mother
    can combine work and family duties more effectively.
de Vries, Peter. Let Me Count the Ways. Little, 1965.
    Parental conflict.
Epstein, Seymour. A Penny for Charity. Little, 1965. In-
    ter-generational attitudes of hate.
Fisher, Dorothy Canfield. The Bent Twig. 1915. Son of a
    possessive "chaste vampire" mother who devours
    everybody.
Gehman, Betsy. Twins: Twice the Trouble, Twice the Fun.
    Lippincott, 1965. Suggestions on how to ease the
    problem of caring for twins and to provide for each
    twin's individuality.
Neisser, Edith. Mothers and Daughters. Harper & Row,
    1967. Suggestions on how mothers and daughters may
    have a more meaningful relationship.
Parad, Howard, ed. Crisis Intervention: Selected Readings.
    Family Service Assoc. of America, 1965. Suggestions
    for the solution of various types of family crises.
Sartre, J. P. The Flies. 1943. Conflict between genera-
    tions--adults may hate youth because they see in youth
    what they have hated in themselves.
Simon, Anne. Stepchild in the Family: a View of Children
    in Remarriage. Odyssey Press, 1964. Suggestions
    to problems and helpful counsel to all types of step
    relationships.
Thomson, Helen. The Successful Step-parent. Harper &
    Row, 1966. Practical suggestions to problems con-
    fronting the step-family.

Inferiority Complex

Banks, Murray. How to Overcome an Inferiority Complex.
Murmil Associates, 1966. Provocative suggestions on
how to use what one has to the best advantage.

Injustice

Malamud, Bernard. The Fixer. Farrar, Straus and Giroux,
1966. A novel about a man trapped by injustice.

Introverted

Butters, Dorothy. Masquerade. Macrae Smith, 1961. Girls
attending an art school learn to be more open and to
solve their problems.

Loneliness

Benet, Stephen Vincent. John Brown's Body. Religion as a
factor in personality and family. Loneliness overcome
through faith.
Faherty, William. Living Alone. Doubleday, 1967. A guide
for the single woman who lives alone.
Shaw, George Bernard. Saint Joan (a play). 1923, 1942.
Religion as a factor in personality and family. Loneliness overcome through faith.

Marriage Problems

Albee, Edward. Who's Afraid of Virginia Woolf? (a play).
Atheneum, 1963.
Aldrich, Bess Streeter. White Bird Flying. 1931. Love or
a career dilemma of a college girl.
Hyman, Mac. Take Now Thy Son. Random House, 1966.
Incompatibility in the marriage of an intelligent woman
and a stupid man.
Lewis, Sinclair. Cass Timberlane. 1954. Incompatibility
in marriage.
Thorn, Ronald Scott. The Twin Serpents. Macmillan, 1965.
Failure--a doctor and his wife.

Mental Retardation

Abraham, Willard. Barbara--A Prologue. Rinehart and Co.,
1958. A prominent leader of society faces trials and
problems caused by birth of a mongoloid daughter.

Buck, Pearl. <u>The Child Who Never Grew</u>. John Day, 1950. An account of the author's attemp to adequately care for her mentally retarded daughter.

Buck, Pearl. <u>The Gifts they Bring</u>. John Day, 1965. An emphasis on love and understanding of the mentally retarded plus suggestions for their care and education.

Campanelle, Thomas C. <u>Counseling Parents of Mentally Retarded Children</u>. Bruce, 1965. Suggestions to parents on how to alleviate the problems of rearing a retarded child.

Egg, Maria. <u>When a Child Is Different</u>. John Day, 1961. Suggestions to parents who have mentally retarded children.

Erno, Richard B. <u>The Catwalk</u>. Crown, 1965. An account of the trials and struggles of a mentally deficient man.

Garton, Malinda. <u>Teaching the Educable Mentally Retarded</u>. Charles C. Thomas, 1961. Discusses the educational objectives, curricula, and methodologies as they apply to the mentally retarded.

Hunt, Douglas. <u>The World of Nigel Hunt: The Diary of a Mongoloid Youth</u>. Garrett, 1967. An autobiography by a 17-year-old mongoloid boy which should provide encouragement to parents of mongoloid children.

Leland, Henry and Daniel E. Smith. <u>Play Therapy with Mentally Subnormal Children</u>. Grune and Stratton, 1965. Methods whereby mentally retarded children can be helped through play therapy.

Levinson, Abraham. <u>The Mentally Retarded Child</u>. John Day, 1965. An outline of the problems faced by the mentally retarded child and by those persons, including parents, who must deal with the child.

Molloy, Julia. <u>Teaching the Retarded Child to Talk</u>. John Day, 1961. A guidebook for parents and teachers of mentally retarded children.

Pollock, Morris P. and Miriam. <u>New Hope for the Retarded</u>. Porter-Sargent, 1953. Suggestions to students, teachers, parents, and laymen on how to deal more effectively with the mentally retarded.

Rogers, Dale Evans. <u>Angel Unaware</u>. Fleming Revell Co., 1953. Story of a mongoloid child born to Dale Evans and Roy Rogers. Suitable for any age.

Seagoe, May. <u>Yesterday was Tuesday</u>. Little Brown, 1964. An account of the thoughts and feelings of a mongoloid boy who lived to the age of 43 years.

Slaughter, Stelia. <u>The Mentally Retarded Child and his Parent</u>. Harper and Row, 1960. Helpful suggestions to parents on how to deal with a mentally retarded child.

Stout, Lucille. I Reclaimed my Child. Chilton, 1959. Story
of a mentally retarded child.

Psychological Sex Problems

Anderson, Wayne J. How to Understand Sex. T. S. Denison,
1966. A straightforward, objective discussion and
guidelines for college students on the various aspects
of sex.
Blood, Robert. Marriage. Free Press, 1962. A discussion
of dating, marriage, and marital problems.
Brenton, Myron. The American Male. Coward-McCann, 1966.
A discussion of the dilemmas faced by both sexes in
attempting to cope with current concepts of masculinity
and femininity.
Greenblat, Bernard. A Doctor's Marital Guide for Patients.
Budlong Press Co., 1964. A guide to healthy sexual
relationships in marriage.
Hofmann, Hans. Sex Incorporated. Beacon Press, 1967. A
discussion of how sex can be incorporated constructively into one's life.
Jaeck, Gordon and Dorothea. I Take Thee. Zondervan Publ.
House., 1967. Suggestions on how to develop a successful marriage.
McGinnis, Tom. Your First Year of Marriage. Doubleday,
1967. A discussion of the problems frequently en-
countered during the beginning of marriage but emphasizes the importance of a constructive interpersonal
relationship.
Robie, W. F. The Raptures of Love. Belmont Books, 1965.
Advice on how to obtain sexual happiness in marriage,
excellent for newly-weds.
Rohner, Louise. The Divorcee's Handbook. Doubleday, 1967.
Advice to the divorcee on how to solve the problems
which usually accompany divorce.
Schaefer, George, and Zisowitz, Milton. The Expectant
Father. Simon and Schuster, 1964. Advice to the
father about his role during his wife's pregnancy.

Psychoses and Neuroses
(These for the bibliotherapist. A few suitable for readers.
Select carefully.)

Borsin, Anton T. Out of the Depths. Harper and Row, 1960.
An account of the author's schizophrenic episode.
Coate, Morag. Beyond All Reason. Lippincott, 1965.
Author's own experience with schizophrenia.

Farberow, Norman, and Schneidman, Edwin, eds. The Cry
for Help. McGraw-Hill, 1965. An interdisciplinary
compilation on suicide by America's leading experts
on the subject.

Grant, Vernon. This is Mental Illness. Beacon Press, 1963.
An interpretation of schizophrenia based upon clinical
case histories.

Green, Hannah. I Never Promised You a Rose Garden.
Holt, Rinehart & Winston, 1964. About a 16-year-old
schizophrenic.

Kesey, Ken. One Flew over the Cuckoo's Nest. New Amer-
can Library, 1962. An absorbing story of life in a
mental hospital.

McKenna, Richard. The Sand Pebbles. Harper and Row,
1962. The story of a withdrawn Chinese sailor and
how he gradually but surely becomes more involved
with the real world and lives a more meaningful life.

Perceval, John. A Narrative of the Treatment Experienced
by a Gentleman During a State of Mental Derangement.
Stanford Press, 1961. A story of the delusions, hal-
lucinations, and bizarreness of a psychotic.

Rubin, Eli Z. Emotionally Handicapped Children and the Elementary School. Wayne State Univ. Press, 1966.
Suggestions to school psychologists, special educators,
and persons in clinics, hospitals, and day-care centers
on how to work more effectively with emotionally
handicapped children.

Rubin, Theodore I. Jordi. Macmillan, 1960. Story of a
boy's struggle against schizophrenia.

Sherburne, Zoa. Stranger in the House. Morrow, 1963.
Kathy has difficulty in accepting her mother as a well,
responsible person upon her return from a mental
hospital.

Smith, Bert. No Language but a Cry. Beacon Press, 1964.
An account of the problems faced by emotionally disturbed children and of the facilities available to help
them.

Stern, Edith. Mental Illness. Harper & Row, 1962. Practical guide for the family.

Winter, J. A. The Origins of Illness and Anxiety. Matrix
House Ltd., 1966. An account of the influence of
emotions upon physical disease symptoms.

Wojciechowska, Maia. A Kingdom in a Horse. Harper and
Row, 1965. David had withdrawn from relationships
with others until his love for a horse brought him back.

Ward, Mary Jane. Snake Pit. New American Library, 1946.
A patient's experiences in a mental hospital.

Woolson, Arthur. Goodbye My Son. Harper and Row, 1960.
    A father's account of his son's struggle to retain his
    sanity.

Religious Conflict

Babin, Pierre. Crisis of Faith. Herder and Herder, 1964.
Gaer, Joseph. How the Great Religions Began. New Ameri-
    can Library, 1956. A comparison of the similarities
    and differences of the major religions of the world.
Kaufman, Walter. The Faith of a Heretic. Doubleday, 1961.
    Honesty in religion.
Lee, Ernest. The Minute Particular. Beacon Press, 1966.
    An English minister discusses his search for a mean-
    ingful religion.
Liebman, Joshua L. Peace of Mind. Simon and Schuster,
    1946. An attempt to integrate psychological insights
    and principles with religious teachings and beliefs.
Life Magazine. The World's Great Religions. Golden Press,
    1967. An illustrated presentation of the major reli-
    gions.
Mann, Stella. How to Analyze and Overcome Your Fears.
    Dodd, Mead, 1962. Suggestions on how to rid oneself
    of fear and anxiety through a belief in the power and
    goodness of God.
Marshall, Catherine. Christy. McGraw-Hill, 1967. A
    young 19-year-old girl searches for maturity and re-
    ligion in Appalachia during the early part of this cen-
    tury.
Montaurier, Jean. A Passage Through Fire. Holt, 1965.
    Religion and crisis.
Mousma, John C., ed. The Evidence of God in an Expand-
    ing Universe. G. P. Putnam's Sons, 1958. Forty
    top scientists say that science does not undermine re-
    ligion but rather that their faith has been strengthened
    by their study and research.
Pollock, John C. Billy Graham. McGraw-Hill, 1966. A
    biography of the famous evangelist.
Swain, Loring. Arthritis, Medicine, and the Spiritual Laws:
    the Power Beyond Science. Chilton, 1962. An account
    of a physician who uses religion along with drugs in
    the treatment of his patients.

Responsibility

Albee, Edward. A Delicate Balance. Atheneum, 1966. A
    drama of human responsibilities and relationships.

Self-Acceptance

Chekhov, Anton. The Black Monk (from Stories of Anton
    Chekhov). Acceptance of one's limitations as a problem.
Dostoevski, Feodor. The Brothers Karamazov. 1880. Con-
    ception of self and others in the development of per-
    sonality.
Sartre, Jean Paul. The Flies. 1943, 1947. Conception of
    self derived from others.
Steinbeck, John. The Wayward Bus. 1947. Conceptions of
    the self and the social mirror.

Sex Education and Marriage

Anderson, Wayne J. How to Understand Sex. T. S. Deni-
    son, 1966. A straightforward, objective discussion
    and guidelines for college students on the various as-
    pects of sex.
Bankowsky, Richard. On a Dark Night. Random House, 1964.
    Sex without love is a cesspool.
Blood, Robert. Marriage. Free Press, 1962. A discussion
    of dating, marriage, and marital problems.
Brenton, Myron. The American Male. Coward-McCann,
    1966. A discussion of the dilemmas faced by both
    sexes in attempting to cope with current concepts of
    masculinity and femininity.
Cather, Willa. My Antonia. 1918. Tender components of
    love and sensual components in contrast.
Duvall, Evelyn. When You Marry. Heath and Co., 1967.
    Suggestions to help ninth- and tenth-grade students look
    at marriage more realistically.
Gordon, Albert. Intermarriage: Interfaith, Interracial, In-
    terethnic. Beacon Press, 1964. A definitive survey
    on intermarriage plus case histories.
Greenblat, Bernard. A Doctor's Marital Guide for Patients.
    Budlong Press, 1964. A guide to healthy sexual re-
    lationships in marriage.
Hettlinger, Richard. Living with Sex: The Student's Dilemma.
    Seabury Press, 1966. An exploration of the sexual
    conflicts facing young adults.
Hofmann, Hans. Sex Incorporated. Beacon Press, 1967. A
    discussion of how sex can be incorporated construc-
    tively into one's life.
Jaeck, Gordon and Dorothea. I Take Thee. Zondervan Publ.
    House, 1967. Suggestions on how to develop a suc-
    cessful marriage.
McGinnis, Tom. Your First Year of Marriage. Doubleday,

1967.   A discussion of the problems frequently encountered during the beginning of marriage but emphasizes the importance of a constructive interpersonal
relationship.

Robie, W. F.   The Raptures of Love.   Belmont Books, 1965.
Advice on how to obtain sexual happiness in marriage,
excellent for newly-weds.

Rohner, Louise.   The Divorcee's Handbook.   Doubleday, 1967.
Advice to the divorcee on how to solve the problems
which usually accompany divorce.

Sakol, Jeanne.   What about Teen-Age Marriage?   Julian Messner, 1961.   A realistic discussion of the various aspects of teen-age marriage.

Schaefer, George, and Zisowitz, Milton.   The Expectant
Father.   Simon and Schuster, 1964.   Advice to the
father about his role during his wife's pregnancy.

Swinnerton, Frank.   Quadrille.   Doubleday, 1965.   Sex attitudes.

Vocational-Inspirational

DeMille, Agnes.   And Promenade Home.   Little, Brown,
1958.   Story of how Agnes DeMille won fame as a
dancer after years of failure.

War

Child Study Assoc. of America.   Children and the Threat of
Nuclear War.   Duell, Sloan & Pearce, 1964.   Answers
to children's questions about nuclear war are arranged
by age level.

Crane, Stephen.   Red Badge of Courage.   Watts, 1965.   A
war novel which illustrates the chaotic conditions during war and how one person conquers his fear.

CHAPTER 5

GENERAL HOSPITALS AND SPECIAL INSTITUTIONS

General Hospitals (including Veterans'
Administration Hospitals)

After the initial growth in the 1930s, patients' library
service in hospitals grew more slowly than other therapies;
Clara E. Lucioli, head of the Hospital and Institutional Department of the Cleveland Public Library, pointed out in
1967 that in the twenty years since 1947 it had not kept pace
in development and acceptance with the growth of hospitals.
Hospitals moved from sixth to fourth place among the major
industries of the United States; and with this growth all the
therapeutic facilities except the library came into their own.
If there were any doubt about this, Lucioli says, one has
only to look for the category of patients' librarian in any list
of hospital or library careers.

Lucioli goes on to quote some remarks of patients
that prove the therapeutic value of libraries. Here are only
a few:

> 'How did you know that writer would save my
> sanity?'

> 'I couldn't have lived through these days without
> books. '

> 'What do people do when they can't read?'

In addition to the need for extension of library service to
hospitals Lucioli stressed the need for expansion into nursing
homes and other extended care facilities. [1]

In an article six years earlier, Lucioli said that the
average librarian knows far too little about the complex social
and educational purposes of the hospital organization which
lend themselves naturally to a broad spectrum of library

services. The librarian's basic purposes in a hospital library, she feels, are the same for all classes of people,
namely:

> To help orient the individual to a new and strange
> world.
>
> To provide a constructive means to escape stress.
>
> Through books to build a bridge over which the
> reader may move back into normal life and
> activity. [2]

Four techniques are basic, according to Burket: to
keep the patient planning ahead; to interest the patient in
others; to provide resources to enable the patient to lead a
rich life in spite of illness or handicaps; and to help the patient ease discomfort and loneliness through reading. [3]

There are probably few situations in which bibliotherapy can be employed to greater advantage than in general
and special hospitals. Because it has most often been used
in the past in hospitals, particularly Veterans' Administration
and mental institutions, it is usually with such institutions
that laymen associate bibliotherapy. There is no doubt that
bibliotherapy has reached its highest development in hospital
situations and that many of its pioneer and present practitioners have been and are librarians, psychiatrists, psychologists, and general doctors connected with hospitals. The
considerable broadening of the field today is a tribute to the
outstanding work done by hospital librarians and other personnel, particularly in Veterans' Administration hospitals.

Because of this past association, however, there are
some librarians and medical staff members who feel that the
use of bibliotherapy must be limited to its scientific aspects
in a medical setting. Such persons, while meaning well,
would deprive many other groups and individuals who are not
hospitalized of the beneficial aspects of bibliotherapy.

Although more has been written on the hospital applications of bibliotherapy than on any other aspect, this book
would not be complete without the inclusion of at least its
basic uses in this most important field. Because the Veterans' Administration hospitals may have many different types
of patients beside mental cases, they are being included in
this chapter on bibliotherapy in general hospitals.

Obviously, in any hospital the long-term patient is likely to receive the most benefit from bibliotherapy. Long-term patients may be orthopedic cases, paralysis or prolonged heart cases, accident victims with serious injuries or amputations, poliomyelitis, encephalitis, or rheumatic fever patients, or any others with diseases or injuries requiring more than a few days' or a few weeks' stay.

If the hospital is large enough to have a library and someone in charge, whether a professional librarian or a volunteer, it is possible to plan group reading activities in the library or the wards, or in a recreation room or lounge for those patients who are ambulatory or can be brought in wheelchairs. If library service is furnished by the public library, or if there is a part- or full-time recreation director, reading aloud sessions with group participation are also possible. In either case, the person conducting such sessions needs to work closely with doctors and nurses and understand fundamental bibliotherapy techniques. If there is no library in the hospital and no one from a public library able to plan and conduct bibliotherapy group sessions, there may be available occupational or educational therapists operating from a permanent agency or under a temporary government program who can include bibliotherapy in their program with patients.

In enlisting volunteers the person coordinating the program should make sure that they have a wide book knowledge, good judgment, and the kind of warm, friendly personality necessary to insure good results. The hospital bibliotherapist has three factors working to his advantage: 1) The long-term patient is often left to himself for long periods, so he is apt to anticipate the visits of the librarian as a pleasant break in the monotony; 2) The bibliotherapist can, hopefully, enlist the help and cooperation of the medical staff and social workers, and sometimes even of the nurses' aides and orderlies; 3) The environment and immediate situation can usually be controlled and the patient is under close enough observation so that any changes or results that could be attributed to the bibliotherapy can be noted and used as a guide for future treatment. These advantages are usually not present when the therapist works with the individual in a non-institutional environment.

Once the patient can be started reading for himself, the advantages of reading over other forms of entertainment such as radio and television soon become apparent. These can be pointed out by the therapist if the patient fails to perceive them for himself, but it must be done in an informal and friendly discussion, not in an argumentative manner. Briefly they are:

1. Reading is a quiet, personal, and private activity which brings its message to the reader alone. It does not annoy or disturb other patients in a two- or three-bed room or a ward.

2. The patient can choose (with help from the therapist) the kind of reading he will enjoy. He does not need to listen to or watch commercials or programs which are not to his liking.

3. Book service in a bibliotherapy program is free. There is no extra charge as there so often is in a hospital for a radio or a television set.

4. Reading material suggested in a bibliotherapy program is more stimulating and helpful than the average radio or TV program.

5. Once secured, the book or other reading material is there to be picked up and laid down at will. Lines or passages of particular interest or beauty can be reread and savored at leisure. The book waits, can be read slowly and absorbed. Radio and TV programs move rapidly and cannot be held still or turned back.

The problem of chronic illness continues to grow as more patients are kept alive through advances in medical skill. A decade ago (1964), it was estimated that there were approximately two million people hospitalized for chronic illness, not counting those in mental or tuberculosis hospitals.

For the patient temporarily ill the experience is merely an unpleasant episode, a comparatively brief interruption in his usual life pattern. Chronic illness, however, is a problem which demands the help of many people. It becomes not only a medical but a psychological and social problem for which a team approach has been developed. This team includes library service as one of the rehabilitation therapies, but a library service which increasingly employs bibliotherapy techniques.

Reading, says Mildred T. Moody, [4] divides itself naturally into four categories: recreation, useful information,
intellectual stimulation, and insight. She examines how each
of these can benefit the hospital patient with a long-term or
chronic illness.

An entertaining piece of fiction read for recreation
can serve as an outlet for hostility, as the reader identifies
with the hero and vicariously works out the problem in the
story. In every book a reader enjoys there is personal identification and personal satisfaction, and communication has
been established.

Reading for useful information is important in bibliotherapy with the chronically ill, because it helps the patient
accept and overcome his handicap. He learns the nature of
his disease, and ways in which he can overcome some of its
limitations, such as how to dress, move about, or keep house
with various types of handicaps. Material on home care of
invalids can make it easier for both the patient and his family
when he leaves the hospital. Books may help him to attain
vocational rehabilitation; and material for formal and informal
education is available so that he may begin training for jobs
requiring little or no physical effort or movement. Such
training can make the patient feel useful and provide him with
a livelihood later when he is back in the mainstream of life.

Reading for intellectual stimulation is not easy and
often requires a great deal of motivation. But it is especially
important for a patient with a chronic illness or handicap
which will restrict his activities for the rest of his life. An
active mind, thinking and exploring, is not confined by a
handicapped body, but it is often in finding and reading this
type of mind-stretching material that the patient needs the
most stimulation and guidance.

Reading for insight is particularly needed when life has
dealt a severe blow, evoking the often heard question, "Why
did this have to happen to me?" Once the crisis of an acute
illness is past there is time for introspective thinking. Books
in this category can be of the greatest help, but if chosen
poorly they can give the greatest offense. Patients today
seem less likely to be satisfied with the superficial "positive
thinking" approach to their religious and philosophical problems. Our present age of tensions and anxieties seems to
demand a deeper and more personal search for answers and
responsibility. [4]

One of the best approaches to interest the chronically ill person in reading is to find a book or books that have some link with his past.   Dr. Joost Meerloo says the most successful rapport is established between patient and biblio-therapist when some past moment of success or happy experiences is a basis for book selection.   As a starting point for reading, the past can also become a means of accepting the present.   The subject to trigger such interest might be the patient's birthplace, a sport or activity in which he excelled, a childhood hero, or any role in which he starred and from which he can gain a feeling of self-esteem, so that he says to himself, "I am still that person.   There is hope for me yet. "[5]

It is unrealistic, Moody says, to expect every hospital to have a professional librarian on its staff; budgets do not permit it and training for hospital librarians is not widespread. Thus, if bibliotherapy is to be used effectively, public librarians must be asked to cooperate and to help train qualified volunteers to understand the general concept, goals, and methods of bibliotherapy.

The benefits of group reading and discussion programs, particularly with the disabled and physically handicapped, whether they be juveniles or adults, veterans in a Veterans' Administration hospital, or long-term patients in a general hospital, are to provide an opportunity for the victims to share experiences and frustrations, develop understanding and foster hope through encouragement.   Often a patient with a physical handicap, seeing others who are cheerful while working to overcome limitations of handicaps far worse than his own, is himself cheered with new hope of regaining a useful and more normal life.

The awareness that they share common problems bring to such a group a feeling of unity, of belonging, a relief of loneliness, greater relaxation, and a means of enjoyable activity.   A group program could consist of at least ten sessions, of one-half hour each, with discussions based on books by persons who have mastered or compensated for the effects of disabilities.   In the case of geriatric patients the librarian can condense materials and encourage personal references and comparisons through discussion.   Self-help devices and audio-visual aids such as page turners, magnifying glasses, recorders and tapes can be assigned to individual patients for follow-up visits between discussion periods.   Throughout the discussion sessions library services, whether in the hospital itself or from the public library, should be demonstrated as a morale force with concern for the individuality of each patient. [6]

Patients who read are usually more responsive to other hospital therapies. Thus bibliotherapy, in addition to affecting the patient directly, may also reinforce the constructive effects of other types of therapy.

At the Veterans' Administration Hospital in Oklahoma City[7] bibliotherapy is one of several therapies, such as occupational, recreational, industrial, and corrective therapy. These, combined with psychotherapy, provide an all-around effort to meet the patients' needs. Therapy group leaders meet once a week to discuss problems and procedures in each group. Although begun as a course of lessons in how to become a better therapist, the meetings have expanded to discussions of patients' problems. Here is an example of excellent cooperation, with other therapists discussing problems with the bibliotherapist. Psychiatrists or psychologists recommend goals for patients so that the bibliotherapist can decide what is most needed in the group sessions. The bibliotherapist also has an opportunity to express his ideas on the progress or lack of progress of individual patients.

A detailed report is written up by the librarian after each bibliotherapy session. It contains information on the extent of each member's participation and action, and on each member's attitudes and appearance.

The bibliotherapist must be objective and factual in these reports and sensitive enough to interpret subtle remarks and gestures which may give extra meaning to what a patient does or says. The psychiatric staff can profit in this way from the bibliotherapist's observational skill. The report then goes to the primary psychotherapists when mental or emotional problems are involved. After it has been read and studied by them, it is placed on the patient's chart to be later reviewed and discussed. If further clarification is required, the psychotherapy leader's group meeting is used for such discussion.

Sadie Peterson Delaney, an outstanding pioneer librarian-bibliotherapist in Veterans' Administration hospitals, while at the Veterans' Administration hospital in Tuskegee, Alabama, motivated use of the library by hanging its green walls with maps, paintings, and pictures of Negro leaders and authors and of leaders in other fields who had attained great heights through books.

As long ago as 1933, when Mrs. Delaney wrote about her work, [8] there were nearly 6, 000 volumes in the library's general collection, plus a separate collection by and about Negroes. Throngs of readers used the library, many choosing a vocation or hobby through books, and some completing their educational preparation. Mrs. Delaney made a personal introductory visit to each new patient, circulating book lists; she also compiled pamphlets, had a weekly radio talk, suggested books and synopses, and gave talks in the wards to keep the patients informed about the library's resources.

In some hospitals library activities may include a stamp club, a patients' forum, and instruction in Braille; and such materials as talking books, booklists in Braille and Braille books are used to help the patients gain self-confidence and afford them an outlet.

When a patient has been struck down by a serious accident or illness, there will often follow a period of time when he will be unable to read; he may be indifferent to reading and even to living. But if he reads a book such as Thomas Mann's The Magic Mountain, or another about people who have been similarly afflicted, he may become absorbed. Or if he is paralyzed and reads a biography of another person who was able to conquer his disability spiritually and make something of his life, he may well be helped to find courage to face his own situation. [9]

"The type of literature depends largely on the person who elicits the patient's interest and provides the right food for thought for him at the right moment, " said Dr. Lore Hirsch, addressing librarians at the Hospital Libraries Division meeting at an ALA conference some years ago. "A patient who does not have the capacity to read a big book can be helped just by reading the daily newspaper. Through it he may become interested again in what goes on in the outside world ... get all sorts of stimulating ideas, work a crossword puzzle, answer some questions, or read about vocational opportunities for disabled people, of which he has never known. If he can do a little more than that he may read a magazine which appeals to his humor, stimulates his fancy, reminds him of pleasurable experiences in the past, and provides amusement. "[9]

What of the patient who is totally or partially illiterate,
the one who knows how to read but does not like to do so, or
the one whose eyes are troubling him so that he can't read
for himself? If the hospital librarian does not have time to
read to such patients she should try to contact some of the
service organizations for volunteers who will read aloud material selected with the patient's interests and needs in mind.
Sometimes, if a literate non-reader can be persuaded to
listen to a story, book, or article, he will become interested
enough to start reading for himself. [9]

Barbara Coe Johnson, Director of Libraries at Harper
Hospital, Detroit, writing in 1969, emphasized that hospitals
need two separate libraries: the professional or biomedical,
and the patients' library. The two should not be combined.
She gives four reasons, two of which relate directly to bibliotherapy:

> 1. Technical service to technical personnel is
>   indirect service to the laity; therapeutic serv-
>   ice to hospitalized patients is direct service.
>   No librarian alive can put both first, and both
>   direct and indirect service to the laity have
>   their necessary place in hospitals. The two
>   needs should be coordinated enough so that
>   each section is aware of what the other is do-
>   ing and cognizant of its importance. But the
>   'Line' librarian who is in direct contact with
>   his separate public must be free to immerse
>   himself in their needs. The Veterans' Ad-
>   ministration and the Mayo Clinic, both leaders
>   in hospital librarianship, recognize this fund-
>   amental fact, and it is time all hospitals do
>   so. If the librarian serving the patients is to
>   do effective bibliotherapy with them her time
>   cannot be taken up serving doctors, nurses
>   and other medical staff. Each is a full-time
>   job.
>
> 2. Ambulatory patients use the lay library, and
>   it is potentially dangerous to allow patients
>   access to technical information which presumes
>   the professional background necessary to place
>   it in context, just as it is unethical for a
>   pharmacist to dispense dangerous drugs with-
>   out medication by the physician. The relation-
>   ship of this to bibliotherapy is obvious. [10]

The other two reasons concern administrative and financial matters and are not pertinent here.

"To see a book free a patient from his cubicle of pain or despair, even temporarily, is to see a small miracle," says Perrie Jones. "That such miracles happen is perhaps more important than how they happen, yet greater knowledge of the factors involved in the process can increase the effectiveness of hospital library service and make it truly therapeutic."[11]

Some do's and don't's for bibliotherapists working with hospital patients, especially for the first time, have been suggested by McFarland.[12] When we use the shorter term "therapist" for bibliotherapist here, we refer to whomever is acting in that capacity--librarian, nurse or layman.

1. Before entering a private hospital room the bibliotherapist should knock.

2. When she enters she should not give the impression that she is going to choose a book for the patient. He himself is going to pick out the book.

3. She should also have a smile when she enters the room. If a smile seems too self-conscious, she should look directly at the patient when she greets him.

4. Some chronically ill patients resent the librarian or the bibliotherapist standing up because it makes them feel more dependent. They may be resentful of too much activity on the part of the visitor. If she sits down, he may resent her because she is sitting in a chair too far away or too close. The therapist needs to watch the patient's eyes and movements closely for his reactions to her every move, and act accordingly. When the therapist comes in there is no telling what mood the patient may be in; he may be disturbed by some minor matter such as having dropped a book on the floor or the sight of a picture hanging crooked. He may be so sensitive to the therapist that such a minor matter as whether she stands or sits, or where she sits,

may determine whether he takes a book or
not. This may seem extreme, but to a bedridden patient who may have little to do but
stare at hospital walls all day such trivial
matters take on an exaggerated importance.

5. The bibliotherapist should give the patient a
    few moments to make his adjustment to her
    before discussing the matters at hand. Matter-
    of-fact remarks about something satisfactory
    that may have happened to the patient, to her,
    or at their last meeting is a good start, if
    there has been a previous contact or contacts.

6. The therapist should speak slowly and on only
    one idea at a time.

7. If the therapist is seeing the patient for the
    first time she should give him the facts about
    herself in a businesslike way--simple facts
    that avoid controversy. The right of the pa-
    tient to the courtesy of this kind of introduc-
    tion is clear.

8. The therapist at this point should watch for
    signs that she is accepted and that the patient
    has become relaxed. This would be revealed
    by the eyes, a smile, easy movements of the
    hands and fingers, natural voice tones, per-
    haps the telling of an anecdote.

9. If the patient does not take the initiative and
    ask about the library, the therapist has to de-
    cide whether the book service should be dis-
    cussed later. Sometimes it is best post-
    poned. Arguments must be avoided. If the
    patient says, 'I never read books, ' the thera-
    pist should not begin giving him a long list of
    reasons why he should. That has no place at
    this point. The therapist should tentatively
    suggest a later visit, but the patient should
    be given the privilege of refusing or commit-
    ting himself to an exact time, accepted by the
    therapist. If he refuses, he may later ask
    for her to come back. This ritual is im-
    portant because by it the patient commits
    himself emotionally to accept the idea of read-

ing.   Nothing should be hurried.   There should
be an atmosphere of leisure and relaxation
about beginning this relationship.   The patient
must not feel that anything is being forced upon him.   His stay in a hospital is first of all
enforced by circumstance; practically all other
hospital services are forced upon him: his
daily bath, his medication, the treatments
prescribed by the doctor, tests, many other
aspects of hospital routine.   It will be a welcome relief to be confronted with a service in
which he has a choice.

10.   The therapist should make clear to the patient
that she would like to spend time talking with
him about things on his mind.   Gradually, as
these conversations develop, even a patient
who has never bothered to read much may pick
out books he wants.

11.   A patient may be reluctant to start reading because he fears disapproval of his reading interests.   The therapist, anticipating this,
should casually talk about the great men who
read mystery, western, and science fiction
stories for relaxation.

12.   When the patient accepts the idea of reading,
he should be handed three or four books, not
just one.   Choice is then made possible. When
the therapist finally identifies his major needs
and interests she will see to it that she brings
books bearing on his problems but still has
enough so she can hand him several and know
that each of them has some constructive value
for this individual patient.   Only two books
may sometimes create an issue in the mind
of the patient--which one?   Given plenty of time
to choose, it would even be desirable to leave
as many as ten or twelve books on the bed, at
which point the therapist would excuse herself
for a few minutes to enable the patient to get
away from the feeling of compulsion created
by another person in the room.   If leaving the
room is not practical, she might read a magazine, standing near a window.   Thus the patient, does not feel he must hurry in order to

let her be on her way.

13. With magazines, the therapist should place a whole armful on the bed, after holding them a moment, getting the patient's attention, and then flipping the pages carefully but without much comment. The therapist should seek every possible way of dramatizing to the patient that he has choice.

14. But the therapist does hope the patient will choose books she has carefully selected to meet his needs. Since she cannot too obviously thrust them upon him, a special device is to arrange the books in a different way on the book cart, so that the eye is inevitably drawn toward those books. One method is to place one of the books flat on the cart shelf, placing the others in their natural position on top so that their height breaks sharply with the others in the row. Or a lone book can be placed flat on top at the very end of a bottom row. Sometimes a patient will assume that such a lone book was purposely isolated so he would not choose it and may then take perverse pleasure in selecting it.

15. One way to personalize non-fiction books in or from the hospital library is to encourage patients to write in them, to make apt remarks for other patients. If they write in ink in the margins and sign their names and the date, the therapist can make an exception and call such books to the attention of the patient. His natural curiosity to see what was written will probably do the rest. Of course, if the books are furnished by an outside agency this cannot be done.

16. The therapist need not despair concerning illiterate patients. She can explain about the library service; if the patient is ambulatory, take him to the reading room and show him the different treasures there. She dramatizes in the patient's mind the fun of looking at piles of magazines, particularly the pictorial

type, and of leafing through them.   He must
think of dictionaries and reference books in
terms of pictures, hundreds or thousands of
them.   When the bookcart comes to a bedridden illiterate the therapist must have
chosen so well she can lift several dozen
magazines with bright covers and pictures,
a major mail order catalog, or even a tool
catalog off the shelves.   Not only will the
illiterate patient usually enjoy looking at the
pictures, he will also get enjoyment out of
using his fingers.

Experience shows that common sense and sensitivity
are the most important factors in the relationship of the bibliotherapist to the patients, in getting them to read, enjoy
reading, and benefit from it.   Reading can be a vital element
in their rehabilitation, even when conducted, as McFarland
recommends, as "indirect guidance."

The Special Problems of Hospitalized Children

Nurses who care for children find that many have great
difficulty in relaxing and adjusting to hospital routines.   Pre-
school children, particularly, cannot understand why they
must be in strange surroundings away from their own homes
and the familiar faces of family. [13]

Books, both in pictures and stories, can help them
adjust to the temporary lack of the things they know and need.
Books can be used either in bed or while sitting at a table;
it is not necessary to move about as it is in certain creative
activities such as painting, working with clay, or playing
simple games.   In some cases moving about too much or at
all can interfere with recovery, particularly in the case of
those with fractures, post-operative or other conditions. Books
also are all in one piece and do not require much room for
storage. [13]

Books serve the nurse, librarian, or other bibliotherapist as a tool in gaining the confidence and friendship of the
young patient.   Any child who is frightened, angry, or bewildered by hospital confinement has an emotional problem
accompanying his physical problem, and bibliotherapy can be
very effective in helping to resolve it and thus hasten recovery.   Children like individual attention, in fact need a

certain amount for security.   The longest picture books usually take no more than ten minutes to read, and even a busy
nurse can often steal that much time to help an unhappy child.

Very young children find security and reassurance in
a somewhat rigid set of daily routines.   Often a child cannot
go to sleep unless his pillow is placed just so, his favorite
stuffed animal is beside him, or he is read to or told a short
story.   He is used to eating at certain times at home, and
hospital meal hours may be different.   When he is in physical
discomfort or pain and is deprived simultaneously of his comfortable, familiar environment, he will inevitably be unhappy.
No hospital can possibly conform to the varying home patterns of many children, but wisely chosen picture books can
provide one familiar element, particularly if the bibliotherapist can ascertain from parents or the child himself titles of
familiar stories or rhymes.   These books can then be supplied by family or librarian, for the young child enjoys the
same stories over and over.   Stories about comfortable,
routine situations can be especially helpful in making the child
feel more at home. [13]

A child is also impelled by curiosity to explore and
learn.   His world of understanding widens as a result of the
information he receives from experience, the communication
among others in his own home, and his own active investigations.   A hospital is not a good place for broadening the in-
tellect through hearing others all day, for the child will usually be in a children's ward or a room with at least one
other child of approximately his own age.   Active investigation
is not encouraged or even permitted.   So the child must somehow satisfy this fundamental need to know.   Books offer the
opportunity to experience things vicariously.   Thus the wise
bibliotherapist will not only include a few simple informational books among the offerings, but will also take a little
time to discuss the material or story after reading it.   Older
children who have read the books or stories for themselves
will also enjoy discussing them afterwards with whomever is
acting as bibliotherapist, whether it be nurse, nurse's aide,
librarian, visitor, or parent.   Everything from how animals
behave to how a rocket is launched can be found in books for
the various age levels and can help satisfy the child's need
for intellectual and sometimes even physical activity. [13]

Stories about a particular family activity can be especially helpful, since everyone tries to identify himself with
a group.   However, sentimental stories about family groups

should be avoided, since they may only increase the child's feeling of abandonment. In most homes the child is praised for each new achievement, such as standing up for the first time, walking by himself, learning to clean his own teeth or put on his shoes. Reading about heroic adventures and everyday happenings may provide a substitute sense of achievement. Matter-of-fact stories with humor are better than excessively tender tales which may only cause the child to feel more lonely. Older children may more readily feel a sense of achievement from stories in which the characters meet various challenges and accomplish their objectives, but even younger children can derive some pleasure from stories of achievement.

Aesthetic satisfaction can also come to the child through books with well chosen illustrations. The illustrations should be in color and tell the story almost as fully as the text. Books should always be chosen that will help satisfy as many of the child's needs as possible. [13]   .

In order to choose books properly for children their developmental needs at various ages need to be considered. The following chart (from Dolch, Elaine T. "Books for the Hospitalized Child." American Journal of Nursing, December 1961.) will help:

Ages	Developmental Characteristics	Type of Books
1 to 2	Liking for the familiar	1. Less complex nursery rhymes.
		2. Finger plays.
	Desire to investigate, including touching things	3. Simple stories about the sounds animals make.
		4. Stories about daily routines with pictures of cribs, play yards, kitchens, living rooms, etc.
		5. Books with samples of cloth, fur or other textures.
		6. Books made of cloth or heavy cardboard so children can handle the book themselves.
		7. Books with simple illustrations and not much detail.

Ages	Developmental Characteristics	Type of Books
3 to 4	Understands more detail. Good sense of imagination. Desire to know how things work. Likes repetition of certain sounds and ideas	1. Books can have simple plots with some suspense and humor. Example: A Very Special House, by Ruth Krauss. 2. May include nonsense words and imaginative happenings. 3. Simple explanatory stories about how familiar things work (4 yr. olds). 4. "Once upon a time" stories about the child himself (his own experiences given back to him--by parent or friend familiar with child's life so far). 5. Books with repetition.
5	Can tell the difference between the real and unreal. Comprehends more complicated plots. Appreciates some paradox and humor.	1. Longer and with more detail. 2. Stories about mechanics and what they can accomplish. 3. Police and fire station stories. 4. Alphabet and counting books.

"It seems wise to give a sick child a simple book, "
Elliott points out.   "He will soon tell you if it is too simple.
'Yes, ' said one little girl, 'I'm in fourth grade but I read
sixth grade books. ' She did, gaily going through the Penny
Marsh books and confiding to the librarian that she intended
to be a nurse.   A hesitant reply when you ask, 'Can you read
the words in this book?' calls for an easier book.   Good
clear print is always best and it is advisable to have some
books in large type. "[14]

The role of the nurse in helping children in a pediatric
hospital adjust to their environment by overcoming tension
and fears through books is described by Amelia C. Lipchak,
School of Nursing, University of Virginia, in Top of the News.[15]

She believes that the most effective method is through sympathetic understanding care by someone whom the child has
come to trust and believe.   Once the child has established a
positive relationship with some one person (a nurse, nursing
aide, or a hospital volunteer) he is then ready to use the
freed energy for constructive growth.   At this point the nurse
or others caring for the hospitalized child will be seeking
types of activities to help him use his time constructively.
Reading, listening to stories told, or hearing books read aloud
can be an important part of this activity.   A child left in a
hospital may have a feeling of abandonment by his parents and
possibly harbor anger toward them.   Although his feeling is
not based on fact it needs to be handled constructively.   Lipchak suggests A Place for Peter, by Elizabeth Yates; Bright
Days, by Madge Chastain, or The Hundred Dresses, by Eleanor Estes, as titles which deal with rejection or anger against
parents and which could cause a child to verbalize these feelings and provide an opportunity for their dissipation.   The
child confined to a bed or to one room in a hospital also
needs to explore the outside world vicariously, gain insight
into interpersonal relationships, pursue interests in natural
science and animals, and learn about people in other times.
A book like Kate Seredy's The Good Master allows him to
explore life in another country, read a good story, and learn
that children in other lands have experiences very much like
his own. [15]

        The fundamental needs of every child for love, se-
curity, achievement and adventure are intensified by illness,
since he feels insecure in his strange and sometimes painful
new environment, and is physically unable to be active and
accomplish anything; if of school age, he may be upset
about being away from school and falling behind; and he has
little chance for adventure.   Books to help provide support
in this time of stress should have the following characteristics:

            Literary merit and a high degree of interest.

            Real-life characters.

            Enough suspense to motivate the child to keep on
            reading and want to finish the book.

            Chosen with the individual child in mind: within
            the scope of his experience.

Chosen by someone familiar enough with children's literature to make a purposeful and intelligent selection to help the child overcome any negative feelings or nagging problems.

Be sufficiently small to make for ease of handling when strength and energy are limited.

Have a type size easy to read.

Have short lines and sentences.

Be attractively illustrated with pictures appropriate to the text. [15]

Examples of books for small children that meet most of these needs are Ruth Krauss's A Hole is to Dig, Dr. Seuss's The Cat in the Hat, Gobel Peterson's First Book of Poetry, Beverly Cleary's Henry Huggins, M. L. Clark's The True Book of Dinosaurs, Dr. Seuss's Horton Hatches the Egg, Munro Leaf's The Story of Ferdinand, Ellen MacGregor's Miss Pickerell Goes to Mars, and Glen Rounds' Ol' Paul, the Mighty Logger.

Carefully selected books on the many phenomena that are a part of hospital experience, particularly those that could help the child understand the work of doctors and nurses, the need for hospital rules, the nature of his own illness (if it is not a fatal or serious one), and functions of the body can make a hospital stay less onerous and give the child a feeling of learning something new. [15]

If hospital library work with children is to include bibliotherapy and be effective it must be both regular and frequent. Books should be distributed at least three times a week, according to Mary Frank Mason. [16] For those children too small to read, a picture book has often helped to restore equilibrium. Picture books with a few lines of text can be read aloud and the personal contact thus formed is more comforting than if he were left alone with the same book. But when the session is finished the book should be collected and put away for the next time. Children who can read can have the books checked out in the usual manner.

In the case of children with a more or less chronic disease, such as rheumatic fever or asthma, it is highly important that they be read to--anything from comics to fairy

tales.   Children confined to bed for long periods need to continue to grow and develop as personalities.   If there is some
emotional problem coupled with or resulting from the physical
illness, the bibliotherapist obviously should choose books that
will help with both types of problems. [16]   In some cases the
emotional problems may, in fact, be the more serious of the
two, since they may hinder normal convalescence.

     Experience has shown that children in a hospital fall
asleep with less fussing if a story is read or told at bedtime.
In one of the largest children's hospitals in Chicago, volunteers come in for this purpose.   As a reward for progress
in reading, one children's hospital has the children read aloud
into a tape recorder, with the tape then given to the parents.
They are always grateful, tearfully so if the child does not recover.

     If a child in a ward loves to read, invariably he has
his ward mates reading too, so that the therapeutic effect
becomes effective for several children instead of just one.
One definite benefit if a child is in for a long-term stay is
that by reading in the hospital he keeps in practice and does
not feel so far behind when he re-enters school.   Perhaps
the greatest therapeutic effect, however, lies in the fact that
reading is a tangible contact with life.   The child who reads
while ill does not lose touch with activity and things of the
outside world.   He projects some of what he reads into his
own future, thinks ahead and looks forward to that future.
He may read about activities he wants to try when he is well
again, things he would like to have, things he would like to
learn more about.

     Nurses may complain that children mutilate or tear
library books which are left with them.   If a child has been
a public library borrower, he has probably been taught to
respect books and take care of them.   If not, a registration
card on which the child signs a pledge of this kind may
help. [16]

               When I write my name on this card I promise to
               take good care of the books I use and to return
               my book to the hospital library before I go home.

     It must be remembered that a highly imaginative or
extremely sensitive child can be emotionally disturbed rather
than helped by stories in which ogres, witches and blood
curdling incidents play an active part.   Fears may not be

evident at the time the story is told or read, but at night,
with all lights out, a child who is far away from the security
of his own home may become almost hysterical with fear or
have terrifying nightmares.   The bibliotherapist who wants to
add to the child's feeling of security, not destroy it, will
select small children's stories with special care.   The Super-
man type of comic, brought by unthinking visitors or parents,
has been known to cause many a nightmare.   Wholesome
stories of normal family, school and sports life are most desirable for children who need a calming influence. [16]

    Unless the librarian or volunteer bibliotherapist knows
her story so completely that it is alive within her, she should
not try to tell it in a hospital ward.   It is better to read
it than to stumble through it in an uncertain manner.   Unrest
or distraction in a children's ward may also make telling a
story or reading it aloud impractical.   If there is a recreation room for convalescent children, this may prove an excellent place for story reading or telling.

The Use of Bibliotherapy by Hospital Volunteers

    In discussing the possible duties of volunteers in a
hospital Mary Frank Mason says,

> Volunteers are apt to be frightened by the form-
> idable term 'Bibliotherapy'; justly so when they
> read professional literature which overwhelms
> them with taboos on the subject.   They learn that
> the full-time trained librarian who is a member
> of the hospital staff is the specialist best quali-
> fied to advise on the contents of books.   She is
> the consultant who cooperates with doctors and
> nurses in prescribing reading diets.
>
> In the face of such facts, what reassurance can
> be offered the volunteer that her services as an
> untrained hospital librarian are desirable?   If the
> volunteer is going to take her avocation seriously
> she will follow the lead of the professional librar-
> ian and enlarge her acquaintance with all sorts of
> books as a daily matter of course.   She will de-
> velop an inquisitive instinct, if she doesn't have
> one naturally, and exercise it on the book trail.
> She will learn how to dip into, scan, skip, or
> digest whatever her instinct prompts her to sample.

> But most important of all, she will not attempt
> bibliotherapy on her own in a hospital situation
> where there is an established procedure of bib-
> liotherapy. She will offer her services to the li-
> brarian and be guided by her. There will be pa-
> tients to whom she can read the books suggested
> by the librarian as therapy. She can assist at
> group reading and self-searching sessions. She
> can be the messenger to bring doctor or librarian-
> recommended books not available in the hospital
> library, but obtainable at a nearby public or col-
> lege library. She can report any interesting pa-
> tient reactions to the medical staff and librarian.
> As she becomes more familiar with the long-term
> patients and books in general, she will be un-
> doubtedly given greater freedom and responsibility
> in bibliotherapy if she has the desirable personal
> traits and shows an aptitude for it. [16]

It is interesting to note that as far back as 1940,
special training for hospital volunteers was being sponsored
by the Junior Legaue of New York City, under the direction
of the Central Bureau of Hospital Libraries. It consisted of
thirteen lectures, covering a two-and-a-half-month period and
included hospital library techniques, story-telling, book selection and bibliotherapy. It is regrettable that such courses
are not now, after thirty-five years, being offered.

The Nurse's Part in Hospital
and Institutional Bibliotherapy

Unless a nurse rests on the conviction that hers is a
significant intermediary position between her patient and the
hospital librarian, she will lose many an opportunity for exercise of her nursing art. Since both librarian and nurse
are primarily interested in the patient it is only logical that
the two should cooperate. [17]

"The tired mind, the irritated disposition, the frayed
nerves, the bewildered heart, the baffled soul"--these, says
Margaret DeLisle, "are the factors with which the nurse has
to labor when the inspections have been made, the medicines
meticulously given, the entries made on the charts. " More
is expected of her than a pair of willing hands and the ability
to direct a group of nurses' aides. Her mind and heart, too,
are sought by the patient who depends for a long or a brief

period on the vitality of other human beings for sustenance of his own.   It is natural, if the patient has liked the nurse, to turn to her when physical convalescence prompts reading; there may not be a patients' library or librarian in the hospital, or if there is, the patient, having seen the nurse more often that the librarian, may well ask her for help first.

If there is a hospital library and librarian, the nurse, unless she has read a certain book herself and knows that its contents will have a good effect on the patient, should contact the librarian and follow her recommendation.   Together they may decide that possibly the physician on the case should be consulted.   If two heads are better than one in such a case, three may be even better than two. [17]

Tuberculosis Hospitals

Although tuberculosis has been so successfully controlled and treated that the number of hospitals solely for tubercular patients has been sharply reduced, the disease is still with us--has, in fact, in the past few years showed an unexpected upsurge.

Since a patient who finds himself in a T. B. hospital is apt to be there for some time, bibliotherapy can play an important role in making that stay more endurable and helping the patient to throw off the depression which such a disease so often brings.   With tuberculosis, as with so many other diseases, if emotional, social and economic problems are not solved or somehow minimized, medical authorities agree that physical repair is slower, and when achieved, less enduring. [18]

During their long stay patients need to be helped to feel that the time is not a waste, a bore, or a torment. The temperament of the patient determines to a large extent which of these attitudes he will be apt to take.   He must be helped to feel that the enforced rest can actually provide pleasure, profit, and achievement.   For those patients who react to the disease and the hospital more severely, resulting in extreme emotional maladjustments, therapy of every possible type becomes even more necessary.

Tuberculosis is apt to set in during late adolescence or early adulthood, just in time to interrupt an advanced education or an early career.   The patient must suddenly give up everything to enter a hospital for a long and uncertain period. The hospital to which he is sent may be far from his home so that friends and family cannot come to visit very often, some not at all. Even for a healthy person, a change from normal to institutional living is difficult; for a sick person it can be traumatic.

The first point at which the librarian may help, then, is in the matter of orientation. At this stage her best procedure is to provide the patient with whatever he wants in reading material, thus giving him at least some sense of gratification. The librarian then needs to study the patient's social history which was written up upon his entrance. From this history she records for her own information the patient's education, employment, family relationships, his activities and interests; in short, everything that will help her to understand his physical and mental condition. Tests have been given to determine his intelligence, social and emotional adjustments, his aptitudes and inclinations. All of this information is of value to the person who will prescribe individual therapeutic reading or group reading and discussion sessions.[18]

With this background information at hand the librarian is ready to become better acquainted with the patient, discuss with him books he may have read in the past, of, if he has not been a reader, try to find some common bonds of interest. If neither of these procedures seems to bring about any degree of rapport, then a few friendly visits with no special purpose may establish confidence and make the patient receptive to reading suggestions made later.

Once the patient's needs have been discovered, the bibliotherapist must then try to assist in the curative process by finding books that will help fill those needs. Needs may be divided into three practical types: educational, cultural development, and vocational training or retraining. In addition, of course, there is a fourth need--recreation, to keep the patient's mind off his troubles.

If the need is to continue an interrupted education, the bibliotherapist may find herself supplying required outside reading to supplement the textbooks, for instruction up to the high school level is usually supplied if the patient is physically able to take the courses offered. There will also be patients who, with or without special motivation from the librarian and hospital personnel, will want to pursue independent study on their own. There may be foreign-born patients

who do not read or write English, or who do so very poorly.
Such patients have been taught to read and write in tubercular
hospitals and may then even take up one of the educational
courses.

Another type of patient needing educational help is the
adult who left school for early employment. Such patients
can often make up their deficiencies in schooling by reading
in such fields as English language and literature, history,
government, contemporary literature of all languages, and
other ordinary secondary school subjects outside of regular
texts. Much of this outside reading can be supplied by the
bibliotherapist-librarian, working in close cooperation with
the teachers. This is indirect bibliotherapy in that the librarian works with and through someone else, has less personal contact with the patient but supplies material which
helps him to achieve and helps prevent discouragement and
depression.

General cultural improvement can be a means of
growth for long-term patients. Such improvement may come
through acquaintance with poetry, appreciation of the standard works of literature, introduction to new authors and new
types of books, an awakening interest in music or art, or
reading philosophy, psychology, and other aspects of the
social sciences. [18]

The bibliotherapist may also work with the vocational
rehabilitation therapist to find new occupations for the patient
whose post-hospital condition will require change of vocation.
After discussion of the patient's interests the bibliotherapist
may be able to offer suggestions arising from the patient's
hobbies. He can provide the patient with both ideas and how-
to-do-it books, while the vocational counselor provides the
materials for experimentation. Often upon his release from
the hospital, the patient must change to some occupation less
strenuous than his former occupation. Watch-making and repair, photography, orchestration, weaving, writing, sewing,
painting, commercial art, shoe repair, bookkeeping, up-
holstery, operating business machines, are just a few of the
vocations a former mover, truck driver, construction worker
or traveling salesman would find required much less physical
exertion. Shorthand, typing, designing of various types are
other possibilities. The bibliotherapist, in cooperation with
the vocational therapist, must discover the aptitudes, preferences and capacities of the patient, and this requires much
more than merely making available books on a variety of

hobbies and occupations.

Thus the bibliotherapist, as a part of the whole therapy and rehabilitation program, endeavors first to help the patient adjust to hospital living; second, to provide pleasurable and profitable employment of time without interfering with the cure; third, to eliminate emotional distress caused by circumstances of life in a hospital; and last to help provide preparation for a continuing cure for the patient without his being a burden on society (vocational training). [18]

The tubercular patient must not only adjust to a long period of medication to be followed meticulously; he must also learn to live after his hospital stay by health rules designed to protect both himself and those who come in contact with him.

Group bibliotherapy can be especially effective in the case of tubercular patients. A well-run therapy group involves three-way interaction--between group members, between therapist and individual group members, and the mass interaction between the group as a whole and the leader or leaders. This provides more avenues for insight and social response than are possible in the one-to-one relationship. Some patients may not have the strength at first to participate in group therapy, for being in a crowd and listening to many voices can be exhausting. The bibliotherapist needs a special skill to control group reading therapy so that it does not get out of hand, arouse arguments, and generate too much excitement or even ill-feeling. Participants must be carefully chosen for their physical condition, personalities, and general readiness. Thus group bibliotherapy should, whenever possible, be preceded by study of records and individual contacts between bibliotherapist and patients, so that she may know the people as well as the books.

Tuberculosis victims, unlike the mentally ill, in that they possess more mental stability, have the ability to think rationally and consistently, and have fewer inhibitions, can usually carry on a more stimulating and fluent group discussion. The feeling of "togetherness" combats loneliness, and the sense of unity with others with the same physical problems can be comforting. If the reading material for the group is well chosen, a feeling of achievement at having learned new facts or ideas reinforces the other positive factors. When patients are sufficiently relaxed and accustomed to the group, a cathartic emotional release may result from the free ex-

pression (sometimes confession) of long-repressed thoughts
or actions. [19]

Consideration of the stage of illness is more necessary
in a tuberculosis hospital or ward.   Among the three stages
of tuberculosis--minimal, moderately advanced, and advanced
--there are many gradations of strength.   People sometimes
do not realize the extent to which mental activity consumes
energy, and that the rest which is imperative for the patient
is impaired by mental strain.   For this reason, books which
require intense concentration should not be given to patients
in the advanced stages.   The intellectual background of the
individual patient, however, is a determining factor in book
selection, for what is difficult for an eighth grade graduate
would be easy reading for a college student.   In cases that
are minimal or only moderately advanced, more serious or
purposeful reading can be encouraged.

In addition to its service to patients the Evansville
Public Library included books for the hospital personnel, from
the pathologist in the laboratories to the cooks and scrub
women in the basement.   Specialized reference service was
supplied for the nurses' training classes and for doctors and
internes. [19]

A trite saying around a tuberculosis hospital is that
which describes the three main parts of the cure: "Rest,
good food, fresh air, and the greatest of these is rest." A
librarian who wishes to do effective bibliotherapy in such a
setting must understand the basic elements and treatment of
the disease, and must realize that while a patient in the
minimal stage may suddenly grow worse, a patient whose
case is far advanced may take a turn for the better and the
disease be arrested.

Even the operations which can give a measure of help
to tubercular patients are only means of giving rest to the
diseased lung.   That rest permits the lung to wall-in the in-
fected dots upon its surface with scar tissue which at first is
delicate and easily torn.   Any movement, even raising the
arms above the head, is likely to destroy this thin membrane
when it is first formed.   Upon entering a sanatorium or hospital even the early tuberculosis patient is put to bed for
several weeks.   This absolute rest, plus plenty of good food,
allows the body to repair its injured area more rapidly.   During this period the patient should not be given books, for
mental activity, as noted earlier, uses energy needed in the

repair process. [20]

Book therapy should be applied in two ways: as psychotherapy to help produce a good mental attitude, and as an early form of exercise. When the doctor first allows the patient to read, he or the librarian should prescribe something light, impersonal, unexciting. Fiction is probably the best first fare, with a theme so improbable or far from the patient's own life that it does not stir him to emulation or too much thought. As the patient gains strength, books requiring more mental exercise may be given, with subjects along the lines of the patient's special interests, always keeping in mind the progress of the disease. Poetry is often a comfort. Biography needs to be selected rather carefully, avoiding the gloomier lives, heavy in tone and heavy to hold. The lives of Emerson, Voltaire, and Ruskin are good because all three lived to advanced ages in spite of tuberculosis. Fighters of Fate, by Myers, is helpful because it tells the life story of many celebrated "lungers."

Special studies for patients with far advanced tuberculosis should not be undertaken without the doctor's permission and should therefore not be suggested directly to the patient. [20]

The best bibliotherapy can be done with patients who are at a moderately advanced stage of the disease. If all goes well they may be helped back to health more rapidly, but if they read a vicious or depressing book at the wrong time, or are overstimulated to study, the medical work of months may be upset. Besides the already-listed objectives of recreation, education, vocational training, and therapy, the tuberculosis patient who has every chance of getting well should read some of the best books on tuberculosis written for lay readers, so that he may thoroughly understand the nature of his disease, the kind of after-care needed and the dangers of advice from well-meaning but uniformed friends and relatives. He should be advised to buy a few of these good books on tuberculosis to refer to after he gets home.

The main therapeutic value lies in books which exactly match his mood, acting sometimes as a sedative, sometimes as a tonic, as needed. "The right book," according to Dr. Josephine A. Jackson, "is an active therapeutic agent, since it actually affects the body chemistry of the invalid. As the sick person's fancy is thrilled with high hopes for the hero, that very mood proves a stimulus to his glands of internal secretion, making the heart less sluggish and the digestion livelier. "[20]

Having an index card for each patient, with notes on his likes, dislikes, physical and mental condition, interests and hobbies, type of reading done in the past, education, and home background, is a great aid to good bibliotherapy service. This information can be gathered from doctors, nurses, psychiatrists, occupational therapists and social workers. These notes, used in conjunction with frequent visits to and observation of the patient, and consultations, whenever possible, with hospital staff in order to keep up-to-date, should provide a sound basis for intelligent bibliotherapy.

Adeline M. Macrum, former librarian of the Tuberculosis League of Pittsburgh, in an address before the American Library Association many years ago, said: "... the reading needs of tuberculous patients vary with their physical ups and downs and with their personal interests. To serve these people adequately, the librarian should flavor her book knowledge with psychology, add a modicum of medicine, a pinch of pedagogy, vocational guidance to taste, and a full measure of real liking for people; for above all else hospital patients need with every book they get a generous share of the librarian's sympathetic understanding. "[20]

One of the chief benefits of bibliotherapy in a tubercular hospital is as a means of combating the non-cooperative frame of mind or mental attitudes that frustrate the best medical efforts. The T. B. hospital library actually has a three-point program: 1) An initial breaking down of nervous tension through books of humor or light verse; 2) an intermediate stage of adjustment via purely recreational reading; and 3) a final phase looking toward a future made more attainable through constructive reading.

> The objectives should be to help the person improve his ability to relate successfully to others, help strengthen his ego and his opinion of himself through the reassurance of skills, increase awareness of community resources, and encourage the use of available educational materials. Specialists involved should include psychologists, social workers, and educators.
>
> One approach could consist of group discussions centering on talking about realistic problems of

living, work habits, and opportunities for development of creativity. Books and films on careers, work habits, and the like are used as a basis for group discussion. Library resources in the community can be presented and explained.

Another approach could work through extension departments of universities. Practical study groups can be set up for homemakers. Volunteers can be trained to teach and discuss services and materials furnished by extension services. The purpose of these discussions should be to present homemaking as a challenge, to bridge the gap between hospital and home, and to lessen the patients' anxiety about reentering the community.[21]

Bibliotherapy with the Narcotic Addict
and the Alcoholic

While there are specialized sanitariums and other rehabilitation centers for alcoholics and drug addicts, such patients suffering the extreme results of either addiction are sometimes found in general hospitals. Bibliotherapy has been effective in working with both these groups, especially when used in connection with such organizations as Alcoholics Anonymous and Synanon.

James Graves[22] writes graphically of the librarian's part in the rehabilitation of narcotic addicts at the United States Public Health Hospital near Lexington, Kentucky, opened in 1935 to treat federal prisoners, probationers, and voluntary patients who were addicted to drugs as defined under federal law. It is a beautiful 1,050-acre Blue Grass farm with a bed capacity for nearly 1500 patients, the main building alone comprising fifteen acres under one roof. The hospital treatment program is based on many years of clinical experience and research.

There are two professional and four patient recreational libraries. The extreme diversity and inconsistency in reading tastes found among the patients may parallel the instability and inconsistency of the addicts themselves. The range of reading habits is extensive because of the variety of cultural, geographical, and educational backgrounds. The two most requested types of reading matter are, strangely enough, the two most diverse: they are, first, magazines and news-

papers dealing most blatantly with sensationalism and saturated with sex and crime (unavailable at the hospital); and,
second, classical, literary, poetic works. Such contrasts in
taste often gradually resolve into a consistent pattern of preference as the patient progresses in the treatment program
or otherwise adjusts and reduces his own conflicts.

At the outset, particularly, an addict is apt to be
suspicious of inquiries; he is strongly aware of his lack of
socially recognized professional achievement or of his inability to maintain proficiency in an area of respected endeavor. The bibliotherapeutic role in such a hospital is
usually indirect, consisting of supplying materials and incentives for vocational education and job training. Since feeding
the habit has generally been a full-time job for the addict,
many of the patients have had little time for reading. The
bookcart is usually eagerly awaited, since most patients are
entirely dependent upon the institutional library services.
Bibliotherapy groups, current events classes, and book review clubs are all under the supervision of the library staff.

The importance of the library program to the narcotic
addict is shown by the fact that at the time of the Graves'
article, sixty-five per cent of the patients at the United States
Public Health Hospital held borrower's cards; an estimated
additional ten per cent read periodicals but did not check out
books. The librarians talked to the patients about books,
magazines and hobbies, letting each one know that they were
interested in them as persons and not just as prospective or
current borrowers. There was more than the usual need to
maintain friendliness, to instruct, and to encourage the use
of library services, for narcotics addicts experience great
mental and physical torment in the course of their withdrawal
and physical and mental adjustment to an entirely new pattern
of living. [22]

Early in 1963 the New York State Correction Department asked the Library Extension Division to conduct a bibliotherapy project for thirty young drug addicts who were
nearing parole and who had been brought to the New York
State Vocational Institution at West Coxsackie. [23] The project
was a four-month demonstration of reading groups similar to
those conducted in many hospitals. Because of their previous experience with reading groups Margaret C. Hannigan
and William T. Henderson were chosen to carry on the demonstration.

Prepared to find a group of withdrawn, passive, un-responsive individuals who were difficult to work with, the two leaders were pleasantly surprised to meet a nice-looking, attentive group of normal-appearing young men, alert, responsive, interested and cooperative, due probably to the fact they had not had access to drugs for some time. Ages ranged from seventeen to twenty-six; their educational classification was from low remedial through high school level. As it turned out, their differences in reading ability seemed to be an asset rather than a deterrent to group progress, for the good readers helped the slow readers, and the latter were able to accept assistance and correction from their fellows without resentment.

At the preliminary meeting officials of the institution explained the special program. The leaders, in turn, talked about the benefits of good reading and cited actual cases where books and reading had helped individuals help them-selves. It must be remembered that, unlike newly-received addicts, this group was past the ordeals of withdrawal and well into the process of rehabilitation. Thus they were receptive and could accept the type of direct approach being used in this project.

Some of the books available for borrowing were shown and book talks were given on titles ranging from The Family Book of Verse, from which Mr. Henderson read Poe's "The Raven, " to Victory over Myself, by Floyd Patterson, Act I, (the incident where Moss Hart as a boy of thirteen worked in the storage vault of a furrier), to Audel's New Automobile Guide and The Occupational Outlook Handbook. After a question and answer period all but three of the men signed up for the program and checked out books. Several requested additional material. At this point, the leader believed that the new books, rather than the reading group itself, were the real drawing card. [23]

The men were divided into four sections, each section meeting with one of the librarians for a fifty-minute period, the major part of which was spent reading aloud short stories, plays, poetry, articles, or excerpts from books. About ten to 15 minutes was allowed for checking out material for recreational reading. The men were encouraged to talk about their reading and to recommend to others books they had enjoyed. Occasional book talks aimed at broadening reading interests and experience were given.

Hannigan and Henderson felt that it would have been better if there had been only two groups with at least two hours of time, so that they could have finished a short story or one-act play at a sitting, with ample time left over for examining, sampling, and talking about books.

Words, ideas, and unfamiliar points were discussed to enrich the men's understanding. The leaders were impressed by the way in which the men entered into the spirit of whatever they were reading. They were often expressive and dramatic and their responses to material beyond their experience were appropriate and intelligent in spite of their limited backgrounds.

Everyone seemed to enjoy short stories and essays; Harry Golden, O. Henry, and Poe were among the favorite authors. One of the most fortunate selections was William E. Barrett's Señor Payroll, a story of Mexicans working in the mills. It gave the Spanish-speaking men a chance to excel in reading the Spanish names and words, which they did enthusiastically. For once they were able to correct the pronunciation of the usually more glib members of the group. Poetry seemed to have a special appeal, the taste of the men ranging from old favorites to modern "beat" verse, and they enjoyed reading it individually and in unison. A hilarious time was had with one session of nonsense verse and tongue twisters from The Silver Treasury of Light Verse.

Play reading proved most popular of all, even though the group had had little or no experience with drama. The men were delighted with the plays and vied with each other for good parts. Such plays as Goodman's Dust of the Road and Benet's The Devil and Daniel Webster stimulated significant discussion of theme and characters. The Lottery, based on Shirley Jackson's eerie and shocking short story, provided an opportunity to talk about scapegoats and superstitions. Most effective of all was Arthur Miller's powerful All My Sons, with situations and relationships which came close to the men's own experiences.

Time was taken to encourage the men to use their own New York Public Library after release (all were from New York). Booklets giving the locations of branches and describing the library services were distributed, and the men were given the name of the Reader Advisor at the central library and urged to go to him for guidance in their future reading.

Efforts were made to evaluate the project as it came to an end, the director of the institution authorizing the newly appointed librarian and two counselors to interview the men about what the reading program meant to them and how they thought it might help them after they left. With due allowance for the men's natural desire to make a good impression, the responses were impressive and meaningful. Many had discovered that they enjoyed reading and learned from it. Some had made lists of books they wanted to read or buy. Books became a topic of conversation among themselves and with other men in the institution.

Considering the project a success, the institution director arranged to have it continued, with the institution librarian in charge and voluntary participation by the inmates. Here are some of the comments of the men:

> On the outside, when you come home from work, a good book will help keep you out of trouble. I won't want to go on the streets so much. I'll stay home now. I feel I'll be able to get closer to my parents.

> I don't believe I ever read a whole book through before. Now I've started reading and I like it.

> Before, I used to think, 'why should I read?' I wandered in the streets. I feel when I get out I'll be able to stay home more and read.

> When we first started I had the feeling that someone cared for me and was trying to help me....

> I thought 'They're helping me. I'll try to do my best.'[23]

Dr. Sadie P. Delaney reported on the following experiment in bibliotherapy for alcoholics in the Antabuse Clinic at Tuskegee, Alabama.

The chief librarian became part of the team of the Antabuse Clinic in its incipiency. The majority of the seven patients in the clinic had been readers in the library and had occasionally attended library activities. Due to their continued alcoholic episodes, their interest had waned. Empirical methods of bibliotherapy were tried with some promising results. Objectives were: to help the alcoholic in the

Antabuse Clinic hurdle the acceptance of a non-alcoholic
future and to obtain the emotional stature of adulthood; to
bolster his will power in his self-made decision never to take
alcohol again; to provide selected books on the subject of
drinking which contained factual material on the effects of
alcohol, but which were free from any preachment or dogma
which might negate the program of re-education; to provide
books which did not depict characters who were drunkards or
which described drinking parties or cited persons covering up
guilt or overt acts by drinking.

One hour weekly was arranged for bibliotherapy in the
Antabuse Clinic on Ward T, where a homelike, friendly atmosphere prevailed. The meetings were opened with poems
read by the chief librarian. Book reviewing and current
events discussions by the patients in the group proved most
beneficial. Each patient felt a pride in presenting news of
the week. An interchange of comments in free forum pattern
after each one had taken part developed interest, and ideas
for following bibliotherapy hours were outlined by the group.
Often a patient who had given a report on current events
offered to review the book he had read. In the library activities such as the Thursday Evening Library Press Club, positions such as sergeant-at-arms or news reporter were given
these patients. The prominence given the patient appearing
before an audience tended to establish pride. Competition became general, and constant absorption of interest served to
guide their thoughts from their past. One book in particular
which provided interest and therapy for the entire group was
You Can Stop Drinking, by Harold M. Sherman, in which the
author sits down with his reader and relates his own experiences in strictly Alcoholics Anonymous fashion. This book
was left in the clinic so that the nurse in charge could read
chapters to the patients. At the bibliotherapy hour in the
clinic, this book was reviewed by four of the seven patients,
and interesting comments were offered by the entire group.

The chief librarian arranged for a visit to the Carver
Museum at Tuskegee Institute as a cultural activity for these
patients in Antabuse Clinic. Accompanied by their nurse,
chaplain, aide and the chief librarian they enjoyed this educational event. One patient wrote an excellent paper on "The
Value of the Visit to Carver Museum." Some of the significant values from bibliotherapy for patients in Antabuse Clinic
cited by Dr. Delaney were:

Competitive book reviews and discussions of

material they have read stimulated leadership and established confidence.

It promoted a feeling of well-being and importance and served as a support.

It helped to establish will power and aided them to face reality.

It opened their minds to new fields of occupation and endeavors.

Exposure to the cultural environment of the library awakened a desire for better living.

The team approach with Antabuse patients provided balance in treatment, giving opportunity for the weighing of various therapies as the patient responded. Acts were revealed and discoveries were not partitioned. Bibliotherapy had a definite place as part of this team effort. Reviewing literature for the alcoholic helped pave the patient's way for interest in the Alcoholics Anonymous Association. [24]

The Hospitalized Physically Handicapped

Dr. Gordon R. Kamman once called bibliotherapy "a science of psychological dietetics, " thus emphasizing its status as a science and as a psychological tool. Dr. Gerald Webb said, "There are times when it is incumbent upon a physician to prescribe not a posset or a purgative but a poem. "

"This doesn't mean, " Helen Webster, then chief librarian of the Veterans' Administration hospital in Fort Harrison, Montana, pointed out in 1948, "that any patient is served a tray with five poems and two biographies on it and told he must read those books for fifteen minutes every day in order to recover. It does mean, though, that a doctor can say to the hospital librarian something like this: 'Mr. Wright on Ward 2 is facing an amputation. Do you have any biographies on handicapped persons that might help him keep his courage or anything that would suggest some new line of work he'll be able to do when he gets out of the hospital?' "[25]

For those who through accident or disease must face an amputation, or those who have crippling diseases such as severe arthritis, multiple sclerosis, infantile paralysis, cerebral palsy, Parkinson's Disease, muscular dystrophy or paraplegia, biography and autobiography about people who have overcome some of the limitations of physical handicaps and have led useful, productive lives can make facing up to their own problem much easier. Such books provide not only moral courage but also may suggest hobbies and occupations that the handicapped can pursue for pleasure and profit.

When hospitalization and testing have confirmed the presence of a serious and crippling disease, with the patient facing only a wheelchair future, the mental shock can be intense. At this time, more than any other, therapy is needed. Such occasions provide a hospital or sanitarium librarian with probably the most important challenge she will ever meet in her work with patients.

Helps in Learning about a Hospitalized Patient

It is not easy for a person who wishes to do bibliotherapy to form a quick and accurate judgment of persons who are ill. Hospital life is a great leveler. In a hospital gown, without makeup or in need of a shave, with hair unbrushed, in a room or ward that is impersonal, people appear much alike. Rose Burket suggests the following as some of the criteria for judging a patient without asking questions:

1. The way one speaks, his use of grammar, will give a clue to educational background. The use of colloquial expressions may indicate an area of the country from which the patient came; an accent may indicate origin from another country.

2. By noticing any clergyman who calls on the patient, the librarian or other bibliotherapist may learn the church affiliation. Catholics may have a rosary or prayer book in their room or be wearing a religious medal. A person's religious affiliation may have a bearing on his taste in reading.

3. Another source of helpful information is family pictures. Children, a well-gardened home, a picture of pets, all may indicate something to

the visiting bibliotherapist. A patient with children may find in books on child care, in Parents Magazine, or in a child's magazine information or stories to carry home and use there. Any reading which helps the patient plan for the time when he can be about his usual duties is good therapy.

4. A cardiac patient may keep his arms notice- ably still; his color may show lack of oxygen, or there may even be an oxygen tank outside the door ready for emergency use. Cardiac patients need material that is light to hold such as Reader's Digest or paperbacks.

People are often more cheerful after the librarian or other bibliotherapist has called. It is as if they thought, "I must be all right or they wouldn't tell her to come in here with something for me to do. "

5. If friends have brought magazines or books or the patient has brought his own, any of these lying about will be an indication of the pa- tient's taste and will also indicate that he is already interested in reading.

6. Perusal of the patient's case history if one has been compiled is always one of the best sources of information, but some hospitals and doctors will not permit non-medical per- sonnel to have access to these records.

7. If by opening the conversation with friendly reference to her own job the bibliotherapist can lead into what the patient's occupation is, it will not seem like a direct question but will be of immense help in deciding what kind of books to bring him. It will also be likely to indicate to the bibliotherapist whether this person will need rehabilitation into a change of occupation because of his injury or ill- ness. 26

Notes

1. Lucioli, Clara E. "Out of Isolation. " Library Journal,

v. 92, April 1, 1967, p. 1421, 1423.

2. Lucioli, Clara E. "Full Partnership on the Educational and Therapeutic Team--The Goal of Hospital and Institution Libraries." American Library Association Bulletin, v. 55, April 1961, p. 313-14.

3. Burket, R. R. "When Books are Therapy." Wilson Library Bulletin, v. 29, Feb. 1955, p. 450.

4. Moody, Mildred T. "Bibliotherapy for Chronic Illnesses." Hospital Progress, v. 45, Jan. 1964, p. 62-63.

5. Meerloo, Joost A. M. Modes of Psychotherapy in the Aged." Journal of American Geriatrics Society, v. 9, March 1961, p. 225-234.

6. Social, Educational Research and Development, Inc. "The Practice of Bibliotherapy--Program Suggestions for Specific Institutions or Types of Individuals." In: Institutional Library Services--A Plan for the State of Illinois. American Library Association Study authorized by Paul Powell, State Librarian, Illinois State Library, Springfield, Illinois, 1970, p. 73-74.

7. Gilson, Preston, and Al-Salman, Janie. "Bibliotherapy in Oklahoma." Oklahoma Librarian, v. 22, July 1972, p. 12.

8. Delaney, Sadie P. "The Place of Bibliotherapy in a Hospital." Library Journal, v. 63, April 15, 1933, p. 307-08.

9. Hirsch, Lore. "Book Service to Patients." Wilson Library Bulletin, v. 27, April 1953, p. 634-35.

10. Johnson, Barbara Coe. "Services an Integrated Hospital Library Can and Cannot Provide." American Library Association Bulletin, v. 63, Dec. 1969, p. 1558.

11. Jones, Perri. "Hospital Library Services Make a Difference." Minnesota Libraries, v. XXXII, Winter 1967.

12. McFarland, John H. "Indirect Reading Guidance." Wilson Library Bulletin, v. 25, Feb. 1951, p. 440-44.

13. Dolch, Elaine T. "Books for the Hospitalized Child. "
     American Journal of Nursing, v. 61, Dec. 1961,
     p. 66-68.

14. Elliott, Mrs. Pearl G. "Bibliotherapy: Patients in
     Hospital and Sanatorium Situations. " Illinois Li-
     braries, v. 41, June 1959, p. 477-82.

15. Lipchak, Amelia C. "Use of Children's Books in Pedi-
     atric Hospital. " Top of the News, v. XIV, Dec.
     1957, p. 36-39.

16. Mason, Mary Frank. The Patients' Library: A Guide-
     book for Volunteer Hospital Library Service. H. W.
     Wilson, c1945, p. 99-101.

17. DeLisle, Margaret M. "You, the Nurse, and I, the
     Hospital Librarian. " Catholic Library World, v. 13,
     April 1942, p. 208.

18. Pomeranz, Esther B. "Aims of Bibliotherapy in Tuber-
     culosis Sanatoria. " Library Journal, v. 65, Sept. 1,
     1940, p. 687-89.

19. Folz, Carolyn. "Pied Piper of the Modern Library. "
     Library Occurrent, v. 11, Apr. -June 1933, p. 42.

20. Macrum, Adeline M. "Supplying the Reading Needs of
     the Tuberculous Patient. " The Modern Hospital,
     v. XXXVII, Sept. 1931, p. 53.

21. Social, Educational Research and Development Inc. "The
     Practice of Bibliotherapy--Program Suggestions for
     Specific Institutions or Types of Individuals. " In:
     Institutional Library Services--A Plan for the State
     of Illinois. American Library Association Study
     authorized by Paul Powell, State Librarian, Illinois
     State Library, Springfield, Ill. , 1970, p. 77.

22. Graves, James A. "The Librarian--A Part of the
     Health Team in the Rehabilitation of the Narcotics
     Addict. " Kentucky Library Association Bulletin,
     v. 24, Jan. 1960, p. 21-22₊.

23. Hannigan, Margaret C. and Henderson, Willam T.
     "Narcotics Addicts Take Up Reading. " The Book-
     mark, New York State Library, v. 22, July 1963,
     p. 281-84.

24. Delaney, Sadie P. "Bibliotherapy for Patients in Anta-
     buse Clinic." Hospital Book Guide, v. 16, Oct. 1955,
     p. 140-41.

25. Webster, Helen E. "The Patients' Library." Pacific
     Northwest Library Association Quarterly, v. 12,
     January 1948, p. 74, 77.

26. Burket, Rose R. "The Patient Approach." Wilson Li-
     brary Bulletin, v. 25, Feb. 1951, p. 438-439.

REFERENCES FOR THE BIBLIOTHERAPIST

Anastasia, Sister M. "Bibliotherapy." Catholic Nurse, 9:34-
     36, December 1960.
         Brief discussion of therapeutic value of books and
reading by hospital patients.

Brendan, Sister Mary. "The Hospital Library in Preventive
     and Curative Medicine." Catholic Library World, 30:
     299-300, February 1959.
         In the modern hospital, interdependence between mind
and body is clearly recognized. The librarian should realize that bibliotherapy is a potent influence and use it for the
patient's welfare.

Darrin, Ruth, ed. "Library as a Therapeutic Experience."
     Bulletin of the Medical Library Association, 47:305-311,
     July 1959.
         Material submitted by participants in a workshop for
institutional librarians. Many of the wide range of suggested
activities are applicable to hospital librarianship generally,
not merely to mental hospital work.

Dunkel, Beatrice. "Bibliotherapy and the Nurse." Nursing
     World, 125:146-147+, April 1951.
         A hospital librarian presents bibliotherapy to nurses.
This excellent article is an admirable introduction for all to
the aims and goals of hospital library work and bibliotherapy.

E. Ignatius, Brother. "Bibliotherapy--Books as Cure-alls."
     Hospital Progress, 22:325-327, October 1951.
         A witty presentation of the value of bibliotherapy for

hospital patients.

Ethelreda, Sister. "Library Meets a Challenge. " Catholic
    Library World, 32:369-372, March 1961.
        Briefly discusses the four "B's" which challenge a
hospital librarian: brains, books, buildings and bibliotherapy.
The author gives a good exposition on the aims and objectives
of bibliotherapy.

Hirsch, Lore, M. D. "Book Service to Patients. " Wilson
    Library Bulletin, 27:634-639+, April 1953.
        Covers patient library work and bibliotherapy under
the following topics: "Librarians can help!"; "Sick children";
"Reading as a clue"; "Release in books"; "Library work for
rehabilitation"; and "Is realism depressing?" Dr. Hirsch
was staff psychiatrist, Veterans' Administration Hospital,
Bronx, New York, when paper was prepared.

Hyatt, Ruth. "Book Service in a General Hospital. " Library
    Journal, 65:684-687, September 1, 1940.
        Excellent and practical suggestions for relating books
to hospital patients. Again this is from the standpoint of
public library cooperation with local hospitals to provide service to patients.

Rey, Margaret and H. A. Curious George Goes to the Hos-
    pital. N. Y.: Houghton Mifflin, 1966.
        The hospital experiences of a mischievous monkey
may be used to help prepare the young child for a stay in
the hospital. For adult use with the child.

Rose Mary, Sister. "Hospital Library for Patients. " Hos-
    pital Progress, 20:82-83, March 1939.
        The author gives a list of favorite authors whose
works interest the convalescing hospital patient. Literary
classics often neutralize bibliotherapy efforts because they
may be difficult reading and emotionally disturbing to the
patient.

Upton, M. E. "Library Service in a Veterans' Administra-
    tion Hospital. " Little Rock Division, Consolidated Vet-
    erans' Administration Hospital, Little Rock. Arkansas
    Libraries, 16:13-17, October 1959.

SUGGESTED READINGS FOR GROUP WORK
WITH NARCOTICS ADDICTS (ADULT)

(Selected stories, poems, plays, and essays from
the collections listed)

Eaton, H. T., ed. Short Stories. N. Y.: American Book
    Company, 1951.
        One Hour of Glory, by Mary R. Rinehart
        One Minute Longer, by Albert P. Terhune
        Some Can't Take It, by B. B. Fowler

Golden, Harry. Only in America. N. Y.: Permabooks, 1958.
        Buying a Suit on the East Side
        Carry-the-books-plan
        Causerie on Death
        The Show Must Go On
        The Vertical Negro Plan
        Why I Never Bawl Out a Waitress

Goodman, R. B., ed. 75 Short Masterpieces: Stories from
    World's Literature. N. Y.: Bantam Books, 1961.
        Absent Mindedness in a Parish Choir, by Thomas
          Hardy
        The Bedchamber Mystery, by C. S. Forester
        Charles, by Shirley Jackson
        Fear, by Rhys Davies
        Señor Payroll, W. E. Barrett

Henry, O. The Pocket Book of O. Henry Stories, ed. by
    Harry Hansen. N. Y.: Washington Square Press, 1959.
        The Cop and the Anthem

Hewes, Henry, ed. Famous Plays of the 1940's. N. Y.:
    Dell, 1960.
        All My Sons, by Arthur Miller.

Kazelka, Paul, ed. 15 American One-act Plays. N. Y.:
    Washington Square Press, 1961.
        The Devil and Daniel Webster, by S. V. Benet
        Dust of the Road, by K. S. Goodman
        The Lottery, adapted from a story by Shirley Jackson

Leacock, Stephen. Laugh with Leacock. N. Y.: Dodd, 1913.
    My Financial Career

Palgrave, F. T., comp. Golden Treasury of the Best Songs
      and Lyrical Poems. rev. ed. by Oscar Williams.
      N. Y. : New American Library, 1961.
            Elegy Written in a Country Churchyard, by Thomas
                Gray
            Invictus, by W. E. Henley
            O Captain! My Captain!, by Walt Whitman
            The Passionate Shepherd of His Love, by Chris-
                topher Marlowe
            The Seven Ages of Man, by William Shakespeare

Poe, E. A. Great Tales and Poems. N. Y. : Washington
      Square Press, 1960.
            Hop-frog
            The Tell-tale Heart

Rapport, Samuel, and Rapport, Kathryn, eds. Light for the
      Road. N. Y. : Harper, 1961.
            Whistle, by Benjamin Franklin

Stefferud, Alfred. The Wonderful World of Books. Boston:
      Houghton, 1952.
            The Book of Books, by Fulton Oursler
            The Joy of Reading, by Holbrook Jackson
            Our Reading Heritage, by T. V. Smith
            Reading Aloud Brings Ideas to Life, by E. C.
                Lindeman
            What Good are Poems?, by Thomas Riggs, Jr.

Williams, Oscar, ed. The Silver Treasury of Light Verse.
      N. Y. : New American Library, 1957.
            Cocaine Lil and Morphine Sue
            The Dying Airman
            Father William, by Lewis Carroll
            Father William Answers
            For Loose Tongues
            Jabberwocky, by Lewis Carroll

(From an article entitled "Narcotics Addicts Take Up Reading, " by Margaret C. Hannigan and William T. Henderson,
in the New York State Library's publication, The Bookmark,
v. 22, no. 10, July 1963, p. 285-86.)

SUGGESTED READING FOR THE ALCOHOLIC

Non-fiction

Anderson, Dwight. The Other Side of the Bottle.
Lovell, Harold W. Hope and Help for the Alcoholic.
Maine, Harold. If a Man Be Mad.
Mann, Marty. Primer on Alcoholism.
Sherman, Harold M. You Can Stop Drinking.
Towns, Charles B. Habits that Handicap.

Fiction (The alcoholic escapes his problems by running to the
    bottle. His escape is analyzed in the following:)

Fisher, Dorothy C. The Bent Twig.
Greene, Graham. The Power and the Glory.
Greene, Graham. Labyrinthine Ways.
Grondahl, Kathryn. The Mango Season.
Holding, Elizabeth. The Innocent Mrs. Duff.
Inge, William. Come Back, Little Sheba (drama).
Jackson, Charles. The Lost Weekend.
London, Jack. John Barleycorn.
Marquis, Don. The Old Soak.
Odets, Clifford. The Country Girl.
Saint-Exupery, Antoine de. The Little Prince.
Schulberg, B. W. The Disenchanted.
Scott, Natalie. Story of Mrs. Murphy.
Stone, Irving. Passionate Journey.

(Comment and fiction list from Mirror for Adjustment by
Austin Porterfield, p. 78-79.)

For the Children of Alcoholics

Sherburne, Zoa. Jennifer. N. Y.: Morrow, 1959. The
    problems a girl faced due to her alcoholic mother.
    Ages 12 up.

Summers, James. The Long Ride Home. N. Y.: West-
    minster Press, 1966. Alateens helps two children face
    the problems caused by their father's alcoholism. Ages
    8-12.

(Above and following titles from Facilitating Human Development through Reading by Joseph S. Zaccaria and Harold A. Moses, Champaign, Ill. : Stipes Publishing Co. c1968.)

Alcoholism (Adult)

Barrymore, Elaine. All My Sins Remembered. N. Y. : Appleton, 1964.

Kent, Patricia. An American Woman and Alcohol. N. Y. : Holt, Rinehart and Winston, 1967. A former alcoholic tells of the problems which face the female alcoholic.

Kessel, Joseph. The Road Back. N. Y. : Knopf, 1962. The author spent many years observing Alcoholics Anonymous in action and reports a number of true cases of persons helped by that organization.

Meyer, Lewis. All About Alcoholism. N. Y. : Doubleday, 1967. An easy to read, witty informal book on alcoholism.

Roth, Lillian. I'll Cry Tomorrow. N. Y. : Frederick Fell, 1954. Story of how a movie star became an alcoholic and how she was helped by Alcoholics Anonymous.

Valles, Jorge. How to Live with an Alcoholic. N. Y. : Simon and Schuster, 1967. Helpful suggestions for the friends and relatives who want to help the alcoholic.

Voldeng, Karl E. Recovery from Alcoholism. Chicago: Henry Regnery Co. , 1962. A doctor's account of an alcoholic patient, from illness to recovery, with suggestions to others for salvaging alcoholics.

Westheimer, David. Days of Wine and Roses. N. Y. : Bantam Books, 1963. Story of two heavy social drinkers who married, became alcoholics, and after seeing the results, took the cure.

Whitney, Elizabeth. The Lonely Sickness. Boston: Beacon Press, 1965. A guide to the treatment and causes of alcoholism, plus a number of real cases of alcoholism which the author helped cure.

Drug Addiction (Adult)

Algren, Nelson. The Man with the Golden Arm. N. Y.:
Fawcett Publications, 1964. A novel about one man's
struggle against dope addiction and his degenerate friends.

Cohen, Sidney. The Beyond Within. N. Y.: Atheneum, 1963.
About LSD.

Mills, James. The Panic in Needle Park. N. Y.: Farrar,
Strauss, 1966.

Smith, Philip B. A Sunday with Mescaline. Menninger
Clinic, 1959. An account of a psychiatrist's experience
with mescaline written in language understandable by the
layman.

Tuberculous Patients

Robison, Mabel. Frank H. Krusen, M. D., Pioneer in
Physical Medicine. Minneapolis: T. S. Denison, 1963.
Biography of how Dr. Krusen overcame tuberculosis
and became a pioneer in the field of physical medicine.

Ticknor, W. E. "Program for Troubled People. " Library
Journal, 84:3078-3080, October 15, 1959. An experiment on the use of bibliotherapy for tuberculosis patients. Outlines a form of group psychotherapy guided
by librarian and psychotherapist, and using books as a
basis for discussion. Examples of discussions are
quoted.

Tucker, W. B., M. D. "How Reading Contributes to the
Treatment of the TB Patient. " Hospital Book Guide,
17:3-4, January 1956. Dr. Tucker feels the best rule
to follow: read and enjoy it. If one does not enjoy
reading, do not read. However the library is a valuable rehabilitation agency and most patients will come
to the point of enjoying reading while in the hospital.

Long-Term Illnesses Requiring Hospitalization

JUVENILE

O'Connor, Flannery, ed. A Memoir of Mary Ann. N. Y.:

Farrar Straus, 1962. Mary Ann remains cheerful
despite her grave illness. Ages 12 up.

Patterson, Katheryn. <u>No Time for Tears.</u> Johnson Publishing Co., 1965. The story of a girl's ill health, her
parents' incompatability, her epilepsy, and finally her
becoming the mother of a hydrocephalic boy. Ages 12
up.

Scott, Jim. <u>Bob Mathias, Champion of Champions.</u> Minneapolis: T. S. Denison, 1963. Story of a small town
boy who overcame anemia to become a great all-around
athlete. Ages 12 up.

Shumsky, Lou. <u>Shutterbug.</u> N.Y.: Funk and Wagnalls, 1963.
Boy who was very interested in sports learns to adjust
to rheumatic fever and appreciate others. Ages 10-15.

ADULT

Brams, William A. <u>Managing Your Coronary.</u> Philadelphia:
Lippincott, 1966. A heart specialist discusses in layman's language the symptoms and causes of heart disease, plus a number of cases of successful treatment
and rehabilitation.

Goodstone, Samuel. <u>The Doctor Has a Heart Attack.</u> Boston:
Beacon Press, 1964. A physician describes his experience with a coronary thrombosis.

Poole, Lynn. <u>I am a Chronic Cardiac.</u> N.Y.: Dodd, Mead,
1964. A story of how one man reacted to a heart condition with suggestions on how others can learn to adjust when faced with similar problems.

Zehnpfennig, Gladys. <u>Melvin J. Maas, Gallant Man of Action.</u>
Minneapolis: T. S. Denison, 1967. Biography of a man
who lived an exciting and productive life in spite of
diabetes, arthritis, ulcers, heart attacks, and loss of
vision.

CHAPTER 6

BIBLIOTHERAPY IN NURSING HOMES
AND HOMES FOR THE AGED

Homes for the Aged

Homes for the elderly vary from the elegant retirement center whose residents are in fair to good health and carry on all the normal activities of a busy, happy individual, to the run down houses or hotels where pensioners of small income eke out a bare existence in one room or even part of a room.

Although individuals who live in plush retirement centers or colonies of individual retirement homes will have some among them whose personal or physical problems indicate a need for bibliotherapy, the greatest need is in those sub-standard retirement homes where about all a resident may expect is a bed of sorts and three meals of dubious quality each day. In spite of state and local standards for such places, many homes exist sub-rosa or operate outside existing laws. Chapter 10 discusses the elderly person who lives alone or who has psychological problems arising out of living with relatives and being dependent upon them. Here we are concerned only with the institutionalized aged, including those in small homes where as few as three may reside under the care of a family or single manager.

Bibliotherapy with the elderly very often involves reading aloud. Although loneliness, lack of family ties, poor health, or unpleasant environment may be causing severe depression, a good many older people are unable to read because of poor eyesight; because they never formed the reading habit when younger and now find it almost impossible to begin; or because they have reached a stage of senility in which reading requires more concentration than their minds are capable of exercising.

For many, a group session in which the bibliotherapist reads aloud, selecting material that has some relationship to

one or more of those present, is the only method.   After
becoming acquainted with those who are mentally able to enjoy having stories, articles or poetry read to them, visiting
them in their rooms, learning about their lives or experiences, families, interests, etc. , the therapist can vary the
material read so that it touches at some point the lives of
each in turn.   For those who are bedridden and unable to
join a group, the bibliotherapist must read individually.

There will not be a large number in the average nursing home who can profit from bibliotherapy, but for those
who can the service will be more than welcome.   Perhaps
nowhere is there a greater need.   For many, a nursing home
is the end of the road.   With no future to look forward to,
time moves slowly and the days grow monotonous.   The therapeutic benefit derived from reading or being read to may
come from one or all of these sources: the companionship
and attention of the therapist, taking the listener's mind off
his troubles, depression and possibly physical discomfort or
pain; or a change in attitudes because of the specific content
of the material.

The larger nursing homes or those which have the
residents' welfare most at heart employ the full- or part-
time services of a recreation director who arranges programs,
bringing in outside entertainers, speakers, or clergymen; sets
up crafts projects, arranges parties, visits each patient often,
and if they can read, brings them books.   Often a recreation
director will collect books and magazines to form a small library, supplementing it with books from the public library.
In some cases public libraries supply collections to nursing
homes, working in cooperation with the recreation director
or management to ascertain residents' needs; or a bookmobile may make regular stops at the nursing home, the librarian choosing books for those unable to come out and
choose their own.

The recreation director, by the nature of her many-
faceted relationship with the residents, as friend, teacher of
crafts, social and recreational director and librarian, has an
unusually good opportunity to do effective bibliotherapy, and
many good recreation directors are doing just that.   Since
such recreation directors are usually chosen for their ability
to get along with people, particularly the elderly, they will
already have one of the two essentials for a good biblio-
therapist--an understanding of people.   If their knowledge of
books is not adequate, there are sources of help available:

local libraries, the bibliographies of books for use in bibliotherapy, the how-to literature on the subject, and the rest of
the nursing home staff.   If the recreation director brings
residents only the books they request or those which have
purely recreational value, with no attempt to match books to
their special but sometimes unexpressed needs, she is not
practicing true bibliotherapy; she is giving shut-in library
service.

Before giving a resident a book, the bibliotherapist
should visit with him for a few minutes to catch up on any
new developments which might affect the choice of books. To
illustrate, here is a case in point:

An elderly resident whom we shall call Miss X had a
pet dog she loved very dearly.   It was being cared for by a
good friend but she saw it frequently, as it was brought to
visit her or she was taken to the friend's home for the day.
She was very proud of the dog, a beautiful little animal, and
kept a picture of it on her wall.

This resident had good eyesight for her eighty years
and was a constant reader.   She especially enjoyed books
about dogs and was brought many such by the recreation director, who often attempted bibliotherapy.   On one visit the
recreation director had brought a dog story which, for the
first time, she had not herself read first, but which she
assumed the patient would like because it contained a true
story of a dog of the same breed as her own.   Fortunately,
she had not yet taken the book out of her bag.

Miss X was very disturbed and informed the recreation director that she had cried all night because her dog was
very sick and was being checked by the veterinarian for a
possible malignant tumor.   Miss X was afraid the dog would
die, and even as she spoke of it, began to cry anew.   The
therapist visited with her for an unusually long time and
finally managed, at least temporarily, to divert her mind to
other things.   She decided not to bring out the dog story at
such a time and took it home with her.   Later, scanning the
contents, she found that it had a very sad ending in which
the dog died and the master's grief was described in short
but very telling manner.   The bibliotherapist-director resolved never to take a resident a book again without reading
it first, and thanked her lucky stars she had not given this
one to Miss X before talking with her.   The emotional impact of such a book at such a time could have been extremely

negative, even possibly dangerous, for among her other ailments Miss X had a weak heart.   As an aftermath to the story, the dog was found not to have a tumor and did eventually get well, actually outliving Miss X herself.

The use of audio-visual aids for therapy, tying in with books whenever possible, is especially good in a nursing home.   Many such homes show movies once a week or so, and an alert manager or recreation director could accompany each showing with a display of books allied to the subject, including as many large print and photographic type books as possible.

This author, who has frequently visited nursing homes, one in particular three or four times a week, has found by talking with residents and staff that the elderly residents who read of their own volition or can be persuaded to read have the following preferences in books:

> Local history about the area in which they live or from which they came.

> Religious material of an inspirational nature, such as the books of Peter and Catherine Marshall, Harry Emerson Fosdick, or Norman Vincent Peale.

> Light romances, especially those with some religious theme, such as the fiction of Grace Livingston Hill.   Here is a perfect example where therapeutic value must be considered first and literary quality second.   Although generally considered by librarians to be of inferior literary quality, the works of Hill and similar writers of light love stories seem to have elements of faith and optimism which appeal to the elderly.

> Men often enjoy good westerns (hard to find these days), semi-historical fiction with a western setting, or adventure tales of the sea, exploration, etc.

> Books about other countries and places in the U. S., with many pictures, especially in color, have their appeal and are easy on those with tired eyes.   One secret here is to try to find

books on the country or area of an individual's
origin.   The little old lady from Sweden who
was given a beautifully illustrated picture book
on modern Sweden was in her element, finding
scenes she remembered from childhood, marvel-
ing at the many changes and the growth of the
cities.   Another bedridden patient loved a book
on the Great Smoky Mountain area of North
Carolina where she had lived for many years.
Reliving those years as she talked with the recreation director afterwards, her eyes glowed
and she seemed transported from her bed and
the four walls of her room into the far reaches
of those famous mountains.   For a few hours
at least she was no longer a prisoner of the
flesh, and the afterglow remained with her for
several days.   After that she often requested
the same book when the bonds of her physical
condition became too oppressive.   She also requested and was brought other books on North
Carolina and Great Smoky National Park, but
the first book remained her favorite.

There will, of course, be some residents who will
read on a variety of subjects--biography, travel, fiction--
whatever their reading tastes were before entering a nursing
home.   These people will read mainly for recreation until
some problem comes along, at which time the bibliotherapist
can draw upon her book knowledge to prescribe something she
thinks will help.

For those patients able to knit, crochet, sew, or in-
dulge in other crafts, books of patterns, instructions, and
how-to-do-it books of various types may help encourage a
hobby and relieve the tedium of nursing home life, besides
furnishing a feeling of usefulness and accomplishment.

Hopefully, a government program sponsored jointly by
the National Retired Teachers' Association and the American
Association of Retired Persons, and funded by a $158,763
grant from the U. S. Office of Education, will bring improved
library services for the elderly, including nursing home
service.   Beginning operations in April, 1973, the program
had as its objectives:[1]

1.   To develop and provide materials especially
adapted to older adult needs such as large print

books and newspapers, talking books, books in braille, and the newest audio-visual aids.

2.   To train library staffs to serve older people.

3.   To develop a model system of library service for the aged which can be duplicated elsewhere.

4.   To explore ways to improve existing physical plants in the areas of lighting and furniture, and to eliminate architectural barriers.

5.   To seek to develop programs and activities for the 'hidden and hard-to-reach' elderly through satellite facilities such as sub-stations, portable reading shelves, and bookmobiles.

The two-year demonstration is being carried out in four libraries in Kentucky, at Louisville, Lexington, Somerset and Hazard.   The sites range from urban to rural and offer a contrast in economic conditions and in racial and ethnic population groups.   Kentucky had more than 371,000 persons over age 65 in 1973.   This figure, compared with the state's total population, is somewhat higher than the national ratio.   The results of this demonstration should be followed up by those interested in bibliotherapy programs for the elderly.

An interesting development in audio-therapy which requires no material other than a standard recorder, tape, and equipment for playback is the so-called geriatric historical interview.   The purpose of these interviews is to sustain self-esteem in the elderly by having them record interesting and important events in their lives, and then to make the recordings available to other patients who have similar interests. [2]   Prior to taping, the subject should be interviewed to develop the most interesting points in the story.   The recorded interview may be conducted with one or more questioners, and with or without an audience.   The tape is then edited and placed on file for replay by groups or individual listeners.

Historical events, dramatic personal experiences, or amusing recollections make good subjects.   Recordings in foreign languages are especially valuable.   Writers of local histories have also found this method of taped interviews with the elderly, particularly their recollections of local historical events, a good means of preserving such events while they are still remembered by actual observers. Since the memories of the elderly can sometimes be faulty, such writers usually try to interview a number of those living at the time in question, and use as a factual record only those events upon which there seems to be general agreement. Being interviewed for material for a possible book has even greater therapeutic effect than doing it for replay only, as the elderly person consulted feels he is contributing something of value, and his self-esteem rises accordingly. A nursing home can provide a fertile field for such a endeavor, as there are usually quite a few patients who are physically unable to care for themselves but whose minds are alert. Bibliotherapy is inherent in this type of program if we think of in as including more than books. For that matter, it is often possible to tie in reading with the replay of a taped geriatric interview so that the listener extends his interest in the subject by follow-up reading. Introductory reading can also pave the way and provide background information before the taped interview.

Clara E. Lucioli points out that studies of access to libraries are incomplete unless consideration is given to the homebound, the institutionalized, the resident of retirement centers and nursing homes; these too are disadvantaged people as far as traditional library services are concerned. Perhaps this fact is clearer, Lucioli comments, to a librarian in a large urban center, but the needs of people who comprise the "new public" may be even greater in smaller communities where other cultural and educational opportunities are scarce. "I always go back," she says, "to the novel, The Journey of Simon McKeever, to recall old arthritic Simon, a wheelchair pensioner in a rural nursing home who 'didn't give a damn for fresh air and quietness.' It was the owner's willingness to haul him to town once a week to use the library that made life bearable."[3]

Lillias Burns, formerly a consultant with the Tennessee State Library, writing in the fall of 1969, pointed out that audio-visual materials and personal contact are particularly helpful in working with geriatric patients.

Dr. Herman Turk, then superintendent of the State Hospital at Lima, Ohio, in an article in Hospitals more than twenty-five years ago, said: "Experiments have shown bibliotherapy to be definitely instrumental in decreasing the amount of sedatives, cathartics, and tonics prescribed for

patients.   In mental cases reading subdues angers, fears,
and intense delusional ideas that may be present. "[4]   When a
physician speaks of experiments he generally refers to those
that are scientifically controlled and are not mere theory or
based on a few cases.   Dr. Turk's remarks highlight some
interesting and tangible effects of bibliotherapy which apparently were definite and measurable.

Since nursing homes find that a large number of their
patients require frequent or regular medication, including
sedatives, cathartics, and tonics; and since non-violent mental
cases are often cared for in nursing homes, not only would
the patient profit from a substitution of reading for pills and
injections, but so would the institution itself.   There have
been frequent cases of mental patients in nursing homes
striking and injuring nurses and aides, even though they were
admitted as non-violent.   Anything that will reduce or eliminate anger, fear and delusions is of immeasurable value both
to the patient and the nursing home personnel.

Retirement and nursing home life could be made much
more bearable for many residents if adequate library service
coupled with the bibliotherapeutic approach were provided.
This writer has asked at several nursing homes in or near
her own community whether anyone was using bibliotherapy
with the patients, only to be met with a blank stare and a
question as to what bibliotherapy is.   For the layman the
mystery needs to be stripped from the term.   He needs to
recognize it as simply a form of extended reading guidance
that tries to help the patient meet a physical, emotional, or
mental problem with the aid of someone whose interest goes
far deeper than just handing out a book.   The word "bibliotherapy, " among the uninitiated, is sometimes confused with
bibliography.   Perhaps we need a simpler term; even plain
book-therapy would be clearer to those unaccustomed to
medical and semi-medical terminology.

After President Nixon withheld approval of amend-
ments to the Library Services and Construction Act and the
National Commission on Libraries and Information Science
Act which would have greatly expanded services to the elderly, another beginning was made when the Bureau of Libraries and Learning Resources (then the Bureau of Libraries
and Educational Technology) moved to attain Associate Com-
missioner Lamkin's priority of strengthening library services
to older adults through agreements with the Cleveland Public
Library, the State of Rhode Island, and the Institutes of Life-

time Learning.

The Cleveland Public Library had completed its initial
survey of library services to older adults; the Office of Education renewed its contract to the library, enabling it to
make a more comprehensive examination of such services.
This second survey was published in December, 1972 as The
National Survey of Library Services to the Aging (Second
Phase).

Many public libraries have nursing and rest home stops
on their bookmobile schedule. Although worthy in its purpose, this service has its limitations, since so many of the
residents in nursing homes are bedridden or physically unable to come out, climb up on a bookmobile, and make their
own selection of books. Only those ambulatory patients whose
eyesight is good enough to read at least large-print books
can make direct use of the bookmobile, so it is often a better
plan to have a collection of large-print and other books in
the nursing or rest home, changed by the bookmobile staff
or a visiting librarian from the central library shut-in service. Bibliotherapy demands personal contact and individual
work with residents or patients. A busy bookmobile, even if
someone on the staff were especially trained in the techniques
of bibliotherapy, affords little time for reader guidance in
depth.

Library service to nursing homes and homes for the
aged should be considered important enough to be a regular
part of the general library service and not an added luxury
to be cut back when budget problems arise. Training active
older persons as volunteers helps to cut down costs, and
one-to-one service can be provided if enough volunteers can
be recruited.

It is almost staggering to consider that the rate of
those becoming 65 or over is increasing at 900 per day or
330,000 per year. These people deserve good service. Involving librarians in bibliotherapy in general and with the
aged raises again, however, the old controversial question of
whether the librarian should become in one sense a social
worker or psychologist, or whether, as Rose Vainstein says,
they should give only such service "as will help attain and
maintain library objectives." Services involving social work
leadership should be the responsibility of other agencies, she
believes. [5]

The sheer numbers of the old and their steadily growing articulateness are making the nation in general more
aware of their significance as a political force. It is thus
more than ever important that librarians and other educators
build programs for the aged which help to maintain mental
resiliency and the ability of older people to think of welfare
in terms of society as a whole, and not of themselves as a
segregated and rejected portion of that society. Herein lies
the need for more study of library gerontology and bibliotherapy for maintaining mental resiliency, and for pursuing
ways of changing attitudes.

Notes

1. News item. "NRTA-AARP Library Project Aimed at
    Improving Services to Elderly. " AARP News Bulle-
    tin, v. XIII, May 1972, p. 3.

2. Social, Educational Research and Development, Inc.
    "The Practice of Bibliotherapy--Program Suggestions
    for Specific Institutions or Types of Individuals. " In:
    Institutional Library Services: A Plan for the State of
    Illinois. American Library Association Study author-
    ized by Paul Powell, State Librarian, Illinois State
    Library, 1970, p. 77.

3. Lucioli, Clara E. "Bibliotherapeutic Aspects of Public
    Library Services to Patients in Hospitals and Institu-
    tions. " In: Monroe, Margaret, editor, Reading Guid-
    ance and Bibliotherapy in Public, Hospital, and Insti-
    tution Libraries. Library School, University of Wis-
    consin, 1971, p. 51.

4. Turk, Herman M. , M. D. "The Psychiatrist Evaluates
    the Hospital Library. " Hospitals, v. 15, Feb. 1941,
    p. 45-46.

5. Vainstein, Rose. "The Role of the Public Library in
    Education for the Aging. " Adult Leadership, v. 9,
    May 1960, p. 10.

SUGGESTED READINGS

Buckley, Joseph. The Retirement Handbook.   N. Y. : Harper
& Row, 1967, or latest edition.   Suggestions to the
retired on how to live a richer and fuller life.

Cagan, Maxwell. There's Gold in Your Golden Age.   Minneapolis: T. S. Denison, 1963.   How to enrich the
later years.

Comfort, Alex. The Process of Aging.   N. Y. : New American Library, 1964.   Written in layman's language.

Gray, Robert, and Moberg, David.   The Church and the
Older Person.   Grand Rapids, Mich. : Wm. B. Erd-
mans Publ. Co. , 1962.   Suggestions on how the church
and older persons can work together for the mutual
benefit of both.

President's Council on Aging.   On Growing Older.   Washington, D. C. : Gov't. Printing Office, Supt. of Documents,
1964.   Useful facts and ideas to help older people
understand the aging process.

Roulston, Marjorie.   Live and Alone and Like It.   N. Y. :
Doubleday, 1967.   A handbook of suggestions to women
past 60 on how they can lead a full and useful life.

Smith, Ethel.   The Dynamics of Aging.   N. Y. : W. W. Norton,
1956.   Suggestions on how older persons can enjoy a
more rewarding life.

CHAPTER 7

PRISONS AND OTHER CORRECTIONAL INSTITUTIONS

For some years the Extension Department of the Detroit Public Library worked with the Detroit House of Correction at Plymouth, Michigan, cooperating closely with Dr. Maurice Floch, the clinical psychologist. Dr. Floch, in an article written in collaboration with Genevieve Casey of the library staff, points out that most prisoners have an extraordinary interest in themselves and their own mental processes, probably because they have been in the toils of various social agencies since they were children. Inmates are quoted:

> We know that somewhere we have taken a wrong turn, and we want books to help us understand where and why.

> Books can sometimes change a man's life, especially his way of thinking. My incarceration and reading good books here have done this for me. I have plans for a much better and more wholesome life. [1]

A most useful publication for the prison official and librarian who are trying to build a meaningful program of bibliotherapy is Objectives and Standards for Libraries in Correctional Institutions (ALA, 1962), which also appears in the American Hospital and Institutions Library Quarterly, Spring 1962 issue, pages 9-19. It clearly states the library's responsibility in the total rehabilitative process, emphasizing that the library is far more than a repository for books and the librarian far more than a mere dispenser of books.

Nowhere is there a greater opportunity for a good librarian-therapist to exercise his or her talents, for here is certainly a "captive" audience twenty-four hours a day. In many prisons and other correctional institutions, except of the most modern type, recreational facilities are far from

151

adequate. The prisoner or correctional institution inmate has more than enough time to reflect and think deeply. Reading the right type of books may well change his thinking from schemes for revenge upon society for his incarceration to constructive thinking and the conclusion that "crime does not pay. "

W. Gray describes a highly successful program of adult education carried on at an Oklahoma penal institution through several years by the Oklahoma City Libraries. [2] The end result of this experiment was a public discussion group demonstration by eight inmates. The author observed real rehabilitation. Of the participants he said, "They had learned to stretch mentally with a good book and found it as comfortable as stretching upon arising in the morning. " He also observed an improvement in the general reading tastes and interests throughout the institution.

Aside from the content value of books recommended by a librarian-therapist, participation in group discussion of a specially selected book has considerable value as social therapy, in prisons just as in mental institutions, for in prisons there are many hostilities, unhealthy relationships, and anti-social attitudes which participation in a normal group discussion may help to alleviate. In hard core cases the results may be negligible or non-existent, but even a miniscule amount of progress is worthwhile. Moreover, no one can be forced to take part in group discussion, even in a prison, so that those who do participate are less likely to be those in whom no changes could be observed.

Obviously the choice of books for group therapy must be a very careful one. The volumes chosen should be relevant, constructive, of as general interest as possible, and just controversial enough to stir up discussion and enliven the meetings. Highly controversial titles might well be avoided at the outset but possibly introduced after group sessions have been held for some time. Otherwise, there may be a tendency for participants to take sides merely because those they consider unfriendly at the start have chosen to champion the other side. Animosities in such cases could flare into possible hatred or violence, to the detriment of the entire program. Here again, the librarian must know the individual inmates, their records and reactions, and be always on the alert for first signs of hostility among participants. He must be able to control the discussion to avoid inflammatory incidents or accusations; yet he must try to maintain the feeling of informality and free exchange of opinion that spells the difference between success and failure of the program.

During his fifteen years as a librarian and teacher at Walkill Prison and at the New York State Vocational Institution, Herman Rudolf observed the following deficiencies in the inmates:[3]

> 1. Their inability to express themselves adequately.
> 2. Their limited range of experiences, and narrow range of interests.
> 3. Their complete lack of objectivity in judging others and themselves which evokes an unrealistic approach to themselves and to the world around them.
> 4. Their lack of knowledge and understanding of their own needs and how to satisfy these needs in a realistic manner.
> 5. Their lack of ability to differentiate in themselves and in others the make-believe world of illusion from the world of reality.
> 6. Their lack of ability to become involved in human relationships on a natural give and take basis instead of on a defensive posture.

Rudolf devised a course in reading, speaking, attitude forming, and critical self-evaluation, the reading part of which was definitely bibliotherapy. The aims of the course were:

> 1. Through a discussion of language to make them aware of the importance and effectiveness of speech. To give them practice in verbalizing about their attitudes and reactions to a variety of problems raised during the discussion periods and by the assignments given. By reading and discussing specific texts in class to provide the students with a broadened vocabulary and background, and to lead them to think about the broad spectrum of life's problems as presented by the text material.
> 2. To have the students develop the criteria necessary in judging a good speech and speaker in order to use these criteria as an objective basis for criticizing the speech of their classmates.
> 3. Through reading a wide variety of books and a discussion of the characters and incidents involved to broaden their range of experiences.

4. To teach the student the fundamental concepts necessary for speech improvement and to permit him to practice giving a formal talk at each session.

5. To have the students use the criteria developed in the speech rating chart as a guide to develop a personality rating chart. To use this chart as a basis for the evaluation of persons they knew and as a basis for the evaluation of themselves according to objective criteria.

6. To stimulate their interests in reading in general and in the use of libraries in particular.

Paperbacks in the course included: Only in America, by Harry Golden; 75 Short Masterpieces (Bantam Classic); The Reading Explosion (Pamphlet published by International Paper Co.); 4 Contemporary American Plays; To Kill a Mockingbird, by Harper Lee; Native Son, by Richard Wright; and Days of Wine and Roses, by David Westheimer.

At a preliminary meeting with all the teachers, Rudolf explained the purposes of the course and asked for their cooperation in finding suitable candidates. The course was held for the entire Friday morning for fifteen weeks. Rudolf also spoke to each of the classes, asking for volunteers. He interviewed the volunteers in order to choose those whom he considered sincere and who could benefit from this course.

For the first session the class met in the library, seated around tables in a semi-circular fashion. The objectives of the course were explained and the following ground rules laid down:

1. No marks would be given.
2. The men would be permitted to smoke.
3. The students were always to address each other as "Mr." (Placecards with their names printed on were in front of each student.)
4. The men were expected to act grown-up and to help each other.
5. Regular classroom procedures were not to be followed.
6. They were expected to take the course seriously and to do the assignments accordingly.
7. The men were expected to help one another and never ridicule each other.
8. Whatever was said by any student would be treated

in strict confidence by the entire group and
nothing would ever be reported unless it trans-
gressed the custody regulations of the institution.

Each of the students was called upon to read selections
from Only in America, by Harry Golden.   Difficult words
were put on the blackboard and explained.   During the twenty-
minute break after the reading session, the men could choose
books from a special selection of new books which were
brought in for this group and could be charged out for the
regular two-week period.   (It is interesting to note that during three different classes, not a single book in this collection was lost).   The books were borrowed from the Mid-Hud-
son Regional Library.

The class was asked to state the different purposes
for which language is used.   As these ideas were developed,
they were written on the board.   Some of the ideas for the
uses of language elicited from the group were: 1. Communication; 2. Expressing ideas; 3. Expressing emotions (acting,
story telling); 4. Entertainment (jokes, songs, etc.); 5. Relating experiences; 6. Bridging new experiences; 7. Propa-
ganda; 8. Teaching.

During the first speaking session, each student was
asked to tell something about himself, his background, hobbies, likes and dislikes, etc.

The first part of the second session was devoted to
"reading for ideas. "

During the last session, we read a number of essays by a famous American humorist describing
his insights into various phases of American life,
mainly of an era long since passed.

Let us see if we can analyze these essays to see
what it is that the author is trying to tell us.
[A brief discussion of the essays follows.]

Following the discussion, each of the men was called
upon to continue reading aloud.   Difficult words were explained and written on the blackboard in advance of each short
essay, and at the close of each session the words were explained again in review.   The men were encouraged to help
one another with their reading difficulties.

The second part of this session consisted of a book selection break of 15 to 20 minutes. (The part of the program and assignments which concerned speaking only are here omitted.)

The third session also began with a reading period:

> In this session we begin reading famous short stories from the literature of the world. As we read these stories you should be using the following questions as guidelines.
>
> 1. In what way can your prejudices prevent you from understanding or enjoying what you read, hear, or see?
>
> 2. Has any story you've read affected your attitudes towards other people?
>
> 3. Is the author merely trying to entertain us or does he have any additional reason for telling us this particular story?
>
> 4. What is the importance of setting the mood for the story by giving us the background and setting of the story in terms of time, place, and circumstances?
>
> 5. Would the hero or the other characters in the story necessarily act in the same way at a different time and place?

Each of the men was called on to read from the selected short story. The difficult words were written on the board and explained.

Among reading assignments was the following, on "What's a Stereotype":

> 1. Do you know what is meant by a stereotype? When we refer to persons as stereotypes we mean those who conform to a fixed or general pattern, who are undistinguished by individual marks as if stamped out of a fixed mold. The dictionary also adds 'a stereotype refers also to a standardized conception or image invested with a special meaning and held in common by members of a group. '

2. Would you agree that the characters in 'westerns' generally conform to this pattern?

3. When you see the hero in a 'western' on a white horse and the bad man on a black horse does this influence your way of thinking about whites and blacks?

4. Would you call a stereotype character true to life? Why?

5. Is it true that very few people indeed are all bad or all good?

6. When you become a member of a group or gang do you become a stereotype?

7. Would you call 'hippies' stereotypes?

8. When would the opinions of one group about another group be stereotypes?

9. What opinions do you have about the Chinese? The Japanese? The Indians? How were these opinions formed?

Another reading assignment was:

1. Which story that you've read did you particularly enjoy?

2. Did this or any other story (or book) that you've read give you any new insights into the lives of other people or any new understanding about human behavior? (Can you explain why the person did what he did?)

3. List briefly what points you particularly enjoyed about any story (or book) that you have read.

4. What in your opinion makes for a great story (or film, or play)? Would the fact that you would be willing to reread, or see the movie or play again be a guide?

Introducing the fourth session, the instructor said:

We continued reading from the collection of famous
short stories illustrating the ideas previously
brought forth, particularly with regards to attitudes
and reasons for actions by the various individuals
in the stories. The men were asked to explain
why they would defend or deplore the reactions of
the characters in the stories.

Each of the men was called on to read a passage.
Difficult words were written on the blackboard and
explained. The men were encouraged to make
comments about what they were reading. This
was again followed by a book selection break.

Bibliotherapy with Delinquent Adolescents

Juvenile delinquents usually have four major problems: 1) They are almost always underachievers, school
dropouts and generally deficient in academic skills; 2) They
usually have severe emotional and behavioral problems; 3)
They have trouble relating to others; and 4) They usually have
low self-esteem, although they may cover this with over-
assertiveness as a defense mechanism.

Rehabilitation programs, including bibliotherapy, must
take all these factors into account. Since, generally speaking, a plentiful supply of material is available, the important
thing is how the materials are used. Books with a social
theme can be of very high interest for these youths. Claude
Brown's Manchild in the Promised Land (Macmillan, 1965) is
a good example. Some commercial films used as audio-
visual therapy, when combined with group discussion, have
been effective; The Loneliness of the Long Distance Runner,
for example. This 16mm film can be rented or purchased
from Continental 16, 241 E. 34th St., New York, New York,
10016. A variety of specially prepared films are available
from the Canadian Film Board, Suite 819, 680 Fifth Avenue,
New York, New York, 10019. [4]

Judge Juanita Kidd Stout's observations substantiate the
theory that the inability to read is the leader of a long line
of negatives for delinquent or troubled children; others include
poor school achievement, truancy, chronic absenteeism,
dropping out, unemployment, dependency and criminality. According to the findings of Dorothy Houseman and Dr. Carlton
W. Orchnick, psychologists of the County Court of Philadel-

phia, and Dr. Bruce Balow, assistant professor and director
of the Psycho-Educational Clinic, College of Education, University of Minnesota, the typical delinquent boy is about three
years retarded in reading.   Sheldon and Eleanor Glueck, when
comparing the average reading quotient of delinquents and
non-delinquents, found a five-point difference in favor of non-
delinquents.   Dr. Robert J. Havighurst, professor of education, University of Chicago, reported that poor reading and
delinquency are partners.   Poor reading is not necessarily
the cause of delinquency but is frequently the first sign of it.
Many others have also noted the high relationship between
delinquency and reading retardation. [5]

Thus the librarian, counselor, or anyone else attempting bibliotherapy with delinquents, either singly or in groups,
faces a double task.   He must overcome the mental "allergy"
to reading which the child or young person usually develops
because of his inability to perform, and he must choose easy
reading on a subject of such compelling interest that the
young person will read it or listen to it read in spite of his
negative attitude toward reading.   The County Court of Philadelphia initiated cultural counseling in conjunction with the
various cultural centers of the city.   Some sessions were
scheduled by joint planning with the Free Library of Philadelphia.   The books for discussion varied in content and were
selected to demonstrate to the counselees the essential value
of books in understanding themselves, in understanding life,
and in preparing to take part in it.   The first discussion,
for example, was on Victory over Myself, by Floyd Patterson, who had been a juvenile delinquent and a poor reader.[5]

The evidence is overwhelming that the inability to read
is a substantial factor in the production of delinquency, criminality, unemployment, and dependency.   Thus the basic act
of teaching a poor reader to read better or to alter a prejudice against reading is in itself a form of bibliotherapy,
and an introduction to the full use of bibliotherapy to change
negative attitudes toward other individuals or society in general.

Although done in 1945, a comprehenseive study of
juvenile delinquency causes, prevention and cure made by
Sister Mary Corde Lorang still has current value, since human nature remains basically the same.

A total of 2,308 students from eight public and
Catholic high schools were asked to list books

they had read recently and periodicals they read
more or less regularly. They were asked further
to state whether or not they had been emotionally
affected or moved to act in any way as a result.

The free response of these young people was
startling, both as to the quality of their reading
and its results. The reading of cheap love magazines and comics was frankly stated to have led
not only to the acceptance of such ideas as that
'crooks are not such bad guys, ' but also to stealing, drinking, use of profane language, and sexual
experimentation. This bore out the evidence of
daily newspapers in which we often read of young
delinquents claiming that they'd 'read it in the
comics' or 'saw it in the movies. '[6]

That books may definitely be used to change attitudes
of delinquent children and youth was further demonstrated by
an experiment conducted by The Public Library of Cincinnati
and Hamilton County with two groups of delinquent youths,
one of boys, one of girls, 12-15 years of age. Under a federal grant, the experiment, which lasted eight months, attempted to discover whether the reading and discussion of
books relevant to the problems of the individuals concerned
would make any difference in their attitudes and self-concepts.
Multiple copies of the books were provided so that all who
wished could read at the same time. The books were reasonably well written and had believable characters and situations with which the boys and girls could identify.

The young people were tested before and after the
study with the Tennessee Self Concept Test. Forty-minute
discussion periods of books read held at three-week intervals,
were led by a young people's librarian. Two books were introduced at each session and the group members could choose
between them. Some read both books, and both were discussed at each meeting. In the eight months about eighteen
books were covered.

Favorite books with the boys were Bonham's Durango
Street, Clarke's High School Dropout, Garst's Red Eagle, and
Harkins' Knockout. The girls liked Eyerly's Dropout, and
A Girl Like Me, Friedman's Ellen and the Gang, Finlayson's
Runaway Teen, Hinton's The Outsider, Hunt's Up a Road
Slowly, and Means' It Takes All Kinds.

Due to a high rate of attrition which made it impossible to give the final tests to some of the youths, little change was noted in one group. However, in the other group, five positive changes were noted:

1. Insight into their own behavior improved;
2. The general physical condition of the group was better;
3. There was less maladjustment;
4. There was less self-criticism, indicating a decrease in defensiveness;
5. There was less neuroticism.

A control group was used, and these differences were more pronounced in the experimental group than in the control group. This experiment was library-initiated and library-conducted, although the cooperation of the hospital was secured.

The wider uses of bibliotherapy were recognized as far back as 1958 in connection with an ever-increasing problem in today's society--drug addiction, so often connected with juvenile delinquency. Maurice Floch, clinical psychologist at the Detroit House of Correction, Plymouth, Michigan, stressed the particular value of two books recommended by the then Chief of Extension of the Detroit Public Library: Long Day's Journey into Night, by Eugene O'Neill, and Let No Man Write My Epitaph, by Willard Motley.

"Long Day's Journey into Night proved to be a veritable treasure trove to me as a psychotherapist, " Dr. Floch said in an article written for the New York State Library's Bookmark. "Willard Motley's Let No Man Write My Epitaph turned out to be even stronger meat. Here was a book that pictured the slum as no photograph or painting ever could. "

Dr. Floch felt that the effects of these two books upon addicts were profound. The strong sense of identification with the main characters and their sufferings led to cautious self-examination, and also raised such philosophical questions as: What is this whole business of living about? What are the aims, the purposes? What other solutions are possible besides escape into the temporary self-forgetfulness brought on by narcotics and liquor?

Willard Motley's book proved even more valuable to Dr. Floch than to his addicts. After reading this tour of the inferno of the addicts' world he felt much closer as a human

being to his addicts than ever before, and was thus able to
reach a better understanding and do a better job of working
with them. [7]

Institutional Library Services; A Plan for the State of
Illinois offers program suggestions for delinquent boys and
girls soon to be discharged from correctional institutions.
Objectives are to inculcate and develop social living skills;
strengthen the self-confidence; develop feelings of independence, ease and relaxation; provide assistance in adjustment
and appreciation of the results of acceptable social behavior
within the group and later in the community; and create a
sense of belonging.

> Librarians, helped by volunteers, can conduct
> group discussions centering upon social relations
> with the use of books, films, filmstrips, and pic-
> tures on etiquette, dating, grooming and the like.
> A series of at least eight to ten 40-minute to one-
> hour sessions should be planned, although there
> need not be a formal limit to these sessions. The
> first two could be introductory and informal dis-
> cussions.   As the group becomes more cohesive,
> role-playing sessions and skits could be used for
> discussions, the latter to be taped and played back
> for evaluation.   Several sessions should be planned
> using the activities room for simulated environ-
> mental situations involving participation in a reality
> situation.
>
> One session can be devoted to library services
> and materials available in the community, how to
> obtain them, how to use the library, and how to
> regard it as a source for help and information
> and as a means for utilizing leisure hours.

We are prone to regard criminals and juvenile delinquents as though they were not among us all; to see them
rather as strangers, intruders upon our world.   The spirit
of revenge is often confused with the idea of justice in American society.   We forget that "but for the grace of God, there
go I. " We are "we, " and they are "they. "   Books to help in
overcoming this "we-they" attitude include Maxwell Anderson's
play Winterset; J. G. Cozzens' The Just and the Triumphant;
Charles Dickens' Great Expectations; Feodor Dostoevski's
Crime and Punishment and The House of the Dead; Hans Fallada's The World Outside, George Eliot's Adam Bede; William

Faulkner's Intruder in the Dust and Sanctuary, Paul Green's
In Abraham's Bosom and This Body the Earth; Victor Hugo's
Les Miserables; Sidney Kingsley's Dead End; John Knittel's
Via Malo; Willard Motley's Knock on Any Door; Charles
Reade's It's Never Too Late to Mend; Jean-Paul Sartre's The
Respectful Prostitute; L. N. Tolstoi's Resurrection, and Mar-
garet Wilson's One Came Out. These novels and dramas re-
flect many aspects of the place of the criminal in society,
and one who reads them thoughtfully must conclude that the
wrong-doer can do no wrong without the hidden will of all.

Zaccaria gives a list of personality traits of juvenile
delinquents which he feels consistently show the same basic
patterns. His list is more comprehensive and somewhat
different from the traits suggested earlier in this chapter in
The Practice of Bibliotherapy in Institutional Library Services:
A Plan for the State of Illinois. Zaccaria cites:

1. Feelings of being rejected, deprived, insecure,
   unloved and misunderstood.
2. Deep feelings of being thwarted.
3. Strong feeling of being inadequate or inferior in
   areas such as home life, school, peer relationships, sports, etc.
4. Intense feelings of discomfort concerning family
   disharmony, parental misconduct, errors of
   parents, etc.
5. Strong hostility toward one or more siblings because of discrimination or favoritism of parents
   in their treatment of their children.
6. Feelings of confused unhappiness due to deep-
   seated conflict.
7. A conscious or unconscious sense of guilt about
   earlier delinquent and/or non-delinquent behavior.

In recent years, says Zaccaria, therapy has played an increasingly important role in the rehabilitation of the juvenile
delinquent, and bibliotherapy has been used as one aspect of
the rehabilitation process. [8]

Craig described the use of books in a bibliotherapeutic
context in a home of juvenile delinquent boys, noting that they
found release of their hostile feelings through reading. [9]

Books were also found useful in the rehabilitation of
juvenile delinquents in a cooperative court-library project described by Slocum. [10] Carefully selected books and maga-

zines were made available to the boys in a pleasant and newly
decorated probation department waiting room manned by
trained volunteer librarians.   Books aided in the total treatment program by providing release of feelings and stimulating
introspection or self-study by the boys.

Honor work camps, both for adult prisoners and juveniles, can provide a good environment for informal bibliotherapy if there is even one counselor, guard, or other official on the staff who will take the time and trouble to select
a group of books for evening reading and see that they are
made readily available to the prisoners.   After a hard day's
work in the woods, in a temporary camp lacking the facilities for most other types of recreation, books may help fill
the time between the evening meal and bed.   Since many prisoners, old or young, who have been non-readers will not
turn to books of their own accord, even in such a setting,
some kind of planned program of group reading and discussion
or special incentives will be necessary.   If the prison from
which the men or boys are sent to an honor camp has a library and librarian, he or she is the logical person to try to
set up a program and to assist one of the regular attendants
at the camp who will actually supervise it.

The type of prisoners sent to honor camps are usually
those whose prison record has been good enough to merit
trust.   Levels of intelligence and education may be superior
to those of the general run of prisoners, and such prisoners
will be likely to profit most from a constructive reading program.

Books on nature, wildlife, philosophy, in readily understood language, such as the works of Thoreau, may help
honor camp inmates to get some pleasure from their surroundings and make them better able to see themselves as others
see them.   Teenagers can gain from books like Frank Bonham's Durango Street, which deals with delinquency and gang
activities in Los Angeles; Emily Neville's The Seventeenth
Street Gang; Floyd Patterson's and Milton Gross's Victory
Over Myself, the story of how Patterson overcame a life of
delinquency and became the world's heavyweight boxing champion; Bill Sands' My Shadow Ran Fast, how one man became
a convict and his attempts to help others who are headed in
the same direction; and Jo Sykes' Chip on His Shoulder, the
tale of a juvenile delinquent rehabilitated on a Montana ranch.

Juvenile detention homes and courts have an even

better oppotunity than honor camps to work bibliotherapy into
their programs, for three reasons: 1) They have better facilities for housing books and a larger collection; 2) The
services of trained counselors and librarians are more readily available; and 3) There are usually public libraries in the
vicinity where groups can be taken for browsing, library orientation, or reading periods.

The use of probationary waiting rooms for displays of
books to be read while waiting, and more efforts like the
joint project of the county court and Free Library of Philadelphia described by Judge Kidd are needed. Also needed
are more cooperation between public librarians and juvenile
officers; and more books purchased or made available in
juvenile detention homes and court anterooms. Some offenders waiting for interviews will pick up a book from pure
boredom, even if they would not read under other circumstances. Others, nervous and fearful, may be able to lose
those fears, at least temporarily, in a book or magazine. A
book chosen and read of one's own free will in such a place
may do more good than one handed out personally by a counselor in the role of bibliotherapist, even though it will probably be obvious to the reader that the books were especially
chosen for their themes on juvenile problems.

In order to work successfully with criminals or juvenile delinquents public librarians will have to change some of
their attitudes. They will have to look at prisoners with the
realization that they are human beings who have landed where
they are because of faulty environment, unhappy home life,
unfortunate experiences in school, or other maladjustments.
Criminals are not born; they are molded by negative factors
the librarians have managed to escape by fortunate circumstances of birth, environment and more constructive associations. Prisoners released and returned to their home communities to work and live especially need the atmosphere of
freedom and friendliness a library can offer if the staff is
properly chosen. Rehabilitation does not stop with release
from prison. The attitude with which society greets and treats
the newly released prisoner or inmate of a training school
may well determine whether he decides to become a constructive citizen in a normal society or whether he will again become a criminal and a recidivist.

David Wineman has pointed out that the effects of a
corrective institution, whether it be a reformatory, training
school, ordinary prison or a maximum security penitentiary,

are deep and far-reaching on an individual. He does not shed
these effects in a day or a week or sometimes months after
release, and perhaps never. As Wineman says, "An orientation to a total therapeutic milieu means an awareness of all
of the identifiable ingredients in it that can presume to have
an effect on its captives."[11] A librarian bibliotherapist must
work with prison officials as a part of the total rehabilitation
program and not as a prima donna performing an isolated
service. A librarian in the community must help smooth the
re-entrance of a freed prisoner into a world he left behind
when he entered prison walls, and which may now prove be-
wildering and frustrating. If he has been behind bars for
many years, he is often a lost creature that the world he
knew has left behind. Library materials can help to bring
him up to date. Library staff can help him feel once more
like a normal human being.

If there is no library in a prison, an understanding
bookmobile librarian may arrange to have a good sized bookmobile stop regularly in a prison yard during the recreation
hour. William Henderson, Institutional Library Consultant,
Michigan State Library, has described a typical day's service
by bookmobile to the Michigan Training Unit, a medium-
security correctional institution with 400 inmates, all youthful
offenders, at the time service began in 1964. There were
both academic and vocational units but no professional librarian on the institution staff. Starting in May, 1966, this bookmobile service was extended to other such institutions until
all but the Michigan Parole Camp were included. Aside from
bookmobile service, collections of from 200 to 3,000 volumes
are selected by an institutional consultant from the state library and left at the institutions, being changed periodically.
A detailed account of the bookmobile service may be found in
Henderson's article "Bookmobile Service to Correctional Institutions: Background and Description of One Day's Service"
(Association of Hospital and Institution Libraries Quarterly,
v. 7, no. 2, Winter 1967, p. 34-36).

Prisoners may suffer from a number of destructive
effects of prison life, or from lack of constructive effects.
Among these, David Wineman points out, are :

> 1. Conditions in some institutions radically abu-
> sive to normal human functioning.
> 2. Too few institutions have a therapeutic central
> guiding philosophy of care and treatment or are
> using the latest and best findings of the behavioral

sciences.

3. The prisoner may experience encounters with sexual deviates, captor-captive relationship with staff, psychic humiliation, physical brutalization, constant exposure to programless boredom, unclean grouping, enforced work routines in the guise of vocational training, violations of privacy, close power and domination of other inmates, the maddening limitations of space; the rigidity and inflexibility of the managerial system; confusion as to the powers and duties of some staff members; loss of communication with the outside world, and symptom-squeezing forms of punishment. [12]

Not all of these harmful factors are to be found in all prisons of course, and prison management has undoubtedly improved in the last decade, though sometimes only after violent revolt and riot among prisoners. But nowhere would there seem to be greater need for bibliotherapy as a release for tensions, a means of keeping up with the outside world, as recreation, as a help to the prisoner in gaining insight into the reasons for his failure in society.

Modern penal institutions increasingly employ the same methods of psychological and educational testing, evaluation and guidance as are in use elsewhere. Many studies have been made to determine what makes a criminal and how he can be diverted into normal channels of behavior. With many types of crimes and persons involved, easy generalizations are impossible. However, Dr. Hector J. Ritey, writing in the Archives of Criminal Psychodynamics, stated, "We find at least one fundamental characteristic that all criminals have in common: the morbid fear of reality. "[13]

The criminal, Mildred T. Moody believes, cannot think of himself as a contributing human being. In fanciful daydreams he is the victor or hero. He sheds all responsibility and is secure in the knowledge that society, not he, is at fault. By acting in direct or violent opposition to the rules by which others live, he is showing other people how wrong they are, and he evokes a response similar to that which caused his early aberration--parental censure, rejection, and punishment. This pattern will continue until he can somehow realize that the source of his social failure lies within himself. Books, carefully selected and followed up with discussion, can help him reach this insight.

Group therapy is used extensively in correctional institutions because there is not enough medical counseling staff to attempt intensive individual psychotherapy on the scale that would be required. The library has been considered one of the valuable adjuncts for group reading therapy. It serves a threefold purpose, actually, as recreation, a source of knowledge, and a means of gaining insight. Correctional journals have carried many articles on libraries, some showing a deep concern for book selection bordering on strict censorship, while another school of thought argues that books chosen for their vitality and honesty need not be censored.

Great Books programs with groups have been used with varying success. Reading and discussion clubs have been formed. The most usable group therapy has been borrowed from the mental hospital. It has been found that an important factor in the prisoner's social failure may be his perception. If he is intelligent enough to learn to see things differently, group sessions may help him develop the needed perception. Then he must participate. A therapist cannot evaluate an individual who fails to participate in group discussion. Finally, the prisoner must be willing to persist until he achieves some measure of reality. A prescribed reading program through which the prisoner gains insight is directed by the librarian. Group therapy necessitates self-probing with the individual doing supplementary 'homework' as he gropes toward an understanding of himself. Beyond the group sessions there is independent reading by which the individual builds his own bridge to reality through the experiences and thoughts of others.

In prison there are not many ways a person can touch the real world other than through books. The impact of this is illustrated in the case of a prisoner who, when released from the Minnesota State Prison after 45 years behind bars, said, 'It took twenty years before I realized I was wrong. It was gradual and came through reading the thoughts and ideas of great men.' This man, who was described as 'the toughest kid in America' when he was convicted of two murders, also taught himself mathematics, engineering, and electronics, and his self-education helped him win freedom and

a career as a mathematician with a west coast
electronics firm. [13]

Unfortunately, although there has been considerable
prison reform in recent years, there are still a few prisons
where terror, not therapy, is the "name of the game." Some
institutions supposed to be curative or correctional are neither.

The staff of a well-run prison or other correctional
institution needs to know the following, says Wineman:

> Which routines and rules are best for which kinds
> of prisoners.
>
> When group rituals are behind squabbles and fights
> among the inmates.
>
> What is the overall atmosphere: scapegoating; sub-
> clique formations; group excitement waves which
> individuals are getting sucked into, acting out the
> needs of the group.
>
> Trait clusters, if any.
>
> Who should be roommates and who not in correc-
> tional institutions for children and young people.
>
> Space, equipment, time, and props available.
>
> The activity structure and the nature of consti-
> tuent performances.
>
> What seepage is coming in from the outside world.
>
> Is there a system of umpiring services and traffic
> regulations between environment and resident?
>
> Is there resiliency in the behavioral management
> system?

Only if he understands these facts and trends can a
correction staff member do a good job of bibliotherapy, especially in the group pattern. An excellent library program
will sail over the heads of the residents if there is such
fussy and rigid control of library space and materials that
the resident begins to feel he needs to know the governor to
get in or out of the library. Nor can the library be allowed

to become the tool of a cruel punishment system, refusing
admittance to the library or withdrawing all reading material
from individual inmates as a means of discipline.

Describing the library service of CIM (California Institution for Men) at Chino in 1955, Abe Oppenheim, [14] the
librarian, pointed out that it was a minimum custody prison
and a significant social advancement in prison management.
The user of the CIM library was a man in the process of returning to normal community life. A strong effort was made
to make these men, the majority of them first offenders, feel
that they were using a normal community library and to make
them feel at ease in the library atmosphere. Many of the men
had more time and inclination to read than ever before. Books
can have an even greater than usual impact when read by
someone who has not been accustomed to reading and who has
a great deal of time to think about what he has read.

Many men, Oppenheim said, get the reading habit soon
enough in prison. The free man who sneered that someday
he might read a book may well find reading a stark necessity
in prison. In reading, restless, imprisoned men can sometimes lose a mounting tension, the insistent pressure of an
emotional bitterness or a corrosive hatred. Sometimes men
who balk at discussing a problem with a counselor will accept
the impersonality of a "book consultation. " Oppenheim used
a publicity technique of putting library advertising squibs on
the back of the men's laundry slips, clothing adjustment
forms, etc. , and at 11 o'clock each night, before the institutional radio signed off, a library-sponsored taped program
called "At the End of the Day" closed the day with a song, a
bit of verse, a pleasant thought--and a library plug. The
program proved very popular. These plugs, like the laundry
slip squibs, kept reminding the men to relax with a good
book, to pleasure read, to read for fun, to be at ease with
a good book.

Oppenheim invited the cooperation of the correction
officers at CIM with a list of so-called "life building books"
on popular psychology, religion, social living, etc. , which
he included in the in-service training programs for new
officers. A notation asked any officer who read one or more
books on the list to indicate titles which he thought would be
most helpful to the inmates. Officers were to make the recommendations as specific as possible, both as to the content
of the book and the type of inmate for whom it would be most
applicable.

Perrine[15] emphasizes an important point regarding library service in correctional institutions: regular and continuous consultation and resource contacts should be maintained with the state, county, and local libraries for assistance, especially in the area of techniques and devices for the motivation of reading. In addition to meeting the individual needs of the men, he says, the library should complement all group and treatment activities of the institution. To accomplish this, the complete incorporation and integration of the library with the academic, vocational, social, education, and mental hygiene programs of the institution is a prime necessity for dynamic and functional service. Only if this integration of all prison services exists can effective bibliotherapy be practiced in the library.

At the New York State Training School for Boys, Jacobs describes the program he found successful with delinquent boys twelve to sixteen years of age. Many of the boys who came into the institution as apathetic non-readers became active users of books, with an accompanying improvement in behavior patterns. Although Jacobs referred to his library work with these young inmates as guidance rather than bibliotherapy, it definitely had all the ingredients of bibliotherapy--boy with problems, careful guidance, and therapeutic results including an improvement in the type of books read and enjoyed.

After each boy admitted had passed through the first stages of classification, a file was compiled of material taken from the social worker's observations, the psychologist's report, the results of a battery of tests, and other pertinent information. A summary of this material went to the librarian, as well as to teachers, recreation leaders, and the vocational men. With this information, supplemented often with conferences with the boy's supervisor, the librarian became familiar with the boy's background, vocational interest if any, reading ability, recommendations from different units of the institution, and other information helpful in setting up an individual reading program.

Each boy had a short interview with the librarian when he first came to the library. Thus was established a one-to-one contact at the beginning rather than the group library orientation used in most general public schools. The boy filled out a questionnaire, was told about the library and its services, and was given a copy of a booklet entitled "Magic Trail To Adventure. "

Jacobs worked on the theory that no matter how low the reading level, there is some interest through which a boy can be reached. A hobby, a vocational preference, even the kind of movies enjoyed provided clues as to what type of reading to offer. A special questionnaire was used to determine movie interest. The "Magic Trail To Adventure" booklist, unlike most library booklists, contained some books with little literary value as well as better titles. The annotations were written in the language the boys spoke, and the list was well illustrated with catchy drawings.

Response to this list was gratifying. Boys who formerly showed no interest in reading called for books listed. The list included many books boys of this type would never have read of their own volition, yet they contained action, suspense, adventure of the kind they had found formerly only in comics, confession magazines, tabloid newspapers, and such publications as Ranch Romances and Inside Detective Stories.

Movies such as "Beau Geste," "Captains Courageous," "Dawn Patrol," and "Gunga Din" were shown once a week and often led into reading the books from which they were adapted, or other books on allied subjects. Reading was never forced on the boys. If they refused the books suggested, they were given magazines or the daily paper. Reading was never made to seem something a teacher was compelling them to do.

Notes

1. Floch, M. and Casey, G. "The Library Goes to Prison." American Library Association Bulletin, v. 49, March 1955, p. 126-218.

2. Gray, W. "Reform Through Reading." Library Journal, v. 85, February 1, 1960, p. 502-503.

3. Rudolf, Herman. Course in Reading, Speaking, Attitude Forming, and Critical Self-evaluation. Mimeographed, n. d. , 15p.

4. Social Educational Research and Development, Inc. The Practice of Bibliotherapy in Institutional Library Services. A Plan for the State of Illinois. American Library Association, study authorized by Paul Powell,

State Librarian, Illinois State Library, Springfield, Illinois, 62706, 1970, p. 71-72, 78.

5. Stout, Juanita Kidd. "Troubled Child and Reading Achievement." Catholic Library World, v. 36, May-June 1965, p. 603-08+.

6. Lorang, Sister Mary Corde. "The Effect of Reading on Moral Conduct and Emotional Experience." Catholic University of America Press, 1945. Described in Catholic Library Practice, Kirchner, Clara J. "Bibliotherapy and the Catholic School Library."

7. Floch, Maurice. "Bibliotherapy and the Library." The Bookmark, New York State Library, v. 18, December 1958, p. 57-59.

8. Zaccaria, Joseph S. and Moses, Harold A. Facilitating Human Development through Reading. Champaign, Ill.: Stipes Publishing Co., c1968, p. 39.

9. Craig, Leila P. "Boys and Books Get Together." The Child, v. 16, March 1952, p. 98-109.

10. Slocum, G. B. "Books for Probationers: A Court-Library Project." National Probation and Parole Association Journal, v. 1, January 1955, p. 20-24.

11. Wineman, David. "The Effects of the Institution on the Person." American Library Association Bulletin, v. 63, Sept. 1969, p. 1087-96.

12. Ibid., p. 1087-88.

13. Moody, Mildred T. "Modern Concepts in General Hospitals and Other Institutions." In: Library Trends, issue on Bibliotherapy. Ruth M. Tews, issue editor. v. 11, October 1962, p. 151-52.

14. Oppenheim, Abe. "Diversion and Direction." Wilson Library Bulletin, v. 30, Nov. 1955, p. 245, 248.

15. Perrine, Charles J. "A Correctional Institution's Library Service." Wilson Library Bulletin, v. 30, Nov. 1955, p. 249-252.

SUGGESTED READINGS:
CRIME AND JUVENILE DELINQUENCY

JUVENILE AND TEEN AGE

Alcock, Gudrun. Run, Westy, Run. Lothrop, Lee, and
     Shepard, 1966. Boys and girls, 8-12. A young social
     worker helps a "nice" boy and his family out of trouble.

Bonham, Frank. Durango Street. Dutton, 1965. 187p. Boys,
     12-18. Parolee's problems with gangs in his own
     neighborhood.

Butters, Dorothy. Heartbreak Street. Macrae Smith, 1958.
     191p. Girls, 12-15. Improvement of a poor neigh-
     borhood.

Carson, John F. The Twenty-third Street Crusaders. Far-
     rar, 1958. 183p. Boys, 12-16. Concerns teenagers
     on probation.

Chandler, Ruth. Too Many Promises. Abelard-Schuman,
     1956. A juvenile delinquent gradually develops ma-
     turity and responsibility. Juvenile-adolescent.

Eyerly, Jeanette. Drop-out. Lippincott, 1963. 189p. Girls
     and boys, 13-18. Problems of dropouts when they try
     to become adults overnight and become involved with
     crooks.

Felsen, Henry G. Hot Rod. Dutton, 1950. 188p. Boys and
     girls, 11-16. Teenagers' speeding and defiance of
     authority.

Finlayson, Ann. Runaway Teen. Doubleday, 1963. 143p.
     Girls, 11-16. Resentment over mother's remarriage
     and involvement with a gang.

Floherty, John J. and McGrady, Mike. Youth and the FBI.
     Lippincott, 1960. 159p. Boys, 12-18. Nationwide
     juvenile delinquency and crime.

Fox, Paula. How Many Miles to Babylon? White, 1967.
     Boys and girls, 8-12. Delinquency.

Friedman, Frieda. Ellen and the Gang. Morrow, 1963.

191p.   Girls, 10-14.   Pre-teen girl becomes dupe of older teenage delinquents.

Graham, Lorenz.   North Town.   Crowell, 1965.   220p.   Boys, 12-18.   Adjustment of a Southern black to Northern city living.

Harkins, Philip.   Knockout.   Holiday, 1950.   242p.   Boys 11-15.   Achieving identity without joining a gang.

Hill, Donna.   Catch a Brass Canary.   Lippincott, 1964. 224p.   Boys and girls, 14-18.   How a Puerto Rican teenager became weaned away from a gang through work in a library.

Hinton, Susan E.   The Outsiders.   Viking, 1967.   188p. Boys and girls, 12 and up.   Written by a 17-year-old who has known life on the streets.   A boy faces harsh realities of life in a big city.

Johnson, Annabel & Edgar.   Pickpocket Run.   Harper, 1961. 185p.   Boys and girls, 12-18.   A restless teenager tempted by crime.   Slangy, realistic.

Lewiton, Mina.   That Bad Carlos.   Harper, 1965.   175p. Boys, 9-12.   Puerto Rican boy's adjustment to New York City life.

Liggett, Thomas.   The Hollow.   Holiday House, 1958. Boys, 12 up.   Al finally found himself after being sent to a camp for delinquent boys.

Parker, Richard.   Killer.   Doubleday, 1964.   201p.   Boys, 14-18.   Tough boys and tough talk about a mass escape of boys from a juvenile institution.

Patterson, Floyd and Gross, Milton.   Victory Over Myself. Scholastic Book Services, 1962.   Boys, 12 up. Story of how Floyd Patterson overcame a life of delinquency and became the world's heavyweight boxing champion.

Riter, Dorris.   Edge of Violence.   McKay, 1964.   245p. Boys and girls, 12-18.   A probationer trying to adjust back into society.

Sykes, Jo.   Chip on His Shoulder.   Funk & Wagnalls, 1961. 186p.   Boys, 12-16.   A city teenager adjusting to country life and from delinquency to going straight.

Verral, Charles S. The Winning Quarterback. Crowell,
    1960. 248p. Boys, 11-14. The far-reaching effects
    of gang membership.

ADULT

Bryan, Helen. Inside. Houghton Mifflin. 1953. Story of
    female criminals and a description of penal procedures.

Farrell, James T. Studs Lonigan. Vanguard Press, 1935.
    The story of a middle-class Irish-Catholic boy's
    wasted life.

Fenton, Norman. The Prisoner's Family. Pacific Books,
    1959. An account of what happens to the members of
    the convict's family and what may be done to help
    them.

Fenton, Norman. What Will be Your Life? American Cor-
    rectional Association, 1955. A book to help in the
    rehabilitation of ex-convicts.

Gibbons, Don C. Changing the Lawbreaker. Prentice-Hall,
    1965. Problems in the treatment and rehabilitation of
    delinquents and criminals.

Knoplen, Gisela. The Adolescent Girl in Conflict. Prentice-
    Hall, 1966. A study of delinquent institutionalized
    girls with suggestions for prevention and treatment.
    Adult only.

Leibert, Julius A. Behind Bars. Doubleday, 1965. A
    chaplain's description of prison life in three major
    prisons.

Lykke, Arthur F. Parolees and Payrolls. Chas. C. Thomas
    Co., 1957. Problems of ex-convicts in finding a job
    and adjusting to life on the outside.

Sands, Bill. My Shadow Ran Fast. Prentice-Hall, 1964.
    How one man became a convict and his attempts to
    help others who are headed in the same direction.

Sands, Bill. The Seventh Step. New American Library, 1967.

A history and explanation of the Seventh Step Foundation and its attempts to rehabilitate ex-prisoners.

(Adapted from Bibliotherapy--Methods and Materials, Association of Hospital and Institution Libraries, American Library Association, 1971, p. 149-157; and Facilitating Human Development through Reading, by Joseph S. Zaccaria and Harold A. Moses, Stipes Publ. Co., c. 1968.)

READING FOR THE BIBLIOTHERAPIST

American Library Association. Objectives and Standards for Libraries in Correctional Institutions. Chicago: American Library Association, 1962.
    A comprehensive guide for the prison official and librarian. Clearly states the library's responsibility in the total rehabilitative process.

Auchincloss, Louis. The Embezzler. Houghton, 1966.
    Upper-class crime. Fiction.

Burnett, William R. Asphalt Jungle, Knopf, 1949.
    Crime, newspapers, and the police.

Camus, Albert. The Stranger. Knopf, 1946.
    Crime and courtroom psychology.

Cochran, M. R. "The Library in a Correctional Institution-Its Contents." American Journal of Correction, v. 23, July-August 1961, p. 14₊.
    Excellent discussion of book selection.

Dostoevski, Feodor. The Brothers Karamazov.
    Criminal behavior. Aggression as adjustment to a sense of frustration. Fiction.

Dostoevski, Feodor. Crime and Punishment.
    Criminal behavior. Aggression as adjustment to a sense of frustration. Fiction.

Faulkner, William. Intruder in the Dust. Random House, 1948.
    Crime and the criminal. Mob law and the innocent. Fiction.

Floch, Maurice and Casey, Genevieve. "The Library Goes
to Prison. " <u>American Library Association Bulletin</u>, v. 49,
March 1955, p. 126-218.
Discusses the program of the Extension Department of
the Detroit Public Library in connection with the Detroit House
of Correction.

Gray, W. "Reform through Reading. " <u>Library Journal</u>,
v. 85, Feb. 1, 1960, p. 502-03.
Describes the highly successful program of adult education carried on at an Oklahoma penal institution.

Leibert, Julius A. <u>Behind Bars</u>. Doubleday, 1964.
A chaplain's description of prison life in three major
prisons.

Malamud, Bernard. <u>The Assistant</u>. Farrar and Straus, 1957.
A criminal tries to find redemption in marriage. Fiction.

Motley, Willard. <u>Knock on Any Door</u>. Appleton, 1947.
Juvenile delinquency with society as the delinquent.
Fiction.

O'Halloran, Wayne. "Group Psychotherapy and the Criminal: An Introduction to Reality. " <u>American Journal of
Correction</u>, v. 23, May-June 1961, p. 26.

Proust, Marcel. "Cities of the Plain. " In: <u>Remembrance
of Things Past</u>. Random House, 1941.
Subcultures of criminal behavior. Aggression as adjustment to a sense of frustration.

Ritey, Hector T. "The Psychological Background of Recidivism. " <u>Archives of Criminal Psychodynamics</u>, v. 1, Fall
1955, p. 898.

Sands, Bill. <u>The Seventh Step</u>. New American Library, 1967.
A history and explanation of the Seventh Step Foundation and its attempts to rehabilitate ex-prisoners.

Slocum, G. P. "Books for Probationers: A Court-Library
Project. " <u>National Probation and Parole Association
Journal</u>, v. 1, July 1955, p. 20-24.
Recounts an experiment with volunteer library and book
service to probationers of the Kings County Court, Brooklyn,
New York. Books were made available in the probationers'
waiting room.

Steinbeck, John. Cannery Row. Viking, 1945.
  Subcultures of criminal behavior; on homosexuality.
Aggression as adjustment to a sense of frustration.

Note: Some of the above would also be suitable for prisoners
  or inmates of other correctional facilities, subject to
  the judgment of the bibliotherapist.

CHAPTER 8

PROBLEMS RELATED TO A SCHOOL SITUATION

In spite of early recognition of the therapeutic value of reading, teachers did not begin to investigate and use the technique of bibliotherapy to any extent in the classroom until the 1940s. Joseph Blake points out that investigations even before 1950 had shown that symptoms of personality maladjustment decrease and in some cases disappear as reading success occurs. [1]

Today, many school libraries are being converted to media centers which contain not only books, periodicals, and vertical file material--the components of the conventional school library of the past--but many types of audio-visual equipment and materials calculated to aid in the learning process. We shall frequently refer to media specialists, therefore, as well as librarians throughout this chapter.

The school media specialist, librarian, counselor, or teacher has a very special opportunity to use bibliotherapy effectively, since he has what may be regarded as a semi-captive clientele. Unlike public librarians, who see their patrons at varying and usually unpredictable intervals, school personnel see their students very frequently; often, as in the case of teachers, five days a week. Moreover, school personnel have access to school records for background information and may confer among themselves concerning problem cases, pooling their information and ideas. They can even learn a great deal about their students through informal, friendly conversations with them and with their friends and acquaintances. Public librarians, too, of course, may sometimes be able to employ this technique. Some very interesting sidelights on character, reading interests, and personal problems may emerge from such conversations.

Although the librarian, media specialist, counselor, or teacher will usually be in the best position to practice bibliotherapy, any other school employee with whom the student feels rapport--the office secretary, a school nurse, the administrator, perhaps even a staff psychologist--may also be involved.   The bibliotherapist in the school situation may well be anyone qualified by personality, human understanding, and knowledge of books.

Bibliotherapy is not a cure-all, nor can it be used with all individuals, but when it can, there seems sufficient evidence to prove that it is an effective method.   According to Zaccaria and Moses, not a single study in a substantial body of research found bibliotherapy to be ineffective in a school setting. [2]

Three goals of education in particular suggest the use of bibliotherapy in a developmental or preventive rather than a remedial sense: education for psychological maturity, for life adjustment, and for character development.   Minor problems that arise in these developmental processes may be helped by bibliotherapy and prevent the formation of more serious problems.   Bibliotherapy, as distinguished from ordinary reader guidance, will be used in cases involving mental, physical, or emotional problems, where the student is immature for his age, poorly adjusted to other people or his environment, or possesses some character weakness likely to yield to treatment.

Bibliotherapy can be particularly useful today because so many young people are groping for answers, seeking their own identity, trying to find their place in the world, refusing to accept a social order in which they have no faith.   Lack of adjustment and inability to face reality is seen in the increasing use of narcotics, tobacco and alcohol, even down into the upper elementary school or junior high school levels. Hostile to "the establishment, " they later turn away from society and seek self-fulfillment in association with others of like mind.   These students may become the school dropouts, the inciters to riot, even the violent type of revolutionary. They become devotees of causes to which they, and not the social order, have given priority.

Many of these non-adjusters have keen minds and special skills.   In school they have been or are good readers. Increasing use is being made of group bibliotherapy, but usually only after the young person has become a drug addict, an alcoholic, a mental case, or a criminal.   Individual or group bibliotherapy practiced earlier in the school setting might well have prevented some journeys down the path of

maladjustment to juvenile delinquency, and from juvenile delinquency to more serious crimes and addictions.   School
personnel have not only a rare opportunity but a special obligation to use every means at their command to prevent such
tragedies.

In the teaching of moral precepts evidence shows that
students usually do not respond as well to direct efforts as
to indirect, more subtle methods.   Let a counselor talk end-
lessly about the dangers of drugs, promiscuous sex, or alcohol, and it may have little effect if a student's peer group
thinks and acts otherwise.   If this same student is subtly and
unobtrusively channeled into reading books which graphically
portray the horrors of drug addiction and the agonies of withdrawal, the degradation of alcoholism, or the tragedy of un-
wanted pregnancies, the impression is more likely to be both
effective and lasting.

The mental hygiene or mental health movement which
has grown so much in importance during the twentieth century
is inseparably linked to education.   Large school systems
may have a staff psychologist or at least the services of a
consulting psychologist or psychiatrist.   Bibliotherapy as used
by such staff members will assume clinical or medical aspects, but school staff members who are in a position to help
with bibliotherapy should be consulted and assigned a part in
the process.

The use of bibliotherapy in education has been discussed at great length in an excellent book by Joseph S. Zaccaria and Harold A. Moses, Facilitating Human Development
through Reading--The Use of Bibliotherapy in Teaching and
Counseling.   Although this work is somewhat technical and
perhaps better understood by the psychiatrist or psychologist,
it does present some practical applications of bibliotherapy
which can be helpful in a school situation.

Reading, especially on the elementary school level,
according to Schrodes, has been too often taught as a skill
in which meaning and value are subordinated to mechanical
facility in recognizing words and remembering facts.   For
those who learned to read in this manner the bibliotherapy
method of reading for ideas and reflection can be a new and
fresh approach. [3]

Most people, especially children and young adults, read
books because they are interesting, exciting, or provide

needed information. They do not think in terms of the potential therapy value, which emerges as a by-product but is
none the less effective.

Four methods of discovering a student's problems have
already been mentioned: consulting school records, conferring
with other teachers or school staff members who have contact with him, talking in friendly fashion with the student himself, and talking with his friends and acquaintances.   Others
may include: observation of behavior in the classroom, the
halls, the library, the media center, the playground, or the
cafeteria; talking with the student's parents; knowing the student through sponsorship of extra-curricular activities such
as sports, clubs, journalism, music, or dramatic activities.
Sometimes, different aspects of a student's personality may
be revealed through these more informal contacts.   A student's problems may also be revealed in an English class,
through his writings or his inability to speak before a class.
Since the reading of a certain number of books is still an
English requirement in many schools, the English teacher has
an added opportunity to influence reading choices and to discuss the books read with the students, either individually or
in groups.

The student who is too inhibited or too shy to discuss
personal problems directly with a teacher, counselor, or librarian, regardless of how much he may like or respect him
or her, can often project his own problems in a much more
impersonal manner through class discussion of book characters with which he has identified.   In such a discussion he
feels that he is not giving himself away, but as the class
members react to his explanation of the actions and attitudes
of a hero or heroine, he secretly applies such reactions to
his own attitudes and conduct.   Or he may discuss a problem
character with friends or acquaintances outside class with
similar effect.   Serious problems will require the help of a
guidance expert, perhaps even a psychiatrist, with whom the
student confers after reading, but the English class can help
the student to gain insight into some of the lesser problems
he encounters from day to day.

Here are some of the situations in which bibliotherapy
may be used in a school setting by a bibliotherapist who knows
people and books:

1) Membership in a library club whose members discuss and recommend books to each other may help

the introverted or shy student to become more
group oriented and to find a solution to a problem
similar to his own.

2) Fiction and biography may be used to show stutterers how others have overcome the habit and
become successful. Since fear and embarrassment
only amplify a stuttering problem, any book which
may allay such fears, minimize the effect of the
stuttering on other people, or give the student self-
confidence, is in order.

3) Reading about people of other races or ethnic
groups can help alleviate problems of prejudice,
hostility, and even anti-social behavior toward
other students.

4) The physically handicapped can be helped by reading about sports heroes, statesmen or others who
have succeeded in spite of handicaps similar to
their own.

5) When there are serious emotional and mental
handicaps the problems usually require that the
bibliotherapist work closely with a psychiatrist or
school psychologist. However, the student can
often be helped by reading, particularly in group
therapy projects. Mental handicaps may include
retardation, the various pychoses and neuroses,
if not serious enough to require special institutional care; inflated egos, inferiority complexes,
sadism, and other maladjustments. A clever
counselor will be able to detect early signs of such
problems and may be able to recommend material
that will prevent the problem from becoming serious.

6) Less serious emotional problems may include over-
aggressiveness, habitual lying, a painful degree of
shyness, lack of courage, a dislike of school, a
bad temper, an unjustifiable sense of guilt, extreme
intolerance, a reluctance to read, inability to get
along well with others of the same age and grade,
difficulty in adjusting to a new neighborhood or
school, coming from a non-English speaking family,
finding insufficient challenge in school because of
being especially gifted, and rebellion against es-

tablished authority (the "discipline cases").

7) Stealing, assault, arson, sex crimes, vandalism,
    drug addiction, and alcoholism are, unhappily,
    rapidly becoming a part of the school scene, es-
    pecially in large cities.   These criminal activities
    are hard to control, but bibliotherapy has been
    used effectively with groups of young drug addicts,
    with boys and girls in correctional institutions,
    with adult alcoholics, and with juvenile delinquents.
    Why not, then, use it in school, before the prob-
    lem has become deep-seated and of long standing?

A student who becomes involved in a serious crime or
personal habit such as trafficking in or using narcotics is
often expelled from school on the theory that he may corrupt
his classmates.   Rehabilitation and a quick return to school,
or perhaps treatment without expulsion, could often be accomplished through systematic and more general cooperation
between school authorities and juvenile delinquency officers,
employing every means at their disposal, including bibliotherapy.   Expelling a student who does not want to leave
school may break down the last barrier between him and a
career of major crime.   Resentment, bitterness, and a desire
for revenge may be aroused.   In a substantial number of instances proper counseling and the recommendation of the right
books have combined to cause a potential school dropout to
change his mind or an actual dropout to return.

The objection is often raised that there are not enough
school counselors, librarians, media center personnel, or
school psychologists to carry on preventive and developmental
bibliotherapy; not enough funds for such highly individual
treatment of problem cases.   The answer is clear: is it not
less expensive in the long run to support such a program than
to support an increasing percentage of our population in jails,
rehabilitation centers, and penitentiaries, or to suffer the
losses caused by their crimes?   Bibliotherapy has an important but too often overlooked role to play in the schools in
the correction of maladjustment and the prevention of juvenile
delinquency and crime.   When a potentially worthwhile young
person becomes a criminal, it is a reflection upon parents,
our schools and our entire social order.   In what way or ways
have we failed him?   At what point did we neglect to give him
the help he needed?

A child is not so plastic a creature that he is easily

changed by what he reads.   Books used should exemplify good
literature and be used in a manner based on sound educational
and psychological principles.

No one would claim that bibliotherapy is a panacea for
all ills, that it has magic powers to straighten out the thinking of a student whose mind has become badly warped.   But,
used in conjunction with the economic, physical, and mental
aids society now has available, it can be an added factor in
reconditioning the student's emotional makeup and completing
his developmental needs.   If it is to be effective it must begin early, at the first sign of an emerging problem; must be
used in conjunction with other types of therapy as necessary;
and must be practiced by a skilled adviser who understands
people, particularly children and young people, and knows
when to be subtle and when to be direct.

Bibliotherapy, therefore, in a school situation may
well be coupled with educational and occupational planning,
with job placement, with parental help, with teacher cooperation, with remedial measures and social reconstruction in
cooperation with outside agencies such as police and probation
officers, the courts, welfare officials, employment personnel,
medical personnel, school or community organizations--anyone
or any group interested in the welfare or rehabilitation of
children and youth.

Only as the student is assisted toward self-understand-
ing and self-direction early in his school career, whenever a
problem arises, can the deepening or multiplication of problems be prevented.   Thus the developmental or preventive aspect of bibliotherapy becomes much more socially desirable
than the traditional remedial aspect applied after a problem
has become serious.   The troubled person is not a good
learner nor does he generally get along well with others.
Maximum growth and self-fulfillment cannot be realized if the
individual has not resolved personal conflict and satisfied his
needs.

If a teacher, librarian, or media center supervisor is
to act as a bibliotherapist and recommend books as a therapy
measure, he must first gain the confidence, even the friendship of the student.   He must be warm, friendly, and outgoing, accept the individual as he is, be permissive to a degree, be sensitive to the feelings of the individual and treat
him as a person capable of slowly taking over direction of
himself.   Bibliocounseling is not advising.   In the permissive

atmosphere created by the therapist a student is helped to interpret circumstances surrounding his problem or need. Advising, by contrast, carries the connotation of supplying the pupil with ready-made solutions.

With this type of relationship the student will feel a sense of security and be receptive to the older person's suggestions. The bibliotherapist will know instinctively when to suggest a book directly related to the problem at hand or whether to casually suggest recreational reading of certain books or types of books. He will do so knowing the contents and how they may influence the student, but the student need not be conscious that the reading material is suggested for its therapeutic value. There are a number of ways in which the school staff member interested in practicing bibliotherapy can indirectly promote the reading of certain materials by the student or students he is anxious to help:

1. Placing in their hands attractive, illustrated booklists which highlight books the bibliotherapist wishes to encourage the student or students to read. If giving the list to him seems too obvious, place a pile of booklists on each reading table or in the classrooms.

2. Talking about new books with the student in a way that makes the student feel he, not the therapist, has made the choice. He should at least feel that it is a joint choice.

3. Giving a book talk on the chosen book in the student's own classroom, focusing eyes and attention very frequently on the particular student needing help. This semi-personal approach gives him a feeling that the speaker is actually talking to him.

4. Displaying jackets of the chosen books on bulletin boards in the student's own homeroom or English classroom.

5. Having table displays of a few selected books and finding a casual way of directing the student's attention toward it.

6. Suggesting a particular title or titles for a book report requirement for English class. The book can be described as particularly adventurous, timely, or likely to be considered a good choice by the English teacher. (Some collusion with the English teacher may be necessary on this, as the teacher may not always consider a good therapeutic choice the best "literary" choice.)

7. Suggesting that the boy or girl read the book and tell you about it, since you do not have time to read all the books but should have a good knowledge of them in order to tell other students. This is an especially good approach, as the student feels he then has more knowledge about something than you do, and is able to reverse the student-teacher roles.

8. A variation of no. 7 is asking the student to read a new book and then write his opinion of it for a scrapbook of student recommendations to other students. The scrapbook should be left in the library and frequently consulted. Many students are more interested in books their classmates or other students have recommended than in what adults recommend.

9. Seeing that the selected book is left on the reading table where the student is accustomed to sit when he comes into the library. If the student sits somewhere else you could talk to any student at that table on some pretext and leave the book lying close to the desired student, seemingly by accident. He may bring it to you, thus giving you a chance to comment on it.

10. Getting another student who has read the book, or who will read it at your request, to recommend it personally to the problem student.

11. Having therapeutic books lying on tables in the guidance office where students will see them and pick them up while waiting to see the counselor.

The therapist's choice of books should be governed by several general principles:

1. Know the student thoroughly before attempting bibliotherapy with him.

2. Choose the right time and place for making the book contact. Timing is important.

3. Know the material thoroughly.

4. Consider the reading level of the student.

5. Try to discuss the book with the student in a friendly and informal manner, perhaps at the time he returns it. This may open the way to further recommendations.

6. In discussing a book with the student the therapist should not try to influence the student's opinion or understanding of the book. Let his reaction be spontaneous. If the book has not had the desired

effect, try another on the basis of what you learn
from his objections or comments about the first.

7. Do not suggest specific books too early in your
relationship with the student. The student should
understand his own problems before specific books
are recommended. Otherwise he may not relate
the material to his own case or identify with the
main character.

8. As bibliotherapy is or should be practiced in connection with other guidance or therapy technique,
it may be more effective to suggest brief articles,
short stories, poems, or pamphlets rather than
full-length novels. The reading of a few chapters
in a book of non-fiction may be more effective than
reading the whole book, since the idea or ideas
the therapist is trying to get across may be lost
in too lengthy a piece of literature which touches
on other matters not related to the problem involved. Some students may prefer to read a whole
piece, and where there is excellent rapport between student and counselor and the student understands his problem, the adult bibliotherapist can
make a direct suggestion and be frank and open in
discussing the material both before and after reading. This ideal situation is not too common.

9. It is usually better to suggest or promote alterna-
tive selections and to give the student a choice.
This seems less like an assignment or prescription, and may give the student an opportunity to
choose something that fits his subconscious or unexpressed interests and desires, as well as those
he has expressed.

10. The practicing therapist should be sensitive to any
physical handicaps of the student which may make
necessary the use of special reading materials
such as large print books, books with the best type
of illustrations for those with visual impairment,
book holders for those whose hands will not support a book, talking books for the blind or near-
blind, etc.

11. Bibliotherapy has been used with individuals within
a fairly wide range of general intelligence, reading ability and personality, but experience has
shown that it is generally most effective with students of average or above average ability. The
poor reader's reluctance to read at all must be

overcome before the reading can have any good
effect. The average or above average student is
generally more comfortable reading and skillful
enough to gain from it both intellectually and
emotionally. The number of high-interest, low-
vocabulary books available for the slow reader is
also more limited than the great variety of books
available for the average or better than average
reader. [4]

Herein lies a particularly important challenge
for bibliotherapy. The number of physical, mental, and economic problems among our so-called
"disadvantaged" children and youth is apt to be
greater than among those from middle class and
wealthy families. These children need help as
much as anyone, and perhaps more than most, but
first they must become readers. Bibliotherapists
in such cases must work closely with teachers of
remedial reading and with English teachers; and
in the case of older children and youth from non-
English speaking homes, perhaps with teachers of
the Laubach method. Emotional problems, physical
problems, and the acquisition of bad habits, however, can occur regardless of economic status, and
some of the worst social problems have arisen
among the over-indulged children of wealthy parents. Problems and habits are no respecters of
status but in addition to the usual variety of problems, for the child of poor parents there is the
problem of economic insecurity.

12. Reading a book, article, pamphlet, or other material is not enough. It should be followed up by
discussion and/or counseling. Here the philosophy
and personality of the bibliotherapist have a strong
influence upon results.

13. Bibliotherapy, while usually effective when practiced properly, should usually not be used independently but as an adjunct to other helping relationships. This involves cooperation among all
those concerned with the welfare of the student--
a fact that cannot be over-emphasized.

Since no one technique works with all individuals, it is
well at this point to list some of the limitations, even dangers, of bibliotherapy which can minimize or nullify any positive effects.

1. The fears and anxieties of some students may be aggravated by reading about mental health problems. They may actually acquire more symptoms as a result.
2. Some students rationalize their problems when reading about them, rather than gaining the needed insight.
3. The bibliotherapist and/or the reader may believe that the problem can be fully resolved merely by reading. In reality, the purpose of the reading is simply to set in motion the thinking and coping behavior which will finally work through to a solution.
4. If the relationship between therapist and student is not somewhat impersonal (though still friendly), the student may show improvement because of his liking for the therapist but be unable to transfer the improvement to other situations or with other people.

Developmental bibliotherapy can help to solve an anticipated problem, one the student mentally feared but which has not happened or which has arisen only in mild form. Remedial bibliotherapy, more often associated with the scientific or clinical aspects, must often be practiced outside the school by psychiatrists or even in an institution. If the school system has a psychiatrist or psychologist on its staff or available for consultation, school personnel who detect problems should refer the student and cooperate as necessary with the psychotherapist. If the latter has not been accustomed to using bibliotherapy, and this technique seems in order, the school librarian or media center head could suggest tactfully that he or she is willing to help in this way if the doctor so wishes. School personnel cannot tell a medical or psychological expert how to treat a patient but they can suggest the possibility of bibliotherapy, perhaps citing other cases of its successful use in alleviating milder but similar problems.

The possibility of combining bibliotherapy with related therapies within the school situation should not be overlooked. Music therapy has been widely used with mental patients; perhaps it can be used for less disturbed children in combination with bibliotherapy. Music may have the soothing effect necessary to put a child in a reading mood. Participation in music activities has also had a therapeutic effect.

Art therapy, both from the production and appreciation

standpoints, may be another good partner for bibliotherapy.
The school setting, with its art and music facilities, lends
itself well to such combinations, not always possible in out-
of-school situations.   Writing has been used as a therapy and
fits in especially well with bibliotherapy.   Suggestions for
specific types of writing include diaries, journals, letters,
essays, poems, short stories.   Some students, after reading
a book, may find it easier to express their feelings and reactions in writing than to the bibliotherapist in person.
Several investigators, according to Zaccaria and Moses, have
reported the use of writing as a sole therapeutic medium. [5]
In conjunction with reading it should be doubly valuable.   Unlike bibliotherapy, with writing therapy it is recommended
that the subject be convinced ahead of time that the writing
and the other help given is truly intended to help him in his
personal growth and development.   In bibliotherapy with the
deaf, the combination with writing becomes almost a necessity, for unless there is an effective hearing aid, all suggestions and communications from the therapist must be in
written form.   .

Bibliotherapy can be used effectively in connection with
recreational or play therapy, occupational therapy and educational therapy.   The therapeutic aspect of educational therapy
may require paramedical help in the form of speech and/or
hearing therapy.

Frustration and emotional problems in a school situation may develop among children from a Spanish-speaking
family whose English-language background at home has been
so restricted that reading difficulties are created and add to
problems of adjustment in a classroom where most other
children may be from different economic and cultural backgrounds.   Next to the Negro, the Spanish-speaking population
forms the largest minority group in the United States.   Although these immigrants have a rich cultural heritage, their
status in this country becomes that of the "cultural illiterate" because of our own ethnocentric pride.   In the last few
years, however, libraries and schools, stimulated by the Library Services and Construction Act programs, American
Library Association efforts, the National Defense Education
Act, "bi-lingual institutes," and Title VII of the Elementary
and Secondary Education Act, have begun to give more adequate recognition to the Spanish-speaking culture.

Nevertheless, there are still many children who face
a problem.   Such a child, in Arizona, California, or Texas,

for example, may speak Spanish at home and with relatives
and friends.   Seldom does he have the comfort and joy of
reading a book in his mother tongue.   The teacher, in his
efforts to Americanize him, may even call him Paul instead
of Pablo, Michael instead of Miguel.   He senses that his
language, even his name, is considered second class.   He is
robbed of his dignity, security, and pride.   He may soon
learn to be secretive, acquiescent and humble until some day
he breaks out in violence. [6]

Bibliotherapy with children from Spanish-speaking homes
can begin in the school library or classroom with a collection
of Spanish books, varied like those in the English collection.
It may be just a corner of the room to begin with.   Not all
the books will be read.   But they will be waiting and one day
Miguel will find them; he will discover a name like his, a
picture that looks like his mother, a story about Juan Diego
or the Virgin of Guadalupe.   The mere presence of the books
may provide the beginning of a bridge between cultures, a
feeling that his own has value in the eyes of the librarian
or teacher.

Compared to the vast output of English titles, there
are few good children's books in Spanish, but they are now
emerging in Spanish-speaking countries in surprising numbers.
They are sometimes moralistic tracts or watered-down versions of adult books, but there are also original works with
fine illustrations such as the Elena Fortun series, built
around a fine family relationship and helpful to the child with
family problems.   There are fairy tales from all over the
world to develop the imagination, and classics of their native
country which can be used to introduce children to Lope de
Vega Carpio, Tirso de Molina, Antonio Lachado, Rafael Al-
berti, and Federico Garcia Lorca while they are still in
grammar school.

The many bilingual books on the market in the United
States can be valuable.   The child exposed to both languages
at once is helped to feel at home sooner in both cultures.   He
will "explore" the language he knows least and his confidence
in the one he knows will carry over into the other.   He is no
longer ashamed of the language of his home and he can move
more readily toward an understanding of the dominant culture.[6]

In many schools there will be someone on the faculty
who understands Spanish.   If not, the help of older Spanish-
speaking students may be enlisted in translating titles and

annotations on buying lists.   Books of therapeutic value for
specific problems may be found among the books in Spanish,
as well as those in English or bilingual text, although with
more difficulty.   Librarians, media specialists, or teachers
will need to consult Libros en Venta, Fichero, use Bro-
Dart's Project Leer (a bibliographic service), or order from
Sanborn's in Mexico City, which carries a large stock of
books both for children and adults.

At the end of chapter 10 a list of books for the Spanish-speaking child or young person is given.   It is adapted
from a list compiled by Toni de Gerez in the article "Books
for Miguel" in the December, 1967 School Library Journal
and therefore does not contain any titles published after that
date.   It is an invaluable list, however, as such selective
lists are very hard to find.   Both United States and foreign
publishers are included.   For ordering information, write to
The Centro Mexicano de Escritores, Valle Arizpe No. 18,
Mexico, 12. D. F.   The Centro is a non-profit organization
which awards fellowships and publishes bibliographic bulletins.
It also serves as a distributing agency, exporting books published in Mexico and other Latin American countries to the
United States.   The Centro will assist in securing titles from
the list given, and also has annotated lists of Spanish-language
children's books and simple books for adults which it makes
available to United States libraries for the price of a self-
addressed envelope, as part of the Centro's selection and
procurement service.

The problem of working with the emotionally disturbed
retarded reader is magnified because he must first begin to
enjoy reading before the therapeutic content of "prescribed"
books can have an effect.   The New York City Board of Education in 1963 had eleven reading clinics primarily to deal
with this type of reader, and also provided teacher training
for such clinics.   When first admitted to the clinics and given
reading tests, the majority of these children showed a high
percentage of errors and indiscriminate marking of answers.
A minority marked only the answers they were sure of. Those
in charge felt that the majority reaction may have reflected
the disturbed child's general impulsiveness and lack of control or his great anxiety regarding his reading failure and his
underlying inadequacies.   In the latter case he seemed to try
to hide his failure by pretending to be working and marking
answers at random.

As the children continued in the reading clinics they

noticeably relaxed and appeared happier. These changes arose
from their reading progress; they adopted better work habits
as reading became a more meaningful and satisfying experience. Although at first typically confused and discouraged,
the children, after experiencing the warmth and understanding
of the reading counselor and profiting from the carefully
planned material based on their diagnosed needs and from the
other benefits of the total program, were able to face up to
the reality of their reading problems. The answering pattern
became more normal, answering the "sure" items, taking a
chance on some doubtful items only partially read, then stopping when encountering the test items that were too hard.
Thus they acknowledged their own limits. Very often, growth
in personal adjustment accompanied the reading progress. [7]

It has been stressed that in order for bibliotherapy to
be effective with retarded readers, whether of the direct or
concomitant type, they first must like to read. How can the
teacher or school librarian stimulate the retarded reader to
read independently? In the reading center of the A. E. Burdick School, Milwaukee, questions written on an index card
and inserted into the pocket of the book with the charge-out
card became the answer to the problem of wide reading in the
reading center. Although the students of grades four through
eight reported a half hour each day to the reading center
where there were more than a hundred "high interest, easy
readability" books easily accessible, the books had rarely been
read, for the poor readers had known reading as a humiliating
and disastrous experience. [8]

A controlled vocabulary comparable to that of the book
was used in the questions. Some were of the simple recall
type; others required thoughtful re-reading, use of generalizations, and judgment. The children were encouraged to read
the questions before reading the book. Looking for the answers thus became a game. As the child flipped through the
pages for possible answers he became more efficient at skim-
ming and looking for key words. The children were encouraged to ask their parents for help. It was more fun to discuss possible answers with someone. Books were chosen to
insure successful reading with a minimum of effort. It was
suggested that the child return the book without reading it if
he began it and found he did not like it, or found it too difficult. The slow readers, as a result of this procedure, were
reading an average of three outside books a week.

A chart listing the names of all the children was tacked

upon the bulletin board. Five or ten points were awarded for
each book read with the questions correctly answered. The
ten-point books were more difficult, usually longer than a
hundred pages, had fewer pictures, and had more difficult
questions. At the end of each month the points were totaled
and the names of the winners posted. Thus competition was
brought in as motivation. The answers were checked and the
scores posted daily while the child was in the reading center,
so the reward was immediate. No reports were returned to
be done over because of untidiness or poor spelling. Only
when an answer showed the child did not understand a concept
was he asked to discuss it. These retarded readers felt that
they had a real reason for doing extra reading. They achieved
success with a minimum of effort and their chart showed them
their daily progress. They were becoming aware of the joy
of reading. Some of their comments were:

> I get more out of a book when I answer the ques-
> tions.

> I like to watch my score get big. It's like a race.

> I know that you really care if I have read the book.

> I like to do the work with my mother.

> I'm learning what to look for when I read a book.

Faith Zentgraf who wrote the article on the Burdick
School experiment, does not believe in oral reporting because
it takes time and does not always reveal sufficient comprehension. Questioning the reviewer in front of the group may
embarrass him if he has not fully read or understood the
book--another block to further reading. Detailed written reports also inhibit extra reading, the author feels. Brief book
reports, she says, tell nothing about the book and encourage
"picture reading" and deception.

Viola Krantowitz, in her article "Bibliotherapy with
Retarded Readers, "[9] says, "After exploring a great variety
of books, magazines, pamphlets, and specialized materials
intended for the problem learner I found that in certain hard-
core problem cases, if one could find meaningful reading that
answered that individual's particular needs, one could achieve
gratifying results in progress in learning different attitudes
toward books, and sometimes even a better self-concept over
a period of time. "

As we give special attention to the retarded emotionally disturbed reader, so must we single out the gifted child whose very superiority may be causing a maladjustment. The slow pace of his classmates and his inability to go at his own pace may create a total unhappiness with school. He may adopt a superior attitude which interferes with good social relationships. Or he may become a discipline problem because he does not have enough to do to present a real challenge.

"Assumption that all children from the inner city are low achievers and that the academic goal for these children should be only some mystical academic norm, is not professionally sound, " according to William K. Durr. "The school has the responsibility of helping each child attain his full potential, and there are children of apparently limitless potential in all walks of life. "[10]

A gifted beginning reader may conceal lack of reading skill by his ability to memorize words. But later, when the number of words has become too great for him to memorize, his mastery of word-attack skills suffers. In respect to his own potential ability, he has become a disabled reader.

Sequential language development can guard against this in the first place. The gifted student must be provided with challenging enrichment experiences. As he is freed from a limited and restricting curriculum, much of his maladjustment to school or his peer group can diminish or disappear. Obviously, the type and specific titles of books for enrichment reading should be chosen with the particular problem of the gifted student in mind. (Not all gifted students, of course, have personal or emotional problems.) Here are specific suggestions for enrichment activities connected with reading, some of which are preventive rather than remedial bibliotherapy.

1. Gifted children fond of a particular writer's work may like to read biographies of that writer and relate them to his works. Where was the author when he wrote a particular book? What life factors seem to account for his interest and style?

2. Encourage the more mature students to organize and run a "Great Books Club. " They should make their own selection of books with a minimum of guidance from adults. Here is an outlet for constructive energies that could turn to destructive activity if not channeled. Discuss books at the

meetings. It is important that students express
their own opinions and defend them, rather than
simply adopt adult-held opinions. The feeling of
freedom from adult domination in this type of
activity can afford release to the gifted student
who chafes against established authority in the
school situation.

3. Have the students read and analyze the characteristics of published book reviews. Using similar
formats, have them write their own analyses of
books.

4. Have gifted children devise a technique for survey-
ing the interests and needs (in and out of school)
of their classmates and then select books for a
suggested reading list which would embrace these
interests. Each child will find certain titles that
answer questions of his own. The lists may then
be pooled, repetitions and books of poor quality
eliminated, and a master list made comprising the
best items of all the lists. This is a developmental activity toward maturity of judgment, with
possible results of self-insight.

5. Have pupils choose an informative current events
article from a newspaper or news magazine and
analyze it word by word, noting how the author's
judgments and choices of words influence the impression conveyed to the reader.

Daniel Fader, in his widely read work, Hooked on
Books, [11] points out that "School librarians should take a useful lesson from operators of paperbound bookstores, who let
their merchandise sell itself by arranging their stores so that
their customers are surrounded by colorful and highly descriptive paper covers." Such an arrangement would be especially
useful for attracting those students who have fallen far behind
in their schooling because of emotional problems. Since
Daniel Fader's program for getting teenagers "hooked on
books" was used in a training school for boys it is discussed in detail in the chapter on crime and juvenile delinquency. However, Fader points out that it is unrealistic to
expect partially literate students "to relate to books through
words printed on their spines," in criticism of the manner in
which most libraries display books.

Judith F. Koon, writing on the teaching of the emotionally disturbed adolescent, [12] suggests that in the case of
disturbed teens who withdraw to fantasy worlds, books about

their particular fantasies will easily "turn them on. " Then
the bibliotherapist can gently tune them in to the realistic
aspects of their fantasies. A boy who lives in outer space
will respond well to science fiction. Later he may be led
to developing an interest in N. A. S. A. and to realize that
greater attention on his part to mathematics and science in
school could eventually bring realization of his fantasy.

A reading interest survey conducted with a class of
twenty-five emotionally disturbed adolescents at John Umstead
Hospital in Butner, North Carolina, substantiated the fact that
disturbed adolescents do respond positively to identification
through literature. To the question, "Do you like to read
books in which you can identify with one of the characters?"
nine students responded "usually, " four checked "sometimes, " one answered "seldom, " and no one responded
"never. " Over half the students indicated that certain books
had influenced their thinking and/or their behavior. Though
situations which too nearly resemble their own traumatic experiences could be threatening for these students to read
about, the teachers found that they would not identify in such
cases. But milder parallels between their own and the
characters' experiences often brought positive therapeutic
results.

Joseph E. Malkiewicz, in an April 1970 Instructor
article, [13] describes the bibliotherapy technique he used successfully with fifth graders. He stresses, however, that each
teacher must find the one best method for her and her class.
Each day Mr. Malkiewicz read aloud a chapter or unit of plot.

> A discussion followed in which the class identified
> the story's main problem, the character who was
> most involved, the secondary problems, and made
> an evaluation of the interaction between them. As
> the reading progressed, the discussion added a
> personal dimension. The class and the teacher
> related themselves to the characters and action.
> In an atmosphere free from disapproval and rid-
> icule, the children were encouraged to share their
> own similar experiences. At first this was pos-
> sible only because the discussion was about a safe
> and remote person, the story character. When
> the children understood that 'others' could discuss
> an individual's problems with compassion and em-
> pathy, acquired defenses were relaxed. Lively
> discussions revealing much insight followed.

As a last step, the children went on to measure
their own attempts to solve their problems against
evaluations and insights gained when discussing the
story.   Thus they were able to take a more critical look at their own behavior.   They no longer
needed face-saving strategies, for no one was
labeling individuals with misleading tags.   Through
the reading all concerned had become interested in
the 'why' of behavior, especially their own.

On the college level bibliotherapy has often been employed in counseling.   At Stephens College it was used by hall
counselors.   It was found that in most cases, after recommending a book which touched upon a girl's problem, follow-
up interviews by the counselor were necessary.   This not only
helped the student relate her own problems to those depicted
in the book but also to work out practical applications of the
suggested solution.   This same technique is equally applicable
to high school students. [14]

Convinced that much juvenile delinquency and many
mental breakdowns later in life are due to the
failure of young people to reach emotional maturity, the Delaware State Society for Mental Hygiene, even before 1947, introduced human relations classes in the seventh and eighth grades in
schools throughout the state.   These classes, conducted weekly, involved the reading of a story by
the teacher, discussion of the problems presented
therein by the pupils and then a correlation drawn
between these problems and the experiences of the
children themselves.   Although reading a story
aloud is more suitable to classroom than to library
procedure, such a program offers much guidance
to the librarian who could have a read-aloud period and use the same method in making the books
on her shelves real to the child. [14]

Inspired by reports that 'bad' girls and boys expressed a desire to read books more than did
'good' boys and girls, the public schools of Mas-
sena, New York, conducted an experiment to see
if this interest in reading could be used as an
opening wedge by which the school librarian could
help problem students reach a higher level of social maturity and more acceptable behavior.   Reading programs were planned for individual children

based upon findings of the Washburne Social Adjustment Inventory. The results, as shown by published case studies, showed a high degree of success. [14]

Sister Mary Agnes, the librarian of Cathedral High School in New York City, reported in 1947 on a study made of the difference in attitude toward racial prejudice among two groups of high school girls. [15] Analysis showed that those girls who had recently read stories in which Negroes were sympathetically portrayed were not quite as prejudiced as those who had done no such reading. Although results were not highly significant, this method seems to offer possibilities for further study. Since prejudicial attitudes have undergone change since 1947, one might hope that results today would be more significant.

The librarian, media specialist, or counselor practicing bibliotherapy must be a prolific reader. The bibliotherapist should also make an annotation for every book read which seems to have application to present or future student problems. These cards, supplemented by the many available therapeutic reading lists for children and young people, should provide rich sources for suggestions. This type of book knowledge, combined with a knowledge of human psychology and the ability to create an atmosphere conducive to confidence and trust, is a good formula for positive results.

The classroom teacher cannot leave the task entirely to librarians, media specialists or counselors. Innumerable cases reported have clearly revealed the unlimited potentialities of bibliotherapeutic techniques for the classroom teacher. G. Robert Carlsen points out, in Literature and Emotional Security, that "in order to make literature vital we have to think in terms of the kind of understanding which students will be ready for rather than in terms of giving student samples of all kinds of literary types. "[16]

A clear distinction must be made between children's and young people's literature of the past and that of today. The older literature was filled with saccharine moralizing in an attempt to change attitudes and behavior. Today's material is much more realistic and complete, facing up to many problems that would not have been mentioned in the ficition or non-fiction of yesterday. "A reader can now see reflected in books his fears and dreams, his problems and experiences in quite a complete and natural way. A good story is of prime

importance, for a child reads because he is interested and
not to be cured. "[16]

The reading program for the gifted child should not
allow him to become so engrossed in books that he cuts himself off from his fellow students and from reality. This type
of pupil will benefit greatly by being able to share his reading experiences with others. In discussion groups of three to
five individuals each can discuss his reading and his opinions
of what he has read, and others in the group should question
or give opinions of the material, also. In forming these discussion groups, the alert teacher should assign people of
varied interests to meet together. In this way new horizons
will be opened to the participants. A gifted student enjoys
talking and is anxious to express his opinions. A book discussion group affords him the opportunity to relate and discuss his readings. It also gives him the chance to quote or
read passages orally to his group. There are many outlets
for his sharing besides the discussion groups. Panel discussions, tape recordings, and dramatization of materials read
are other ways for a student to impart his reading knowledge.

The gifted student should be trained to discuss, state
his views, and be able to support his ideas. This type of
student does not need as much detailed instruction because of
his alert mind. However, he does need guidance about seeking and finding materials, locating needed information, and
reviewing and reporting his findings. This reading program
should definitely be formed with the idea that the student is
working not for a credit or grade but for an individual
achievement. In organizing a reading program for the gifted,
it is extremely important that the program have the sanction,
sympathy, and cooperation of the school's administration,
counselors, and teachers. [17]

Bereiter and Englemann made a study of children of
very low socio-economic status who were taught in an intensive, fast-paced and highly-structured program in basic language arts skills, reading and arithmetic, plus singing. The
children moved from teacher to teacher every fifteen or
twenty minutes. Because the children came from poor language functioning areas, language was used to maintain social
relationships in satisfying material needs and not to obtain
and transmit information or monitor behavior. The fundamental goal of the program was to get children to understand
a teaching language. The language of these children, according to project directors, seemed to consist not of distinct

words but rather of whole phrases or sentences that function like "giant" words. [18]

According to Jean Osborn, a pre-school teacher, these "giant" words are not taken apart by the child and recombined and transformed into questions. If this theory is correct, the child will have much difficulty dealing with sentences as a sequence of meaningful parts. Osborn lists the following characteristics of the language of the disadvantaged four-year-old:

1. He omits articles, prepositions, conjunctions, and short verbs from statements.
2. He does not understand the function of NOT in a sentence.
3. He cannot produce plural statements correctly and cannot produce actions implied by plural statements.
4. He cannot use simple tenses to describe present, past, and future action.
5. He is able to use HE and SHE for male and female figures but cannot use the pronoun IT to refer to inanimate objects.
6. He does not understand many of the common prepositions and conjunctions, such as BETWEEN and OR.
7. He can often perform direction but is unable to describe what he has done.
8. He does not realize that two or more words can describe one object. [19]

James J. Bigaj, of the Milwaukee Public Schools, believes that application of the following basic principles of instruction should make reading more interesting and challenging for the gifted pupil in the primary grades:

1. Emphasis must be placed on individualizing instruction for the gifted pupil.
2. The gifted pupil is often more capable of self-directed learning. He may want to go ahead under his own steam in reading if he is provided with some very simple directions and adequate materials.
3. The gifted pupil at the primary level also needs flexible reading assignments, the pupil who is forced to conform to general reading assignments for the entire class may become bored and

disinterested.

4.   The gifted pupil may not need as intensive and extensive a readiness program at any level as average and slow-learning pupils may require.

5.   The gifted pupil also needs guidance in critical and creative reading skills since his powers to do logical and critical thinking may easily become much greater than the average student's.

6.   Since the gifted reader often can think, generalize, and solve problems at a higher level than other children, he must be challenged constantly if learning is to take place and interest maintained. Emphasis on drill in reading should be avoided.

7.   Since the gifted child at the primary level can gain a great deal of self-fulfillment through reading, instruction should not only assist him in developing information-gathering skills but also in becoming a confident happy individual by enlarging his pleasure in reading.

8.   The gifted pupil should not be penalized by expecting him to complete huge assignments merely because of his potential.   More of the same is not what is needed.   An important consideration in all the reading he is required to do should be quality, not quantity.

9.   The gifted pupil frequently has a longer attention span than the average learner.   Therefore, one may be able to teach him for longer periods of time.   He often does not require as many repetitions when mechanical or other reading skills are presented as other children in the classroom may need.

10.   Emphasis during reading instruction should be placed more on inductive rather than deductive instruction.

11.   The gifted pupil often displays more diversified reading interests than do other pupils. Teachers, therefore, should build on these interests during reading instruction. [20]

Disadvantaged children will need illustrations depicting characters with whom they can identify.   In other words, the color bars must be broken; the pictures should show non-white people in as favorable a light as white people. Whipple recommends that each illustration or sampling be inspected to see the extent and character of the integration, and that tabulations of the results should be made. [21]   For example, is

there any built-in discrimination such as depicting blacks as
bystanders, naming white characters only, putting the stories
of blacks at the back of the book, presenting blacks in menial
positions, and not depicting the professional black and others
of high status? These facts concerning illustrations are
known:

1. Illustrations may exert a negative as well as a
    positive appeal.
2. The larger the total number of illustrations in the
    book, the higher the interest value. This point
    holds true up to an undefined point of saturation,
    at which a textbook becomes a mere picture book.
3. The larger the average size of the illustrations,
    the higher the interest value, other things being
    equal.
4. An illustration in several colors has greater merit
    than one that is black-and-white. The artificial
    use of a single color other than black is less
    appealing than the realistic use of several colors.
5. An illustration with a center of interest that draws
    the eye to a particular point offers greater appeal
    to children than a picture with no recognizable
    center of interest or one subordinated by too many
    details.
6. The more action and the more interesting the
    action, the more appealing is the illustration.
7. The subject matter of the illustration has a marked
    effect upon its interest to children. Eventful topics
    depicted in the illustration have greater merit than
    still-life topics. [21]

After having guided the learner in the selection of materials for both reading instruction and recreational reading,
the teacher may extend activities to the area of bibliotherapy.
Through this phase the teacher may aid the disadvantaged
child in solving certain of his personal adjustment problems.
This form of aid may be rendered by having youngsters discover that they are not alone in their dilemma of development
and by encouraging them to seek a better environmental atmosphere to continue their complex growth. It is often a
shock for a child to see another person in his own or similar
circumstances. When working with the disadvantaged, this
removed type of identification with the problems of others can
help to remedy or alleviate some of the problems the child is
experiencing, without damaging or threatening an already
strained ego. Bailey, in Education (May 1956), lists five

general types of insecurity that reading can help the child to
overcome:

    1.   Those based on his relations with his peers.
    2.   Those based on family relationships.
    3.   Those resulting from repeated failures.
    4.   Those based on economic factors.
    5.   Those based on physical factors.

Many critics of bibliotherapy warn that by using this
method one may encourage children to forget or divorce
themselves from reality, and thus one may promote poorer
personal adjustment and in turn encourage the manifestation
of even more limited reading maturity.   One can only respond
that sound professional judgment will meticulously balance the
child's exposure to materials of reality and those designed to
promulgate personal improvement. [22]

Remedial reading services in a secondary school may
be divided into three pupil categories: 1) the slightly retarded; 2) the seriously retarded; and 3) the non-reader.
One must decide how much concentrated effort to put into
helping each group and how many extra classes one can afford
to establish.   Where should the most emphasis be put?

Slightly retarded readers can be handled in regular
English classes, doing work specially planned by reasonably
skillful teachers.   Seriously retarded readers need special
reduced-sized classes in English or, better still, additional
classes for reading instruction.   Non-readers must, if there
is any hope of helping them, be placed in clinics of only four
or five pupils.   The clinics will be programmed in addition
to, or instead of, regular English classes.   There will be
more hope for the severely retarded if they can have more
than one clinic period each day.

However, members of this latter group may need
special medical and psychiatric help which is beyond the scope
or the ability of the most skilled classroom teacher.   Every
school system should be able to provide these services, but
few can.   These pupils, however, cannot be abandoned; even
when failure seems certain, the teacher must keep trying, if
not for total reading success, then for success in human
communication to lead them to happy, successful lives. They
need to know how much the school system wants to help them.
This knowledge alone will start some of them on their way to
success in reading--and in living. [23]

61 WAYS TO TELL ABOUT BOOKS

1. Hold a panel discussion when several students have read the same book or a group of similar ones.

2. Organize a pro and con panel made up of some students who liked the book and some who did not.   Let one person represent the author.   Try for an impartial chairman.

3. Dramatize an incident or an important character.   The student may relate an incident in the first person.

4. Make radio announcements, student-prepared, to advertise books.

5. Have individual conferences in which students talk about favorite books with the teacher.

6. Appoint a committee of pupils who are avid readers to conduct peer discussions and seminars about books.

7. Hold a mock trial permitting the defendant to tell the story of a book of his choosing.   The class renders decision on its merits.

8. Reproduce artist's interpretations of important scenes on slides for the whole class to enjoy.

9. Make brief oral talks--limit five minutes each--at an after-school Coke party or a meeting of a library club.

10. Get the plot down to a succinct nugget.   It takes practice to do this in one paragraph.

11. Conduct dialogs between several students revealing the style and story of the book.

12. Prepare book jackets that really illustrate the kind of book as well as the story.

13. Write a precis--but don't do this too often.   It can be dry as dust.

14. Compose a telegram, trying to give the essence of a book in 15 words.   Then expand it into a 100-word "over-night telegram. "

15. Try your hand at a publisher's "blurb" to sell the book.

16. Read orally an interesting part, stopping at a strategic point.

17. Make a sales talk, pretending your audience are clerks in a bookstore and you want them to push a new book.

18. Have questions from the audience, or let three children be challengers.

19. Make comparisons with the movie and radio versions of the same book.

20. Create a poster advertising the book and maybe others by the same author.

21. Build a miniature stage setting for part of the story.

22. Design costumes for characters in miniature or life size.

23. Write a book review for a newspaper or magazine, and really send it for possible publication.

24. Make a rebus of a short story and try it on your friends.

25. Write a movie script to sell to Hollywood.

26. For a "How to Make" book, bring something you made according to the directions.

27. If it is a travel book, prepare a travel lecture.

28. Write an original poem after studying a book of poetry for both style and choice of subjects.

29. After reading a book of poems, learn a verse, or read one to the class.

30. Tell your best friend why you did or did not like a book.

31. Explain how the book could be used in social studies or science.

32. Make sketches of some of the action sequences.

33. Describe an interesting character--make him come alive

to your audience.

34. Write or tell a different ending to the story.

35. Write or tell the most humorous incident; the most exciting happening: the most interesting event; or the part you liked best.

36. Select a descriptive passage and read it aloud to the class.

37. List interesting new words and expressions to add to your vocabulary.

38. Describe a scene to orient your audience--then show it in true Red Buttons pantomime style.

39. Write a letter recommending the book to a friend.

40. Give a synopsis of the story but don't give away the climax.

41. Make a scrapbook suggested by information in the book.

42. Construct puppets and present a show of an interesting part of the story.

43. If it is a geographical book, make a map, including on it brief information gathered from the book.

44. Have a friend who has read the story try to stump you with questions.

45. Make a list of facts you learned from reading a story.

46. Write questions you think everyone should be able to answer after reading the book--then try them on others.

47. Dress as one of the characters and act out the part you play.

48. Broadcast a book review on your school P. A. system.

49. Write a note to the librarian suggesting why she ought to recommend the book to other students.

50. Review the book you read before another class.

51. Look up the biography of the author and tell about his
     other books.

52. Make a clay, soap, or wood model to illustrate a phase
     of the book.

53. Construct a diorama to illustrate a phase of the story.

54. Dress paper dolls as characters in the book, for a
     bulletin-board exhibit.

55. Prepare a chalk talk, or better still, use an overhead
     projector.

56. Do an illustration for the story.

57. Make a mural to illustrate the book--get others who
     have read it to help.

58. Build a diorama or table exhibit to represent a part of
     the story.

59. Rewrite an incident in the book, simplifying vocabulary
     for a lower grade.

60. If it is a science book, plan a demonstration of what
     you learned.

61. If it is an historical book, make a time line, listing
     events in sequence.

Book reports can range from the casual to the formal,
but their primary use is not to check up on students or to
give them a mark.   The goal should be to get them to talk
about books as a natural part of their day-by-day conversation.

Archie Lejeune, Associate Director of Student Aid,
Scholarships, and High School Relations at Louisiana State
University, discussing "Bibliocounseling as a Guidance Technique,"[24] says, "Bibliocounseling is viewed ... as the clinical
use of books in guidance and counseling situations that involve
personal-social needs and/or problems of individuals--or
groups for that matter.   Of course, bibliocounseling is synonymous with bibliotherapy in this context."   Bibliotherapy,
he says, is essentially the vehicle or means by which bibliocounseling is effected.   Lejeune mentions that one method
the counselor might employ in assisting a student is to re-

commend desirable books or other reading matter that provide
the student with ego-strengthening and self-actualization experiences. Lejeune emphasizes the need for closer ties between the school guidance department and the library. If
there is no guidance department the school librarian may undertake as much guidance as time allows.

Social problems such as shyness, lack of dates, not
being popular, or not being good looking are helped more by
pertinent articles in such magazines as Scholastic, Seventeen,
Ingenue, Practical English or Teens than by the pat answers
found in "Dear Abbie," or "Ann Landers." Books may help
a young person find out who he is, what is truth--questions
so many seem to be trying to solve these days.

Lejeune says, "In this day and time of the impact of
television and the other mass media of communication, there
seemingly is a popular misconception which holds that books
are futile objects with very limited power and influence....
On the contrary, books are dynamic and vital, capable of
changing the whole direction of events, sometimes for good,
sometimes for evil. Throughout history the incidence of book
burning, banishment and murder of writers, and the suppression of ideas and opposition by dictators ... bear mute testimony to the power-the explosive forces pent up in books."

Pioneer bibliotherapy work with children was done by
Dr. Thomas V. Moore at the Child Center of the Catholic University of America. The children were too old for play
therapy and not mature enough to discuss their problems as
an adult would. Bibliotherapy seemed called for, and with
the help of Clara Kirchner a list of 263 books, Character Formation through Books, was compiled, the titles ranging in age
from about six years through the senior high school. [26] This
annotated list, revised and enlarged in 1945, was widely used,
and still has value for the large number of titles still available. It contains a character index--which enables the bibliotherapist to select titles under such headings as selfishness, tolerance, sportsmanship, etc.--an author index, and
a title index.

Porterfield cautions that the teacher's own role, status,
social position, and reference groups influence him so greatly
in his literary appreciations, that to be an objective analyst
he must be aware of these factors and make allowances for
them in prescribing books for students. [27]

Sister M. Bridget points out that divorce statistics are constantly rising in families with children. Some young people go through the experience unscathed; others may seem untouched but are deeply troubled within themselves; still others develop serious exterior difficulties. Bibliotherapy of the non-technical type is especially called for in such situations, she feels, the bibliotherapist not putting himself in the place of a psychologist or psychiatrist but using good common sense, coupled with a warm interest in students. [28]

Little research has been done on the actual clinical results of bibliotherapy with children in ordinary school situations, and much of what has been done is highly theoretical. A search of periodical literature on the subject in the early 1960s, however, bore out Sister Bridget's conviction that there was little difference between the preventive type of bibliotherapy and specialized reader guidance by a trained librarian. [28]

Ruth Hutcherson[29] suggests that one of the ways to help children build a wholesome, self-confident, self-respecting, effective, and happy personality is through telling stories which fit the developmental needs of a group of students, followed by group discussion of the characters in the story and why they reacted as they did, and what social values may be found in the story. The technique is particularly useful with reluctant readers.

As the child reads himself into the characters he may come to see himself as others see him, and the mirror image helps him see his own weaknesses without directly threatening his ego. Even if there is no immediate problem, individual or group preventive bibliotherapy can help a student be better prepared to deal with problems he has previously met in books. He passes through a trial and error process of choosing and rejecting behavior patterns, while avoiding the suffering and disaster such experimentation would involve if carried on in real life. This, of course, is the ideal situation--prevention rather than cure. In group bibliotherapy of this sort, not all students will benefit, but if only one or two should do so, the effort is still worthwhile.

Bibliotherapy, as applied to reading problems in a school situation, may be said to have the following goals:

1. To develop a new attitude of optimism and accomplishment toward the reading problem.

2. To develop new attitudes toward all of the people in whose eyes he feels himself a failure.
3. To use the emerging new attitudes in improving his reading skills in the most direct way acceptable to him. [30]

NOTES

1. Blake, Joseph. "Reading and the Problem of Children." High School Journal, v. 34, May 1951. p. 157-170.

2. Zaccaria, Joseph S., and Moses, Harold A. Facilitating Human Development through Reading--The Use of Bibliotherapy in Teaching and Counseling. Champaign, Ill.: Stipes Publishing Co., 1968, p. 41.

3. Schrodes, C. Bibliotherapy: a Theoretical and Clinical Study. Ph.D. Dissertation. University of California, 1950, p. 325-326.

4. Zaccaria, Joseph S., and Moses, Harold A. op. cit., p. 80-81.

5. Ibid., p. 90.

6. de Gerez, Toni. "Books for Miguel." School Library Journal, v. 92, Dec. 1967, p. 45, 46, 47, 51.

7. Cohn, Stella M., and Fite, Margaretta W. "Personal-Social Changes Reflected in Reading Accuracy Ratings." The Reading Teacher, v. 17, Nov. 1963, p. 97-99.

8. Zentgraf, Faith M. "Promoting Independent Reading by Retarded Readers." The Reading Teacher, v. 17, Nov. 1963, p. 100-101.

9. Krantowitz, Viola. "Bibliotherapy with Retarded Readers." Journal of Reading, v. 11, Dec. 1967, p. 205.

10. Durr, William K. "Let's Not Neglect the Gifted." Instructor, v. 79, April 1970, p. 58.

11. Fader, Daniel. Hooked on Books. N.Y.: G. P. Putnam's Sons, 1966, p. 52.

12. Koon, J. F. "Cues for Teaching the Emotionally Dis-

turbed: Turn On, Tune In, Drop Out. " Clearing House, v. 44, April 1970, p. 497.

13. Malkiewicz, Joseph E. "Stories Can Be Springboards." The Instructor, v. 79, April 1970, p. 133.

14. Kircher, Clara J. "Bibliotherapy and the Catholic School Library. " In: Martin, Brother David, ed. Catholic Library Practice. Portland, Oregon: University of Portland Press, 1950, p. 177-179.

15. Sister Mary Agnes. "Influence of Reading on the Racial Attitudes of Adolescent Girls. " Catholic Educational Review, v. 45, Sept. 1947, p. 415-420.

16. Blake, Joseph. "Reading and the Problems of Children." High School Journal, v. 34, May 1951, p. 159-160.

17. Case, Rosemary Hart. "A Reading Program for Gifted Students in the Senior High School. " In: Figurel, J. Allen, editor. Reading and Realism, Proceedings of the 13th Annual Convention, International Reading Association, Newark, Delaware, c1969, v. 13, part 1, p. 151-153.

18. Bereiter, Carl, and Engelmann, Siegfried. Teaching Disadvantaged Children in the Preschool. " Englewood Cliffs, N. J. : Prentice-Hall, 1966, p. 52.

19. Osborn, Jean. Teaching and Teaching Language to Disadvantaged Children. Mimeographed Report, University of Illinois, n. d.

20. Bigaj, James J. "A Reading Program for Gifted Children in the Primary Grades. " In: Figurel, J. Allen, editor. Reading and Realism, op. cit. , p. 145-46.

21. Whipple, Gertrude. "Practical Problems of School Book Selection for Disadvantaged Pupils. " In: Figurel, J. Allen, ed. Reading and Realism, op. cit. , p. 195, 196.

22. Brennan, Joseph T. "Selecting Appropriate Materials for Disadvantaged Junior High School Students. " In: Figurel, J. Allen, editor, op. cit. , p. 199-200.

23. Mosby, Josephine C. "Planning Remedial Reading
    Services in a Secondary School." In: Figurel, J.
    Allen. Reading and Realism, op. cit., p. 177-81.

24. Lejeune, Archie L. "Bibliocounseling as a Guidance
    Technique." Catholic Library World, v. 41, Nov.
    1969, p. 156-164.

25. Ibid., p. 159.

26. Kirchner, Clara J. Character Formation through Books:
    A Bibliography. 2nd ed. Catholic University of
    America Press, 1945.

27. Porterfield, Austin L. Mirror for Adjustment: Therapy
    in Home, School, and Society for Seeing Yourself and
    Others in Books. Leo Potisham Foundation, Texas
    Christian University, c. 1967, p. 154.

28. Bridget, Sister M. "Divorce and Children's Literature."
    Catholic Library World, v. 34, Dec. 1962, p. 202-
    204+.

29. Hutcherson, Ruth E. "Books that Help Children: A
    Discussion of Bibliotherapy." Library Journal, v.
    88, May 15, 1963, p. 2083.

30. Potter, Muriel. "The Use of Limits in Reading
    Therapy." Journal of Consulting Psychology v. 14,
    August 1950, p. 250-55.

SUGGESTED READING
(SCHOOL PROBLEMS)

Academic Achievement and Study Problems

Beim, Jerrold. Thin Ice. Wm. Morrow, 1956. Leo real-
    izes the importance of knowing how to read when it
    enables him to save his brother from an accident. Pri-
    mary.

Beim, Jerrold. A Vote for Dick. Harcourt, Brace and
    World, 1955. Dick's guilty conscience forces him to

confess that he cheated on an exam.   Juvenile.

Bell, Norman, Burkhardt, Richard, and Lawhead, Victor,
    eds. Introduction to College Life. Houghton Mifflin,
    1966. A selection of readings representing various
    viewpoints on the importance of academic achievement.
    Ages 16 up.

Bernstein, Theodore M. The Careful Writer. Atheneum,
    1965. A guide to the use of the English language cover-
    ing among other things, spelling, grammar and punctu-
    ation. High school and college.

Breck, Vivian. Hoofbeats on the Trail. Doubleday, 1959.
    Girl learns to accept herself even though she is not a
    good student. Juvenile, adolescent.

Brownstein, Samuel, and Weiner, Mitchel. How to Prepare
    for College Entrace Examinations. Barrons Educational
    Series, 1965. Information on colleges and scholarships
    plus subject reviews and practice tests. Adolescent,
    adult.

Carlson, Esther. Sixes and Sevens. Holt, Rinehart and
    Winston, 1960. Gail refuses to accept the proper atti-
    tude toward study and school until her father steps in
    with some restrictions. Juvenile, adolescent.

Carlson, Natalie. School Bell in the Valley. Harcourt, Brace
    and World. 1963. Belle learns that the problems of
    not having an education are greater than those faced in
    acquiring proper training. Juvenile.

Carter, Homer, and McGinnis, Dorothy. Reading: A Key to
    Academic Success. W. C. Brown, 1967. Practical
    procedures on how to improve the college student's
    reading ability. Ages 16 up.

Cretan, Gladys. A Gift from the Bride. Little, Brown, 1964.
    Mari's desire for an education was so great she over-
    came the many problems standing in her way. Primary
    child.

Downs, Robert B. How to do Library Research. University
    of Illinois Press, 1966. Guide to services and research
    facilities of libraries. Ages 16 up.

Elliott, H. Chandler. The Effective Student. Harper and
    Row, 1966. Guidebook to a constructive method of study.
    Ages 12 up.

Finkel, Lawrence S. How to Study. Oceana Publications,
    1964. Helpful hints on studying and preparing for exams.
    Ages 12 up.

Flesch, Rudolf. How to Write, Speak, and Think More
    Effectively. New American Library, 1960. Instructions
    on how to communicate. Ages 12 up.

Forley, Maurice. Public Speaking without Pain. David
    McKay, 1965. Practical advice on formal and informal
    public speaking. Ages 12 up.

Gilbert, Doris. Study in Depth. Prentice-Hall, 1966. A
    workbook designed to help the college student improve
    his study skills. High school and college.

Gladstein, Gerald A. Individualized Study: A New Approach
    to Succeeding in College. Rand McNally, 1967. A
    program for student self-evaluation and suggestions for
    improvement. Ages 12 up.

Harkins, Philip. The Day of the Drag Race. William Mor-
    row, 1960. College requirements change a drag-racing
    teen-ager's views. Juvenile, adolescent.

Henderson, Robert, ed. Helping Yourself with Applied Psy-
    chology. Prentice-Hall, 1967. Suggestions on how one
    can lead a richer life through the help of psychology.
    High school and college.

Herr, Selma. Effective Reading for Adults. W. C. Brown,
    1966. Suggestions and lessons to improve the adult's
    reading skills. High school and college.

Hersey, John. Too Far to Walk. Knopf, 1966. College life
    and students--self indulgence and frustration among
    Faustians. Ages 16 up.

Leaf, Munro. Robert Francis Weatherbee. J. B. Lippin-
    cott, 1935. Robert Francis finally realizes the ad-
    vantages of learning the things which are taught in
    school. Primary.

Pabley, B. G. Building for Tomorrow. Allyn and Bacon,
    1966. A book designed to help junior high school stu-
    dents adjust to school, self, and others, and make more
    realistic plans for the future. Ages 12 up.

Pauk, Walter. Successful Scholarship. Prentice-Hall, 1966.
    A selection of articles designed to help students develop
    better reading skills, gain insight into learning, and
    understand the process of scholarship. Ages 12 up.

Rivlin, Harry, et al. The First Years in College. Little,
    Brown, 1966. Essays by noted educators on what to
    expect in college and advice on adjusting to the college
    environment. Ages 16 up.

Williams, Raymond. Second Generation. Horizon Press,
    1966. Stress in the life cycle. Ages 16 up.

Adjustment to a New School and Neighborhood

Baker, Laura. Somebody, Somewhere. Knopf, 1962. Girl
    faces the problem of adjusting to a new school. Ages
    8-12.

Biesterveld, Betty. Run, Reddy, Run. Thos. Nelson &
    Sons, 1962. A migrant logging family lacks a feeling
    of security and love. Ages 8-12.

Binzen, Bill. First Day in School. Doubleday, 1972. Tale
    of opening day at a New York kindergarten will reas-
    sure five-year-olds and their parents.

Bulla, Clyde. Indian Hill. Crowell, 1963. An Indian boy
    finds it hard to adjust to living in an apartment after
    having lived on a reservation. Ages 8-12.

Bulla, Clyde. Open the Door and See All the People.
    Crowell, 1972. The family of two young girls, sisters,
    moves into the city from the farm. Adjustment to a
    new type of neighborhood becomes very difficult. Ages
    7-10.

Carlson, Natalie S. The Empty Schoolhouse. Harper & Row,
    1965. A Negro girl in a small Louisiana town endures
    loneliness as first to integrate her school.

Cohen, Miriam. Best Friends. Macmillan, 1971. Beginning of the school day at a new school. Kindergarten and nursery school. Pre-school and primary.

Commager, Evan. Valentine. Harper & Row, 1961. Girl fails to make friends in a new community until she forgets herself in trying to help others. Ages 12 up.

Craig, M. Jean. New Boy on the Sidewalk. Norton, 1967. Primary age. Boy adusts to a new neighborhood.

Epstein, Beryl. Lucky, Lucky White Horse. Harper & Row, 1965. Ellen overcomes her shyness and makes friends in a new community. Ages 5-8.

De Leeuw, Adele. Linda Marsh. Macmillan, 1943. Girl learns to make friends in a new high school. Ages 12-16.

Douglas, Gilbert. The Bulldog Attitude. Crowell, 1957. Mark faces many adjustment problems when he transfers from a small high school to a large one. Ages 12-16.

Erdman, Loula. Room to Grow. Dodd, Mead, 1962. A French family settles in Texas and the children are faced with the problems of adjusting to new people and a new country. Ages 8-12.

Felt, Sue. Hello-Goodbye. Doubleday, 1960. Two girls learn that moving from one house to another can be fun. Ages 5-8.

Fox, Paula. The Stone-faced Boy. Bradbury Press, 1968. A sensitive boy puts on a "stone-face" because of teasing at school. Ages 8-12.

Greene, Constance C. The Unmaking of Rabbit. Viking Press, c1972. An eleven-year-old boy, lonely and left adrift in today's disjointed world suddenly realizes that it is he who must make his own life happen.

Harkins, Philip. The Day of the Drag Race. Morrow, 1960. College requirements change a drag-racing teen-ager's views. Ages 12-16.

Haywood, Carolyn. "B" is for Betsy. Harcourt, Brace and World, 1939. Betsy changed her mind about school and found it to be a pleasant experience.   Primary age.

Haywood, Carolyn.   Back to School with Betsy.   Harcourt,
   Brace, and World, 1943.   Betsy experiences a good
   year during the third grade.   Primary age.

Head, Gay.   Hi There, High School.   Scholastic Book Services, 1961.   This book answers the questions a typical
   pre-high school student might have concerning what to
   expect in high school.

Holland, Isabelle.   The Man without a Face.   Lippincott, 1972.
   A young boy needs a tutor because he is failing in
   school.   The homosexual problem enters here.   Ages
   14 up.

Lewiton, Mina.   That Bad Carlos.   Harper & Row, 1964.
   Carlos has to learn self-reliance, respect for property,
   and adjustment to a new environment when his family
   moves to New York.   Ages 8-12.

Little, Jean.   Mine for Keeps.   Little, Brown, 1962.   A
   cerebral palsy victim must adjust to her family after
   being in a special school.   Ages 10-14.

Marino, Dorothy.   Moving Day.   Dial Press, 1963.   Two
   children hate to leave their old friends when they move
   into a new home but find that they make other friends
   in the new community.   Ages 5-8.

Sachs, Marilyn.   The Bear's House.   Doubleday, 1971.
   School problems and problems of mental illness in the
   family.   Ten-year-old finds escape from unhappy reality
   in a dream world she creates at school.   Ages 8-12.

Samuels, Gertrude.   Run, Shelley, Run.   Crowell, 1974.
   Homosexuality.   A girl put in a correctional school is
   sexually assaulted by other girl inmates.   14 up.

Spencer, Eleanor.   The Nothing Place.   Harper & Row, 1973.
   A boy almost fails school because of his partial deafness.

Sterling, Dorothy.   Mary Jane.   Doubleday, 1959.   A black
   girl must face the problems of being black in a newly
   integrated school.

Summers, James D. Senior Dropout. Westminster Press,
    1965. A boy has problems in school when his father
    remarries. Ages 14-18.

Thompson, Vivian. Sad Day, Glad Day. Holiday House, 1962.
    Kathy is sad because she is moving away and leaving
    her nice yard, but she is pleased with her new home.
    Ages 5-8.

Wells, Rosemary. The Fog Comes on Little Pig Feet. Dial
    Press, 1972. Rachel never wanted to go to boarding
    school, and she was constantly in trouble. Ages 10-15.

Zolotow, Charlotte. A Tiger Called Thomas. Lothrop, Lee
    and Shepard, 1963. Thomas discovers that people in
    his new community do like him. Ages 5-8.

Language Barriers

Bouchard, Lois K. The Boy Who Wouldn't Talk. Doubleday,
    1969. Puerto Rican boy whose family move to New
    York, refuses to talk because people make fun of him.
    In school he learns English and his troubles disappear.
    Ages 7-11.

Brenner, Barbara. Barto Takes the Subway. Knopf, 1961.
    Ages 5-8.

Ets, Marie H. Bad Boy, Good Boy. Crowell, 1967. Mex-
    ican pre-schooler tries to adjust in an English-speaking
    country. Everyone thinks he's bad because he doesn't
    understand English. Primary to age 9.

Speevack, Yetta. The Spider Plant. Atheneum, 1965. Ages
    8-12.

Peer Relationships

Anderson, Ethel. High Apple on the Tree. Funk & Wagnalls,
    1957. Helping a paralyzed friend helps a girl to con-
    sider others. Ages 10-15.

Beim, Jerrold. Trouble After School. Harcourt, 1957. The
    problems of apperance and reality are central to Lee
    Emerson's initiation into maturity. The need to belong

focuses on a frequent problem of intermediate grade
youngsters.   Ages 8-12.

Beyer, Ernestine.   The Story of Little-Big.   Reilly & Lee,
    1962.   Little-Big finds a playmate in his own wigwam.
    Ages 5-8.

Bonsall, Crosby N.   It's Mine.   Harper & Row, 1964.   Two
    children learn that they can have more fun when they
    share things and do not quarrel.   Ages 5-8.

Bradbury, Bianca.   Two on an Island.   Houghton Mifflin, 1965.
    Two children learn during a stress situation that each
    is more friendly than the other had thought.   Ages 8-12.

Bragdon, Elspeth.   There is a Tide.   Viking Press, 1964.
    Boy who has been expelled from a number of schools
    learns to consider others.   Ages 8-12.

Burch, Robert.   D. J.'s Worst Enemy.   Viking, 1965.   Boy
    at odds with peers and family.   Ages 9-12.

Burnett, Hallie, ed.   Sometimes Magic: A Collection of Out-
    standing Stories for the Teen-Age Girl.   Platt & Munk,
    1966.   Twenty-one short stories written by outstanding
    authors and covering many of the problems faced by
    adolescent girls.   Ages 12 up.

Byars, Betsy.   The 18th Emergency.   Viking Press, c1973.
    Ezzie lives in terror of a larger, older bully in school,
    until he learns to face up to fear, terror ... and honor
    when he is a "man" of twelve.   Ages 8-12.

Estes, Eleanor.   The Hundred Dresses.   Harcourt, 1944.
    Wanda Petronski's one hundred drawn-on-paper dresses
    focus on a multi-fold problem: acceptance or rejection
    by a group; peer disapproval; responsibility of leader-
    ship.   Ages 5-8.

Fitzhugh, Louise.   Harriet the Spy.   Harper & Row, 1964.
    Peer relationships.   Ages 8-12.

Frick, C. H.   The Comeback Guy.   Harcourt, Brace, and
    World, 1961.   Boy overcomes his arrogance and in-
    creases his popularity.   Ages 8-12.

Friedman, Frieda.   Ellen and the Gang.   Morrow, 1963.

Girl faces the problem of choosing between her friends and her principles.   Ages 8-12.

Goddin, Peggy.   Take Care of my Little Girl.   Dutton, 1950. An account of the problems faced by a girl when she joins a college sorority.   Adolescent and adult.

Hahn, Emily.   Francie.   Franklin Watts, 1951.   An attractive but spoiled 17-year-old girl is transferred to a boarding school where she learns self-control and tolerance. Ages 10-15.

Holberg, Ruth.   What Happened to Virgilia?   Doubleday, 1963. Girl learns how to overcome jealousy and make friends during the year she spends with an aunt.   Ages 8-12.

Little, Jean.   Look through my Window.   Harper, 1970. Getting along with others.   Ages 12 up.

Scott, Sally.   Jenny and the Wonderful Jeep.   Harcourt, Brace and World, 1963.   Girl learns that she should be willing to give others the same treatment she wishes to receive.   Ages 5-8.

Udry, Janice.   Next Door to Laura Linda.   Albert Whitman, 1965.   Laura finds that when no girls are available to play with, boys make good substitutes.   Ages 5-8.

Wilcox, Jessica.   Time to Grow Up.   Harper & Row, 1962. A guide for girls on many of the problems faced by most adolescents.   Ages 10-15.

Zolotow, Charlotte.   The Three Funny Friends.   Harper & Row, 1961.   When a little girl finds a real friend she is glad to give up her three imaginary ones.   Ages 5-8.

Miscellaneous School-Related Problems

Lexau, Joan.   Olaf Reads.   Scholastic Book Services, 1961. Olaf becomes enthusiastic about reading after discovering some of the values in it.   Ages 10-15.

Stolz, Mary.   The Noonday Friends.   Harper & Row, 1965. Problems faced by an 11-year-old girl at home and at school are finally resolved.   Ages 8-12.

Stoutenburg, Adrien. The Blue-Eyed Convertible. West-
    minster Press, 1961. A number of unexpected events
    almost wreck the college plans of two young men. Ages
    16 up.

Sports and Sportsmanship

Gault, William. Dirt Track Summer. Dutton, 1961. An
    exciting story of racing which also deals with adoles-
    cent values, prejudices, and sportsmanship.   Ages 12
    up.

Sources of titles and annotations on this list:

Suggestions to author from children's librarians (verbal).

Zaccaria, Joseph S. and Moses, Harold.   Facilitating Human
    Development through Reading.   Stipes Publishing Co.,
    1967.

Hendrix, Margaret M.   Fiction Books that Deal with Children's
    Problems.   Mimeographed list produced by Oregon State
    Library, Salem, Oregon, compiled by Margaret M.
    Hendrix, Consultant in Children's Services, Public Li-
    brary Development Division.   October, 1970.

Walters, Gerald.   Teachers' List of Books on Problems of
    Children.   Mimeographed list prepared by Jerry Walters,
    Springfield, Oregon, 1974.

Author's personal examination of many titles.

CHAPTER 9

THE ROLE OF THE PUBLIC LIBRARY
IN BIBLIOTHERAPY

Bibliotherapy should not be considered the prerogative only of the hospital librarian, teacher, school librarian, or counselor. Public librarians have been using bibliotherapy for many years whenever they have, consciously or unconsciously, helped a patron toward the solution of some psychological, physical, or emotional problem through suggested reading. They have done this in the name of reader guidance and many will continue to prefer to use that term. However, as stated earlier, the distinction between reader guidance, or reader advisory services, and bibliotherapy lies in the presence of a problem, something other than the conventional search for information for its own sake. A student seeking material on Egyptian history may be doing so to fulfill an assignment or do a paper or report. He is not necessarily in need of therapy.

By whatever name we designate it, public library reading guidance or bibliotherapy, especially with children, is becoming increasingly important, particularly in cities where the clientele of a main library or branch is changing from middle or upper class to low economic, less advantaged groups or where the library is losing a large proportion of its former borrowers. The task in inner-city libraries and libraries that serve migrants, Indians, Negroes, Mexican-American or other racial or ethnic groups is now to encourage non-readers or reluctant readers to learn to like reading and to use libraries. This will require more and more of the one-to-one approach and offers a practical opportunity for the application of bibliotherapy.

In reporting on the bibliotherapy workshop held June 25-27, 1964, as an American Library Association pre-conference program, Orrilla T. Blackshear, assistant director of the Madison, Wisconsin, Public Library, said:[1]

As a consultant in this workshop, I should like to
have been able to sit down with public librarians
who are interested in bibliotherapy and learn about
their concerns.   Since this was not possible, I
tried to examine the role of the public library in
the practice of bibliotherapy.   There is very little
mention of its role in the professional literature
... An examination of the principles and standards
of public library service reveals the framework
within which the service might be offered.   That
framework sets up certain guidelines which include
the authority to establish a positive program of
guidance to individuals in the use of educational,
informational and recreational materials by the use
of verbal, visual or other interpretative means.
The scope of services may extend to groups and
institutions.   Standards also indicate that the public
library 'should seek to bring its services' to the
attention of those who may need them.   Materials
are to be selected to meet 'the needs of various
age and interest groups in the community' ... and
'must go beyond the requests of particular groups
who come to use the library regularly and reach
out to segments in the population which do not as
readily turn to this facility. '

There are a number of considerations which the
public librarian must examine: first, the need for
training in the necessary skills; second, the parts
of the public library program that would be improved if bibliotherapists were members of the
public library staff; and third, what additional
services ought the public library consider in
strengthening the bibliotherapy program? ...

Public libraries are presently giving service to
individuals and groups with specific needs.   Much
of this service might involve bibliotherapy to some
extent: assistance to the blind person in directing
him to talking book service, direct assistance to
the visually handicapped person who is not eligible
to receive the talking books, delivery of books to
nursing and retirement homes and to other homebound individuals, special service to psychiatric
wards in hospital service, club projects for the
aging and the handicapped, cooperation in programs
preparing people for retirement and the prepara-

tion of reading lists, study guides and exhibits for various uses. None of these activities could presently be considered successful as therapy, except incidentally.

It seems reasonable to believe that the public library might fit into the [adjunctive] role.... Certainly, it is the public librarian's place to assist in developing community understanding about the values of the bibliotherapy program for patients and their families. To perform this function he must be informed about bibliotherapy, he must keep in touch with developments and research about bibliotherapy and he must realize that he cannot engage in bibliotherapy until he has received the training for it.

More specifically, public librarians need to know the answers to such questions as these: What is the public librarian's responsibility to the patient who has been mentally ill and is returning to the community? What kinds of information and materials will be needed in the public library for the adjunctive role it may serve in the bibliotherapy program?

Forty years ago Elizabeth Pomeroy appealed to public libraries to initiate hospital library work in local hospitals on the premise that such service offered the library the chance to extend its educational program; the opportunity to gain friends, and to practice therapeutic restoration and improvement of community health. [2] Such emphasis has been placed in most writing on the benefits to the patients that the reciprocal benefits to the library itself have seldom been pointed out. Yet they are undeniably present and should be counted by any library contemplating beginning hospital service. Many public libraries now offer service when the hospital does not maintain an adequate patient library. When public librarians man the bookcarts within the hospital they have ample opportunities to practice constructive informal bibliotherapy. The public librarian who has direct contact with patients should, however, know the nature of the patient's illness before recommending books as therapy; he should seek an opportunity to talk with an authoritative member of the medical staff, preferably, of course, the patient's own doctor. When this is not possible, the physician's advice may be sought through the head nurse or an intern. If the public library staff member has an unusual understanding of books and patients, sees the same long-term patients frequently, and obtains a medical briefing on a patient's condition and any special precautions to be observed, there is no reason why such a staff member should not render bibliotherapy where a need is sensed.

Emerson Greenaway, for many years librarian of the Free Library of Philadelphia, believes public librarians can perform three separate but related functions in service to handicapped persons, all of which have direct or indirect applications to bibliotherapy. These are: 1) Create a favorable climate of opinion towards the handicapped (indirect); 2) Entertain and inform the handicapped themselves (direct); and 3) guide those specialized people who work with the handicapped through library resources (indirect).[3]

Margaret Hannigan, an authority in the hospital library field, has said that in its broadest sense bibliotherapy, as institutional librarians practice it, is closely related to reader guidance service in public libraries and to the use of books and reading for character formation and guidance by many literature teachers at all levels. Here is a direct statement by an institutional librarian that bibliotherapy need not be confined to the scientific or medically-related aspects, but can be extended into broader fields.[4]

The public library director who believes that a library has no social responsibility toward its borrowers beyond supplying them with library materials, will probably feel that bibliotherapy has no place in his operation. As the emphasis upon public library work with the disadvantaged grows, however, the progressive and humanitarian librarian must show more interest in the patron as an individual rather than just as another statistic to boost the annual report.

In a large library the majority of patrons come and go rapidly, and often infrequently. But there are some who stand out because they come very often, are obviously unhappy, troubled or lonely, or who long desperately to find answers to physical, emotional or psychological problems through the right book. Finding the right book for the person with a problem is the essence of bibliotherapy. Who can deny that the library staff member who finds John Button's Hope and Help in Parkinson's Disease for the little old lady who lives alone, who is afflicted with the first stages of this ailment and lives in daily fear of what the future may hold, is not better fulfilling the library's true function than the one who recommends the newest Mary Stewart suspense novel to the Gothic novel fan simply because she knows this reader will enjoy such a book? This is not to decry the latter. Recommending any book is part of good library service, but in order to help the elderly Parkinson sufferer to allay her fears, it is necessary for the staff member to know that this particular volume by Button is one which can truly help, which is written in terms a layman can understand, and which has a cheering, encouraging effect despite its accurate presentation of the problems. It is also necessary to know that the patron has the disease, how she feels about it, and whether she is likely to welcome a suggestion that she read a book about an affliction she already spends too much time worrying about. The factor which makes the first case bibliotherapy is the presence of a physical problem, obviously disturbing to the patron; the second case is a commonplace example of reader advisory or reader guidance service.

Clara E. Lucioli, head of the Hospital and Institutional Department of the Cleveland Public Library, says that the patients' library is usually last in the total planning of both hospital and public libraries because the psychological needs of the ill and handicapped come last in the great hierarchy of concern for physical care on the part of hospitals, and in public libraries often the more obvious demands of the general public take and hold precedence. Notable exceptions are the New York State Library Extension Division and the Hospital and Institutions Department of the Cleveland Public Library, Veterans' Administration libraries, and the United Hospital Fund of New York. [5]

Some librarians and library workers possess instinctively a high degree of understanding of human nature and may more readily sense deep-seated patron needs than a less understanding person with training in the behavioral sciences. Such instinctively understanding people are to be treasured on any public library staff, and they should never be discouraged from doing constructive book-related therapy because they lack formal library training or a wide knowledge of the social sciences. The librarian, after all, does not attempt to practice direct psychiatry. He or she is only the link between the person and the book. As Dr. Floch points out, "Psychotherapy is basically nothing but personal influence exerted by one person on another, and books are substitutes for people. As one pores over a book, it is almost as if one held a conversation with the author. "[6]

The public librarian, when reading or checking reviews on a book, must go one step further if she wishes to practice successful bibliotherapy. She must analyze the book in terms of the problem or problems it deals with, and of the patron or patrons for whom it may be appropriate. The alert librarian-bibliotherapist will build up a bibliography arranged by the nature of the problems, and will draw upon it as needs arise. She will also secure and file all available lists of titles already suggested as bibliotherapy aids, many of which are broken down by the nature of the problem. The advantage of compiling one's own list is that it will contain only books the library has or can easily borrow, and the process of compilation will enable the librarian to remember titles better when a need arises.

Among things the public library can do are:

1. Establish a delivery service to shut-ins which includes periodic visits by a staff member equipped by personality and training to make use of bibliotherapy as the need is indicated. If a shut-in service is already in effect, reassess the qualifications of the staff who do the visiting. Try to choose people with the best possible background for the practice of bibliotherapy; if no such staff members are available, encourage one or more to take special courses in psychology, counseling, techniques of rehabilitation, elementary psychiatry, medical and social problems of illness, medical, psychological and psychiatric terminology, and the psychology of the physically handicapped.

2. Work closely with juvenile officers, heads of training schools for boys and girls, homes for unwed mothers, sanitariums for alcoholics or drug addicts, and general and special hospitals, to supply booklists, a deposit of books, book-cart services, individual visits to rooms. Recommend bibliotherapeutic reading after discussing cases with those in charge. Suggest and supply books to staff personnel that will help them to do bibliotherapy.

3. Help a newly-released patient from a mental institution to find his old place in the community. Make him feel welcome in the library. Get well acquainted with him, suggest reading that will overcome discouragement or despair; help him regain confidence. Provide material which will help him find a job more easily.

4. Assist blind persons by securing or helping them

secure talking book service, and by choosing talking books
that will emphasize the accomplishments of the blind in overcoming their handicap.

5.   Cooperate with school counselors and psychologists
to help the troubled or maladjusted child or young person.
Suggest material on bibliotherapy for the counselor's own
reading.   Don't urge titles on a school counselor but make
bibliotherapy sound so worthwhile and interesting that he will
want to read for himself and work with both the school and
public librarian to learn more about it.   School people are
often even busier than librarians, and the librarian may have
to take the initiative in such cooperation.

6.   Observe special problems among the children who
attend story hours.   Select stories that deal with problems
such as shyness, over-assertiveness, fear, sloppiness, etc.
Set up displays of picture books that have some relevance to
the problems of known individuals.   Work with the children
and their parents if there is any possibility of direct contacts, for example if a parent brings the child to the library
between story-telling sessions.   This must be handled very
carefully.   Some parents cannot or will not recognize behavior problems in their own children and resent anyone else
implying that such problems exist.

7.   Form retirement or senior citizens' clubs.   Use
group therapy and individual bibliotherapy in program planning
through further acquaintances formed with club members.

8.   Sponsor a series of pre-retirement lectures. Seek
the acquaintance of group members and recommend books on
retirement problems.

9.   Work out a program using children's literature in
group therapy.   This program is designed to facilitate reentry
of the mother into the family group upon discharge from a
mental hospital, to help rebuild a close family relationship
and to provide a means for family recreation and resocialization.   A group of women patients who have young children
at home may be referred to the librarian for group activity.
A wide variety of children's literature is made available for
reading and browsing.   Each member of the group chooses
books and magazines she feels will appeal to her children.
Excerpts are read aloud.   Television programs for children
are also discussed.   Use of the public library by all the
family is discussed and a visit to the public library should be

arranged. These sessions will hopefully lead to a discussion
of family problems in general, but specific problems should
be referred to the physician, psychologist, or social worker
for additional counseling. In addition to a general collection
of children's books for several age groups and interests, some
good books on storytelling are useful in such a program. For
example: Sawyer, Ruth. Way of the Story Teller (Viking,
1962); and Shedlock, Marie L. Art of the Story Teller (Dover,
1951).

10. "In smaller communities in which hospitals do not
have many adjuncts for the care of the sick, bibliotherapy
assumes an even more important role, " says Dr. Gordon
Kamman. Almost every community has its public library and
librarian; there may not be a therapist trained in the other
auxiliary branches of medical treatment, but the librarian is
always available. If she understands the fundamental principles of bibliotherapy she can perform a service of great
importance. She could be invited to consult with members of
the hospital staff on reading assignments for individual patients. Group projects could be promoted, planned reading
programs worked out, and patients embarked upon a wholesome, diverting, instructive, and constructive reading program.

How should the public librarian go about planning a
reading program for a patient? Here are the steps suggested
by Dr. Kamman, some of which require the active participation of the doctor:

> A. Before seeing the patient the librarian should have
>   an interview with the attending physician and as-
>   certain important facts about the patient's illness,
>   such as the nature of the illness, how long the
>   patient will be incapacitated, the prognosis, and
>   whether he will be permanently handicapped.
>
> B. She should familiarize herself with any peculiar-
>   ities or personality traits that will influence her
>   approach to the patient.
>
> C. She should discover the presence or absence of
>   suicidal tendencies or paranoid ideas.
>
> D. She should learn something about the social and
>   educational background of the patient as well as
>   his special aptitudes and interests.

E. The physician should tell the therapist what results he expects from bibliotherapy (whether he wants the patient to be diverted, amused and educated along certain lines, or whether he wants him to engage in a reading project that will indoctrinate him with certain principles and ideas which have therapeutic effect).

F. The physician should take the therapist to the patient and introduce her in person. He should arrange a preliminary interview between the therapist and the patient at which she can verify and supplement the impressions she received in her conference with the physician. At the same time the patient has a chance to become acquainted with the therapist. Many patients are difficult and self conscious. Many are in the hospital against their own wishes and they could be resentful. Some are suspicious and hostile. Sometimes the bibliotherapist must make several daily visits to the patient in order to arouse interest in reading projects. [7]

11. The public librarian can help hospital staff set up book displays (jackets, lists, and posters on bulletin boards), and table displays in wards or solariums. An exhibit in a library corridor, a hospital lobby, a downtown window or bank lobby can call attention to public library services available for the ill, the handicapped and the shut-ins. Samples of the latest equipment to facilitate reading for paralytics, for readers with poor eyesight, or for those with a hand in a cast or other physical problems which make normal use of a book difficult, could be included in the displays. Examples include mechanical page turners, ceiling projectors, special magnifiers, large print books, book holders, etc.

12. A ceiling projector or an ordinary slide projector can be used to inform the public of the therapeutic and educational services available both from the library and the hospital for the special needs of the long-term patient. [8]

When a public library extends service to a hospital which does not have its own library it must, of course, have the consent and cooperation of the hospital administrator and staff. To help convince a busy administrator that the service is needed, and that it will be worth the time required for nurses to collect books of patients being discharged, to write

down special requests, or to report to the librarian and doctors a patient's special reaction to any books, it is well to
stress that books that might help the administrator and other
staff members in their own work can also be obtained and
brought to the hospital along with the patients' reading material. [9]

Ann Matthews, a public librarian, stressed the following important rules for the librarian offering public library
service to a hospital.   Observing these rules should insure
good relations with both administrator and staff:

1. Always check at the nursing station before enter-
    ing a room.
2. Never reveal any information seen or heard within
    the hospital.
3. Know the reading material.   The wrong book can
    cause harm to patients.
4. Keep adequate records of the books, talking books,
    recorders, films and ceiling projectors on loan.
5. Supply the materials from the library with no
    overdue charges.   Special subject materials such
    as interlibrary loan from other libraries will need
    a time limit.   Due date and any fine charges im-
    posed by the other libraries should be explained
    to the patient.

In turn, what can the public librarian expect from the
hospital?   Mrs. Matthews lists the following:

1. The hospital should give the librarian a simple
    diagnosis of patients the nurse recommends to be
    visited.   Certain patients--heart patients, for ex-
    ample--should not be given fiction so exciting that
    it could upset them.
2. Books returned by nurses to nurses' stations
    should be kept in a safe place to be picked up by
    the librarian when she comes each week.   Books
    are only given to the nurses if the patient is re-
    leased before the librarian returns.
3. The hospital should assume financial responsibility
    for lost books.   The hospital could demand the
    right to be given weekly records of all loans if
    they are to assume this responsibility.   Some
    hospitals would not accept the service if they had
    to pay.   In such cases the public library should
    not refuse service, but if possible should absorb

the loss or itself contact the patient at his home, and attempt to secure its return.

Mrs. Matthews found, during her three years of work with hospitals in Jackson, Michigan, and from the results of a questionnaire submitted to hospital administrators, that the public library plan was received enthusiastically by those administrators who had been served well by organized library facilities.   Conversely, bad library service caused administrators to be violently against any library service.   Thus, administrators and library directors should thoroughly understand any program before it is put into operation.   Book loss in the Jackson operation was found to be negligible.   The efficiency hinges upon the cooperation of the nurses, and their cooperation will depend a great deal upon their directive from the head of nursing services. [9]

As far back as 1945, the Gravois Branch of the St. Louis, Missouri, Public Library, which was in a good neighborhood, found juvenile delinquency a very definite problem.[10] Four group activities were instituted in a special effort to combat this growing trend.   The first was in cooperation with one of the neighborhood schools located approximately ten blocks away, where a special summer reading club was organized for nineteen sixth, seventh, and eighth grade students who were problem children and poor in their school work. Although not labeling it bibliotherapy, the teachers and principal felt that reading the right kind of books would be beneficial to these children.

The nineteen children were given to understand that they would pass into the next grade in September if they read a book a week chosen by the children's librarian.   The children's librarian was given the confidential case history of each pupil; then the group was brought to the public library by one of the teachers for personal interviews and to be organized into a club.   The librarian and each individual boy or girl discussed together the type of book or magazines the child had been reading.   These turned out to be of a generally poor type, but the children's librarian, now in the role of bibliotherapist, did not disparage their former reading choices. Instead they discussed some of the most interesting library titles about boy and girl friendships and some of the love stories for older girls.   Authors included were Lambert, Boylston, Ferris, Snedeker, and Worth.

The children read the suggested books with enthusiasm

and discussed them with the children's librarian. Several of
the children felt that orphans were social outcasts and as a
defense mechanism had become belligerent bullies or sullen
unhappy individuals.   With no discussion of their problem,
books were suggested and enough of the story told to interest
them, the only motive given being to remove the conditioned
grade.   Enough books were carefully selected during the
summer to help change their mental attitudes.   Another problem was a girl with a hairlip who had developed an overpower-
ing inferiority complex.   Such books as Helen Keller's Story
of My Life, Pyle's Otto of the Silver Hand, Fox's Lona of
Hollybush Creek, and Hatch's Bridle Wise were suggested to
her.

A definite empathy had to be established with each
child before much progress could be made.   The librarian
and the children became good friends, and at the end of the
summer the school principal and teachers were well pleased
with the results of this cooperative plan.   These pupils continued to come to the library and seek the help of the children's librarian in selecting their books, even into high school
years.

Opportunities for bibliotherapy on the part of the
children's and young people's librarians can also open up as
they come to know Girl or Boy Scouts who do reading for
merit badges.   They can learn the interests of the young
people, tell stories at their social gatherings, establish the
type of friendly, sympathetic, interested association that invites confidences and makes it possible to help solve family
or individual problems through books. [10]

Clara E. Lucioli, in a paper on the "Bibliotherapeutic
Aspects of Public Library Services to Patients in Hospitals
and Institutions" in 1968, pointed out that some hospital administrators and their department heads are frankly skeptical
of the value of reading for their clientele; even "free" services may be questioned on the basis of time and space requirements and as an interruption of the treatment programs. [11]

The public librarian who embarks on an outreach
service in this milieu, which may be strange to him, worries
about bibliotherapy both as a term and how he can equip himself for it.   This, Lucioli says, should not be the first but
the last concern, the one which comes as a culmination of
experience after one has acquired a solid footing in the insti-

tution. Before this can happen both the personnel and the
clientele must be convinced of the public library's interest in
them and the total treatment program. Long before the librarian is given an opportunity to work with the staff on the
well-being of any patient or inmate, she must have demonstrated an interest in the individual employee; the way to a
place in the circle of care begins with good service to people
in every category of employment in the institution.

Since public library services and librarians do not
operate on a full-time basis in any institution, they are outsiders, in a sort of in-between position, Lucioli maintains.
They are not volunteers, who are seen as financial assets and
receive gratitude as such, nor are they special workers provided by "grants-in-aid" obtained by the hospital. They are
a community resource that is "free" and they can be overlooked or their efforts minimized unless they develop a warm
climate of acceptance and respect. What librarians lack in
the support they would get as employees of the institution
must be compensated for by strong ties to their libraries and
by developing impact through competence and personality.
The librarians should tailor their talks to the interests of
hospital personnel and through them to the patients too. A
talk with the hospital director may well begin with an explanation of the public library's role as the information center
for the community, and how he can use it as an educational
resource for board members, for in-service training programs and for the staff in general. Lastly, he should be told
what it can do for the patients. If he thinks of it only as a
nice adjunct for patients but never sees it as a help to him,
he will be less likely to generate the kind of appreciation that
comes from knowing it is a real resource in saving time and
investigating problems.

Discussing the services an integrated hospital library
can and cannot provide, Barbara Coe Johnson, in 1969, emphasized that hospital libraries have not kept pace with the
times and the growth in number and size of hospitals, and
that accordingly public libraries need to step in and fill the
gap. She says:

> After all, public libraries have long accepted the
> responsibility of providing trained personnel versed
> not only in general service to the public but also
> in specialized service to various segments of the
> population. Public librarians dealing with pa-
> tients might need some special training in the

psychology of illness, but oviously this kind of
service can be performed well by public librarians, as witness the experience of the Cleveland
Public Library. I think public librarians feel a
responsibility in this area, but I do not think they
have been very aggressive about making their
talents known; equally, I think those in hospital
libraries have not been very forward in asking for
the help they need.

Johnson explains her concept of an integrated hospital
library as follows: "I am inclined to think that lay and professional collections can only be coordinated, probably by
sharing the same administrative librarian, while all services
to technical and professional personnel can truly be integrated
(combined, shared, consolidated, whatever word one wants to
use). " Because she believes that it is potentially dangerous
to allow patients access to technical information which pre-
sumes the professional background necessary to place it in
context, she does not favor having the library for patients
combined with that for the medical and nursing personnel. [12]

Carolyn Folz, as hospital librarian of the Evansville
Public Library in 1933, carried on a very successful extension service from that library to the city hospital. [13] Collections of books were placed in the hospitals and changed at
regular intervals. She, as librarian, took book carts to the
hospital rooms, visiting with the patients, and subtly influencing their selection of books to fit their needs and help
solve their problems.

In a public library, says Mrs. Folz, the patron's
purpose in reading, his educational background, what he has
already read, and what is available in the library (or obtainable through interlibrary loan) are all factors to be considered
when recommending reading material. Hospital library service to patients presents additional considerations: the nature
of the illness, the stage of convalescence, and the mood,
taste, intelligence and general background of the patient.
There are also the physical requirements that the books be
light in weight, of large clear print, of a convenient size for
reading in bed, and of attractive makeup.

Mrs. Folz notes that as soon as a book was slightly
soiled it was sent back to the general extension department.
Only immaculate books were used with patients, the library
believing that it should maintain the same standard of clean-

liness that was observed in the various departments of the
hospital. Moreover, the clean, colorful backs and front pages
created a cheerful effect and were more inviting to patients
than shabby, soiled volumes would have been.

While many readers will prefer love stories, westerns,
or mysteries, it is important that a well-chosen group of distinctive books be available for discriminating readers. The
bibliotherapist must be able to recognize such readers and
select books for them intelligently. Although the main purpose
of the librarian-bibliotherapist is not to try to raise reading
standards, the books supplied will not satisfy or do the greatest possible good unless they meet the patients' standards.
On the other hand, in bibliotherapy the content of a book or
other reading material and the degree to which it meets the
patient's needs must take precedence over literary value. [13]

When the Agnews State Hospital in San Jose, California was closed to mentally ill patients in June, 1972, the
bibliotherapy program which had been conducted for four years
with LSCA funds, was taken over by the Santa Clara County
Library; mental health facilities such as alcoholic and drug
treatment centers, half-way houses, board and care homes,
and psychiatric hospitals are visited by two bibliotherapists,
Clara Lack and Bruce Bettencourt, who conduct reading and
discussion groups.

At the community facilities most of the patients are
not as disturbed as those who were at the hospital; therefore
the results make an interesting comparison. For further information on the progress of this program, which is rela-
tively new for the community, it is suggested that the reader
write the bibliotherapists named at the Santa Clara County
Library. Here is an example of a public library doing a
comprehensive job in bibliotherapy with an organized program. [14]

Notes

1. "A Bibliotherapy Workshop." Wisconsin Library Bulletin,
     v. 60, Sept.-Oct. 1964, p. 296-298.

2. Pomeroy, Elizabeth. "Hospital Libraries." American
     Library Association Bulletin, v. 25, Sept. 1936, p.
     430-435; Bulletin of the American Hospital Association,
     v. 6, Oct. 1931, p. 68-77; Medical Bulletin of the

Veterans' Administration, v. 77, Oct. 1931, p. 986-994.

3. Greenaway, Emerson. "Library Service to the Blind and other Handicapped Groups." American Library Association Bulletin, v. 55, April 1961, p. 320-23.

4. Hannigan, Margaret C. "Bibliotherapy: Its Part in Library Service." The Bookmark (New York State Library), v. 15, March 1956, p. 127-28.

5. Lucioli, C. E. "Out of Isolation: The Patients' Library." Library Journal, v. 92, April 1 1967, p. 1421-23.

6. Floch, Maurice. "Bibliotherapy and the Library." The Bookmark (New York State Library), v. 18, Dec. 1958, p. 59.

7. Kamman, Gordon R. "Balanced Reading Diet Prescribed for Mental Patients." Modern Hospital, v. 55, Nov. 1940, p. 80.

8. "The Library and the Hospital Can Jointly Plan Exhibits." Hospital Management, v. 95, Jan. 1963, p. 58.

9. Matthews, Ann. "Bibliotherapy Gives a New Lease on Life." Hospital Management, v. 95, Jan. 1963, p. 57.

10. Eagle, Opal Cole. "Combating Juvenile Delinquency through Group Activities in the Public Library." Wilson Library Bulletin, v. 19, May 1945, p. 607-09.

11. Lucioli, Clara E. "Bibliotherapeutic Aspects of Public Library Services to Patients in Hospitals and Institutions." In: Monroe, Margaret E., editor, Reading Guidance and Bibliotherapy in Public Hospital, and Institution Libraries. Library School, University of Wisconsin, Madison, 1971, p. 51-52, 54-55.

12. Johnson, Barbara Coe. "Services an Integrated Hospital Library Can and Cannot Provide." Library Journal, v. 63, Dec. 1969, p. 1556, 1558.

13. Folz, Carolyn. "Pied Piper of the Modern Library." Library Occurrent, v. 11, Apr. -June 1933, p. 39, 42.

14. Lack, Clara, and Bettencourt, Bruce. "Bibliotherapy in the Community." *News Notes of California Libraries*, v. 68, Fall 1973, p. 372.

CHAPTER 10

THE NON-INSTITUTIONALIZED DISADVANTAGED

In 1971 the handicapped represented over 22,000,000 people in the United States, a figure being increased annually by the birth of 100,000 or so babies with crippling physical defects, and by hundreds of thousands maimed by war, age, traffic accidents and other accidents or handicapping illnesses. Approximately one out of seven people in our nation has a permanent physical disability.

The non-institutionalized handicapped who are homebound offer a growing challenge. More must be done for this group than merely delivering and picking up books, though even this service is rendered by far too few libraries. The handicapped are often lonely; they can become depressed, discouraged, tired and apathetic from chronic pain. Visits from an understanding person who not only brings books and magazines to suit their tastes but will also take time to talk and to discuss the books after they are read, or to read aloud if the person is blind or has poor eyesight, can bring untold happiness to shut-ins and others whose normal activity is hampered by physical handicap or infirmity, or who suffer from the deprivations of poverty with its oft-accompanying psychological and emotional problems.

The non-institutionalized disadvantaged may include those crippled by multiple sclerosis, arthritis, asthma, heart conditions, cerebral palsy, birth defects, polio, paraplegia, paralysis, or any other crippling disease, as well as the deaf, blind, mute, or those with speech defects of any kind. Some of these who have a folding wheelchair or can get about with a walker would enjoy an occasional trip to their local library so that they may browse and select titles for present or future reading.

Many libraries now offer service to the homebound, but much of it is merely a delivery and pickup and includes no element of bibliotherapy. While such service is undoubt-

edly better than nothing, it falls far short of the full book
therapy such people need in today's society. Today's uncer-
tainties and anxieties may affect the aged, infirm, poor and
physically handicapped even more than those not afflicted because, being less active, they have more time to think, to
brood and to compare conditions today with their own less
complicated early lives. Thus the right choice of books,
magazines, phonograph records, tapes, talking books or other
materials, plus visits by a person able to practice bibliotherapy, can help to soothe anxiety, encourage hope for the
future, and emphasize the positive aspects of life today.

If a library does not have sufficient funds or personnel able to provide homebound library service to shut-ins and
others who find it difficult to get to libraries, the services
of volunteers from organizations such as R. S. V. P. , Friends
of the Library, Soroptomist, Junior League, Lions, etc. ,
may be solicited by the library. It is important to stress to
presidents or heads of organizations that the personality of
the members picked for such library service is all important;
that they should be outgoing, perceptive, sympathetic, and
warmly understanding of other people's problems; if they are
well read that is also highly desirable. Many lonely elderly
individuals who live alone may respond well to people near
or in their own age bracket, while others will prefer the re-
freshment of a young person's vitality and youthful outlook on
life. Experimentation may be necessary at the outset to find
the type of person who is best suited to the one visited, and
no one visitor will be equally successful with all types of
persons.

If volunteers are used or the local libraries have no
one versed in bibliotherapy, the library should offer a training course, preferably at night, and including lectures by a
practicing bibliotherapist, a psychiatrist or psychologist, an
expert in geriatrics, a social worker, and a doctor. Participants should read widely in the material available on bib-
liotherapy--carefully chosen articles and case studies covering a variety of the problems encountered, especially the
mental and emotional problems of the elderly and the physically handicapped, those suffering from poverty and the
chronically ill. Must reading would include:

Bibliotherapy: Methods and Materials. Chicago: American
        Library Association, 1971.

Bibliotherapy.   October 1962 issue of Library Trends,

Urbana, Ill.: University of Illinois, Graduate School
of Library Science.

Facilitating Human Development through Reading.   Joseph
        Zaccaria and Harold A. Moses.   Stipes Publishing Co.,
        1968.

Reading Guidance and Bibliotherapy in Public, Hospital and
        Institution Libraries.   Madison, Wis.: Library School,
        University of Wisconsin, 1971.

Library Service to the Disadvantaged, by Eleanor F. Brown,
        Metuchen, N.J.: Scarecrow Press, 1971.   Chapters
        on Services to the Elderly and the Physically Handi-
        capped.

Porterfield, Austin L.   Mirror for Adjustment: Therapy in
        Home, School, and Society for Seeing Yourself and
        Others in Books.   Leo Potisham Foundation, Texas
        Christian University, c1967.

Selected articles from American Libraries, Library Journal,
        Wilson Library Bulletin as indexed in Library Litera-
        ture, and selected articles from some of the leading
        geriatric periodicals.

Those taking the course should also be acquainted with
and know where to get the various reading lists and bibliographies available.   Copies of reading lists recommended in
the above publications and other sources, especially those
dealing with the problems of physical handicaps, old age, and
chronic illness, should be made available to students in the
training course.   These should be lists of books to recommend to persons visited and are not to be confused with the
background reading for the would-be bibliotherapists themselves.   Two films useful for such a course are Lisa's
World and Stress--Parents with a Handicapped Child, since
they depict frankly, even starkly, the difficulties of handicapped people and their families.

It may not be easy to secure a coordinator, lecturers,
and enough students for such a training course, which would
include at least ten sessions and ample homework, but if the
library administration works with heads of volunteer organizations to interest members in the value of bibliotherapy and
the need for orientation in it, there should be sufficient response.   The coordinator of the course need not be an expert

in bibliotherapy.   His or her task is to find people who have experience and background in it and who are willing to help. If such courses could be sponsored by public libraries in all the larger cities and taught in expanded form in library schools, bibliotherapy might come closer to achieving the status it deserves.

Dr. David Chambers, a Los Angeles physician, speaking before an annual convention of the California Library Association in 1963, stated that many adults would require less post-operative medicine if their minds could be occupied sooner with interests outside of themselves.   Much the same is true of the handicapped person: getting his mind off of his own problems and on to outside interests and the problems of others through books is probably the very best service a bibliotherapist can render.

In order to prepare the way for intelligent use of bibliotherapy the librarian or other therapist needs to read the medical case history of the person, if it is possible, to gain access to it.   He should communicate with the person's physician, explaining the service, to see if there are any special directives or precautions; find out from families or the person himself if there are times unsuitable for visits, and obtain reading lists recommended for the particular handicap involved.   Such lists will, of course, have to be supplemented as emotional or psychological problems are discovered through continued contact and acquaintance with the individual. Once the bibliotherapy has started, a careful reading record and notes on interesting or significant facts arising out of conversations should be kept.   The latter should never be made in the presence of the patient but recorded as soon as the visit is over.   If volunteers are assisting they should provide a complete report on each visit to the person responsible for recruiting them for the service.

The physically handicapped who are homebound are more likely to be adults, since handicapped children are most often institutionalized or attend special schools.

The Unemployed Handicapped

The bibliotherapist working with a handicapped person who is unemployed must determine if the person is in any way employable.   The physical rehabilitation counselors and the person himself can help in this determination.   In the case of a person on Social Security disability the person making the periodic checkups could provide information on this point.   The bibliotherapist may help in any one or all of these ways:

1. By providing reading material and instructional material on jobs or crafts a handicapped person may do.
2. By helping the person uncover hidden talents through reading (a person confined to a wheelchair who has a good mind and the willingness to study may find he can paint or write and produce a marketable product; or at least may find a catharsis for his frustrations and barriers).
3. By putting the employable person with ability or talent in touch with prospective employers.
4. By encouraging the person to avail himself of rehabilitation agencies.

Employment suitable to the handicapped can sometimes be found within the library sponsoring the shut-in service. Book mending, routine cataloging, and typing are among tasks which certain types of handicapped persons can perform. There is no greater therapy than work if it is enjoyable, and books can be used to help the employee gain the needed skills both before and after employment.

If there is a language barrier which makes communication difficult and bars a person from employment, bibliotherapeutic techniques should be applied by a bilingual librarian or counselor to reassure the individual, to get him started in a class for learning English, and to find him books on appropriate subjects in his native language.   Many of the Mexican-Americans and Puerto Ricans now in the United States have need of this kind of help--far more than the average social worker can give him.   Outreach bookmobile staffs work closely with such people, helping them to preserve their pride in their native customs, literature, language and general heritage, and at the same time helping them adapt to their adopted country.   Learning and employment can be deterrents to crime; illness breeds it.   Many a bookmobile or branch librarian in the ghetto is daily practicing bibliotherapy with patrons, without ever labeling it or thinking of it as such.

The Blind or Those with Impaired Vision

The blind or those with impaired vision receive more

help from more sources than do those with many other types
of handicap.   Agencies that help are the Regional Centers of
the Library of Congress for the Blind and Physically Handicapped, The American Foundation for the Blind, the American
Printing House for the Blind, state and local agencies, service
organizations, federally funded programs providing service
through the National Eye Institute and deaf-blind centers, and
private philanthropies.   Guide dogs, braille, tape recordings,
large-print books, talking books and talking book machines,
volunteer readers, optical-tactile reading aids, the Rand-
sight closed-circuit television machine known as Magnavision,
a seeing-eye pen developed in 1971--all these devices and
methods are already available to help the blind or partially
sighted.   However, the bibliotherapist or media-therapist is
often needed to help teach the use of machines, to read aloud,
to help the newly blind adjust through understanding help, to
assist in locating agencies or equipment the blind person will
need, and to perform other therapeutic services.

The Deaf or Those with Impaired Hearing

No deaf child can really read until he can achieve a
fundamental knowledge of language.   His early schooling must,
therefore, consist of extending his experience and vocabulary
and learning to associate symbols and lip movements with
communication.   For him, the pre-reading period must be
prolonged considerably beyond that of his hearing contempo-
raries; and the reading lag as his education progresses can
often be three or four years behind the normal grade level.
Here is where the outside bibliotherapist or the teacher employing bibliotherapeutic techniques can help--not only to
speed up the child's progress but also to prevent the formation of a deep-seated inferiority complex, or to alleviate it if
it already exists.   The child who is able to attend a school
for the deaf is progressing at somewhere near the same rate
as his fellow students; the non-institutionalized child attending
a public school is not so fortunate.   Finding himself so backward in reading, he may feel conspicuous and stupid.   If he
has a good hearing aid the problem usually does not become
so acute, but certain types of deafness are not helped by a
hearing aid, and in other cases therapy is necessary in order
to persuade a child to wear one.   At this point a book like
Tim and His Hearing Aid can be used effectively (see reading
list at end of chapter).   Since the teacher is usually too busy
to give the child the special attention he needs, the aid of the
school librarian and/or public librarian should be enlisted.

Often, a severe emotional disturbance has built up in a child before it is discovered that he is becoming hard of hearing. The knowledge that this is happening can be a traumatic experience. Books should be found that he can read himself about men and women who overcame deafness to achieve great success; one of the easy accounts of the life of Helen Keller would be especially appropriate.

For the child who has been deaf from birth the problem is different. If he is not in a special school or a special class for exceptional children in a public school system, it will be because none such are available or perhaps because his parents are itinerant. Outreach bookmobiles often reach itinerant workers in agricultural and construction camps, and special cases there should be noted and given special attention and special books. Bibliotherapy in depth may be impossible in such a situation but a service that goes beyond ordinary reader guidance to get to the heart of special problems is needed. A deaf person, child or adult, may be withdrawn, shy, or sometimes even over-aggressive and resentful at being deaf. Communication with such a child in writing may be necessary if he cannot read lips. A resourceful librarian, social worker, or school counselor wanting to use the therapeutic approach will find a way to communicate.

The bibliotherapist working with deaf children in the pre-reading or early reading period should use simple picture books showing familiar objects and scenes--family life, pets, city and country life, toys, children at play, etc.; such books as Papa Small by Lois Lenski, or Where's the Bunny? by Ruth Carroll. Storytelling, with the child lip reading, should center about these everyday things and activities, with the storyteller speaking slowly and enunciating each word very clearly. Storytelling to a group of deaf children should be carefully planned and the group kept to not more than seven or eight children so that the storyteller's lips can be easily observed. Storytelling in this manner is a form of bibliotherapy in itself.

Pictures held up and shown from the book will provide the needed visual expression. Uncluttered simple pictures should be used. Mrs. Patricia Cory, former librarian for the Lexington School for the Deaf, recommends supplementing pictures in the book with blackboard stick figures when more explanation seems necessary. The children will lip-read only key words and if the storyteller is in doubt about having conveyed an idea, it might be well to rephrase or repeat. The children should be involved if possible by an occasional question relating to their allied experiences.   Picture books should continue to be used for storytelling and the children's own reading into the intermediate years, with the stories gradually becoming more complex.

The Economically Disadvantaged

An economically disadvantaged person is often in need of bibliotherapy, for poverty is frequently accompanied by psychological and emotional problems.   Modern outreach programs initiated by libraries have been aimed at bringing library service to the economically deprived--a group which usually includes the under-educated, the culturally deprived, those suffering from racial discrimination, and those with language barriers.

Many among the economically disadvantaged have not formed the reading habit; some are illiterate, others at best are poor readers.   Bibliotherapy, which goes one step further in working with the underprivileged as individuals and friends, by discovering their emotional and psychological problems and endeavoring to help at least partially solve them through books, is the connecting link between the prospective patron and his actual use of the material offered.   An outreach service, to be truly effective, needs bibliotherapy more than most other types of service, and it needs the kind of personnel able to practice it.

The non-institutionalized, as a result of their handicaps, whether physical, mental, or emotional, are apt to be sensitive, quick to resent patronage, suspicious of free services, and sometimes antagonistic toward libraries as institutions, seeing them as part of "the establishment."

One of the best opportunities for real bibliotherapy occurs in bookmobiles, for whatever its service area there is more informality, more regular contact, more opportunity for staff to get to know the patrons.   The bookmobile patron is not awed or confused by an imposing building, a large collection, or so large a staff that he meets a different person on duty almost every time.   Patrons may come to bookmobiles just as they are, in work clothes at the close of the day, in house dresses and aprons, in patched jeans; and they can feel comfortable as they often do not in a large and more formal structure.   The staff and regular patrons soon become

such good friends that patrons often confide their problems
and fears unreservedly, particularly if only they or a few
others are on the bookmobile at the time.   A bookmobile librarian needs to understand the principles of bibliotherapy
and use them in "prescribing" books that will help with problem cases.   The author personally knows of a case where
the understanding sympathy of a bookmobile librarian and her
recommendation of just the right books averted a suicide by
a teenage girl, an only child who had just lost both parents
in an automobile accident and had no other relatives to whom
to turn.

The handicapped, regardless of the nature of the handicap, have certain basic needs which the bibliotherapist can
help to supply through books and the personal touch.   These
include the need to feel a part of the community, to escape
from stresses, to feel security, to maintain as much independence as possible, to feel useful, and to realize their
fullest potential.

The extent and number of the needs will depend upon
the individual, but any reading that will help to meet these
needs is good therapy.   Books that will help the handicapped
find a useful occupation or hobby, or which describe methods
and equipment to make him more self-sufficient will all contribute to his feeling of usefulness and independence.   Ideas
for ways in which he can serve the community--through
wheelchair visits to patients in hospitals, handiwork to make
and contribute to institutions for others who are handicapped,
telephone soliciting for local United Fund or other charitable
drives, serving on committees where a physical handicap is
no deterrent, making stuffed animals for children of the poor
at Christmas (if fingers are not too arthritic to sew) etc. --
can be supplied by the bibliotherapist herself or through the
books she supplies.   Recreational reading of the relaxing type
can help relieve stress; a feeling of security can only be
achieved through lack of fear and a feeling that people care.
Sometimes the bibliotherapist needs to work with a family or
provide them reading to help them understand their handicapped member better or to give him more affection.

One means of locating the homebound or non-institutionalized handicapped is through the local or state chapter
of the National Easter Seal Society which provides free wheelchairs to many of the crippled, including those in institutions
and homes.

Most handicapped readers who are not institutionalized are partially or wholly dependent upon their local libraries for library service.   Thus it becomes highly important that public libraries make the effort to train at least one staff member with the right personality in at least the rudiments of bibliotherapy techniques.   Obviously, the more training the better.

Katherine Reebel, Professor of Social Work at the University of Michigan, says that any librarian or other professional or lay person attempting to work with the handicapped must ask himself what his reaction to abnormalities of face and figure will be.   When actually confronted with a marked or repulsive facial disfigurement, twitching or shaking limbs, or an uncontrollable drooling often found in Parkinson's Disease, will he betray repulsion, pity, or marked surpise by facial expression or voice?   There are some people who cannot work with one type of disablement but can with another.   Anyone who finds that he has a negative reaction to any disablement or disfigurement has no business attempting bibliotherapy, for he may do more harm than good. The handicapped are especially sensitive to others' attitudes toward them.

When working with the handicapped the bibliotherapist should ask the person what is needed and help him get it-- but only if the person cannot do it for himself.   The main principle of any kind of therapy is to strengthen the individual's abilities to accomplish.   Many a patient who has achieved great independence in a rehabilitation setting reverts to a dependent role at home because the family and others may at first smother him with attention.   Then, when this phase passes, the handicapped individual often feels neglected; his feeling of security is at a low ebb.   At this point the bibliotherapeutically-minded librarian, social worker, rehabilitation counselor, visiting nurse, or friend, by suggesting the right reading and by talking with him, may help him regain the independence he has temporarily lost.   With that independence comes a greater feeling of security.   The tactful therapist may be able to prevent such early over-attention by suggesting appropriate reading for the family before the patient comes home.   If nothing is done, the handicapped person may become depressed and more serious problems arise, the physical disability becoming complicated by emotional disturbances.

For the handicapped person able to come to the library but who needs special help because he cannot reach the

upper drawers of the card catalog or high or low shelves in
the bookstacks, or for a cerebral palsy child who needs a
thicker pencil or a larger card, Reebel suggests that a
special welcome and a readiness to supply the unusual items
or assistance is a necessity.   Quietly supplying the special
help or needs of a handicapped person who comes to the library is subtle bibliotherapy if it makes him feel comfortable
and prevents him from feeling that he is imposing on the time
and patience of the staff.   Either special training in the psychological approach to the handicapped, via workshops or
staff meetings, is needed for all the staff who come in contact with the public, or, if the library is large enough, a
special staff member best able to do bibliotherapy should be
available during most of the hours the library is open.   The
daylight hours are usually more important since persons who
are lame, on crutches, or in wheelchairs are more apt to
come during the day than at night.   The important thing is
for the staff to feel comfortable in working with the handicapped.   Then they in turn will feel comfortable working with
the staff.

The reading of the handicapped is as varied as that of
the general reader except that they may read more books
about people who have surmounted their handicaps to live
successfully.   Even though many activities are barred to
them, they like to read about those activities and share in
them vicariously.   The handicapped can be expected to read
more than the normal reader because they have more free
time and are often lonely.

A recent study by John McCrossan found that the
average homebound reader borrowed from 65 to 70 items
yearly from the public library, considerably more than the
average sighted and ambulatory user.   Many librarians who
work with the handicapped can confirm this heavier usage.
Magazines are particularly popular as a means of keeping up
with current events and because they are light in weight.

A study by Nelson Associates in 1968 of the users of
selected Regional Libraries for the Blind and Physically
Handicapped showed that over half the readers indicated a
strong interest in novels, best sellers, general interest magazines, and current events.   Slightly less than half were interested in 19th and 20th century classic authors, short
stories, biography and history.   A large proportion of the
readers, 43 per cent, were 65 years of age or older.   The
older readers were less likely than younger ones to be in-

terested in instructional or how-to-do-it materials, special
interest magazines, science fiction, or books which give frank
treatment to sex or violent action.   The older readers, mainly
because of their age, were likely to be retired or unemployed
and so had less interest in vocational, technical, or professional reading materials. [1]   These are facts that a good bibliotherapist should keep in mind in selecting material to bring
the homebound.

Table 1

Handicapped Readers Indicating Desire to Read Materials Often[1]

Type of Material	% of Total Readership
Fiction	
Pleasant novels, family stories & light romances	52. 2
Best sellers	51. 7
Outstanding authors of the 19th & 20th centuries	46. 9
Short stories	42. 7
Science fiction, mysteries, & western	35. 3
Books in which sex, violent action, and/or strong language are treated frankly	12. 5
Non-Fiction	
General interest magazines	63. 9
Current events: news, popular culture	57. 4
Biography	45. 3
History	44. 5
Bible, religious reading	40. 6
Animals and nature	34. 5
Science	23. 0
Philosophy, psychology	21. 7
Special interest magazines	21. 2
Music, poetry, performing arts	20. 7
Recreational: hobbies, crafts, sports, games, ham radio	17. 4
Instructional: music, language, public speaking, vocational	17. 0
Collections of essays: political, cultural, economic	14. 0

The Aged

In 1970, over 19 million people in the United States were 65 years of age or older. The total was increasing at over 1,000 a day. Many of these are lonely, have family relationship problems and poor health, and are confined to homes or one-room apartments.

The bibliotherapist who would work with the elderly must first of all have a natural affinity for old age. He must be prepared to make an unhurried approach and spend more time in establishing rapport with individuals. The therapist who can admire pictures of grandchildren carried in wallets or billfolds, listen to reminiscences and repetition without being bored, and be a good listener for almost any topic the older person wants to discuss, will work harmoniously and profitably with older persons. She must be extremely tolerant of the traits of old age, patient, and sensitive to their needs. [2]

Retirement at age 65 or 70 is often a difficult experience, especially for men. Judicious reading and suggestions for retirement activities may smooth the adjustment for those who do not look forward to it. They should also be encouraged to use the public library as a means of further education and creative activity. Librarians in industrial firms often have a good opportunity, through talking with foremen and supervisors, to discover workers who are likely to have a problem on retirement. Although the firm's library collection may be mainly for the research people, supervisors and technical personnel, in many cases the industrial librarian will conduct a few pre-retirement sessions in which she can work both with the group and individual workers to suggest and discuss material that will make retirement easier. Such sessions can also be offered by the local public library. In either case, only books obtainable at the public library should be suggested.

As noted earlier, tape recorded interviews with old-timers who are pioneers in their areas not only provide interesting local history but can help the diminishing ego of an older person who feels he has been "put on the shelf."

Libraries have produced a good many booklists of suggested reading for senior citizens and these will be helpful to bibliotherapist and reader alike. They deal with everything from health and emotional readjustment to hobbies,

recreation, and travel. Separately shelved collections for
senior citizens are sometimes available in public libraries but
are not widely used because many older persons do not like
to be set apart from others.

For senior citizens, particularly those of advanced age,
modern disturbing material may be a mistake.   The familiar
old classics such as Swiss Family Robinson, Robinson Crusoe,
Alice in Wonderland, Treasure Island, etc., may revive pleasant memories if they were read while growing up, and re-
reading them may be a comforting and present pleasure. The
perceptive bibliotherapist, by discussing some of the books
that the person has read in earlier years, will soon find out
what titles strike a responsive chord or bring back pleasant
memories.   The conversation can be brought around to a point
where the individual can be asked frankly what books he enjoyed as a child or young person, and if he would enjoy re-
reading them.   This approach may not be the best for all
elderly persons, particularly those who are ill, but exploring
it can do no harm and may bring constructive results.

Elderly individuals whose eyesight is poor may require
large-print books, in which case the choice of subjects and
titles is limited, and special care and extra time will be required to find just the right book.   The newer type of stand-
ard-sized book is preferable to the large, heavy volumes
which appeared during the first decade of the publication of
large print books.   Some of the earlier type are still being
published, but the variety of titles available in the smaller
format is increasing from month to month.   The large, heavy
volumes may repel older people or those averse to reading,
for they are not only difficult to handle, but their very size
and conspicuousness only makes the fact of poor vision more
painfully apparent to the person and those about him.   This
is a subtle matter, but to some old or sick persons a small
thing may become a major area of sensitivity.

Next to the blacks, the Spanish speaking population
forms the largest minority group in the United States. Their
extraordinarily rich cultural heritage is too often relegated
to the status of "cultural illiteracy" by our own ethnocentric
pride. A child of Spanish-speaking parents rarely has the
comfort and joy of reading a book in his mother tongue.
Soon, this child senses that his language is a second-class
language, says Toni de Gerez, writing in School Library
Journal.   The child feels that it would be best to forget it,
pretend it never existed.   Everyone is trying to Americanize

him. Even his name now seems second class.

This situation can be traumatic. If Miguel is to have
a sense of dignity, security and pride, he must retain the
best of his own culture. The many bilingual books on the
market in the United States can be valuable in helping the
child feel at home in both cultures. Once he is no longer
ashamed of the language he speaks at home, he will move
with pride and dignity toward an understanding of the dominant culture. Here is an opportunity for bibliotherapy, both
preventive and curative. Furnishing the child, even the adult,
with books in Spanish by familiar authors, books to meet their
needs, has definite therapeutic value.

Toni de Gerez, children's librarian in San Miguel de
Allende, prepared an excellent list in 1967, which is repro-
duced at the end of the chapter. As Mexican publishing has
grown in the past few years, more good books will be available. The Centro Mexicano de Escritores, Valle Arizpe no.
18, Mexico, 12, D. F. is both an exporting agency and a
publisher of bibliographic bulletins. Contact them for new
annotated lists, free except for the price of a self-addressed
envelope.

Notes

1. Library of Congress. Division of the Blind and Physically
    Handicapped. A Survey of Reader Characteristics,
    Reading Interests, and Equipment Preferences; A
    Study of Circulation Systems in Selected Regional Li-
    braries. Nelson Associates, Inc., 1969.

2. Brown, Eleanor Frances. Library Service to the Dis-
    advantaged. Metuchen, N.J.: Scarecrow Press, 1971,
    p. 302.

3. de Gerez, Toni. "Books for Miguel." Library Journal,
    v. 92, Dec. 15, 1967, p. 4587-89, 4593.

BOOKS FOR THE SPANISH-SPEAKING CHILD

Please note that both U. S. and foreign publishers are

included in the list below, which samples the range of available Spanish-language materials, and that the prices are given at times in American dollars, and others in terms of Mexican pesos. Since both currencies use the "dollar" sign as a symbol, be careful to note where Mexican prices in pesos are given for books published in Mexico (M), Spain (E), and Argentina (A). For ordering information write to the Centro Mexicano de Escritores.

Dictionaries-Encyclopedias

Daroqui, Julio. Mi Primer Diccionario (My First Dictionary). Buenos Aires, Sigmar, $1. 20 U. S.
Enciclopedia Barsa: De consulta facil (For Easy Reference). Mexico, Encyclopaedia Britannica, 1957. 21v. $3, 820 M.
Enciclopedia de Oro (The Golden Encyclopedia). Mexico, Novaro. 16v. $560 M.
Yo Sé Todo (I Know Everything). Enciclopedia documental en colores (Documentary Encyclopedia in Color). Buenos Aires, Larousse, 1962. 12v. $1400 M.
Mi Libro Encantado (My Fascinating Book). Mexico, Cumbre, 1959. 12v. $1266. 50 M.
Mi Primer Larousse en Colores (My First Larousse in Color). 4000 palabras (words). Buenos Aires, Larousse, 1945. 189p. $3. 90 U. S.

Picture Books-Easy Reading-Bilingual

Aventuras De Una Ardilla (The Adventures of a Squirrel). Chicago, Encyclopaedia Britannica, 1964.
Basurto, Carmen. Mis Primeras Letras (My First Reader). Libro de lectura y escritura para primer año (Book of reading and writing for the first year). Mexico, Trillas, 1963. 63p. $9 M.
Belpré, Pura. Perez y Martina. New York, Frederick Warne, 1966. $2. 95 U. S.
Brunhoff, Jean de. La Infancia de Babar (Babar's Childhood). Barcelona, Ayma. $20 E.
Chispa, El Pequeño Pony (Spark, The Little Pony). Buenos Aires, Sigmar.
El Circo (The Circus). Madrid, Aguilar, 1963. 48p. $90 E.
Las Cosas Que Vemos (The Things That We See). Madrid, Aguilar, 1957. 68p. $80 E.
Dupre, Ramon. Demasiados Perros (Too Many Dogs.)

Chicago, Follet. $1. U. S.

Duvoisin, Roger. El Molinero, Su Hijo y El Borrico (The
    Miller, His Son and the Donkey). New York, Whittlesey
    House, 1962. $2. 50 U. S.

Elkin, Benjamin. El Hombre Que Caminó Alrededor Del
    Mundo (The Man Who Walked Around The World).
    Chicago, Children's Press, 1961. $2. 50 U. S.

El Flautista De Hamelin (The Pied-Piper of Hamelin). Bar-
    celona, Molino, 1961. $16 M.

Freixas, Emilio. Mi Visita Al Zoo (My Visit To The Zoo).
    Barcelona, E. Meseguer, 1963. $11. 50 M.

La Gallinita Roja (The Little Red Hen). Barcelona, Molino,
    1961. $16 M.

Los Gatitos Mellizos (The Little Twin Cats). Buenos Aires,
    Sigmar.

La Llave Magica (The Magic Key). Barcelona, Timun Mas.
    $15 E.

Leaf, Munro. El Cuento De Ferdinando (The Fable of Ferdi-
    nand). New York, Viking, 1936. $2 U. S.

Norma, Carmen. Rosita y Juanito. Libro primero (First
    Book). Mexico, Trillas, 1965. 109p. $9 M.

Ollé, Maria Angeles. Un Renacuajo En La Escuela (A Tad-
    pole in the School). Barcelona, La Galera, 1964.
    $17. 50 M.

Politi, Leo. El Angel De La Calle Olvera (The Angel of
    Olvera Street). New York, Scribner, 1961. $2. 76
    U. S.

Pollitos y Patitos (Chicks and Ducklings). Barcelona, Molino,
    1961. $12 M.

Prieto, Mariano. El Gallo Sabio (The Wise Rooster). New
    York, John Day, 1962. $2. 86 U. S.

Puntita Se Escapó De Casa (Puntita Escaped From Home).
    Barcelona, Timun Mas. $15 E.

Rey, H. A. Jorge El Curioso (Curious George). Boston,
    Houghton Mifflin, 1941. $3. 25 U. S.

Ritchie, Barbara. Los Cambios De Ramon (Ramon's
    Changes). Berkeley, Parnassus, 1959. $3. 25 U. S.

Scarry, Richard. Ver y Leer (See and Read). El libro de
    las palabras y las imagenes (The book of words and
    pictures). Barcelona, Bruguera, 1966. $84. 50 M.

Soler, Carola. El Pajaro De Nieve (The Snow Bird). Madrid,
    Aguilar, 1957. 147p. $25 E.

del Vado, Maria Luz. ¿ Qué Será? (What Shall I Be?). Bar-
    celona, Ramon Sopena, 1961. $7 M.

Vigil, Constancio C. La Escuela De La Señorita Susana
    (Miss Susana's School). Buenos Aires, Atlantida,
    1941. 110p. $100 A.

Watts, Mabel. Esto Para Ti, Esto Para Mi (This Is For
You, This Is For Me). Barcelona, Lumen. $8 E.

Legends-Heroes-Folklore

Berdiales, German. El Alegre Folklórica De Los Niños
(The Gay Folklore of Children). Buenos Aires,
Hachette. $1 U. S.
Campanillitas Folklóricas (Little Bells of Folklore). Decires y
cantares de los niños en Puerto Rico (Tales and songs
of the children of Puerto Rico). Illinois, Laidlaw.
La Canción De Roldan (The Song of Roland). Buenos Aires,
Atlantida. $. 80 U. S.
Casonia, Alejandro. Flor De Leyendas (Flower of Legends).
Madrid, Aguilar, 1959. 154p. $125 E.
Gauchos y Gauchitos (Big and Little Cowboys). Buenos Aires,
Sigmar, 1964. $1. 50 U. S.
Hernandez, Jose. Martin Fierro. Madrid, Aguilar, 1962.
78p. $35 E.
Leyendas Mexicanas (Mexican Legends). Madrid, Aguilar,
1959. 85p. $125 E.
Leyendas Del Rio De La Plata (Legends of the Silver River).
Madrid, Aguilar, 1958. 89p. $125 E.
Morales, Rafael. Leyendas Del Caribe (Caribbean Legends).
Madrid, Aguilar, 1959. 103p. $125 E.
Santa Cruz Osa, B. Cuentos Chilenos (Chilean Stories). San-
tiago, Zig-Zag. $. 50 U. S.
Sapina, Juan Manuel. Leyendas Indigenas Americanas (Native
American Legends). Mexico, Renacimiento, 1965.
114p. $80 M.

Fairy Tales-Classics

Carroll, Lewis. Alicia En El Pais De Las Maravillas (Alice
in Wonderland). Barcelona, Juventud.
Cervantes, Saavedra, Miguel de. Don Quixote De La Mancha
(Don Quixote of La Mancha). Buenos Aires, Sigmar.
Cuentos De Andersen (Stories of Andersen). Mexico, Renaci-
miento.
Fabulas De La Fontaine (Fables of La Fontaine). Mexico,
Renacimiento, 1959. 142p.
Jimenez, Juan Ramon. Platero y Yo (The Silversmith and
I). Madrid, Aguilar, 1963. 157p.
Perrault, Charles. La Bella Durmiente Del Bosque. (The
Beautiful Dreamer of the Forest). Barcelona, Ed. Cer-
vantes.

El Lazarillo De Tormes (The Blindman's Guide of Tormes).
    Madrid, Aguilar, 1961. 85p.
El Poema Del Cid (The Poem of the Cid). Madrid, Aguilar,
    1961. 102p.
Pulgarcito y Otros Cuentos (Little Thumb and Other Stories).
    Mexico, Renacimiento.

Biography

Diaz-Plaja, Aurora. El Doctor Schweitzer (Doctor Schweitz-
    er). Barcelona, Juventud.
Espina, Antonio. Carlomagno (Charlemagne). Madrid,
    Aguilar.
José Marti (Joseph Marti). Buenos Aires, Biblioteca Billi-
    ken, Atlantida.
Mallorqui, José. Cristobal Colon (Christopher Columbus).
    Barcelona, Molino.
Murray, Jean. El Juramiento De Davy Crockett (Davy
    Crockett's Vow). Buenos Aires, Kapelusz.
Ronda Gonzalez, Marisa. Santa Teresita Del Niño Jesus
    (Saint Teresa of the Child Jesus). Bilbao, Cantabrica,
    1963. 26p. $17.40 M.
Sarmiento. Buenos Aires, Biblioteca Billiken, Atlantida.
Simon Bolivar. Buenos Aires, Biblioteca Billiken, Atlantida.

Science-Nature

Binder, Otto. La Luna: Nuestra Vecina Mas Cercana (The
    Moon: Our Closest Neighbor). Mexico, Novarro, 1965.
    54p.
Herrera, José Luis. El Libro Del Desierto (The Book of the
    Desert). Madrid, Aguilar.
Jiminez-Landi, Antonio. El Libro Del Mar (The Book of the
    Sea). Madrid, Aguilar, 1960. 99p.
Korn, Jerry. Atomos: El Corazon de Toda la Materia
    (Atoms: The core of all matter). Mexico, Novarro,
    1965. 54p.
May, Julian. En El Mundo De Los Cohetes (In The World of
    Rockets). Mexico, Herrero Hermanos.

Stories

Alcott, Louisa. Mujercitas (Little Women). Buenos Aires,
    Peuser, $180 A.

Denneborg, Heinrich Maria. La Burrita Grisela (Grisela,
    The Donkey). Barcelona, Molino.
Fortun, Elena. Celia Madrecita (Little Mother Celia). Madrid,
    Aguilar, 1953. 208p. $80 E.
Fortun, Elena. Matonkiki Y Sus Hermanos (Matonkiki and
    His Brothers). Madrid, Aguilar, 1957.
Ibarbourou, Juanade. Chico Carlo (Little Carlo). Buenos
    Aires, Kapelusz.
Ionesco, Angela. De Un Pais Lejano (From A Distant
    Country). Madrid, Doncel, 1962. 144p. $80 E.
Kurtz, Carmen. Color De Fuego (The Color of Fire).
    Madrid, Cid.
Lawson, Robert. La Colina De Los Conejos (The Rabbit
    Hill). Buenos Aires, Kapelusz.
Saint-Exupery, Antoine de. El Principito (The Little Prince).
    Mexico, Fernandez 1964. 85p.
Sanchez Coquillat, Maria M. Un Castillo En El Camino (A
    Castle On The Road). Barcelona, Juventud.
Sucksdorff, Astrid Bergman. Chendru y Su Amigo El Tigre
    (Chendru and His Friend the Tiger). Barcelona,
    Timun Mas, 1964. $170 E.

Reprinted from School Library Journal, December, 1967,
published by R. R. Bowker, copyright, 1967.

SUGGESTED READING
PHYSICAL HANDICAPS

JUVENILE AND ADOLESCENT

Amputation

Viscardi, Henry. A Man's Stature. John Day, 1952. A
    congenitally deformed boy conquers his disability.
    Ages 12-16.

Asthma

Norris, Gunilla B. The Top Step. Atheneum, 1970. Ages
    8-12.

Blindness and Impaired Vision

Aldis, Dorothy. Dark Summer. Putnam, 1947. Girl is
    forced to spend summer vacation indoors with band-
    aged eyes but overcomes her fears and disappointment.
Bawden, Nina. The Witch's Daughter. Lippincott, 1966.
    Ages 8-12.
Bjarnhof, Karl. The Good Light. Knopf, 1960. A partially
    sighted boy gradually becomes blind but transcends his
    handicaps.
Brown, Marion. The Silent Storm. Abingdon Press, 1963.
    Story of Helen Keller, her trials and triumphs. Ages
    12 up.
Chipperfield, Joseph. A Dog to Trust. David McKay, 1964.
    A blind boy's friends help him adjust to his handicap.
    Ages 10-15.
Clewes, Dorothy. Guide Dog. Coward, 1965. Ages 8-12.
Dahl, Borghild. Finding My Way. E. P. Dutton, 1962. A
    woman's trust in God and self-reliance help her to
    live with blindness. Ages 12-18.
Ericsson, Mary. About Glasses for Gladys. Melmont Pub-
    lishers, 1962. Gladys learns to adjust to impaired
    vision.
Garfield, James B. Follow My Leader. Viking, 1957.
    Ages 8-12.
Griffiths, Helen. Wild Horse of Santander. Doubleday, 1970.
    Ages 12 up.
Hunter, Edith. Child of the Silent Night. Houghton Mifflin,
    1963. Story of a deaf and blind girl and how she
    learned to talk. Ages 12 up.
Rau, Margaret. Dawn from the West: The Story of Genevieve
    Caulfield. Hawthorne Books, 1964. Woman who was
    blinded as an infant adjusted to her handicap and spent
    her life in helping others with the same affliction.
    Ages 8-12.
Russell, Robert. To Catch An Angel: Adventures in the
    World I Cannot See. Vanguard, 1962.
    Autobiography of how a boy blinded at the age of five
    managed to live a full and meaningful life. Ages 12
    up.
Vance, Marguerite. Windows for Rosemary. Dutton, 1956.
    Ages 8-12.
Whitney, Phyllis. Secret of the Emerald Star. Westminster
    Press, 1964. A mystery which helps develop respect
    for, and understanding of, a blind girl and of others
    of different races, religions, and socioeconomic levels.
    Ages 12 up.

Wilder, Laura Ingalls. By the Shores of Silver Lake. Hale,
    1939. Ages 8-12.
Witheridge, Elizabeth. Dead End Bluff. Atheneum, 1966.
    A boy proves that being blind doesn't keep one from
    having courage and ability. Ages 8-12.

Cerebral Palsy

Killilea, Marie. Karen. Prentice-Hall, 1952. Ages 12 up.
Killilea, Marie. With Love from Karen. Prentice-Hall,
    1962. Karen and her family fight a courageous battle
    against cerebral palsy which threatens Karen's ability
    to live a satisfying life. Ages 12 up.
Little, Jean. Mine for Keeps. Little, Brown, 1962. Girl
    learns to adjust to cerebral palsy by developing a
    helpful attitude. Ages 8-12.
Newfeld, John. Touching. Phillips, 1970. Ages 12 up.

Crippled

De Angeli, Marguerite. The Door in the Wall. Doubleday,
    1949. Ages 8-12.
Forbes, Esther. Johnny Tremain. Houghton Mifflin, 1943.
    A boy with overbearing pride suffers from a crippled
    hand, then learns something of humility, loyalty, and
    idealism and makes a contribution to the American
    Revolution. Ages 12 up.
Savitz, Harriet M. Fly, Wheels, Fly. John Day, 1970.
    Paraplegic. Ages 12 up.
Southall, Ivan. Let the Balloon Go. St. Martin's, 1968.
    Ages 12 up.

Deafness and Hearing Deficiencies

Caudill, Rebecca. A Certain Small Shepherd. Holt, 1965.
    Ages 8-12. Deafness.
Montgomery, Elizabeth. Alexander Graham Bell. Garrard
    Publishing Co., 1963. Story of the invention of the
    telephone, an account which offers encouragement to
    deaf children. Ages 8-12.
Robinson, Veronica. David in Silence. Lippincott, 1965.
    About a brave deaf boy. Ages 8-12.
Ronnei, Eleanor, and Porter, Joan. Tim and his Hearing
    Aid. Dodd, Mead, 1951. A small boy overcomes the
    difficult period of adjustment to a hearing aid. Ages
    7-12.
Waite, Helen. Make a Joyful Sound. Macrae Smith. Story

of Alexander Graham Bell and his deaf wife.   Ages
10-16.
Wojciechowska, Maria.   A Single Light.   Harper, 1968.
Ages 12 up.

Handicaps, General

Allen, Mel, and Graham, Frank Jr.   It Takes Heart.   Harper
and Row, 1959.   The stories of a number of athletes
who overcame handicaps to become champions.   Ages
12 up.
Burnett, Frances.   The Secret Garden.   J. B. Lippincott,
1962.   A story of how one handicapped shut-in found
happiness.   Ages 8-12.
Gelfand, Regina and Patterson, Letha.   They Wouldn't Quit.
Lerner Publications, 1962.   Brief biographies of 14
people who achieved their goals in spite of their handicaps.   Ages 8-12.
Little, Jean.   Mine for Keeps.   Little, 1962.   Ages 8-12.
Miller, Floyd.   The Electrical Genius of Liberty Hall:
Charles Proteus Steinmetz.   McGraw-Hill Book Co.,
1962.   The story of the hunchbacked mathematical
genius who helped develop the electrical industry in
America.
Montgomery, Elizabeth.   Tide Treasure Camper.   Ives Washburn, 1963.   Betsy learns that it is better to face up
to one's handicap and not try to conceal it from others.
Ages 8-12.
Patchett, Mary.   The Proud Eagles.   World, 1961.   The
story of a crippled child in Australia and how he
raised an eagle and trained it for falconry.   Ages 12
up.
Splaver, Sarah.   Your Handicap--Don't Let it Handicap You.
Julian Messner, 1967.   Information which focuses upon
the opportunities and abilities rather than the disabilities of handicapped students.   Ages 12 up.

Mute Child

Cunningham, Julia.   Burnish Me Bright.   Pantheon, 1970.
Ages 8-12.
Henry, Marguerite.   King of the Wind.   Rand, n. d. Ages 8-12.

Poliomyelitis

Armer, Alberta.   Screwball.   World, 1963.   Mike, who has been
crippled by polio, avoids facing up to his problems until

he finds an absorbing interest which changes him. Ages
12-16.

Beim, Lorraine. Triumph Clear. Harcourt, 1946. Polio.
Ages 12 up.

Berry, Erick. Green Door to the Sea. Viking, 1955. A
16-year-old girl learns to be useful in spite of polio.
Ages 12-16.

Bothwell, Jean. The Mystery Gatepost. Dial, 1964. A
mystery story which also illustrates how one boy overcame the effects of polio. Ages 8-12.

Chaput, Richard. Not to Doubt. Pageant Press, 1964. Autobiography of a person stricken with polio at the age of
nine and of his struggles to lead a meaningful life although he is paralyzed from the neck down and dependent upon an iron lung. Ages 12 up.

Christopher, Matthew F. Sink It, Rusty. Little, Brown,
1963. A story of how one boy adjusted to polio. Ages
8-12.

Kriegel, Leonard. The Long Walk Home. Appleton-Century-
Crofts, 1964. Autobiographical memoir of a 20-year
struggle with polio which began at 11 years of age.
Ages 12 up.

Poverty and Cultural Deprivation

Angelo, Valenti. Look Out Yonder. Viking Press, 1943.
Story of a poverty-stricken family and their struggles
to own a farm.

Burch, Robert. Tyler, Wilken and Skee. Viking Press, 1963.
Three boys grow up on a farm in Georgia and have
fun in spite of the Depression.

Estes, Eleanor. The Hundred Dresses. Harcourt, Brace,
and World, 1944. A story of an immigrant girl who
was teased for wearing the same dress.

Estes, Eleanor. The Moffats. Harcourt, Brace, and World,
1941. A story of how one poor family still had fun
and family unity.

Lenski, Lois. Strawberry Girl. Lippincott, 1945. A story
of one family's attempt to overcome poverty in the
early 1900's.

Seredy, Kate. A Tree for Peter. Viking Press, 1941. The
story of how a poverty-stricken little boy overcame
his fears and shyness.

Speech Defects

Cunningham, Julia. Burnish me Bright. Pantheon, 1970.
Story of a mute child. Ages 8-12.

Henry, Marguerite. <u>King of the Wind.</u> Rand McNally, 1948.
Story of an Arabian stallion that founded a new line of
thoroughbreds, and of his mute but devoted and loyal
stable boy. Ages 8-14.

Lee, Mildred. <u>The Skating Rink.</u> Seabury, 1969. Speech
impediment. Ages 12 up.

Lowery, Bruce. <u>Scarred.</u> Vanguard, 1961. Jeff is sub-
jected to adolescent cruelty because of a cleft lip scar.
Ages 12 up.

ADULT AND ADOLESCENT

Amputation

Tribelhorn, Joan. <u>The Challenge and the Triumph.</u> Cape
Town, South Africa: Tafelberg Publishers, 1962. A
true account of how one woman overcame the loss of
a leg.

Viscardi, Henry Jr. <u>A Letter to Jimmy.</u> Eriksson-Tap-
linger, 1962. A book of encouragement and hope to
the disabled written by a man who succeeded in life
in spite of the fact that he was born legless.

Blindness and Impaired Vision

Austin, Alex. <u>The Blue Guitar.</u> Fell, 1965.

Barnes, Eric S. <u>The Man Who Lived Twice: The Biography
of Edward Sheldon.</u> Scribners, 1956. A playwright
who becomes physically helpless due to arthritis and
blindness remains at the center of theatrical life.

Bigman, Sidney. <u>Second Sight.</u> David McKay, 1959. A
story of one man's reaction and adjustment to blindness.

Blackhall, David S. <u>This House Had Windows.</u> Ivan Obo-
lensky, 1962. True story of a poet's blindness and
of the struggles he faces.

Caulfield, Genevieve. <u>The Kingdom Within.</u> Harper and Row,
1960. Story of a blind woman who established schools
for the blind in Japan and Thailand.

Chevigny, Hector. <u>My Eyes Have a Cold Nose.</u> Yale University Press, 1946. Story of how a writer for radio
met and surmounted many of the problems caused by
blindness.

Clifton, Bernice. <u>None so Blind.</u> Rand McNally, 1962.
Story of how a female designer-decorator fights against
resentment and meets the challenge of life after sud-

denly becoming blind.

Crawford, Fred. Career Planning for the Blind: A Manual
for Students and Teachers. Farrar, Straus and
Giroux, 1966. A book for students and teachers to
provide vocational guidance for the blind.

Kelley, William Melvin. A Drop of Patience. Doubleday,
1965. Blindness and minority group status.

Moore, Virginia. Seeing-Eye Wife. Chilton Co., 1960. An
autobiography of a woman who married a blind man,
an account which should help dispel many common misconceptions of the blind.

Yates, Elizabeth. The Lighted Heart. E. P. Dutton, 1960.
Story of how one couple adjusted to a peaceful New
England life to meet the problems caused by the hus-
band's blindness.

Cerebral Palsy

Dornfeld, Iris. Jeeney Ray. Viking Press, 1962. A novel
about the struggles of an adolescent spastic girl.

Freeland, S. P. Dear Ann. Johannesburg, South Africa
Central News Agency, 1962. A missionary describes
the growth and development of a cerebral palsied
daughter.

Miers, Earl. The Trouble Bush. Rand McNally, 1966. An
autobiography of a man who has lived a meaningful
and productive life in spite of cerebral palsy.

Deafness and Hearing Deficiency

Bender, Ruth. The Conquest of Deafness. Western Reserve
University Press, 1960. A history of the struggle to
enable persons with a hearing problem to lead normal
lives.

Bloom, Freddie. Our Deaf Children. London: Wm. Heine-
mann Ltd., 1963. A mother relates her experiences
with her deaf child and gives practical suggestions to
others.

Boatner, Maxine. Voice of the Deaf. Public Affairs Press,
1959. Biography of Eduard Gallaudet.

Dale, D. M. C. Deaf Children at Home and at School.
Chas. C. Thomas, 1967. Suggestions to parents and
teachers on how to provide for the needs of deaf
children.

Davis, Hallowell, and Silverman, S. Richard. Hearing and
Deafness. Holt, Rinehart and Winston, 1960. Expla-
nations of causes of deafness, ways of improving

hearing, and answers to many other questions.
Field, Rachel. And Now Tomorrow. Macmillan, 1942.
    Emily, who is pitied because of her deafness, finds
    her loyalties divided during a threatened labor strike.
Van Itallie, Philip H. How to Live with a Hearing Handicap.
    Paul S. Eriksson, 1963. Inspiration for the hard of
    hearing.
Warfield, Frances. Cotton in My Ears. Viking, 1948. An
    account of the author's attempts to conceal her hearing
    difficulty before she finally decides to wear a hearing
    aid.
Warfield, Frances. Keep Listening. Viking Press, 1957.
    The story of the author's struggle against deafness.
Wright, Anna. Land of Silence. Friendship Press, 1962.
    A description of the problems faced by the deaf and
    how they may be helped.

Handicaps, General

Arthur, Julietta. Employment for the Handicapped. Abingdon
    Press, 1967. A valuable discussion of the factors
    which the handicapped person should weigh when con-
    sidering job application, training, and type of employ-
    ment plus references to further sources of information.
Dishman, Pat. Ten Who Overcame. Broadman Press, 1966.
    An account of ten physically handicapped persons and
    the part that religion played in helping them achieve
    their goals in spite of their disabilities.
Eckhardt, Elizabeth, et al. Homemaking for the Handicapped.
    Dodd, Mead, 1967. Practical suggestions to the dis-
    abled homemaker.
Fabricant, Noah D. 13 Famous Patients. Chilton, 1960.
    Biographical sketch of 13 famous patients, including
    Franklin Roosevelt.
Fraser, Ian, ed. Conquest of Disability. St. Martin's Press,
    1956. Biographies of how persons have learned to
    cope with various disabilities.
Garrett, James F., and Levine, Edna, eds. Psychological
    Practices with the Physically Disabled. Columbia
    Univ. Press, 1962. Deals with the incidence, psy-
    chological aspects, and rehabilitation of a variety of
    disabilities.
Greenberg, Joanne. The Monday Voices. Holt, Rinehart and
    Winston, 1965. A realistic portrayal of the problems
    and satisfactions of a vocational rehabilitation counselor.
Henrich, Edith and Kriegel, Leonard. Experiments in Sur-
    vival. Association for the Aid of Crippled Children,

1961. A collection of 33 essays about persons with a
wide variety of handicaps.

Hunt, Paul. Stigma: the Experience of Disability. Prentice-
Hall, 1966. A collection of essays written by 12 victims of various handicaps about their experiences and
social status.

Knowles, John. A Separate Peace. The Macmillan Co.,
1959. Two roommates come to an understanding of
themselves and others after one cripples the other.

Maugham, W. Somerset. Of Human Bondage. 1915. Handicapped child.

May, Elizabeth, et al. Homemaking for the Handicapped.
Dodd, Mead, 1966. Guidebook in home management
for the physically handicapped.

Musgrave, Florence. Merrie's Miracle. Hastings House,
1959. An account of some of the victims of the blast
and radiation burns in Hiroshima.

Plumb, Beatrice. Edgar James Helms, the Goodwill Man.
Story of how a young minister conceived and developed
the plan for Goodwill Industries.

Scully, Frank. Cross My Heart. Greenberg Publishers, 1955.
A breezy autobiography of a 60-year-old man who has
spent most of his life as an invalid.

Veterans Administration. To Work Again--To Live Again.
Supt. of Documents, U. S. Government Printing Office,
1965. True accounts of 206 severely handicapped,
homebound men who become home earners in a wide
variety of occupations.

Viscardi, Henry, Jr. A Laughter in the Lonely Night.
Erikson-Taplinger, 1961. The true story of how 15
crippled persons set out to prove their value to themselves and to the world.

Warshofsky, Fred. The Rebuilt Man: the Story of Spare-
Parts Surgery. Thomas Y. Crowell, 1965. A history
of organ and tissue transfer.

Zehnpfennig, Gladys. Charles F. Kettering, Inventor and
Idealist. T. S. Denison, 1963. Biography of a remarkable inventor who achieved in spite of his physical
handicap.

Paralysis

Hodgins, Eric. Episode. Atheneum, 1964. The author tells
of his struggles to regain voice and muscular control
following a stroke.

Kenney, Lona. A Caste of Heroes. Dodd, Mead, 1966. A
novel concerning the rehabilitation of paraplegics in a
veteran's hospital.

Nolan, Alan T. As Sounding Brass. Houghton Mifflin, 1964.
A 19-year-old boy, who is accidentally shot by the
police and made a paraplegic, struggles to regain his
morale and to find a charity organization that will
finance his desperately needed surgery.
Ritchie, Douglas. Stroke. Doubleday, 1961. A stroke patient
writes of his struggles with asphasia and of the assistance he received from his speech therapist.
Valens, Evans G. A Long Way Up: the Story of Jill Kinmont.
Harper & Row, 1966. The biography of an expert who
becomes a quadriplegic and of her struggles to rebuild
her life.
Wilson, Dorothy. Handicap Race. McGraw-Hill, 1967. A
young track star became a paraplegic and not only lived a
full and productive life but helped others to do so.
Wilson, Dorothy. Take My Hands. McGraw-Hill, 1963. A
biography of how a woman surgeon reconstructed her
life after she became a paraplegic.

Poliomyelitis

Chappell, Eleanor. On the Shoulders of Giants. Chilton,
1960. An account of one woman's struggle and eventual
victory over polio.
Gould, Jean. A Good Fight. Dodd, Mead, 1960. How
Franklin D. Roosevelt conquered polio.
Kingery, Kenneth. As I Live and Breathe. Grosset and Dunlap, 1966. Autobiography of one man's heroic struggles against the effects of polio.
Peare, Catherine. The FDR Story. Thomas Y. Crowell,
1962. Story of President Roosevelt's struggle against
polio, the depression, and international conflicts.

Poverty and Cultural Deprivation

Adams, Jane. Twenty Years at Hull House. Macmillan, 1910.
An account by its founder of the first 20 years of Hull
House, a refuge for the poor and handicapped.
Bagdikian, B. H. In the Midst of Plenty. New American,
1964. The poor in an affluent society.
Ferman, Louis, editor. Poverty in America: A Book of
Readings. University of Michigan, 1965. A collection
of articles on the effects of poverty written by pro-
fessionals from various disciplines.
Levenson, Sam. Everything but Money. Simon and Schuster,
1966. A delightful account of a slum family and how
they managed to be very happy in spite of poverty and

to eventually obtain material success as well. Biography.

Smith, Betty. A Tree Grows in Brooklyn. Harper and Row,
1947. A description of life in a Brooklyn tenement in
the early 1900's. Fiction.

Steinbeck, John. The Grapes of Wrath. Viking Press, 1939.
The story of an itinerant agricultural worker and his
family and the conditions of poverty they endured.

Retirement and the Problems of the Elderly

Bromley, Dennis. The Psychology of Human Aging. Penguin
Books, 1966. Suggestions to the layman and student,
and those directly involved with older persons.

Buckley, Joseph. The Retirement Handbook. Harper and Row.
Latest edition. Suggestions to the retired on how to
lead a richer and fuller life.

Cagan, Maxwell. There's Gold in Your Golden Age. T. S.
Denison, 1963. Suggestions to older citizens on how
to enrich their later years.

Carp, Frances. A Future for the Aged. Univ. of Texas
Press, 1966. A study of the physical and psychological
effects of housing conditions upon the elderly.

Comfort, Alex. The Process of Aging. New American Library, 1964. A discussion of the aging process written
in layman's language.

Cormier, Robert. Take Me Where the Good Times Are.
Macmillan, 1965. Care for the aged and need for entertainment.

Donoso, Jose. Coronation. Knopf, 1965. An aged invalid
and the mental health of the family.

Gray, Robert and Moberg, David. The Church and the Older
Person. Wm. B. Eerdmans Publishing Co. , 1962.
Suggestions on how the church and older persons can
work together for the mutual benefit of both.

Hemingway, Ernest. The Old Man and the Sea. Scribner's,
1952. Courage in old age. fiction.

Llewellyn, Richard. How Green Was My Valley. 1940. The
aged remember.

Merrill, Toni. Activities for the Aged and Infirm: A Handbook for the Worker. Charles C. Thomas, 1967. A
how-to-do-it manual containing explicit directions for
various types of activities.

Roulston, Marjorie. Live Alone and Like It. Doubleday, 1967.
Suggestions to women past 60 on how they may lead a
full and useful life.

Tanizaki, Junichiro. Diary of a Mad Old Man. Knopf, 1965.

Rich old man and the gold-digger.

Speech Defects

Holdsworth, W. G. Cleft Lip and Palate. Grune and Stratton, 1963. A discussion of the function and development of cleft lip accompanied by clear, self-explanatory
   illustrations and case records.
Johnson, Wendell. Stuttering and What You Can Do About It.
   University of Minnesota Press, 1961. Suggestions to
   adult stutterers and to the parents of child stutterers.
Palmer, Charles. Speech and Hearing Problems. Chas. S.
   Thomas 1961. Professional information addressed to
   the lay public.
Van Riper, Charles. Your Child's Speech Problems. Harper,
   1961. A helpful book when counseling parents of
   children with speech problems.

RACIAL AND ETHNIC PROBLEMS

JUVENILE AND ADOLESCENT

Archibald, Joe. Outfield Orphan. Macrae Smith, 1961. A
   story of baseball and a Negro boy's growth to maturity.
   Ages 10-15.
Arora, Shirley. What Then, Raman? Follett, 1960. Ages
   8-12.
Bannon, Laura. The Other Side of the World. Houghton
   Mifflin, 1960. An American boy and a Japanese boy
   learn about each other and discover that each has
   strange ways of living. Ages 5-8.
Barrett, William. Lilies of the Field. Doubleday, 1962.
   Story of how a young Negro veteran helped a group of
   nuns build a chapel. Ages 12 up.
Bates, Daisy. The Long Shadow of Little Rock. David
   McKay, 1962. A description of the problems faced by
   the first Negroes who attempted to enroll in Little
   Rock's Central High School. Ages 16 up.
Black Star Editors and Photographers. To Do Justice.
   Pyramid Publications, 1965. An account of a number
   of Negroes and whites who have struggled to obtain
   equal rights for everyone. Ages 16 up.
Borland, Hal. When the Legends Die. Lippincott, 1963.

A Ute Indian finds himself rejected by both the whites
and his own people. Ages 12 up.

Brodsky, Mimi. The House at 12 Rose Street. Abelard-
Schuman, 1966. A Negro boy and his family struggle
to win acceptance in a white neighborhood. Ages 8-12.

Brown, Jimmy, and Cope, Myron. Off My Chest. Doubleday, 1964. Story of the famous Negro football player
and some of the problems that he had to overcome.
Ages 16 up.

Cavanna, Betty. A Time for Tenderness. Wm. Morrow,
1962. Peggy falls in love with a Brazilian boy and
they face the problems of adjusting to diverse cultures
and backgrounds. Ages 12 up.

Chandler, Ruth. Ladder To the Sky. Abelard-Schuman, 1965.
Chip faces the usual problems of a seventh-grade boy
but he has an additional one--he is a Negro.

Chow, Chung-Cheng. The Lotus Pool. Appleton-Century-
Crofts, 1961. A Chinese girl is forced to fight tradi-
tion and her family in her quest for an education.
Ages 12-16.

Christopher, Matthew F. Baseball Flyhawk. Little, Brown,
1963. Chico finally learns that it is not the fact that
he is a Puerto Rican that is causing his lack of acceptance by others. Ages 5-8.

Cieciorka, Bobbi and Frank. Negroes in American History:
a Freedom Primer. Student Voice, Inc., 1965. A
collection of accounts of famous Negroes since the
American Revolution. Ages 8-12.

Franklin, John. Three Negro Classics: Up from Slavery: the
Souls of Black Folk; the Autobiography of an Ex-
Coloured Man. Avon Book Division, 1965. Three
important Negro classics in one volume. Ages 16 up.

Gregory, Dick. From the Back of the Bus. Avon Book Division, 1966. Humor which contains a large amount
of thought concerning contemporary social issues.
Ages 12-16.

Gregory, Dick. What's Happening. Dutton, 1965. A photographic and gag book with a number of funny take-offs
on recent national events. Ages 12-16.

Griffin, John H. Black Like Me. New American Library,
1961. Story of a white man's account of what it is
like to live as a Negro in the South. Ages 16 up.

Guy, Anne. William. Dial Press, 1961. A fifth-grade Negro
boy faces the problems encountered in a newly integrated school. Ages 8-12.

Haugaard, Kay. Myeko's Gift. Abelard, 1966. Ages 8-12.

Hoffine, Lyla. Jennie's Mandan Bowl. McKay, 1960. Jennie

learns to appreciate her Indian ancestry when she learns more about it. Ages 8-12.

Hughes, Langston, and Meltzer, Milton. A Pictorial History of the Negro in America. Crown, 1966. A history of the Negro which should help the Negro reader to identify with and take pride in his race. Ages 12 up.

Justus, May. New Boy in School. Hastings House, 1963. A Negro boy faces the problems of adjusting to an integrated school. Ages 8-12.

Kim-Young-ik. Blue in the Seed. Little, Brown, 1964. A young Korean boy is discriminated against because of his blue eyes which he inherited from his mother. Ages 8-12.

Lexau, Joan. I Should Have Stayed in Bed! Harper & Row, 1965. Sam and Albert develop a friendship in an integrated school. Ages 5-8.

Lincoln, C. Eric. My Face Is Black. Beacon Press, 1965. An explanation by a sociologist of the feelings experienced by the American Negro of today. Ages 16 up.

Lovelace, Maude. The Valentine Box. Crowell, 1966. A little Negro girl finds a new friend and a valentine upon moving to the suburbs. Ages 8-12.

Low. Alice. Kallie's Corner. Pantheon, 1966. Two city girls from contrasting socio-economic backgrounds learn to get along with each other. Ages 8-12.

McKone, Jim. Lone Star Fullback. Vanguard, 1966. A Negro football player wins acceptance in a Texas high school and community. Ages 12-16.

Mather, Melissa. One Summer in Between. Harper & Row, 1967. Story of how a southern Negro girl who spends a summer with a northern white family gradually changes her perceptions. Ages 12 up.

Meltzer, Milton. In Their Own Words. Crowell. Vol. 1, 1619-1865, 1964; Vol. II, 1865-1916, 1965. A history of the Negro in America. Ages 10-15.

Montagu, Ashley. Man's Most Dangerous Myth: the Fallacy of Race. Meridian Books, 1965. A classic which dispels the myth of superior and inferior races. Ages 16 up.

Mulzac, Hugh. A Star to Steer By. International Publishers Co., 1963. Autobiography of the first Negro to become the commander of his own ship. Ages 10-15.

Neville, Emily. Berries Goodman. Harper, 1965. Ages 8-12.

New York Board of Education. The Negro in American History. New York Board of Education, 1964. Short sketch of the Negro's position in American history. Ages 12 up.

Newell, Hope. A Cap for Mary Ellis. Harper & Row, 1963.
Negro girl faces the responsibility of increasing the
acceptance of her race. Ages 10-15.

Oterdahl, Jeanna. Tina and the Latchkey Child. Macmillan,
1963. Tina becomes friends with an underprivileged
child and increases her understanding and acceptance
of those who are different. Ages 5-8.

Parks, Gordon. A Choice of Weapons. Harper & Row, 1966.
Story of how a Negro photographer overcame prejudice
and poverty. Ages 12 up.

Patterson, Lillie. Booker T. Washington: Leader of His
People. Garrard, 1962. Story of a slave boy who
grew up to become president of Tuskegee Institute.
Ages 8-12.

Patterson, Lillie. Frederick Douglass. Garrard, 1965.
Story of a slave who becomes a leader of his people.
Ages 5-8.

Porter, C. Fayne. Our Indian Heritage: Profiles of Twelve
Great Leaders. Chilton, 1964. Biographical stories
of interesting but not widely known facts concerning 12
famous American Indians. Ages 12 up.

Quarles, Benjamin. The Negro in the Making of America.
Collier, 1964. An account of Negro influences and
contributions to the American way of life. Ages 16 up.

Redding, J. Saunders. On Being Negro in America. Bobbs-
Merrill, 1962. A Negro describes the frustrations
and humiliation of being treated as a second-class
citizen. Ages 16 up.

Robinson, Jackie. Breakthrough to the Big League. Harper
& Row, 1965. Story of the problems faced by the
first Negro who played major league baseball. Ages
10-15.

Rodman, Bella. Lions in the Way. Follett, 1967. Fic-
tional account of the desegregation of a southern
school. Ages 10-15.

Rose, Peter. They and We. Random House, 1965. A study
of racial discrimination and prejudice. Ages 12 up.

Rydberg, Ervie. The Dark of the Cave. McKay, 1965. When
the cataracts are removed from his eyes, Ronnie dis-
covers that his best friend is a Negro who is not very
well accepted. Ages 8-12.

Sachs, Marilyn. Peter and Veronica. Doubleday, 1969.
Ethnic differences and prejudice. Ages 8-12.

Seuberlich, Hertha. Annuzza, a Girl of Romania. Rand
McNally, 1962. Account of a class-divided society
where one has little chance of changing his original
station in life. Ages 10-15.

Snyder, Zilpha K. The Egypt Game. Atheneum, 1967. Ethnic
    differences and prejudice. Ages 12 up.
Sommerfelt, Aimee. Miriam. Criterion Books, 1963. Story
    of the persecution of the Norwegian Jews during the
    German occupation of that country. Age 16 up.
Sterling, Dorothy, and Quarles, Benjamin. Lift Every Voice.
    Doubleday, 1965. An account of the lives of four
    famous Negroes. Ages 10-15.
Sterling, Philip, and Logan, Rayford. Four Took Freedom.
    Doubleday, 1967. Life stories of four Negroes born
    into slavery who became famous. Ages 10-15.
Stevenson, Janet. Singing for the World: Marian Anderson.
    Encyclopaedia Britannica, 1963. Through hard work
    Marian Anderson overcomes many problems, including
    social injustice, to make her dreams come true. Ages
    10-15.
Warren, Mary. Walk in My Moccasins. Westminster, 1966.
    A young Sioux girl learns that other children have
    problems, too. Ages 10-15.
Wier, Ester. The Rumptydoolers. Vanguard, 1964. Boy
    learns to appreciate others even if their backgrounds
    are different. Ages 10-15.
Wish, Harvey, ed. The Negro Since Emancipation. Prentice-
    Hall, 1964. Anthology of selections by a number of
    famous Negroes. Ages 16 up.

ADULT

Baldwin, James. The Fire Next Time. Dial Press, 1963.
    A Negro discusses the racial crisis in our country.
Baldwin, James. Notes of a Native Son. Dial Press, 1963.
    A Negro writer searches for identity abroad and in
    America.
Bassani, Giorgio. The Garden of the Finzi-Continis. Athe-
    neum, 1965. A young Jewish couple in love experience
    prejudice and indignities in Fascist Italy.
Belfrage, Sally. Freedom Summer. Viking, 1965. An
    account of the activities of various groups working for
    civil rights in Mississippi plus a discussion of the
    merits of violence and non-violence.
Bontemps, Arna. American Negro Poetry. Hill and Wang,
    1964. An anthology of American Negro poetry.
Boyle, Sarah. The Desegregated Heart. Wm. Morrow, 1962.
    The story of a southern white woman's crusade for
    civil rights.
Brown, C. Manchild in the Promised Land. New American

Library, 1966.   Story of a Negro growing up in Harlem during the 40's and 50's.

Carroll, Ted.   White Pills: a Novel.   Crown, 1965.   Crossing the color line.

Clark, Kenneth.   Prejudice and Your Child.   Beacon Press, 1963.   An explanation of the detrimental effects that racial prejudice has upon children.

Coles, Robert.   Children of Crisis.   Little, Brown, 1967. A study of the fear and tension in Negro children during racial strife in the South.

Duberman, Martin B.   In White America.   New American Library, 1964.   The text of a play depicting discrimination against the Negro in America.

Evers, Mrs. Megar.   For Us, the Living.   Doubleday, 1967. A biography of the slain NAACP official written by his wife.

Gass, G. Z. , and Rutledge, A. L.   Nineteen Negro Men. Jossey-Bass, 1967.   An account of how 19 disadvantaged Negroes were retrained for work as practical nurses.

Ginzberg, Eli, and Eichner, Alfred S.   The Troublesome Presence.   New American Library, 1964.   A history of the American Negro's struggle from colonial days to the present.

Glazer, Nathan and Moynihan, D. P.   Beyond the Melting Pot.   M. I. T. , 1963.   Discussion of how culture has affected the achievement, political action, and attitudes of five major ethnic groups in New York City.

Gordon, Albert.   Intermarriage: Interfaith, Interracial, Interethnic.   Beacon Press,   1964.   A definitive survey on intermarriage plus case histories.

Green, Paul.   In Abraham's Bosom (a play).   1926.   Racial discrimination, Negro-white.

Handlin, Oscar.   Fire Bell in the Night.   Little, 1964. Racial conflict and minority groups.

Himes, Chester.   Cotton Comes to Harlem.   Putnam, 1965. Mobility and racial conflict.

Himes, Chester.   Pink Toes.   Putnam, 1965.   Racial conflict and status-seeking.

Holt, Len.   An Act of Conscience.   Beacon Press, 1965. An account of how segregation was attacked in one city.

Javits, Jacob.   Discrimination--U. S. A.   Pocket Books, 1962. A discussion of discrimination and segregation both from a historical and a legal viewpoint.

Kaplan, Benjamin.   The Jew and His Family.   Louisiana State Univ. Press, 1967.   Story of the influence of family life upon the history of the Jewish people.

Killens, John. And Then We Heard the Thunder. Pocket
      Books, 1963. Frustrations and disappointments of a
      Negro during World War II.
King, Martin L. Why We Can't Wait. New American Li-
      brary, 1964. Dr. King describes the problems and
      reasons for the Negro's quest for civil rights.
Lewis, Oscar. La Vida. Random House, 1966. Disadvant-
      aged Puerto Ricans tell of their problems and strug-
      gles.
Lubell, Samuel. White and Black: Test of a Nation. Harper,
      1966. Discussion of the opinions of various persons
      about racial tensions.
Luthull, Albert John. Let My People Go. McGraw-Hill,
      1962. Minority groups and apartheid.
McCarthy, Agnes, and Reddick, Lawrence. Worth Fighting
      For. Doubleday, 1965. Account of the Negro during
      Civil War and reconstruction days.
McWilliams, Carey. Brothers under the Skin. Little, Brown,
      1964. Minority group problems are national problems
      and deserve the attention of the federal government.
Madsen, William. Mexican-Americans of South Texas. Holt,
      Rinehart & Winston, 1964. Discussion of the his-
      torical and current status of Latins and their relation-
      ships with Anglos.
Paton, Alan. Too Late the Phalarope. Scribner, 1953.
      Race hatred, also anomie, marginal man, and mixed
      marriage.
Potok, Chaim. The Chosen. Simon & Schuster, 1967. A
      story of Jewish life in Brooklyn during World War II.
Silberman, C. E. Crisis in Black and White. Vintage
      Books, 1964. An historical, sociological, and factual
      reporting of the Negro's position in American life.
Sutherland, Elizabeth, ed. Letters from Mississippi. New
      American Library, 1965. Letters of students who
      worked for Negro rights in Mississippi in 1964.
Uris, Leon. Mila 18. Doubleday, 1961. Story which illus-
      trates how prejudice led to the slaughter of millions
      of Jews.
Wakefield, Dan. Island in the City: the World of Spanish
      Harlem. Citadel Press, 1960. A realistic portrayal
      of the problems faced by Puerto Ricans living in New
      York City.
Westheimer, David. My Sweet Charlie. Doubleday, 1965.
      Race and the unmarried white mother.
White, Walter Francis. How Far the Promised Land?
      Viking, 1955. Minority groups: a question of time.
Wright, Richard. Black Boy. 1946. Racial rejection.

Young, Jefferson. <u>A Good Man.</u>   Bobbs Merrill, 1963.
    Dilemma of segregation--Negro tenant farmer wanted
    to paint his house white.

CHAPTER 11

THE QUALIFICATIONS, TRAINING, AND DUTIES
OF A BIBLIOTHERAPIST

It is interesting to note that when hiring a patients' librarian McLean (mental) Hospital at Belmont, Massachusetts, selected a man who was not a professional librarian but who had had a varied background in working with people. His duties included supervision over eight to twelve patients working in the library; conducting group sessions in reading short stories, plays and poetry; meeting with a writer's group of patients; acting as advisor to the patient-written and/-edited magazine, and working with individual patients in a therapeutic capacity. [1]

The person selected held a B. A. in religion, had studied creative writing for four semesters and had written a novel for a thesis. He had studied more literature than religion, more religion than psychology, had taught physical education in grades one, two and three; religion in six, seven, and eleven; and English in ten and twelve. This background revealed much about how the patient librarian is expected to function at McLean. Something akin to a bibliotherapist was in the minds of those responsible for the hiring, though the terms "bibliotherapist" and "bibliotherapy" were never used to describe his role.

McLean practices mileu treatment in which the whole range of a patient's hospital experience, from ward life to work programs to informal and recreational activities, is seen as adjunctive therapy. That philosophy, the librarian's position in the Activity Therapies Department, and the qualifications of the person hired as librarian indicated an important preconception: that the therapeutic use of a patients' library was not believed to be dependent on the professional training of the librarian.

The man hired for this position at McLean had had no

library science training whatsoever. He found this to be a
handicap when teaching patients how to use the library, but
an asset in preventing him from devoting his energies to
clerical and routine work. Margaret Hannigan has suggested
that adequate performance as a bibliotherapist "may demand
streamlining or even abandoning some routines presently performed by the librarian. "

It seems significant to this writer that McLean apparently placed more emphasis on training in the intellectual,
physical, and ethical aspects of living than on library technology. No one person can be all things to all people. Some
knowledge of books and what titles are best to recommend in
active bibliotherapy practice can be acquired by diligent reading and use of available lists, but the essential deep understanding of and compatability with people is not as easily
acquired.

When Agnews State Hospital at San Jose, California,
embarked on a two-year program of bibliotherapy under a
special grant to demonstrate the value of bibliotherapy and it
became evident that their librarian would not have time to
conduct the sessions, it was generally felt that any sensitive
person with a knowledge of books and empathy with patients
could become a competent bibliotherapist. Good human relationships are more effective in working with people than all
the technical training in the world. Who has not met, for
example, at some time in his life, a brilliant technical
"expert, " perhaps even a highly trained librarian or nurse,
whose personality repelled rather than attracted, and whose
expertise could not be communicated effectively to others?

If a bibliotherapy program, either with groups or an
individual, is to be successful, it is very necessary that the
bibliotherapist possess certain personal qualifications. These
are:

Emotional stability.
A willingness to recognize the misfortunes of others
    and the ability to provide help.
A good psychological adjustment.
Ability to cooperate with others in a therapeutic team.
Respect for the reader's own wishes and rights.
Willingness to accept responsibility.
Tolerance.
Ability to be objective and not be influenced by per-
    sonal prejudices.

Ability to supervise and direct others.
Willingness to learn.
Relative freedom from personal problems of one's own.
Cheerfulness.
A high degree of perceptiveness and sensitivity.
Patience.
Mature judgment.
Ability to communicate clearly.
Ability to be a good listener.
Powers of intelligent observation.
Flexibility.
The type of mind that can organize facts for making
    relevant records and clear reports for the medical
    personnel that may be involved.
Competence to instruct when necessary.
Ability to channel personal feelings and direct them to
    the best interest of those to be helped.
The discernment to discard the erroneous and irrele-
    vant and draw only warranted and valid conclusions.
A deep and abiding interest in other people as indi-
    viduals. [2]

Here it seems, is the picture of a paragon.   No one
person is likely to possess all of these attributes in large
measure, but the degree to which any individual possesses all
or part of them will be a significant factor in determining
success or failure in using books as therapy.

Motive is also an important factor.   The would-be
bibliotherapist must face up to himself and his motives
squarely.   He must ask himself these questions:

Am I interested in practicing bibliotherapy because I
    genuinely want to help others, or is it to satisfy
    my own ego?
Do I only enjoy influencing others as a manifestation
    of power?
Am I motivated by pity rather than a sympathetic un-
    derstanding?
Will I allow sentiment to overrule good judgment?

Unless the motive is clearly humanitarian rather than
self-satisfaction, bibliotherapy should not be undertaken. Much
time is involved; results may be slow to appear or outwardly
seem almost non-existent.   The individual being helped may
show little or no gratitude.   Cooperation from others may be
hard to obtain.   At times the whole task may seem frustrat-

ing.   Nevertheless, in the final analysis, if the approach and
technique employed by a personally qualified bibliotherapist
have been right, there will be positive results.   When constructive results are shown, the therapist may then feel a
legitimate inner sense of satisfaction; self-satisfaction as a
motive and satisfaction at a favorable outcome are two different matters.

Patients and others in need of therapy are often quick
to sense whether the bibliotherapist has their true interest at
heart, and they respond or fail to respond accordingly. Most
of the personal traits listed as requisites for practicing good
bibliotherapy are inextricably a part of a person's makeup,
but many of them can also be cultivated or improved.

The value of formal training is not to be questioned.
However, few formal courses in bibliotherapy are available,
and the candidate must instead rely on courses in psychology,
particularly as it pertains to techniques of guidance, diagnosis, and counseling the physically handicapped and the
emotionally disturbed; principles of motivation and remotiva-
tion; techniques of testing and the interpretation of test results; sociology as it relates to medical and social problems
of illness, techniques of rehabilitating the aging, training in
statistics and report writing; elementary psychiatry, the
biological sciences of anatomy and physiology; and definitely,
of course, literature for children, young adults, and adults.[2]
A few courses in bibliotherapy are offered by library schools
and some organizations, but the training opportunities are
still very scarce and there is a great need both for more
courses and for established standards as to their content.

A new program in poetry therapy was conducted by
Dr. Gilbert Schloss in the summer of 1971 at The Institute
for Sociotherapy, New York City.   An inquiry to this institute
(39 East 20th St.) would reveal if and when future courses
will be offered in this special aspect of bibliotherapy.   In
September of 1971 Long Island University gave a course in
poetry therapy, under the title of Guidance 651, at its
Brooklyn Center.   It was offered in the graduate program of
the Department of Guidance and Counseling by Dr. James
Murphy.   Professor William J. Kirman is chairman of the
department.   Inquiries should be directed to him personally
or to the department.

In most instances, even in the library schools, courses
are content courses directed toward information search and

retrieval, literary content, reading level, and descriptive and subject bibliography. There is little emphasis on the effect of reading upon the individual. However, traditional library training is changing with needs and pressures of a changing society, and the interdisciplinary approach is now being applied to many aspects of the curriculum.

Bibliotherapy will undoubtedly become a part of the graduate program of library schools as its use becomes even more widespread. Its demonstrated success in varied fields cannot fail to be recognized by those in charge of library education, even if belatedly. The strange anomaly is that librarians, who of all people should be aware of the impact of reading upon their patrons, young and old, have not been quick to accept bibliotherapy as either a science or art; though one must except those institutional librarians who have worked closely with it, especially those in mental and Veterans Administration hospitals.

School guidance personnel have often been receptive to the idea of bibliotherapy, especially when the school librarian recognizes its value. However, librarians are beginning to take increasing interest as time goes on, and through the work of the Bibliotherapy Committee of the American Library Association and the efforts and writings of outstanding practicing librarian-therapists, interest should continue to grow. Workshops on bibliotherapy have been organized in recent years and these can be expected to increase in number. A key workshop was an American Library Association preconference program at St. Louis, June 25-27, 1964, on "Bibliotherapy--What It Can Do for Mental Health. "

Margaret M. Kinney says, "The bibliotherapist is primarily a librarian who goes further in the field of reader guidance and becomes a professional specialist. " Miss Kinney emphasizes that such a librarian must have training in greater depth in library materials and their selection. It is imperative that the public librarian recognize the more specialized knowledge that must be acquired: understanding of the principles of clinical psychology and the basic skills of the psychologist, a wide knowledge and understanding of medical, psychological and psychiatric terminology, elementary psychiatry, psychology of the physically handicapped, the psychology of reading, techniques of rehabilitation, techniques of diagnosis and counseling, medical and social problems of illness. [3] Thus Margaret Kinney, writing in 1962, and Louis A. Rongione, writing in 1972, agree very closely on the courses recommended as a foundation for bibliotherapy.

Field service training should be an important part of
the preparation of a bibliotherapist. It should be organized
as a part of social service, or supervised on-the-job training
in hospitals and clinics of clinical psychologists. In a school
situation it could be part of a teacher-aide or librarian-aide
program. It could be organized in cooperation with medical
and mental hygiene clinics and hospitals near the campuses
of colleges and universities having library schools, so that
library science students can gain practical experience while
taking the regular courses for their library degree. The
clinical or hospital field experience should be extended to
readers' advisory service in the children's, young adult or
adult departments of a large public library or in conjunction
with a school library and/or the work of school guidance
counselors. [3] Practical field work of this kind, with careful
reports from supervisors, would help to weed out early those
who do not meet the personal and social requirements for
effective bibliotherapy.

Sister Eileen Liette, in an article entitled "Reading
Guidance: In-Service Procedures and Techniques," says:

> The person who accepts the responsibility for di-
> recting the program must be able to work with
> groups and individuals; must have a good background
> in the psychology of children, youth, and adults;
> must have a thorough knowledge of the process of
> reading, methods, books, and reading materials, as
> well as exhibit an adeptness in locating and using
> resources; must have an almost innate ability for
> organization, and a love for and understanding of
> people. The entire staff must show deep interest
> and enthusiasm as they initiate, develop, and finally
> evaluate a program which attempts to promote per-
> sonal and social growth through reading. [4]

It is not possible to emphasize too strongly the necessity for the bibliotherapist to know a great deal about the
physical and emotional condition of the subject. Without a
considerable knowledge of his educational and cultural background, his hobbies and interests, and his temperament, the
therapist is in no position to know what types of books or
specific titles to recommend, nor can she anticipate in any
degree how he will react to the material read.

In the absence of formal courses in bibliotherapy a broad academic background, with emphasis upon the subjects already mentioned, provides the best foundation. Although many of the important personal traits are difficult to acquire if the would-be bibliotherapist does not already possess them, the broad academic background and field experience can usually be acquired if the individual has sufficient determination. However, since opportunities to use bibliotherapy often come unheralded there is no time to go back and fill in the gaps. Thus, the selection of a bibliotherapist should be carefully made by those in authority and should fall to the person who comes closest to meeting the desirable specifications. If there is no one who can even approach the ideal, bibliotherapy should not be attempted in any complex situation, for it could do more harm than good.

While the common assumption is that the librarian is the most likely bibliotherapist, the question has been raised whether the bibliotherapist should be a librarian trained in clinical methods or a clinician trained in library methods? This is not basically as important as that the bibliotherapist know his material thoroughly and understand the person he is treating; given these factors, his chances of success are fairly high. Since library schools are the logical institutions to provide training courses, it would seem more practical for bibliotherapists to be librarians trained in clinical methods. This choice may be arbitrary, but knowledge of books, an indispensable ingredient for successful bibliotherapy, is more apt to be found among "bookish" people who attend library schools than among clinicians who might take a few courses in library methods because they are recommended or required. The very wide knowledge of books the bibliotherapist needs to be most successful cannot be acquired in a few semesters of formal training but is the product of many years of reading.

Untrained people working under supervision can do much to assist in bibliotherapy with groups, since diagnostic skill is not needed for interaction. A few library schools have developed courses specifically for persons who plan to work in hospital and institutional libraries, but such courses are not labeled as "bibliotherapy." Needed are library school courses in sensitivity training for interpersonal relationships and courses in the psychology of reading as a form of communication.

Sometimes the bibliotherapist must also possess the

attributes of a good salesman, for some people with problems (institutionalized or not) have not been habitual readers and are not immediately amenable to the idea of group or individual reading. Knowing how to conduct and interpret surveys is also an asset for any bibliotherapist.

In working with people in or out of hospitals the bibliotherapist often finds it important to interpret past experiences, to provide a healthy dose of positive verbal reinforcement, and supply appropriate social models for imitation. [5]

M. E. Roberts has stressed that the personal qualities of the librarian, more than training or number of books read, are responsible for a successful bibliotherapeutic program in a mental hospital where patient rapport is of special importance. [6] Other writers reinforce this statement. J. J. Michaels, discussing the attitude of the librarian toward the neuropsychiatric patient in an army general hospital, said, "Understanding, neutral sympathy, patience, and warmth are the prime requirements for the proper approach to the patient. "[7]

Beyond the inherent personal traits and the acquired knowledge and skills required of bibliotherapists there are ethical considerations involved:

1. Willing assumption of the limitations of both himself as bibliotherapist and of bibliotherapy as a practice.
2. An acknowledgment of the actual and potential contributions other professions are making and can make to bibliotherapy.
3. A strict observance of professional secrecy commensurate with the confidential nature of the responsibilities assumed.
4. A willingness to be guided by medical authority where medical personnel are involved. [8]

As stated earlier, it is a rare individual who possesses all of the personal and professional qualities and skills desirable in a bibliotherapist. What is necessary is that the bibliotherapist must be an individual who goes beyond bibliocounseling or reading guidance and becomes a specialist. He should also avail himself of the services and competencies of other professionals outside the field of librarianship. Certainly there is a need for coordination of the efforts of the physician, the psychiatrist, the spiritual advisor, the nurse,

the sociologist, the physiotherapist, the librarian and others
who must become involved if bibliotherapy is to be beneficial
and effective. [8]

One of the best uses of bibliotherapy, as pointed out
in Chapter 8, is in the school.   School counselors trained in
guidance techniques, and school librarians, working singly or
together, will usually be able to take the additional steps required to use bibliotherapy as an extension of reading guidance.   Teachers may lack sufficient reading background or
interest to make adequate use of bibliotherapy, but since a
good teacher with a genuine concern for her students as individuals may know them better than any other staff member
in the school and may inspire their confidence, he or she is
often in a position to do more effective bibliotherapy than
either the librarian or the school guidance counselors.

For teachers who are willing to learn the techniques
of bibliotherapy, in-service training should be offered through
workshops or institutes.   Here is a suggested plan for preparing for and conducting such a workshop:

Development:

1.   Establish a steering committee composed of the librarian
      or librarians, principal, counselor, and a teacher at
      large.

2.   The steering committee should assess the needs for bib-
      liotherapy by oral reports from teachers and by checking
      student information folders.

3.   Subcommittees should compare and analyze the report
      and suggest a format for the workshop.

4.   Assemble a panel made up of a psychiatrist, general
      medical practitioner, librarian in a Veterans' Adminis-
      tration or mental hospital, guidance counselor, school
      librarian, and a resource person who is well acquainted
      with bibliotherapy.   Such a person should act as moder-
      ator.   Some preliminary assigned reading should be done
      by each member of the panel.

5.   An outline of the material to be discussed should be made
      and duplicated.   Here is a suggested outline:

      A.   What is bibliotherapy?   How is it distinguished from

reader guidance or reader advisory work?

B. Who is responsible for bibliotherapy in a school situation? Librarians, counselors, teachers?

C. When is bibliotherapy useful?
(1) Emotional problems.
(2) Mental problems.
(3) Physical problems.

D. How can the classroom teacher help?
(1) Encourage reading in every possible way.
(2) Bring groups of books to the classroom for browsing or reading during reading periods.
(3) Suggest to individual students books that will have a therapeutic effect.
(4) Read aloud stories or books with a theme that will apply to the problems of one or more children.
(5) Discuss the books afterwards with individual students and with the group. Note individual reactions of students.
(6) Be on the alert for signs of potential delinquency.
(7) Cooperate with school psychologists, counselors, librarians on the prescription of reading to help cure student problems.

E. As a project pick out one problem child in your classroom, find out all you can about his family background, describe the case in writing; tell what books you would suggest for this child and what follow-up measures you would take.

The workshop could be held during one full day, with students excused for that day; in several after-school shorter sessions, or on a Saturday.

Once teachers have background information about bibliotherapy, the reading consultant, through the in-service workshop, should encourage them to try the technique. Some teachers will prefer to work with individual students; others may want to make their first attempt with a group. From the outcome of the personal-social evaluation techniques, the teacher should know both the general needs and the individual needs of her students. From these, one of the most important should be selected, and reading material found which will be pertinent to that need. Then a lesson plan can be formulated centering on the theme in question.

Here is a sample lesson plan such as a teacher might use in a classroom (or a librarian in a group book discussion) when it is known that some of the individuals in the class or group have shown intolerance or antagonism toward black people.   It was suggested by Sister Eileen Liette. [9]

1.   Description of class or group need: Intercultural understanding--black people.

2.   Statement of objectives or purposes:
   a. To develop sensitivity to other human beings, particularly the black--sensitivity to his needs, aspirations, abilities.
   b. To stimulate interest in reading about black people.
   c. To develop skill in critical reading.

3.   Story title: <u>Jazz Country</u>, by Nat Hentoff.

4.   What parts of situations of the story are particularly appropriate (for use with this group)?
   a. Tom Curtis' attempt to join the black jazz band.
   b. The people whose influence helped shape Tom's life.
   c. Why Tom Curtis made the decision to go to college.

5.   Will you use the complete story or only parts? [Complete story.]

6.   Class period or time during which you will use the story.   [Reading period or book discussion hour.]

7.   Use of story planned for.   [Total group.]

8.   Plans for presenting the story:
   a. Give background of author.
   b. Introduce the book.
   c. Read the book to the class--daily, part by part.
   d. Have students note particular happenings which they would like to discuss at the end of the reading.

9.   Related activities planned: class discussion, out-

side reading of other books related to the theme,
if time permits, a panel discussion to serve as
part of evaluation.

10.   Specific questions to help pupils relate reading to
personal situation:
    a. In what ways did the black jazzmen influence
Tom Curtis?
    b. What was the predominant positive trait of the
black jazzmen as a group? Discuss.
    c. If you were Tom Curtis, what would you have
done when Tom was rejected as a member of
the band?
    d. How will a college education--such as Tom
Curtis chose--help to build better cultural and
racial understanding?
    e. What other things might Tom Curtis have done?
Discuss what you would probably have done.

<u>Evaluation:</u>   Questions, comments, or reactions made by the
group or individuals regarding this story.   Note especially
how members of a group reconstruct the story.   Have participants give suggestions for changes in planning or approach
for further use of this book.

A reading consultant should help a teacher by observing as she carries out the bibliotherapeutic lesson plan and
by holding a conference to help her make evaluations.

In any workshop session the potential bibliotherapist
should have some degree of introduction to bibliotherapy as a
concept, depending upon his background of acquaintance with
it as a method and his previous general experience.   He may
also need to know what research offers, and what are the
present applications and implications for the future.

The bibliotherapist who will be working in an institution needs to have a fundamental understanding of the goal,
methods, and techniques applied in rehabilitation.   He must
be well oriented to the institution and the methods and duties
of all the staff, whether it is a prison, a delinquency home,
a mental hospital, a medical center, or an institution for the
handicapped.   The librarian-bibliotherapist must know each
individual patient's ability, comprehension, interests, intelligence, and the social setting from which he comes.   He must
establish a good working relationship with all the other staff
members--the psychiatrists, educators, physicians, social

workers, and other professionals. [10]

The institutional librarian-therapist should also serve as a link between the institution and the public library for both the residents and the professional staff. He should be able to use a variety of audio-visual equipment, and to make interlibrary loan arrangements with the state library, the public library, and professional schools and universities.

The institutional librarian should reach out to become involved with the wards, cell blocks, recreation rooms, and any other places where patients gather. He must use methods and techniques which stimulate, encourage, and motivate residents and staff to use the library services.

He must be able to show the relationship of the book to life and of the book's content to overt behavior as it can be related to therapy. Being able to evaluate changes in behavior and attitudes is important, as is the ability to keep accurate records and make clear reports. Literature must be analyzed not only for its objective content but also for its subjective emotional content as it fits the patient's need and provides support in individual and group therapy.

Flexibility--the ability to adjust the program quickly as a patient suddenly reacts adversely or an entire group mood changes--is essential.

And as the librarian-bibliotherapist is also usually the head and perhaps the only librarian in an institution, he must be able to perform the usual duties of administration, such as purchase, processing, and distribution of library materials, record keeping, and working with a library committee and/or supervisory officer. [10]

The bibliotherapist in a public library may be a children's librarian, an adult services head, or any qualified staff member. The desirable situation would be to have a full time bibliotherapist who compiles reading lists of material on the various problems likely to be encountered; teaches staff members individually and in regular group training sessions how to practice bibliotherapy with shut-ins, the elderly, children, or any patron who seems to have a problem and needs help; and who in cooperation with other agencies, arranges and conducts group therapy in the guise of reading clubs with juvenile delinquents, narcotic addicts, alcoholics, and nursing and rest home patients. Especially difficult cases requiring in-depth counseling and much follow-up would be handled by the bibliotherapist personally.

Some study is needed as to the effect of the term "bibliotherapist" or "bibliotherapy" on the individual or on groups with which such a person would work. Someone will be sure to ask the meaning of the terms if he has not been previously acquainted with them. Would the use of the correct terminology cause the individual recipient or members of the group to confuse this procedure with psychiatry and psychoanalysis? Would it cause a fear reaction or a feeling of stigma? Perhaps, in some instances, the bibliotherapist should simply be called a reading advisory or reading guidance specialist to whom a patient or patients would be referred by the general staff.

The results of a 1961 questionnaire sent out by Ruth Tews as Chairman of the AHIL Committee on Bibliotherapy to 120 individuals (35 hospital and institution libraries, 9 psychiatrists, 4 library consultants, 6 library educators, 2 educators in languages, 2 educators in nursing, 1 educator in adult education, 1 sociologist, 1 elementary school teacher, 1 chaplain, 23 federal librarians, 15 general hospital librarians, 9 state hospital librarians, 4 nursing school librarians, 3 volunteer library workers, 2 library administrators, and 2 public librarians) might seem to indicate that bibliotherapy is limited to group reading activity with patients, conducted by a librarian in association with a member of the medical staff. Ninety per cent of the persons surveyed agreed with a questionnaire definition of bibliotherapy in these terms; no other definition received such a uniform response. [11] It should be noted, however, that 97 of the 120 persons to whom the questionnaires were sent were medically-related institutional librarians or psychiatrists. This figure is correct, at least, if the 23 federal librarians were connected with Veterans' Administration Hospitals, although this is not indicated specifically. Even if they were not, however, the total is heavily weighted with medically-related individuals who would be likely to define and confine bibliotherapy to its traditional medical-oriented role. Public librarians and library administrators (the type of library administered is not shown) are a very small percentage of the total.

Even in 1961, had school counselors, social workers, probation officers, social welfare workers, and many more public librarians been included, the results might well have indicated that bibliotherapy need not be confined to so limited a field. Ruth Tews herself, discussing trends in the introduction to the October, 1962 issue of <u>Library Trends</u> which was devoted to bibliotherapy, had this to say:

> Interest in bibliotherapy is spreading. It is no longer confined to physicians and librarians in hospitals and institutions. As the subject has developed, the educator, the public librarian, and others interested in mental health are showing increasing concern. [She quotes Evalene Jackson:] 'Education is not clearly separable from therapy.... It is unlikely that (the librarian) can ignore the therapeutic aspects of reading. '
>
> Other evidences of the spreading interest are the recommendations for study and research in the use and effectiveness of books by such agencies as the White House Conferences on Children and Youth and on the Aging, and National Conferences on action for mental health. Notable progress in bibliotherapy is being made each year in a number of foreign countries. [12]

We have previously noted the growth of a specialized aspect of bibliotherapy as evidenced by the formation of a national association for poetry therapy. Thus the assumption by some institution librarians that the term bibliotherapy applies only to medically-related therapeutic activity with reading materials is not in keeping with today's trends. Certainly, bibliotherapy is not to be used indiscriminately by the unqualified, but if practiced by individuals who understand human nature and enjoy people, who know how to communicate and are sensitive and discerning, whose motives are altruistic, whose knowledge of books is wide and varied, and who have the ability to analyze, evaluate, report, and cooperate with either medical or non-medical personnel, there is no reason it cannot be applied increasingly in many different situations. The traditionalists, the dogmatists, may disagree and criticize, but this is the sincere conviction of this writer, who, both as a teacher and librarian, practiced individual bibliotherapy for years whenever a need was evidenced. The results were definitely positive and easily observable, and were verified by friends and relatives of the recipients who knew them well.

The need for and value of formal training cannot be denied, however, especially for those would-be bibliotherapists or librarian-therapists who have not had courses in

psychology and the other social sciences. If the candidate is
a non-librarian, library or literature courses are usually
essential unless the individual is an inveterate, compulsive
reader who has read widely since childhood.

What are some other duties the bibliotherapist can
perform which will indirectly aid in the bibliotherapy process?
In Institutional Library Services, a Plan for the State of Illinois, the following services are suggested, in addition to
those already mentioned in this chapter:13

> 1.   Have a professional library for the continuing
> self-education of the workers in the hospital.   As
> they learn more about bibliotherapy they will be
> better able to help.   This is possible, of course,
> only if there is a library and a librarian-therapist
> permanently attached to the hospital itself.
>
> 2.   Make interlibrary loan arrangements with the
> State Library, the public library, and with profes-
> sional schools and universities.
>
> 3.   Reach out and become involved in settings other
> than just the library--the wards, cell blocks, rec-
> reation rooms, and the like.
>
> 4.   Establish rapport with all other staff in the in-
> stitution--the psychiatrists, educators, doctors,
> social workers, others.

Ruth Tews, in The Librarian's Role on the Interdisciplinary Team, adds the following:14

> 5.   Relate to the public library and serve as a link
> between the institution and the public library for
> the residents and the professional staff.
>
> 6.   Be able to make use of a variety of audio-
> visual equipment to supplement the use of books.
>
> 7.   Use methods and techniques which create a
> stimulating environment for library services to en-
> courage and motivate residents and staff to use
> them.
>
> 8.   Try to form a staff committee for all the pro-
> fessional services in the institution on an ongoing

basis, so that experiences with and knowledge of the residents can be pooled for the best help in bibliotherapy.

9.   Make it a point to know each individual's ability, comprehension, interests, intelligence, and the social setting from which he comes.

10.   Show the inter-relatedness of the book to life; of the book's content to overt behavior as it can be related to therapy.

11.   Evaluate the changes in behavior and attitude, and keep records and make reports with intelligent observations and evaluations.

12.   Be able to analyze literature for its emotional content to fit the patient's need and to act as support and reinforcement in individual and group therapy.

13.   Be flexible.   Be able to re-evaluate the program to fit the emotional situation; as when a patient suddenly regresses and all plans must be changed.

The institutional librarian, in addition to all of the above, must carry on the usual duties of administering and operating a library, working with the library committee, supervising acquisition of materials, processing, distribution, record keeping and the possible training of patient aides to assist in routine library procedures.

Notes

1.   McDowell, David J.   "Bibliotherapy in a Patients' Library."   Bulletin of the Medical Library Association, v. 59, July 1971, p. 450.

2.   Rongione, Louis A.   "Bibliotherapy: Its Nature and Uses."   Catholic Library World, v. 43, May-June 1972, p. 497-498.

3.   Kinney, Margaret M.   "The Bibliotherapy Program: Requirements for Training."   In: University of Illinois, Graduate School of Library Science, "Bibliotherapy,"

     Library Trends, Ruth M. Tews, issue editor, v. 11, October 1962, p. 130-132.

4.   Liette, Sister Eileen. "Reading Guidance: In-Service Procedures and Techniques." In: Figurel, Allen J., ed., Reading and Realism. Indiana University Northwest. Proceedings of the 13th Annual Convention, International Reading Association, Newark, Delaware, c1969, p. 424, p. 426-427.

5.   Lejeune, Archie L. "Bibliocounseling as a Guidance Technique." Catholic Library World, v. 41, November 1969, p. 159.

6.   Roberts, M. E. "Libraries in Mental Hospitals." Mental Health, v. 7, February 1948, p. 70-71.

7.   Michaels, J. J. "Approach of the Librarian to the Neuropsychiatric Patient in an Army General Hospital." Special Libraries, v. 37, July/August 1946, p. 180-183.

8.   Rongione, Louis A., op. cit., p. 497-498.

9.   Liette, Sister Eileen, op. cit.

10.   Tews, Ruth M. "The Librarian's Role on the Interdisciplinary Team." Mayo Clinic Library, Mayo Clinic, Rochester, Minnesota. Mimeographed, 10 p.

11.   Tews, Ruth M. "The Questionnaire on Bibliotherapy." In: Tews, R. M., ed., "Bibliotherapy," Library Trends, v. 11, October 1962, p. 217, 222.

12.   Tews, Ruth M. "Introduction." "Bibliotherapy," Library Trends, v. 11, October 1962, p. 100-101.

13.   Social, Educational Research and Development, Inc. "The Practice of Bibliotherapy--Program Suggestions for Specific Institutions and Types of Individuals." In: Institutional Library Services--A Plan for the State of Illinois. American Library Association. Study authorized by Paul Powell, State Librarian, Illinois State Library, Springfield, Illinois, 1970, p. 69-83.

14.   Tews, Ruth M. "The Librarian's Role on the Interdisciplinary Team," op. cit.

CHAPTER 12

TYPES OF LITERATURE USED IN BIBLIOTHERAPY

Surveys of the reading habits of patients, particularly those in Veterans' Administration Hospitals, have usually shown that there is little difference between their tastes and those of the general public when freedom of choice is offered. Illness or disability has little influence on what a person wants to read. The same background factors that influence the well or normal individual in his reading or non-reading will usually apply. However, what the patient wants to read and what he should read are not always synonymous, for certain types of material can have a depressing or debilitating effect on a person with serious physical or mental problems. Therefore the bibliotherapist must thoroughly understand the patient's condition and use discrimination in selecting the material to offer. The advice of the doctor should be sought when there is any doubt as to the possible effect.

Biographies have been found by hospital librarians to be especially useful, for they so often reveal the subject's problems and frustrations, and, because they are the life stories of real rather than imaginary people, they are often more convincing to the reader. It is often easier for a reader to identify with someone he knows exists or has existed, and biographies may show failures as well as successes in their true proportions. Gloomy, depressing biographies, and large, heavy volumes are usually to be avoided as too taxing for the patient's physical strength and state of mind.

Zaccaria and Moses, as well as other writers, believe that for purposes of insight therapy, imaginative literature has greater power to effect changes in the reader than non-fiction. For studying the dynamics of reading and even as a basis for psycho-diagnosis, they add, one might well use an occasional piece of didactic literature. They list the following types of literature as among the most effective:

1. Short stories for all ages.

    2.   Poetry (valuable in providing a release for the emotions). The necessary economy of words in poetry lends dignity, order and restraint.

    3.   Science fiction which takes the reader away from immediate problems, many of which may solve themselves by the time he gets back to thinking about them.

    4.   Fables for elementary children and very small children. The obvious moral usually contained in such tales is easy for children to understand and can more easily trigger discussion than more complex material. [1]

Kindergarten-age children (two to six) like to have material concerning familiar events read to them. By ages six to eleven there is increasing interest in fantasy, tales of imagination and adventure.

According to Carlsen, in Books and the Teen-age Reader, twelve to fifteen year-olds prefer animal stories, adventure, science fiction, mysteries, tales of the supernatural, sports, growing up around the world, home and family living, slapstick, and stories with a background of history and pioneer life. In later adolescence, fifteen to eighteen years, war stories, romances, stories of adolescent life, and general adult material are popular. In young manhood or womanhood, eighteen to twenty-two years, personal values, social significance, strange and unusual experiences, and themes of transition to adult life are often preferred. [2]

To provide even a partial list of the books that can help in solving or diminishing emotional, physical, or mental problems would require a volume many times this size. We can, however, cite a few pertinent examples especially helpful in specific types of situations.

Problems such as overt discord, open quarreling, poverty, alcoholism, irresponsibility in money matters, or lack of emotional support, can cause serious emotional upheaval among individual members of a family group, particularly children. In such cases it is often helpful to read books that mirror a stable and happy family life. Adolescents who may have gone through childhood in a discordant home may have no concept of how good family life can be when everyone tries to make it so. Books like Emily Kimbrough's Our Hearts Were Young and Gay, John Druten's I Remember Mama, Frank and Ernestine Gilbreth's Cheaper

By the Dozen, Forbes' Mama's Bank Account, or Clarence
Day's Life with Father, provide a new slant on how problems
are handled in families where there is a spirit of love and
cooperation. It has happened more often than is commonly
supposed that the influence of one family member who gains
insight into how to surmount inescapable problems has been
the lever for improving an entire pattern of family relationships. [3]

    For some individuals in need of therapy, however,
reading about the almost ideal family might serve only to
accentuate the contrast between that happy relationship and
his own home life. Situations like this emphasize the bibliotherapist's need to know the individual thoroughly before suggesting books or other material. The bibliotherapist must be
able to predict his subject's reactions with reasonable certainty.

    A teenager confined temporarily in a hospital or con-
valescent facility will obviously enjoy the same books as a
completely healthy young person in his age range. He will
gain from them some solace for his pain, discomfort, isolation from family, or whatever combination of circumstances
he faces, providing the books offered by the librarian-bibliotherapist are along the lines of his interests and are relevant
to his problems.

    Teenagers in a highly emotional state have been known
to commit suicide because of an unrequited love. Reading a
book like Maureen Daly's Seventeenth Summer might well be
a decisive factor in preventing such a tragedy, for the young
person learns that unrequited love at an early age is quite
common, perhaps even necessary--par for the course, so to
speak--and that the search for love is an eternal one. [3]

    Fiction about speeding, drinking while driving, and
other traffic violations which end disastrously have been effective with teenagers who are taking risks. The books of Gregor
Felsen are outstanding in this field and have proved extremely
popular with young people.

    Problems of adolescence are also well presented in
such books as James Branch Cabell's The Cords of Vanity,
Joseph Conrad's October's Child, Thomas Mann's Joseph and
His Brothers, Booth Tarkington's Seventeen, Angela Thirkell's
The Demon in the House, Gilbert Frankau's Wreath for the
Enemy, Willa Cather's My Antonia, James Joyce's Portrait

of the Artist as a Young Man, Rebecca West's Cress Dela-
hanty, Ann Emery's Going Steady, Rosamund DuJardin's
Class Ring, Double Date, Boy Trouble, and Wait for Marcy.

Emotionally disturbed adolescents at John Umstead
Hospital, Butner, North Carolina, were found to like best
fairly sophisticated books about dramatic human confrontations,
such as Catcher in the Rye, Of Mice and Men, Manchild in
the Promised Land, True Grit, and A Farewell to Arms.
They did not often read newspapers and magazines because
appealing ones were not immediately available, and they did
not use the library of hard-backed books. [4]

In selecting books for the Hamilton County (Ohio)
Youth Center, where boys and girls who have been law offenders are detained until their trial by the Judge of the
Juvenile Court, the librarians of the Cincinnati and Hamilton
County Library realized that these young people, ten through
seventeen, were in a disturbed state while there, that their
interest span was likely to be short, and that many would be
poor readers. They therefore chose books with inviting formats, many of them generously illustrated; collections of
short stories, short fiction titles, and biographies, including
problem situations, and other non-fiction on the general problems of all teenagers. Among titles that circulated most
frequently were Ben and Me, East o' the Sun and West o'
the Moon, Twixt Twelve and Twenty, and Rockets, Satellites
and Space. [5]

Poetry as Therapy

One of the most interesting and surprising elements in
the development of bibliotherapy has been the increasing popularity and use of poetry. It is showing increasing use, for
example, in bibliotherapy with mental patients. The surprise
element lies in the fact that poetry, although perhaps the
most beautiful and significant form of written expression, has
rarely been a generally popular form. The experience of
many teachers has been that the majority of students shy away
from poetry; only a few are interested in reading it or become interested in writing it.

But proof of poetry's growing use and efficacy in bibliotherapy is the formation in recent years of a National Association for Poetry Therapy, with headquarters at 799 Broad-
way, New York City. This organization, known as APT, pro-

motes the establishment of programs in poetry therapy, is
developing training programs and standards of accreditation,
and encourages research and publications on the subject. It
sponsors presentations of poetry therapy panels, symposia
and workshops, an annual meeting of the association and, in
conjunction with it, Poetry Therapy Day. The first annual
meeting held in Brooklyn, New York, April 16, 1971, was
sponsored by the Department of Psychiatry of the Cumberland
Hospital Division of the Brooklyn-Cumberland Medical Center
and the Association. Dr. Jack J. Leedy, APT president in
1971, is the editor of a book, Poetry Therapy, the major
book in its field, and also edited Poetry the Healer: Poetry
and the Therapeutic Experience.

In a representative list of 107 members, 34, or approximately 32 per cent in 1971, were doctors. Included
were some of the country's leading psychiatrists. Thus there
is medical recognition of the value of poetry as a therapeutic
tool. Its advantages for bibliotherapy are becoming recognized not only in the United States but in other countries as
well. Lynne Gordon, one of the APT members, stimulated
interest in poetry therapy and discussed its value and techniques at the Universities of Vienna, Rome, and Genoa. Dr.
Parviz Farvardin, a member in Teheran, Iran, wrote five
books of poetry in the Persian language and translated portions of Poetry Therapy for the Iranian Psychiatric Journal.
A number of magazine articles on the subject have appeared,
and a symposium on poetry therapy was a part of the 34th
Convention of the California Psychologists Association, March
12, 1971.

Eloise Richardson, librarian of the Crownsville State
(mental) Hospital in Maryland, after setting up the library at
that institution a decade ago, realized that if the library was
to fulfill its role within the hospital's rehabilitation function,
it must offer services significant in the institution's therapy
program. She assembled a bibliography of references on
bibliotherapy from Index Medicus, obtained the materials from
the National Library of Medicine, and began intensive research. As she developed her program of bibliotherapy she
learned that poetry served as a most powerful agent for rehabilitative therapy. She gave this specialized area the name
of poetry therapy. Mrs. Richardson says:

There are more ways than one to program poetry
therapy and usually no two therapists work alike.
However, group participation on the basis of indi-

vidual sensitivity aroused by poetry content is a
technique of confrontation which usually brings about
communication.   Interpretation and questions during
the line of communication within the group has a
distinct rehabilitating effect upon the patient. Poetry
gives nourishment to the psychological health of the
patient.   It tunes into the inner self of the patient
because it is written out of the emotions of those
who write it.   Consequently it reaches out to the
emotions of those who read it or hear it read.   It
influences the mental patient because it is a certain
way of using words.

These words take on a vitality which exists in no
other use of them.   Significance which words carry
in speech or prose is intensified in poetry--quality
of sound, shades of meaning, symbolic importance.
They work with a secret potency and they take on
a new personality and can be of bare simplicity. [6]

Mrs. Richardson believes that poetic thoughts can
serve as messages.   The 23rd Psalm, for example, carries
a strong hope for survival to a person who may be despairing
and without hope.   ("Yea though I walk through the valley of
the shadow of death, Thou art with me ... Thy rod and thy
staff, they comfort me.")   Communication can often follow
easily after a revival of hope and belief in a person who is
troubled and withdrawn.

Among other positive results of poetry therapy Mrs.
Richardson has found demonstrated in her work with mental
patients are the following:

1.   It can motivate them in their efforts to overcome
     emotional disorders.
2.   It can help them to develop a philosophy of life
     that makes it easier for them to adjust to their
     misfortune.
3.   It can make it easier to adjust more readily to
     society upon their release from the hospital.
4.   It can help the patient to become more spontane-
     ous, thereby providing a release for pent-up
     emotions.
5.   By reflecting the past, poems can lift a patient
     out of a present dilemma into realities of living
     in moments of ecstasy.
6.   Poetry can establish communication more readily

than other forms of literature because fewer words,
often more poignant and significant, are used to
express an emotion or idea.   A poem is said to
be the shortest distance between writer and reader.

7.   Reading or hearing poetry read can often inspire
the patient to try to write some verse of his own,
giving him a creative activity of great therapeutic
value and providing a means of communicating his
own feelings and emotions to others.

8.   Poetry helps to broaden the scope of interpersonal
relationships and experiences of the patients.

At Crownsville State Hospital small groups of patients
met together weekly with the librarian and volunteers for a
discussion of poems.   The patients were given books or
sheets of poetry from which they selected poems which were
meaningful to them.   The poems were read aloud in this
program.   The therapists realized that the poems were selected for specific reason and were sensitive to their content.   An individual patient might be asked, why this particular poem?   In the ensuing discussion, hidden thoughts or
problems not revealed in any other way were sometimes uncovered.   Such information, conveyed to the psychiatrist, can
be very helpful.   Usually the sessions were pre-stimulated by
music, poetry on records, humor, or perhaps an inspiring
talk by the librarian or a volunteer.   At the beginning of the
work with poetry therapy at Crownsville, listening only sessions were held and were also found to be effective.

Regular sessions of poetry therapy are usually scheduled for mornings, as patients have been more susceptible to
this type of program before lunch and meditation periods.   It
is important, says Mrs. Richardson, that the sessions be
held in the library or some other specially selected area, as
the environment has special rehabilitative significance.   On
one occasion a group of patients was taken to a historical
spot on the Eastern shore of Maryland, where a session held
under a 400-year-old oak tree was particularly effective.

Sometimes resource people are brought in to conduct
programs, and one special activity was a poetry workshop
conducted by several patients who were regular participants
in the poetry therapy sessions.   Participants presented original and other favorite poems, gave their ideas as to why
these poems created a sensitivity or why they wrote them,
and discussed the "why" of poetry in general.   Patient response was extremely gratifying, and the emotional impact

created by this effort stimulated excellent communication.

Resource people who have read their own or patients'
poems to audiences of patients averaging about 100 at each
session at Crownsville have included Ogden Nash, America's
classic humorous poet; Vincent Godfrey Burns, poet laureate
of Maryland; Mary Roberts Finch, poet, artist and professional photographer; Jean Sterling, poet laureate of the Ches-
apeake Bay Country, and other notables.   Through all these
programs, talent is discovered among the patients in the
audience, and the patients' response provides evidence that
poetry is "a powerful agent of therapy," Mrs. Richardson
declares.   At one of these sessions several patients spontaneously requested the privilege of reading poems they had
written.   One young man revealed for the first time that he
had written 70 poems; he later came to the library with a
loose-leaf notebook full of them. The attention of the patients
at these sessions has been remarkable.   There have been no
problems of restlessness, disinterest, or distraction.   When
background music was used as an inspiration to the patients
to write poetry, the Strauss waltzes proved to be the most
popular.

Care should be taken in any such programs to keep
evaluation at a social level.   Psychological interpretation
should be left to the physician, psychologist, or psychiatrist.
Objectives in any poetry reading program planned for restless
or depressed patients should be to provide social contact and
diversion, foster an atmosphere of friendship relating to the
individual's need of belonging, encourage relaxation, establish
an atmosphere of acceptance, stimulate interest, focus attention on a new idea or experience, and project the patients'
feelings.

Mrs. Richardson speaks from experience, not theory.
She has been active in civic affairs for many years in Maryland and was children's librarian for twelve years at the Anne
Arundel County Library.   Among other honors bestowed on
her for her outstanding work in poetry therapy was the Paul
Laurence Dunbar Award in 1969.   This award, presented by
the National Poetry Day Committee, cited her for "outstanding achievement in the use of poetry for the rehabilitation of
mental patients." She has been working with other leaders
to develop a state-wide program for poetry therapy in mental
hospitals.

Evidence that poetry therapy is a potent specialized

branch of bibliotherapy is found in such events as a Demonstration Workshop in Poetry Therapy, held at the annual meeting of the American Society of Group Psychotherapy and Psycho-drama, April 1-4, 1971 in New York City; the Poetry Therapy Symposium at the 34th Convention of the California Psychologists Association, in San Diego January 29-31, 1971; a five-session series in poetry therapy conducted by Mike Larkin, psychotherapist and poetry therapist at Post-Graduate Center for Mental Health, New York, at the Aureon Institute, New York City, in March, 1971; a seminar and workshop sponsored by the Department of Mental Hygiene of Maryland and the Department of Education, Division of Library Development and Services of Maryland, on October 22, 1971; a panel discussion on "Poetry Therapy for Suicidal and Addictive Patients" at the annual meeting of the American Psychiatric Association May 5, 1971; and the writing of several theses in recent years on such subjects as "The Value of Poetry as a Communication of Truths in the Therapeutic Process." Lillian Kristal's research project in poetry therapy was recently accepted by the New York City Board of Education, and Dorothy Kobak has been doing poetry therapy with seven and eleven year old groups of emotionally disturbed children in New York City schools and the "600" schools.

The late Dr. Smiley Blanton, a psychiatrist and author of The Healing Power of Poetry, used poetry with his patients for more than forty years. His book includes an anthology of the poems he used in his practice. He was one of the most distinguished pioneers in the promotion and use of poetry therapy. Dr. Jack Leedy has organized and conducted panels in poetry therapy at the meetings of many professional organizations, including the American Psychiatric Association, the American Society of Group Psychotherapy and Psychodrama, and the New England Librarians' Association. He has organized and conducted programs in poetry therapy in hospitals, schools, clinics, and many other institutions and agencies. Dr. Leedy is the founder and was first president of the Association of Poetry Therapy and is on the staff of the Brooklyn-Cumberland Medical Center Cumberland Hospital, Brooklyn, New York.

Further proof of the rising importance of poetry reading as a specialized branch of bibliotherapy is the offering of a course in poetry therapy by Dr. James Murphy at Long Island University. Beginning in September, 1971, the course was offered in the graduate program in the Department of Guidance and Counseling, Professor William J. Kirman,

Chairman.   A new training program in poetry therapy was
conducted by Dr. Gilbert Schloss at the Institute for Sociotherapy in New York City during the summer of 1972.   The
New York Library Association held a panel discussion on
poetry therapy at its annual meeting in October, 1971.   The
Association for Poetry Therapy held its second annual Poetry
Therapy Day meeting on April 7, 1972, the first one in 1971
having been a great success. [7]

A few pioneers in poetry therapy were using it as far
back as 1929.   A. L. Craigie, writing on the place of poetry
in a veteran's hospital library in Modern Hospital at that
time, stated that the patients seemed to enjoy all types of
poetry except free verse. [8]

The reading of poetry can have a marked therapeutic
effect when done in a group with children.   In Bangor, Pennsylvania, a group of fourth graders, after reading and writing
poetry for several weeks, began to talk about their "feelings," as they expressed it.   To the teacher's surprise, the
children revealed such feelings as misery, disgust, rejection,
confusion, boredom, loneliness and sadness.   Having gained
an insight into their hitherto unexpressed problems, the
teacher was in a much better position to help her children
through bibliotherapy and other techniques.

The rhythm of a poem seems to have the effect of
freeing pent-up feelings as much as do the ideas expressed.
It is well at first that the poetry be read aloud to a group
by an adult who is a good reader and loves poetry.   How
well the rhythm sings out to the listeners will depend on their
ability to hear the poet's melody and make it their own.   "If
a poem is read haltingly or in a deadly sing-song, it has as
little melody as a Chopin prelude clattering from the falter-
ing fingers of an untrained and unfeeling pianist."[9]

When first introducing poetry to children as therapy,
either to a group or individually, it may help to explain that
a poem is actually very much like the rhythm of living.   Tell
the child that there is rhythm in his own body: in his pulse,
his heart beat, the way he breaths, runs, speaks, even if he
is sitting still and dancing with his feelings.   Poetry is only
rhythm put into words.   He must not confuse rhythm and
rhyme in poetry, for there can be, and often is, a rhythmical
cadence without rhyme.   The child should be made to realize
that many kinds of rhythms surround us every day of our
lives, of which we may be unaware until a poem comes along

to bring out the hidden music into verbal expression. The
therapist can point out that there is rhythm in the change of
seasons, the daily exchange of light and darkness, the man-
made rhythm of motors, the rise and fall of the tides, the
cycle of a seed growing, and finally the universal human experience of life, death and new generations arising. Be sure
that the terminology used is within the child's comprehension. [10]

Such comparisons may also be effective with adults who
have read little or no poetry or who have avoided it because
of some unhappy former experience such as having been forced
to memorize too many long poems, sometimes even as a
punishment in school.

Poetry, like music, can give a full range and spread
of tones through the skillful combination of rhythm, meter,
and rhyme. For a child particularly, it may help to point
out that a musical effect may be gained through alliteration--
examples must be shown and a simpler word than "allitera-
tion" used to explain the effect. Most children understand
and enjoy repetition, and this can be pointed out as another
way in which poetry, like music, is pleasing and effective.
The use of word images can be compared to painting, for
most children understand and love pictures. You can show
the child how the very sound of words can express their
meaning (onomatopoiea). Give them examples like "drip,
drip, drip," "murmur," "musty fust of a dusty road," but
avoid the technical term unless you are dealing with an
adult. [10]

The child may wish to write some verses of his own
when poetry is presented as a fascinating game like creating
something with paint, sand, or paper. Such verses, read by
other children in a group or shown to individual children, may
stimulate the over-shy child to express himself, or the hyper-
active or frustrated child to expend some of his surplus
energy or hidden frustrations in words. [10]

Science Fiction as Therapy

For some people at least, said the Reverend Louis A.
Rongione in Catholic Library World, science fiction can serve
as bibliotherapy, particularly in its psychological aspects.
Rev. Rongione believes this special form of fiction accom-
plishes bibliotherapy in the following ways: [11]

1. With its interest in outer space it compensates for our disappointment in a shrinking world.
2. Delving as it does so expertly into matters concerning space travel and other scientific and technical miracles, it restores or revives confidence in American know-how, allaying fears that the United States might become a subject or dominated nation or be destroyed by the technological accomplishments of others.
3. Science fiction can offer some solace for the frustrations of modern man's greatest embarrassment, namely that his probing into age-old problems has created so many more seemingly unsolvable problems. Science fiction is satisfying because it solves problems.
4. Science fiction can offer a refuge from personal problems, for the reader can escape into a book without social disapproval. [This does not seem to be an exclusive property of science fiction. It could be said of any "escape"-type reading.]
5. Space exploration and the amazing accomplishments of science fiction heroes give lavish scope to man's mind, to his courage, and to his aspirations.
6. The further revelations through space travel of the complexity of the universe may strengthen the religious faith of an individual, adding to his sense of security, for much of the science fiction of the past is the reality of the present. (Note the works of Jules Verne.)

Perhaps the basic appeal of science fiction for most patients, whether they are mentally ill, physically ill, or have only disturbing emotional problems, lies in their common desire to escape from the unpleasant reality of their situation. What other type of literature can carry the reader so far from reality--not only from the reality of the patient's immediate environment and condition but from the reality of life as we all know it? The reader may come face to face with disturbing ideas or even horrors in the unreal, but they do not have the same effect as the unpleasant reality he faces every day. No matter how absorbed he becomes in the science fiction plot he knows that this horror or evil is unreal and poses no threat. For patients, however, who have reacted adversely to anything with an element of horror, science fiction should be carefully screened.

Science fiction seems to have special appeal for psychiatric patients. This is perhaps because they have often become mentally ill as a subconscious escape from an unsatisfactory or hated environment. A story in which the environment is invented provides not only vicarious escape but a vicarious sense of power to bring about change.

Isaac Asimov, defining science fiction, calls it "that branch of literature which deals with the response of human beings to advances in science and technology." Since male patients are usually more interested in science and technological advances than women, science fiction finds more fans among men, although there are many exceptions.

Science fiction can be serious or humorous, satirical or didactic, thus suiting the tastes of a variety of patients. According to Robert Plank, there is a similarity between the content of published science fiction stories and private schizophrenic fantasies. Both have suspended the rules which the writers of most other types of fiction do not break. [12]

Patients who have neuroses or psychoses stemming back into unhappy relationships with women--domineering mothers or sisters, venomous, deceitful, or unfaithful wives, jilting sweethearts--may find science fiction particularly to their liking, Plant says, for it is mainly a man's world. Sex is rarely mentioned, and women are conspicuously absent. If romance is introduced it is usually an unimportant element of plot. If there are sexual relationships, the result is often disastrous or nearly so. The men in the story are held together by bonds of duty, ambition, hostility, or solidarity, and a male reader may well gain pride in his own masculinity and a vicarious sense of supernatural accomplishment. There is also little of family life in science fiction, and for a patient who has had family problems of a serious nature this may well be a welcome relief.

For patients who have inferiority problems or physical weaknesses, the power put into the hands of the average science fiction hero, the ease with which he performs superhuman feats or works miracles, can vicariously give the reader a temporary feeling of power, almost of omnipotence. As he identifies subconsciously with the hero, this feeling may even have some carryover to help increase his self-confidence.

Since much science fiction is prophetic it provides

hope for those who have become disenchanted with the present
world and have withdrawn from its reality. Since some of
these prophecies, as in the works of Jules Verne, have become fact, the patient reasons that some of the better worlds
outlined in the utopian type of science fiction may someday
also become fact.   Plank suggests that the works of Edwin
E. Brown, prominent in physical science; Isaac Asimov, expert in chemistry; and the late C. S. Lewis, renowned the-
ologian, can have special therapeutic connotations. [12]

Light Fiction, Magazine Articles, Essays

Light fiction and suspense stories, mysteries of the
conventional type, Gothic mysteries are all good fodder for
the patient whose primary need is to relax.   Escape reading
of this type is usually neither involved nor disturbing unless
one mistakes a macabre horror story or one involving sadism
for a simple mystery or suspense piece.   The bibliotherapist
needs to know his authors well and will stick to such sure-
fire writers as Phyllis Whitney, Mary Stewart, Dorothy Eden,
Daphne Du Maurier, Joan Aiken and other well-known Gothic
novelists.   For light fiction he will turn to Temple Bailey,
D. E. Stevenson, Elizabeth Cadell, Kathleen Norris, Mary
Roberts Rinehart, Emilie Loring, Lida Larrimore Turner
and their ilk.   One recent trend in the Gothic mystery has
been toward Satanism, witchcraft, sacrificial cults, demon-
ology, and supernatural events; such elements may arouse
fear, repulsion, and emotional disturbance.   For the most
part, they should be passed over by the bibliotherapist in
favor of milder fare.

Connell says that many sick people have energy enough
only to read something short, and they like to be able to
finish it.   Short stories and magazine articles, occasionally
essays, can be used in such cases.   The typical who-dun-it
is good escape reading for patients able to read an entire
book, but Connell believes that horror stories should be kept
from mental patients.   Completely engrossed in a fascinating
puzzle, the reader focuses his thoughts away from himself,
his environment, and his illness.   For the western fan, tales
of "hosses, guns, and outlaws" answer the same need.   The
Ellery Queen Mystery Magazine or paperback who-dun-its are
useful for the patient who enjoys stories of this type but does
not feel physically able to hold or read an entire hardbound
book.   Those with tired eyes will appreciate the so-called
"easy-eye" large print paperbacks on non-glare paper.   A

mystery fan who is ill can easily overtax his eyes, sit up in
a reading position too long, or find the concentration too tiring
if given a lengthy volume, for it is very difficult to lay down
a good mystery once one has started it.   The therapeutic
effect of taking a patient's mind off his pain or discomfort
can be dissipated if he becomes over-tired and feels worse
physically after too long a session of reading. [13]

Sister Mary Rose, writing in Hospital Progress more
than thirty years ago, remarked that literary classics often
neutralize bibliotherapy efforts, because they may be difficult
reading and emotionally disturbing to the patient. [14]   Since
human nature seems to change very little, if at all, this
comment may still be valid so far as many patients are concerned.

General Fiction

Sofie Lazarsfeld, a psychologist writing out of more
than 25 years' experience, noted that her attention had been
arrested from the outset by the extent to which people read
fiction to answer their own emotional problems.   Those who
sought her help would refer her to this or that book they had
read, saying that she would find exactly their problem in its
pages.   When she read the books cited, Lazarsfeld seldom
found the identical problem, but she did find her client's personality and his problem portrayed as he imagined them.
This was very valuable in revealing to the psychologist the
individual's total personality and obscured goals.   Many of
the client's conflicts came to light in the ensuring discussions
of the literature with which he identified himself.   "Merely
the act of holding the attention of maladjusted persons on the
question of why certain books impressed them, " Lazarsfeld
said, "often achieves the end result of enabling them to discover certain basic personal characteristics of which they
were unaware. "[15]

Lazarsfeld began to use books as psychotherapy with
clients and, in twenty years of case histories, showed almost
unfailingly constructive results.   She found that clients often
gained insight into their faults, the causes of maladjustments
in their relationships with others, and their wrong attitudes
more easily from reading carefully selected books than
through consultation or other psychological means.   The patient's suspicion that the analyst is out to "sell" him a pre-
conceived idea may become a barrier for proper rapport,

and this, Lazarsfeld says, provokes resistance and blocks
emotional response.   By contrast, the author of a book is
neutral.   He does not know the reader; thus his interpretations can be accepted as genuine and trustworthy.   They are
offered without any analytical purpose and therefore are
easier to accept without reserve.   The patient may not realize
that the book has been especially selected for him because of
its message or the characters it portrays.   Phases of resistance and stagnation of progress were often broken in this
way when other expedients had failed, Lazarsfeld says.

In a Veterans' Administration Hospital survey[16] of
four months' duration conducted in all of the agencies in
1955-56--some 176 hospitals and domiciliary homes--it was
found that V. A. patients read six times as many books as
the general public.   Fiction was a two-to-one choice over
non-fiction, except in the case of neuro-psychiatric patients,
who read almost as much non-fiction as fiction.   In the fiction category, westerns were first choice, followed by mysteries and historical novels; science fiction and sports stories
were the least read.   In non-fiction, the most popular categories, in order, were biographies, history, travel, religion,
philosophy, and science; books on the fine arts and hobbies
were less popular.   Magazines and pocket books, not included
in the survey, were a first choice of many neuropsychiatric
patients, because they were convenient to carry about.   In
the light of current interest in science and science fiction,
and the declining publication of westerns, it is very likely
that a survey taken today would produce different results.

In contrast to the preference for fiction found in some
surveys, Duncan Leys, honorary consultant of Farnsborough
Hospital, Kent, England, states from his experience as a
hospital patient, it is the rather solid kind of book, not very
light or romantic books, which relieves the tedium or anxiety
of hospital stays.   He does not think that light humor has
much appeal to really ill people, if only because many illnesses are painful and it may hurt to laugh.   You have to be
in a very special kind of mood to enjoy the nonsense of
Thurber, he believes.[17]

Of one thing Leys is certain: people who have looked
to a stay in hospital to undertake the kind of serious study
they believe they have always wanted to do, but for which
they think they have never had the time, are always dis-
appointed in their hopes.   They just do not get down to it.
Either the wish was fanciful, and they never did have more

than a romantic view of themselves as a student, or they lack
the energy to carry it through because of the illness and the
conditions of hospital life.

Those who cannot or will not read prefer pictures, but
most heavily illustrated books are large volumes which are
not easy to manage in bed, Dr. Leys says. He recommends
some manageable books with good illustrations and books
wholly about pictures, such as Kenneth Clark's Landscape into
Art, Gombrich's Art and Illusion, and that magnificent collection of photographs, The Family of Man. A collection like
the latter, Leys maintains, is better than books of pictures
of scenery, because it gives scenes from daily life as a universal experience--scenes of lovers, pregnancy, motherhood
and childhood, work, holidays and prayers, illness, sorrow
and death. This kind of book is much more likely to contain
something with which the patient can identify.

Self-help Books

Dr. Lore Hirsch, long a champion of bibliotherapy and
a prolific writer on the subject, said it is almost possible to
diagnose psychiatric patients from the choice of books they
have at their bedside. The more intellectual neurotics frequently read about personality, inner conflicts, and problems
of living; the more anti-social psychopathic is likely to choose
books with gruesome titles such as The Corpse Came Home,
Blood on the Hatchet, or possibly a cartoon book with a se-
ductive picture on the cover. [18]

Dr. Hirsch believed that one cannot assume a maladjusted individual will cure his neurosis or psychosis by
reading How to Relax, How to Stop Worrying, How Never to
be Tired, or others with similarly intriguing titles. Such
publications, and the numerous articles written in magazines
like Psychology, Journal of Living (widely circulated at that
time) and similar self-help periodicals, are widely read, she
says, because they seem to provide simple answers to very
complex problems--problems which cannot be so easily solved.

If a patient reads recommended self-help books and
then discusses them with his doctor, a good basis for an
approach to personal problems can be established, the discussion being the important factor for therapy. Dr. Hirsch
rarely told a patient to read anything, however, preferring to
find out what he read of his own accord and then encouraging

him to talk about his reaction to it.   For the bibliotherapist
to recommend self-help books without an assurance from the
doctor that such a discussion will follow might well be a
waste of time.

Among books written by psychiatrists which can be
used to advantage and read by lay people because they con-
tain a minimum of technical language are: Menninger's The
Human Mind and Love vs. Hate; Saul's Emotional Maturity;
Wertham's Dark Legend and Show of Violence; Horney's Our
Inner Conflicts; Fromm's Escape from Freedom and Man for
Himself; and Reik's Listening with the Third Ear.

For people who have frequent physical disturbances
caused by emotional problems, such books as Psychosomatic
Medicine by Weiss and English, or Carl Bingen's The Doctor's Job, in which the relationship between the function of
the various body systems and the emotions is discussed with
great clarity in simple understandable language, can often
give a patient insight into the cause of his physical problems. [18]

Sometimes sex problems are helped by books like the
Kinsey reports or Margaret Mead's Male and Female.   For
those who can't reconcile religion and psychological concepts,
or where they overlap, books like Liebman's Peace of Mind,
Harry Emerson Fosdick's On Being a Real Person and On
Being Fit to Live, or the works of Peter Marshall may help.
These older titles have proved their efficacy over the years,
and many public libraries still have them available.   Many
new self-help titles are available, of course, some of them
written by reputable doctors, pastors, and understanding laymen, but their effectiveness in bibliotherapy should be tested
carefully.

Sarah P. Delaney, a pioneer bibliotherapist in Veterans' Administration hospitals, found that special group
reading, book reviews, forums, and the study of books on
alcoholism all helped groups of alcoholics toward recovery,
indicating that there is also a place for the informative non-
fiction on the patient's problem. [19]

Most people can read a murder mystery without qualms
because the victim's death is a routine part of the pattern.
However, an account of death outside of a mystery--on the
operating table or from disease--is usually distressing to a
hospital patient or any ill person.   Such books are termed

"pathological, " particularly when they deal with diseases which
are fatal.   In this category also are books which include
maternity deaths or abnormalities, accidental deaths, un-
successful operations, books with emotionally depressing situations or suicides, or those that may shake the patient's
faith in hospitals and the medical or nursing professions. [20]
A patient who is ill or facing an operation needs all the faith
and hope he can muster.

Favorite Non-fiction

        Beside biography (which we have mentioned frequently),
self-help books and factual material on such subjects as alcoholism, humor has its place with certain patients and at
certain times, especially if it can be shared with visitors or
others in the hospital.   The danger of making a patient laugh
too much, if he has been stitched up after an operation, has
already been pointed out.   (It depends, of course, on what
part of the anatomy has been stitched.)   A non-operative
patient may find his whole day brightened by humorous stories or cartoons, and the good humor may spread throughout
the ward.   Satire on the sardonic type of humor, however,
may not appeal to some patients.

        The Bible is often requested by those who are ill.
Just as they need something to make them laugh and forget
their troubles, they may also need something serious, particularly if religion occupies a large place in their lives.
Travel is good because it allows the imagination to roam
even while the physical body is confined to bed.   It brings a
certain sense of freedom which no other type of book or
periodical can produce.   A few patients, though, may find
that travel books only increase their dissatisfaction with being
inactive or bed-ridden and unable to travel as they would like.
This is more likely in the case of a patient who is disabled
for a long period.

        Elderly patients often enjoy history, particularly local
history which may arouse memories of their own early lives.
Generally, they find popular, easy-to-read narrative-style
history easier to understand than dry-as-dust, although perhaps scholarly, tomes overburdened with detail and docu-
mentation.   The Rivers of America series, the Landmark
series, books on the early days of railroads and robber
barons, histories of their own state, are all possible choices
to take an older patient away from his troubles.

Writers whose works have much to offer the reader with vocational or marriage problems include Louis Bromfield, James Branch Cabell, R. P. T. Coffin, Frank Craven, Rachel Crothers, Warwick Deeping, Viña Delmar, Martin Flavin, Rose D. Franken, Ellen Glasgow, Isabelle Holt, Sidney Howard, D. H. Lawrence, Josephine Lawrence, Dorothy Canfield Fisher, Hugh MacLennan, John Phillips Marquand, W. Somerset Maugham, Edith Olivier, Eugene O'Neill, A. N. Ostrovski, Ann Douglas Sedgwick, George Bernard Shaw, L. Tolstoi, Jess Lynch Williams, Barbara Stephens, Ruth Suckow, and Morton Thompson. [21]

Writers who have dealt with parent-child relationships --for example, parental overprotection of children, parent-child conflicts, parental anxiety, filial respect or disrespect, attempts to control the child through claims of sickness, dignity of the child, exploitation of the child, exploitation of the parents by the child, the rejection of the child by the parents or the reverse, father withdrawal into his occupation--include Garzia Deledda, Franz Kafka, Henry James, John Phillips Marquand, Louis Beach, Sylvia Warner, Taylor Caldwell, Maxim Gorki, William Shakespeare, Ivan Turgenev, Feodor Dostoevsky, André Maurois, S. N. Behrman, Honoré de Balzac, Stephen Vincent Benet, Hope Williams Sykes, and others. [21]

Egocentrism (extreme egotism) is a problem with some individuals, old or young. This trait is the theme of Louis Bromfield's A Modern Hero, John Phillips Marquand's B. F.'s Daughter, Oscar Wilde's The Picture of Dorian Gray, Storm Jameson's The Voyage Home, William Saroyan's Sam Ego's House (a play), Louis Auchincloss' Romantic Egoists, John Selby's The Man Who Never Changed, Thomas Hardy's The Mayor of Casterbridge, and Anne Douglas Sedgwick's Tante. Some of these older titles may be a bit difficult to find but should be available through inter-library loan.

A United Hospital Fund of New York publication, Essential Books for Patients' Libraries: A Guide, produced in 1969, mentions several pertinent criteria for choosing books for hospital patients. It points out that while the kinds of material are not as rigidly prescribed as in the past, a few hospitals, particularly those with religious affiliations, still have strong guidelines as to what is acceptable. Even if there is no rigid hospital policy, it is recommended that the administrator and medical and psychiatric chiefs be consulted for their approval or suggestions. The guidelines are

usually similar to the criteria of other libraries but there is
greater emphasis on: books with larger type; books of a size
and weight manageable by the patient; and non-fiction that is
authentic and readable.   Medical texts are excluded specifically. [22]

A handy reference for bibliotherapists is the Fiction
Catalog, (H. W. Wilson) to be found in most public library
reference collections of any size.   Fiction titles are listed
under general subjects.   Although a short summary is given
of each book, these are not complete enough to furnish all
the information the bibliotherapist will need; he should read
any book with which he is not familiar.   The Fiction Catalog
can be a great help, however, as a starting point for making
up a list of books for further investigation.   The Subject
Guide to Books in Print (R. R. Bowker) will also furnish
leads for further study.

Carolyn Folz gives examples of what not to give certain patients:

> Thyroid cases, for example, tend to be nervous
> and easily excitable; such patients should not be
> given books which would intensify this condition....
> On the other hand, patients with broken limbs may
> read the most exciting thriller with no restrictions
> except the general one that it not be depressing in
> effect.   Mental cases are rare in a general hos-
> pital, but there are obvious taboos: any suggestion
> of suicide, murder, or of the particular phobia of
> the patient.
>
> Discernment on the part of the librarian or biblio-
> therapist is necessary in giving out so-called
> cheerful books, for while one person would be
> strengthened by an optimistic philosophy like Mon-
> roe's Singing in the Rain, the Pollyanna type of
> book would annoy the reader who detests being
> obviously cheered.   If the bibliotherapist makes a
> false step here, he could cover his tracks by giving
> an objectively interesting story which will have the
> desired effect but which is not labeled 'cheerful. '[23]

How can all this reading, whether for amusement, escape, or self-analysis, be called bibliotherapy?   Only if the
bibliotherapist--librarian, doctor, nurse, or just good friend
--takes the trouble to know the patient, his interests, tastes,

and present needs; only if each book or piece of reading material to be given the patient is read and analyzed for possible good or bad effect; only if the bibliotherapist works in harmony with medical staff, family, or others responsible for the patient's welfare; only if he has a deep and abiding love for people--only then is it bibliotherapy. The patient has a problem--his illness. Any book that will help him feel better, comfort him, get his mind off his pain or worry, has therapeutic value, and the person who brings patient and book together is practicing bibliotherapy whether he realizes it or not.

A statement made by E. Kathleen Jones many years ago, but as true today as then, may well sum up the type of literature most needed in bibliotherapy: "Bibliotherapy is positive and active. Not content with the distribution of recreational and harmless books, it seeks to supply those which may actually change for the better a patient's viewpoint or philosophy of life. "[24]

Notes

1. Zaccaria, Joseph S. and Moses, Harold A. Facilitating Human Development through Reading. Champagne, Illinois: Stipes Publishing Co., c1968, p. 1.

2. Carlsen, G. R. Books and the Teen-age Reader. Bantam Books, 1967. p. 23-28.

3. Bruell, Edwin. "How to Block the Reading Blocks? Read!" Peabody Journal of Education. v. 44, Sept. 1966, p. 115-17.

4. Koon, Judith. "Cues for Teaching the Mentally Disturbed: Turn on; Tune in; Drop out!" The Clearing House, v. 44, April 1970, p. 500.

5. Limper, Hilda K. "The Public Library at Work with Children in Hospitals and Institutions." American Library Association Bulletin, v. 55, April 1961, p. 330-31.

6. Richardson, Eloise. Poetry Therapy at Crownsville. Mimeographed article. 9p. n. d.

7. APT News (Association for Poetry Therapy News). Un-

signed articles.   April 1971, p. 1-8.

8.   Craigie, A. L.   "Cheering Stimulus of Poetry in Vet-
     erans' Bureau Hospitals. " Modern Hospital, v. 33,
     Nov. 1929, p. 85-88.

9.   Larrick, Nancy. "Children and Poetry. " International
     Reading Association Conference Proceedings: Reading
     and Realism, J. Allen Figurel, editor. v. 13, part 1,
     c. 1969, p. 30.

10. Merriam, Eve.   What Can a Poem Do?   An Explanation
     for Children and Those Who Work with Children.
     Pamphlet. Atheneum House, c1962, p. 1-2.

11. Rongione, Louis A.   "The Psychological Aspects of
     Science Fiction can Contribute Much to Bibliotherapy."
     Catholic Library World, v. 36, Oct. 1964, p. 96-99.

12. Plank, Robert.   "Science Fiction. " American Journal
     of Orthopsychiatry, v. 30, Oct. 1960, p. 801-03, 809.

13. Connell, Suzanne M.   "Books in the Land of Counter-
     pane. " Wilson Library Bulletin, v. 27, April 1953,
     p. 690.

14. Rose, Sister Mary.   "Hospital Library Service for
     Patients. " Hospital Progress, v. 20, Mar. 1939,
     p. 82-3.

15. Lazarsfeld, Sofie.   "The Use of Fiction in Psycho-
     therapy. " American Journal of Psychotherapy, v. 3,
     Jan. 1949, p. 26-33.

16. Kearns, Mildred M.   "Observations on Bibliotherapy in
     a VA Hospital Library. " Kentucky Library Associa-
     tion Bulletin, v. 25, April 1961, p. 22-27.

17. Leys, Duncan.   "Literature in Healing. " Library As-
     sociation Record, v. 66, April 1964, p. 161, 165-66.

18. Hirsch, Lore.   "How a Doctor Uses Books. " Library
     Journal, v. 75, Dec. 1950, p. 2046-49.

19. Delaney, Sarah P.   "Bibliotherapy for Patients in Anta-
     buse Clinic. " Hospital Book Guide, v. 16, Oct. 1955,
     p. 140-143.

20. Mason, Mary F. The Patients' Library. H. W. Wilson
     Co., 1945. p. 82.

21. Porterfield, Austin L. Mirror for Adjustment: Therapy
     in Home, School, and Society through Seeing Your-
     self and Others in Books. Leo Botisham Foundation,
     Texas Christian University, c. 1967, p. 31-32.

22. United Hospital Fund of New York. Essentials for Pa-
     tients' Libraries: A Guide. The Fund, 3 East 45th
     St., New York, N.Y. 10022, 1969, p. 43.

23. Folz, Carolyn. "The Pied Piper of the Modern Hos-
     pital." Library Occurrent, v. 11, April-June 1933,
     p. 42.

24. Jones, E. Kathleen. Hospital Libraries. American
     Library Association, 1939, p. 3.

MATERIAL USEFUL FOR POETRY THERAPY

Angoff, Charles. Prayers at Midnight. Maryland Books,
     Inc., 1971. A book of verse, many of which have
     been found to be therapeutic and can be used in
     poetry therapy groups.

Barshay, Helen. Psalms of a Psychotherapist. Christopher
     Publishing House, n.d. A book of verse, one third
     of which relates to the mentally ill.

Leedy, Jack, ed. Poetry Therapy. Lippincott, 1969.

Leedy, Jack. Poetry the Healer. Lippincott, 1973.

Locke, Wende. Split Hairs. New York University Press,
     1970. A book of verse with special relevance to
     poetry therapy.

Schloss, Gilbert A., Siroka, Robert, and Siroka, Ellen, eds.
     Sensitivity Training and Group Encounter: An Intro-
     duction. Grosset and Dunlap, 1971.

Wolman, Benjamin B. "Poetry and Psychotherapy." Voices,
     Summer 1970.

For Poetry Therapy with Children

These poets who have produced some of their work especially for children have, with few exceptions, written in a simple, direct style the child can understand and enjoy. Obviously, however, not just any poem will do. The particular verses must be selected by the therapist with the child's age, mood, background, and special needs in mind. The works of authors underlined are of special value.

Adams, Franklin P.
Aiken, Conrad
Aldington, Richard
Auden, Wystan Hugh
Behn, Harry
Benet, Rosemary
Benet, Stephen Vincent
Benet, William Rose
Blake, William
Brooke, Rupert
Browning, Elizabeth
Browning, Robert
Bynner, Witter
Carman, Bliss
Carroll, Lewis
Coatsworth, Elizabeth
Coffin, Robert T.
Colum, Padraic
Crane, Nathalia
Cullen, Countee
Cummings, E. E.
Daly. T. A.
Davies, W. H.
De La Mare, Walter
Dickinson, Emily
Doolittle, Hilda
Dunbar, Paul Laurence
Eliot, T. S.
Farjeon, Eleanor
Field, Eugene
Fletcher, John Gould
Frost, Robert
Fuller, Ethel Romig
Guiterman, Arthur
Henley, William Ernest
Hodgson, Ralph

Housman, Alfred Edward
Hughes, Langston
Jeffers, Robinson
Kilmer, Joyce
King, Stoddard
Kipling, Rudyard
Lear, Edward
Le Gallienne, Richard
Lindsay, Vachel
Lowell, Amy
McGinley, Phyllis L.
MacLeish, Archibald
Markham, Edwin
Masefield, John
Masters, Edgar Lee
Meynell, Alice
Millay, Edna St. Vincent
Miller, Alice Duer
Milne, A. A.
Nash, Ogden
Neihardt, John G.
Noyes, Alfred
Pound, Ezra
Reese, Lizette W.
Robinson, Edwin A.
Rossetti, Christina
Sandburg, Carl
Sarett, Lew
Seeger, Alan
Service, Robert
Sitwell, Edith
Spender, Stephen
Stevenson, Robert Louis
Teasdale, Sara
Thomas, Dylan
Thompson, Francis

Untermeyer, Louis
Van Doren, Mark
Warner, Sylvia T.

Whitman, Walt
Wylie, Elinor
Yeats, William Butler

CHAPTER 13

POSSIBLE ADVERSE EFFECTS

Throughout this volume we have emphasized the importance of the bibliotherapist knowing thoroughly both the individual he is trying to help and the contents of the books he prescribes. If he does not know the individual well, he cannot predict his reaction to certain ideas or types of literature. No two persons react to any stimulus in precisely the same way. If the bibliotherapist has been able to observe how the person reacts to similar ideas or materials he has a fairly reliable indication of how he may react to the particular reading material to be suggested.

If this acquaintance with the material is only superficial, the bibliotherapist may suggest a book which could have the opposite effect from the one he hopes to produce. He must have read and analyzed the material in terms of the possible interaction between the subject matter and the individual. If group therapy is planned he must analyze the contents in relation to members of the group as individuals.

A too-introspective person reading highly philosophical books may be separated more than ever from reality. His dream world may be intensified and enlarged by contact with ideas which are conjectural and nebulous. Some persons, absorbed in religion, may brood about their real or imaginery sins as a result of reading the wrong kind of religious literature. A person dissatisfied with the way of the world as he sees it may find an outlet in reading books about murders or revolutions, but may also end up more dissatisfied than ever. Depressing books may further the depression of a manic-depressive or very unhappy person.

An unskilled bibliotherapist may try to force a certain book on a person, causing him to dislike the whole idea of reading. Follow-up, so essential to successful bibliotherapy, may be lacking, and the whole effort can become pointless. Psychosomatic ailments may be intensifed or even induced by reading about them, and anyone with hypochondriac tendencies should not be given material of this type. [1]

In cases of acute illness a reading program is usually of little or no value, as any reading done by such patients is simply for entertainment or diversion; rarely does he read for a proper understanding of his disease. Also, a person acutely ill is often sedated or is so conscious of his own pain or condition that he cannot concentrate sufficiently to gain insight into his own problems. He may forget his physical problems for short periods if he is physically able to read at ail, but light, diverting material ("escape reading") will very likely be all that he will want or that can benefit him. Thus a bibliotherapist who tries to work with a too-ill person may only confuse or irritate him and is unlikely to receive any cooperation from the patient. [1]

Another danger is overdoing the amount of reading. It should be just enough to help the individual cope with his problem but not enough to surfeit or confuse him. For example, a diabetic suffering from marked insecurity was troubled rather than helped when he read so much on diabetes that he discovered discrepancies between caloric values found in various charts. His insecurity was increased as he worried about which chart he should really be using.

Harmful effects also followed in the case of a young mother of a child with rheumatic fever. She collected and read all the information she could find and developed an over-protective reaction which caused a cardiac neurosis in the child.

Another case was that of an elderly person in a nursing home who suffered from Parkinson's Disease. A devoted friend read everything she could find on the subject and felt that the physician was not doing enough for the patient. She gave much of this material to the patient to read, thinking it would help her understand her problems. Although this doctor may not have been doing all he could, he was the only one who would visit the nursing home, and the patient had faith in him. She was making some progress in her attempts to walk alone, but the reading and her friend's attitude made her doubt the doctor. Becoming worried and insecure, she regressed physically.

To be effective, bibliotherapy requires that the patient or recipient be willing to accept counsel concerning the material to be read. He must be prepared to read the material thoroughly, not merely scan it, and he must think about what he has read and try to arrive at its real meaning. He must be willing to discuss the material with the bibliotherapist just as he would discuss a physical ailment with his doctor. [1]

Since adverse effects usually result from wrong choices of material or a wrong understanding of the material by the patient, the post-discussion between patient and therapist is of the utmost importance. It is in this discussion that the bibliotherapist has the opportunity to clear up any misunderstanding the reader may have gained from the content. The importance of knowing the patient or recipient and his condition thoroughly is illustrated in several cases quoted by John F. Briggs M. D. , [1] in which feelings of guilt or depression were strengthened rather than relieved by the bibliotherapist's failure to recognize the extent of these conditions. Two patients cited by Dr. Briggs developed obsessions concerning their heart disease after reading widely in this field, and their conditions worsened from worry and wrong eating habits. One of the patients, a professional man, became obsessed with fear of too high a cholesterol rating and literally starved himself. Failure to recognize the compulsive and obsessive nature of this patient resulted in a cholesterol neurosis.

An emotionally immature patient or subject offers a special risk. Very often, bibliotherapy, unless it is a group effort by a skilled bibliotherapeutic team, should not be tried in such cases. Emotionally immature individuals usually cannot respond constructively because they fail to apply the material to their own case, or they cannot grasp the ideas brought out in the material as it is read. Thus the therapist must consider not only the disease but also the patient's ability to understand and accept bibliotherapy.

If the bibliotherapy to be practiced is medically-related, both the therapist and the physician should know the content of the material to be used. It may be necessary to point out to the patient beforehand that some of the material does not apply to his problem. If he is in doubt about certain portions of it applying to himself, he should consult with either the doctor or the therapist.

Failure on the part of the therapist to recognize that sickness brings increased suggestibility can result in too intense an effect. With the forces of the body below par, the patient is less self-assertive, less opinionated, more recep-

tive.   The mind is nearer to the state just before sleep when
the conscious mind yields to the ever-ready and wholly competent subconscious.   As the nearness to the subconscious
increases, there is less and less of the intermediary conscious mind to modify the impact of any message received
from reading.   It is highly important, therefore, that the
message be one of constructive import.   The subconscious,
when this hypnagogic state of sleepiness or illness exists, is
at the surface, naked and unguarded.   Without the capacity
for interpretation and the braking effect of the fully conscious
mind, an impression may become so intense as to be disturbing, even though in modified form it is only mildly and
constructively stimulating to the emotions.   Thus, in cases
of physical illness where the patient's resistance is low,
special care must be taken in the selection of material. [2]

Intensity of emotion, so often found in well-written
fiction, can affect the actual functioning of the body.   As the
reader experiences the emotions of the characters vicariously
his blood pressure may rise, his heart beat faster; he feels
fear, sorrow, intense joy, perhaps even sexual response.
The physically ill patient, then, should not be given reading
that will draw upon his already depleted life resources.   Material which is inducive to serenity and peace of mind, assurance rather than conflict, gentle humor or pleasurable
narrative rather than dramatic passion and violence, is more
suitable for such physically ill patients, if indeed bibliotherapy is needed at all.

If useful in such cases, bibliotherapy becomes mainly
a soporific, something to get the patient's mind away from
his pain or worries.   This is the basis upon which light fiction, non-sensational biography, and entertaining travel
should be used, and obtuse or intense material avoided.   No
bibliotherapy at all is preferable to bibliotherapy which has
the possibility of an adverse rather than a positive effect.

In dealing with a mental patient even more caution is
necessary.   This does not mean that all mental patients
should have only light, non-disturbing material.   On the contrary, some may well profit from disturbingly controversial
material which stimulates their minds and opens channels of
communication.   But in this type of situation, perhaps more
than in any other, the bibliotherapist must have learned all
he possibly can concerning the patient and his background.
He must have examined records, conferred with doctors and
nurses, observed the patient for some time and in a number

of different situations.   For a murder mystery may serve to
give a would-be murderer a nonviolent vicarious outlet for
his murderous compulsion; but it may, on the other hand, inspire another patient to attempt murder.

With brain-damaged persons, material which is too
difficult can only have an adverse effect.   If the reading materials are not on an elementary level and are not understood, frustration will result.   The brain-damaged individual
has difficulty grasping abstract ideas, so stories chosen for
reading aloud should be short and of the action type rather
than those which rely on character development or are psychological in theme.   In group work the patients' attention
spans are short, and long descriptions slow down story action
so that they lose interest.   Vocabularies are often limited.
The comprehension level will not be the same for all listeners, and if some do not understand while others do, the
feeling of frustration and inferiority on the part of those who
cannot comprehend is greatly increased.   They will be unable
to take part in the discussion which follows and will feel left
out.

As one grows old one's memory returns more and
more to happy periods and events of childhood.   The elderly
ill person reads more slowly as a rule, has less power of
concentration and less capacity for sustained interest, especially for what is unfamiliar.   To offer such individuals
new and stimulating material may be a mistake; the familiar
old classics may be of more comfort and pleasure.

To the old and sick who show no interest in the books
of their earlier years or whose years of growing up may have
held a minimum of reading, any book or other reading material which requires too great a mental effort becomes a
stumbling block rather than recreation.   In such cases the
use of light fiction, short stories, anecdotes, or popular
magazines is often appropriate, particularly material with
illustrations.

On the other hand, persons with prolonged illnesses,
whether old or young, may be seeking in literature, whether
consciously or subconsciously, reassurance about themselves
and the world.   They often find what they want not in light
fiction but in biographies, history, travel, or in novels which
are biographical in essence and have an element of the universal. [3]

For the ill person with certain types of ailments, or for one recovering from an operation leaving a recently stitched incision, an adverse effect from the wrong kind of reading can actually be physical. Humor could be the wrong type of material to give such a person, for it may be painful to laugh, or, worse, laughing too hard could even open an incision. The person attempting to use bibliotherapy with a hospital patient must ascertain from the medical staff his exact physical condition.

Some patients should not read but should be read to. They may be people who are very helpless for a limited time because of some severe illness or operation, or more or less permanently because of some relentlessly worsening disease. They often cannot make the limited effort necessary to hold a book or to keep their eyes focused on the print, but can listen if they can lie flat in as relaxed a state as their physical condition will allow. The one who does the reading should have an agreeable voice and the choice of the material must be made as painstakingly for its therapeutic effect as if it were to be put directly into the patient's hands. There is one slight advantage in this type of reading: the reader must have read the material over beforehand in order to make a proper choice. It is hard to omit portions of a story without changing the sense or making the omissions obvious, but the reader may wish to mark beforehand and omit any passages or ideas which he feels might have an adverse effect. This is censorship, of course, but justifiable under the circumstances, for the physically or mentally ill person is not always capable of judging for himself what is best for him at a certain given time.

The person who reads aloud must bring the material with him and must take it away with him if it contains deleted passages, for the patient may decide to pick up the material later and look at it for himself. The omissions would then be conspicuously evident and would create the very effect to be avoided. Again, it is obvious that the bibliotherapist, if he is to know what should be suppressed and what read aloud, must understand the patient thoroughly and be able to predict his reactions with reasonable accuracy. Reading aloud to a very ill patient or one who is mentally depressed should not be attempted at all by those who do not have the qualifications of a good bibliotherapist or by anyone who is only slightly acquainted with the patient.

Reading aloud can become a point of contact and a

discovery to those who cannot read or have never cared to
read.   There are foreign born persons who speak English but
have never learned to read it with any facility; those for
whom reading has been difficult since childhood; and those in
whom a dislike for or indifference to reading has long been
a way of life.   Such persons may watch television or listen
to the radio if these are available, and will not wish to be
read to.   Reading cannot be forced on these people.

E. Kathleen Jones stresses the fact that book selection
for any hospital includes the careful reading of every book
before it is made available to patients.   Indiscriminate circulation of books depicting illnesses and pathological characters, often found in today's publishing output, may be injurious.   Book reviews found in library publications and current periodicals, she says, cannot be relied upon to reveal
all the information a bibliotherapist needs.   Jones cites as
an example a review of Obscure Destinies, by Willa Cather,
as found in Booklist:[4]   "This volume is made up of three long
short stories: 'Neighbour Rosicky,' 'Old Mrs. Harris,' 'Two
Friends.'   The scene of all three is the west of Miss Cather's earlier novels, and the outstanding figures are similar
to the characters in 'My Antonia,' 'O Pioneers!' and 'The
Lost Lady.'"

A hospital librarian's notes on the same book, says
Jones. might read something like this: "In this volume which
is a collection of three short stories, the first story, 'Neighbour Rosicky' tells of the life of Anton Rosicky, a Bohemian
exile who after many years' experience in London and New
York lives out his life on a prairie farm.   The story opens
with the doctor telling Mr. Rosicky that he has a bad heart
and must stop farm work.   Throughout the story his suffering is grippingly told and his death at the end from angina
brings to a close a complete and beautiful life.   A truly delightful tale but not for cardiac patients.   Recommended for
doctors and nurses interested in the study of angina."

The difference is obvious here.   The bibliotherapist
has always in mind the needs and problems of the individual
he is trying to help, whereas the book reviewer writes for
a more general audience.

To illustrate what can be cruel books in relation to a
patient's problem, Jones discusses Warwick Deeping's Sorrell
and Son and Two Black Sheep, which concern the problem of
cancer.   Because he was a doctor before becoming a writer,

Deeping writes with feeling and understanding of patients'
problems, and the stories are usually given enough lift at the
end to keep them from being depressing.   Nevertheless, since
these and others of his books go into great medical detail,
they should be read carefully beforehand and circulated with
caution.   In Sorrell and Son, for example, there is a tragic
and agonizing description in the last chapter of Sorrell's ill-
ness--cancer of the liver--and his devoted son, Kit, gives
him an overdose of morphine to put an end to his unbearable
suffering.   In Two Black Sheep, Elsie's mother, stricken with
cancer, invites pneumonia to hasten the end.   Reading either
of these could be a traumatic experience for a cancer patient
and might even incite him to attempt self-destruction.

Thus a person who gives any book to any individual
without knowing all of its content is not practicing bibliotherapy.   Indeed, he may be hindering recovery or inducing
a negative or even dangerous effect.   This does not shut the
door upon the layman practicing bibliotherapy.   It only emphasizes the point made consistently throughout this volume, that
one who attempts the science or art of bibliotherapy must
understand the person and know the material before attempting
to bring them together.

The importance of the follow-up discussion after the
reading is finished cannot be over-emphasized.   It is then
that the therapist notes reactions, finds evidence of increased
insight, or has an opportunity to help correct any possible
misconceptions the patient may have formed.

Stories having insane, degenerate, epileptic or otherwise mentally affected characters are not suitable for a
mental patient; nor are books in which suicide is attempted
or accomplished, Jones points out, especially if the actions
leading up to the suicide are carefully described, as in H. G.
Wells' otherwise delightful History of Mr. Polly.   Morbid or
depressing novels, tales which deal with unhappy childhood,
marital unhappiness, physical deformities which warp a man's
nature, or horror stories should also be excluded.

The patient with delusions or paranoid ideas represents
the most difficult and at the same time the most interesting
problem for he will read his own delusions into whatever is
given him; one must therefore be very careful to avoid his
pet aversions, and, when they are harmless, cater to his
ideas.

In Lloyd Douglas' book, <u>Green Light</u>, a senior surgeon
bungles an operation and the patient dies on the operating
table.   His young assistant, to protect his superior, assumes
the blame for the mistake.   This would not do to give to a
preoperative case in a hospital.   Any type of book which tends
to undermine a patient's faith in doctors, nurses, or hospitals
is poor psychology for any hospital patient, regardless of the
type of hospital, and is likely, also to have detrimental value
for the non-hospitalized person who requires frequent medical
attention or is facing a possible operation.   Placing such
books in the hands of patients would also not set well with
the medical staff.

Can books <u>really</u> have any bad effect on patients?
E. Kathleen Jones gives a striking answer in the following
example:

Under protest from the librarian in one mental hospital the chief nurse (an army nurse of the old conservative
type) deliberately gave Philpott's <u>The Grey Room</u> to a ward.
In this story everyone who slept in the grey room was found
to be dead in the morning; the cause, bedsprings filled with
poison.   To the absolute vindication of the librarian, who had
declared that books <u>did</u> influence patients, the entire ward
refused to go to bed that night!   This is an extreme case,
but almost any hospital librarian can give testimony to the
unwholesome effect badly chosen books have had on certain
types of patients.

Another bad effect can result if a number of people
representing various hospital services--such as the physician,
the medical social worker, the occupational therapist, a
nurse, and the librarian--all question a patient regarding his
background.   He will become resentful and suspect that he is
being made a guinea pig for research or experimentation.
This is why the librarian and medical staff must cooperate
and pool their knowledge.   The librarian must gather and
correlate all this information before visiting the patient to
become acquainted and form a personal relationship.

Medical texts are not appropriate for a hospital patient,
whether his illness be physical or mental.   However, on the
recommendation of a patient's own doctor, special books are
sometimes used to help a patient understand his illness.   Few
doctors would ever "prescribe" a book of this type without
being thoroughly familiar with it.   This type of books should
definitely be suggested or authorized by the doctor before

being used.

Expectant mothers who have become unduly fearful over an impending birth should never be given a book like Hemingway's A Farewell to Arms with its prolonged account of death in childbirth. Other books which depict difficult deliveries should likewise be avoided.

The subject of death need not be completely taboo for all ill patients. It is how the death account is handled that matters. Most bibliotherapists, for example, would avoid Lael Wertenbaker's Death of a Man, a non-fiction work in which the author gives a detailed description of her husband's losing fight with cancer and his ultimate suicide. John Gunther's account of the death of his son, in Death Be Not Proud, could be given to some patients but withheld from others; whereas James Agee's Death in the Family would usually require no restriction because it is concerned with family relationships, not with the details of dying. [5]

For elderly and conservative persons, books or other materials which contain obscenity or near obscenity are obviously not a wise choice. Many older people are shocked and disturbed by much of today's literature which features sex or contains episodes considered risqué in their younger days. Such material can upset and worry the reader more than may be realized.

Paperbacks are a good choice in cases where a patient has difficulty holding a book, but some older people have a mental bloc against paperbacks because they associate them still with the early westerns, mysteries, romances, and science fiction which often had somewhat lurid covers (not necessarily indicative of the contents). Some paperbacks also have too small print for those whose eyesight is poor. Some individuals who have been poor readers or non-readers, however, find paperbacks less formidable than hardbacks.

Another precaution for the bibliotherapist is not to recommend any book which may be offensive to the patient's religious beliefs. Books which are offensive to any group, ethnic or religious, are best not given to anyone, since they will likely arouse anger and hostility. If such books are not weeded out by the bibliotherapist through careful reading beforehand, he may find that any possibility of helping the subject has come to an abrupt halt. The person to whom the book is given usually associates the book with the person who

suggested it, and the antagonism aroused by the book will
probably be transferred to the bibliotherapist.   The latter
must know his subject's prejudices, religious beliefs, and
literary tastes and antipathies.

Successful bibliotherapy may require more than the
right book for the right person at the right time.   The bibliotherapist may need to arrange for reading aids so that the
person will be able to read what he is given.   The bibliotherapist should be cognizant, therefore, of any physical handicaps
not immediately apparent to the eye and should help make
available prismatic lenses, bookstands, ceiling projectors,
recorded books, page turners or other devices required by
the individual's physical condition.   Giving reading material
to a handicapped person or to one with poor eyesight without
also supplying such equipment, may serve only to convince
the subject that the bibliotherapist does not understand his
needs and therefore can be of little help.   No aid should be
used, however, without the doctor's or head nurse's permission, in case it conflicts with treatment.   The simplest aid
possible is the least likely to prolong the patient's dependence
on it.

Dr. Karl Binger in his book, The Doctor's Job, said,
"It is almost as important to know what kind of patient has
the disease as it is to know what kind of disease the patient
has."[6] Unfortunately, hospitals, nursing homes, and rest
homes are so understaffed and doctors so overworked today
that there is little opportunity for the cooperative contacts
needed with nurses and doctors.   The bibliotherapist, therefore, must take the initiative and persist in her efforts to
see and talk with the medical personnel and examine case
histories.   Armed with the needed background, the librarian
or other bibliotherapist is then in a position to approach the
patient, pleasantly and casually but alert to any signs that
will give further clues to the subject's interests and personality.   A danger here is that curiosity, rather than the
desire to be a friend and help in any way possible, may seem
to the patient to be the motive.   Hospital patients often resent what they consider prying into their personal affairs by
a stranger.   Before any real bibliotherapy can begin there
must be friendship, empathy, and understanding.

An adverse effect can occur if the bibliotherapist ex-
presses or implies any criticism of the subject's literary
taste.   The bibliotherapist must constantly ask himself whether
or not his own taste and prejudices, rather than the patient's,

are influencing his choices of material.   One may do this
subconsciously without realizing it, and even though the material may have therapeutic value, the effect is lost if all
the elements in the short story, novel, essay, or poem relate
more to the therapist than to his subject.   She should not try
to educate, and she must realize that literary values may
have no therapeutic concurrence. [6]

Reading of difficulties outside his own experience may
bolster a person's courage if he applies the general idea of
overcoming any difficulty by courage and persistence.   However, an unfortunate recommendation can break down morale:
if the hero's or heroine's circumstances are identical to the
patient's, the outcome can be disastrous.   A case in point
occurred when a librarian recommended I Begin Again, by
Alice Bretz, to a middle-aged woman waiting for an operation.
It is a simply written little book which tells the story of a
woman struck blind in middle life who reconstructed her life
with fine courage and distinction.   It seemed just the right
book to recommend, but the librarian did not know an important fact about the patient; namely, that her pending operation was for a thyroid condition.   The author of the book
had become blind after a similar operation.   The patient, obviously, was badly upset. [6]

For children with a weak heart, too exciting a story
can present dangers.   The keenly imaginative child may be
disturbed by giants, witches and ogres between the daylight
and the dark.   Lights are out soon after the supper hour in
most children's wards and there is nothing for a child to do
but lie awake and wait for dreams to come.

With tubercular patients, of which fortunately there are
fewer these days, books like Conrad Richter's The Trees or
Thomas Mann's The Magic Mountain may have a detrimental
effect.   Sometimes, however, the denial of a request for a
certain book can have an injurious effect, too, for the person
who knows definitely what he wants can become frustrated or
irritated at the denial; some in such cases have even been
known to run up a temperature. [6]

Robert Tyson felt that direct advice books, whether in
academic or popular style, are not suited to serious mental
illness. [7]   He cites Thorne: "Logical persuasion can rarely
be effective when emotions so dominate personality dynamics
that behavior is impulsive rather than rational.   A serious
mental case may support his self-destructive or aggressive

tendencies by distortion or misapplication of the material he
reads. "[8] If used at all in such cases, bibliotherapy should
be applied only on the basis of very cautious individual prescription and careful supervision.

Control and perspective must be maintained by anyone
working as a member of a therapeutic team. He or she must
realize that at times reading may be less important for the
patient than becoming mobile once more. [9]

Although the types of material chosen for general hospital patients are not as narrowly prescribed as they once
were, a few hospitals, particularly those with religious applications, still have strong guidelines as to what is acceptable.
Even if there is no rigid hospital policy, it is recommended
that the administrator, medical and psychiatric chiefs be consulted for their suggestions.

In a hospital or other institution the librarian will
meet the new patient soon after his admission. The patient
needs every help he can get toward adjusting to his new environment, and the importance of this first contact between
librarian and patient cannot be overstressed. The patient's
whole attitude toward the library and subsequent efforts at
bibliotherapy will be colored by his first acquaintance with the
librarian and with the library itself. Care must be taken to
make the interview friendly, informal, and disarming.
Wherever the first contact occurs, whether in the library itself, or a ward or room, a generous amount of time should
be given to orientation and to determining the needs and interests of the patient. Otherwise the ability of the librarian-
bibliotherapist to help the patient may be minimized or prevented altogether at the outset.

Notes

1. Briggs, John F. "Adverse Effects from Bibliotherapy. "
      Hospital Progress, v. 45, July 1964, p. 123-125.

2. Jackson, Josephine A. "The Therapeutic Value of Books."
      The Modern Hospital, v. XXV, July 1925, p. 50-51.

3. Leys, Duncan. "Literature in Healing. " Library Asso-
      ciation Record, v. 66, April 1964, p. 164-165.

4. Jones, E. Kathleen. Hospital Libraries. American

Library Association, 1939, p. 8-9, 15+.

5. United Hospital Fund of New York. <u>Essentials for Pa-
tients' Libraries: A Guide.</u> The <u>Fund, 3 East 45th</u>
<u>St.,</u> New York, New York., 10022, 1969, p. 43-44.

6. Mason, Mary Frank. "What Shall the Patient Read?"
<u>The Modern Hospital,</u> v. 66, February 1946, p. 74-77.

7. Tyson, Robert. "The Content of Mental Hygiene Litera-
ture." <u>Journal of Clinical Psychology,</u> v. V, April
1949, p. <u>112.</u>

8. Thorne, Frederick C. "Directive Psychotherapy. XIII:
Psychological Antidotes and Prophylactics." <u>Journal</u>
<u>of Clinical Psychology,</u> v. 3, Oct. 1947, p. <u>356-364.</u>

9. Going, Mona E. "Therapeutic Value of Reading."
<u>Assistant Librarian,</u> v. 63, July 1970, p. 108.

CHAPTER 14

THE USE OF AUDIO-VISUAL AIDS
AS A STIMULANT IN BIBLIOTHERAPY

Although group reading programs to stimulate use of
the library by neuropsychiatric patients are fairly common,
especially in Veterans' Administration hospitals, the use of
audio-visual materials for this purpose is less common. A
notable example of successful use of slides and filmstrips
occurred at a Veterans' Administration Hospital in Pittsburgh,
Pennsylvania. The program began in February 1956. [1]

Sixteen groups of closed-ward patients made a weekly
visit to the library for a one-hour period. Some liked all
the programs and took seats near the screen as soon as they
entered the library; others took part only in those that particularly interested them. The program was held in a corner
of the library where the blinds were drawn and the lights
turned out. A librarian operated the projector, commented
on the pictures and asked questions. Whenever a geographic
area was the subject of a program patients were asked if
anyone present was familiar with it. If so, they were invited
to participate.

Books on the subject under discussion were first dis-
played on a pegboard near the screen; later they were laid
out on a library table, and patients then used them more
freely. Each weekly program was shown for all wards, but
accompanying comments were modified to meet patients' needs.
They were simple for regressed patients, more complex for
the ones in good contact.

Patients asked a considerable number of questions or
remarked on experiences which tied in with the pictures. The
interest aroused in some patients frequently led them to read
up on the subject in the library for as much as several weeks.
Henry Dreifuss, who described the program, cited a number
of instances of patients who formerly had been consistently
silent and who reacted to the pictures and discussions and

established verbal contact with their associates once again. Discussion at times became so lively the librarian did not need to question or comment at all.

Many of the filmstrips used were produced for schools and were accompanied by manuals containing some of the facts needed for presenting the program.   These are usually easily available through a state or local library, sometimes through cooperation with county or city schools.   However, special effort is required to formulate comments that will arouse interest and good judgment must be used about the proper time to make them.   It is important to avoid anything like a schoolroom atmosphere, as many neuropsychiatric patients are oversensitive and tend to resent anyone treating them as other than intelligent adults.   The librarian-therapist conducting the discussions must demonstrate a willingness to be contradicted or corrected.

Once the projector, screen, and a small stock of filmstrips and slides has been purchased, the cost of such a program should be slight, since other films can be borrowed. Dreifuss believes, however, that a small stock of institution-owned films and slides is necessary because there are a few occasions when a borrowed film does not arrive on time or proves unsuitable for showing after arrival.   A vague title may not give a real clue to the contents; thus all films or slides to be used should, if possible, be given a preview by the librarian and any others on the therapy team who can possibly attend, so that any possible ill effects can be detected and the film not used if it is likely to be harmful.

Dreifuss pointed out that at the Pennsylvania Veterans' Hospital where the showings took place, there was a considerable increase in the use of library books, mainly in the library itself; and from the bibliotherapy standpoint, the pictures and books together gave patients new interests, induced many patients to speak up in a group situation, and generally helped them in their resocialization.

The use of radio, television, or any other audio-visual media in bibliotherapy should not be ruled out, but they should be used under controlled conditions and be associated with the use of books and other reading material.

Gilson and Al-Salman, writing on bibliotherapy, said, "Bibliotherapists now realize that various forms of media must be used to reach and stimulate different patients."[2]

Thus the "biblio" prefix may be outmoded, and we may come
in time to use some more general term such as "media
therapy." Recordings, even selected radio and television
programs that are repeats or that emanate from educational
stations and that are thoroughly familiar to the therapist,
may be used if the opportunity presents itself. Obviously
such programs cannot be pre-arranged, but if taped by the
therapist when they occur, they may be used later. In the
case of a repeat TV program, arrangements can be made for
the patient to view it if this seems beneficial. We do not
denigrate audio-visual materials merely by citing the advantages reading may have over certain other forms of communication. The two working together may be more effective than
either alone.

"At various times, " Gilson and Al-Salman point out,
"slides, films, poetry, records, pantomine, puppet shows,
and plays as well as the popular 'book' form have been used
in bibliotherapy. Video tape is used to film some bibliotherapy sessions at the Veterans' Administration hospital in
Oklahoma City. It is then shown to those patients who participated so that they may appraise their own personalities.
Patients criticize their own appearances and personalities as
well as the faults of the others in the group. However, they
also praise those qualities which they feel show good judgment. The video tape is then shown in the psychotherapy
group leaders' meeting where constructive suggestions are
given for various approaches to the same situation. "[2]

By means of storytelling hours a beginning can sometimes be made with patients whom it is very difficult to interest in active reading. Listening to a story is passive,
and even the completely withdrawn patient may be reached by
the storyteller. The inter-personal relationship with the librarian in a storytelling experience helps convince a mentally-
ill patient that there are people of whom he need not be
afraid.

Ward cart service is usually not enough for long-term
patients. Many Veterans' Administration libraries use the
added techniques of word games, story hours, quizzes, music
appreciation hours, talking books, viewmasters, slides, pictures, maps, and all kinds of audio-visual aids used in connection with talks, lectures, and other programs. [3]

Among methods described in Bibliotherapy Methods
and Materials, a 1971 American Library Association publi-

cation, audio-visual materials only were used in a group developmental program on manners, courtesy, and grooming for
retarded or disadvantaged youth in order to build self-aware-
ness, confidence and poise, and to observe the ability of the
group to respond to factual learning, attitudinal learning and
concept learning.   However, books and articles clipped from
magazines were recommended for individual reading.   Materials used included Everyday Courtesy, (Coronet Films);
Mind Your Manners (Coronet); and Manners Make a Difference (Filmstrip House). [4]

An institutional Who's Who Club meeting in the library
to increase understanding and appreciation of the contribution
of various racial and ethnic groups to our national life made
use of pictures, films, filmstrips, music, and a display of
arts and crafts.   Choral speaking to improve articulation and
expression in pupils or patients who have speech problems
may be used as a group activity, as may a modified form of
psychodrama.   Tape recorders are used for geriatric personal interviews (described in Chapter 6); orientation to psychotherapy treatment may make use of books, films, pamphlets, and clippings from periodicals. [4]   Seeing a motion picture may arouse interest in reading the book from which it
was adapted.

As listening to music, looking at pictures, watching a
play, or reading can have therapeutic value, so also can
playing an instrument, singing, painting, acting in a play,
writing poetry or prose, or participating in any creative activity.   By encouraging such activities, bringing books into
the picture either as a stimulant to the activity or as a how-
to-do-it source of information, the bibliotherapist may perform double service for the individual or patient--assisting
him to solve some of his current problems and at the same
time helping him to build a skill or hobby which may give him
pleasure for the remainder of his life.

Writing autobiography as therapy has considerable potential value if the individual has the opportunity to consider
the written material in a counseling relationship.   If the autobiography is to have therapeutic value there must be careful
orientation before the document is written and a follow-up
with the counselor afterward. [5]   Writing autobiography may
not only help the writer gain self-insight; it may also help
him establish a lost sense of identity, the realization of his
own unique self.

The mood or the temperament of a person is so often expressed in the way he plays an instrument, particularly the piano or organ. Hearing a patient play may often help a physician to judge a patient's personality. To a psychiatrist or psychologist, the kind of pictures a person likes or the subjects and style of the way he creates drawings or paintings can also provide very definite clues as to his personality and problems. It is not often possible to get a mental patient or handicapped person to exhibit a talent or skill he may possess, however, until rapport has been established between him and the therapist. The patient must be thoroughly at ease, sure enough of himself to perform before another person. Time and patience may be needed to bring about the desired result.

In art therapy, wherein the individual creates a painting, drawing, or sculpture which through pictorial images enables him to express his thoughts and feelings, emotions are released, communication improved, and ideas given expression. Art becomes a medium of catharsis. Paintings or drawings which are more copies of someone else's art cannot have the same creative and cathartic effect. Patients, both adults and children, should therefore be encouraged to create original artistic forms of art, regardless of how amateurish or crude such efforts might turn out to be. Art therapy can also be used in group counseling, and sometimes added benefit is obtained by members of the group discussing their emotional reactions to the work of other group members. Art appreciation, as opposed to production, may also be revealing both to the bibliotherapist and to the patient himself, as his reactions to various subjects and types of painting are noted and discussed. [5]

Music has many uses in therapy. It may be employed to change the mood of an individual, first by playing music to match his mood, then gradually changing it to influence and alter his mood. It may help to build a counseling-like relationship; or the process of participating in music can become a therapeutic activity. When used with emotionally disturbed children it had a relaxing effect, made a withdrawn child more outgoing, and helped resocialize a severely disturbed child completely withdrawn into himself. With such severe cases a long period of time is required, however. [5]

Play therapy, in which toys are used as a vehicle for catharsis, self-expression and self-insight, is of course mainly useful with children, but music and art have been used successfully with all ages.

Creative writing is therapeutic, regardless of the form of expression, although two forms seem to have particular value--the writing of autobiography, as pointed out previously, and the writing of poetry. Poetry especially seems to express the writer's inner feelings and emotions and affords the bibliotherapist some excellent clues as to the writer's hopes, aspirations, inner conflicts and frustrations.

For a detailed and very interesting discussion of audio-visual, play reading, creative writing, play therapy and other related therapies, see Chapter VI, "Summary, Related Techniques, and Prospectus, " in Facilitating Human Development Through Reading--The Use of Bibliotherapy in Teaching and Counseling by Joseph S. Zaccaria and Harold A. Moses (Stipes Publishing Co. , c1968, p. 86-96). Some of the projects described therein were based upon scientific experiments. These authors have discussed the application of audio-visual and related therapies in more comprehensive terms than any other material this writer has come across.

Notes

1. Dreifuss, Henry. "Listening and Viewing: a Group Picture Program for Neuropsychiatric Patients. " Recreation, v. LIII, Jan. 1960, p. 43.

2. Gilson, Preston, and Al-Salman, Janie. "Bibliotherapy in Oklahoma. " Oklahoma Librarian, v. 22, July 1972, p. 12.

3. Baatz, Wilmer H. "Patients' Library Services and Bibliotherapy. " Wilson Library Bulletin, v. 35, Jan. 1961, p. 379.

4. American Library Association. Association of Hospital and Institution Libraries. Committee on Bibliotherapy and Subcommittee on the Troubled Child. Bibliotherapy. Methods and Materials. Mildred T. Moody and Hilda K. Limper, chairmen. American Library Association, 1971, p. 49-53.

5. Zaccaria, Joseph S. , and Moses, Harold A. Facilitating Human Development through Reading. Stipes Publishing Co. , c. 1968, p. 91.

CHAPTER 15

RESEARCH AND EXPERIMENTATION

Although bibliotherapy has an ever-increasing potential
it has not taken its rightful place in current practice as a
distinct science or art. Three reasons can be given for this
situation: 1) the lack of bibliotherapy courses taught in
schools of library science; 2) the little solid research which
has been conducted in this area since the early 1950's when
the Veterans' Administration libraries conducted efficient and
effective research; 3) "reluctance on the part of librarians to
have interaction with the psychiatric profession. Librarians
perhaps have a slight neurosis to the term 'psycho' anything."[1]
Librarians have often remarked that the psychiatric profession is not cooperative, and while this may be true in a few
cases, Gilson and Al-Salman believe that the psychiatric professional in general is more than willing to work with librarians in bibliotherapy programs. The psychiatric profession, unlike librarians, has long recognized the value of
bibliotherapy as a useful aid in the recovery of patients.

Psychiatric and medical personnel in general, however, adopt a purely scientific attitude toward bibliotherapy.
When they are skeptical about its potential, this may well be
because of lack of research proof of its efficacy. Often,
too, individuals in the medical profession may not be reluctant so much as lacking in time for conferences. Some
doctors, psychiatrists, and psychologists have not been able
to cooperate regardless of how willing they may be.

The need for more and better research is critical.
Results of so-called "experiments" have often been inconclu-
sive because of inability to isolate the bibliotherapy treatment
from other factors and conditions. When constructive results
are shown in an individual patient with whom bibliotherapy is
being employed, how can it be determined positively how much
progress is due to the bibliotherapy, how much to a pleasant
hospital or home environment, how much to medical or psychiatric treatment, how much to the love and support of

344

friends and relatives, how much to other factors? There is constant interaction between the patient and any number of persons and conditions. In a truly scientific study it would be necessary to have two groups of people, identical or similar in educational and social backgrounds, physical or mental conditions, age, sex, and interests. They would need to be in the same institutional or home environment with surrounding conditions closely controlled. The experimental group would receive bibliotherapy; the control group would not. How difficult it would be to set up such an experiment is readily apparent.

Nevertheless, as close an approximation as possible to scientific methods and clinical applications must be attempted in studying the effects of bibliotherapy. Two possible pitfalls must be avoided, however: 1. the danger that science may straitjacket and inhibit bibliotherapy; and 2. the danger of succumbing to the subtle fallacy that a thing is not true unless proven to be so scientifically. Quite the reverse is the case. It is only because a thing is true that it ever becomes possible to prove it so scientifically.

So far, while there has been no well-articulated, coordinated, systematic program, there have been five basic types of "research":

1. Exhortatory studies (not true research). These present the general uses of bibliotherapy and recommend more extensive use.

2. Attempts to relate bibliotherapy to other aspects of practice (Theoretical research). This may be an historical approach or the role of a specific practitioner, a taxonomy of problems, and a bibliography of pertinent books for individuals having these problems.

3. General descriptive research. This type describes how bibliotherapy has actually been used in a particular type of work setting: classroom, neuropsychiatric hospitals, juvenile delinquency settings, or private practice of counselors, psychiatrists, psychologists, librarians, etc. Detailed descriptions of techniques used are given and results cited.

4. Case study research. Case studies are used to

illustrate principles, or to describe use of specific
types of literature, the effectiveness of various
types of bibliotherapy with particular types of peopl
or problems, unique problems of a given individual
and the specific use of bibliotherapy for that individual.

5.   <u>Experimental research studies</u> (Genuine research).
     a.   Before and after studies--one group measured
          twice.
     b.   Controlled experimental studies.   Two matched
          groups, measured to be sure they are similar.
          One group (the experimental) receives the
          normal experience plus a bibliotherapeutic ex-
          perience.   The other, or control group, re-
          ceives only the normal or typical experiences.
          Both groups are tested before and after the
          prescribed period of time encompassing the
          bibliotherapeutic experience. [2]

As stated before, much of the research and experimentation was done during the 1950's in Veterans' Administration Hospitals.   Sadie P. Delaney describes how patients
in the Veterans' Hospital at Tuskegee, Alabama, were observe
for study and their progress evaluated by psychologists and
psychiatrists. [3]   For readers who desire to look up these older
studies, references are given at the end of the chapter; space
does not permit full descriptions of the projects in this
volume.

A study made by Nila B. Smith of children in grades
four through eight in five widely separated schools showed
that in response to a question asking them whether they remembered any books, stories, or poems which had changed
their thinking or attitude in any way, 60. 7 per cent of the
children reported a change in attitude, and 9. 2 per cent a
change in behavior.   No two children in any one grade mentioned the same book.   Among classics mentioned, the reading of which had effected a change in attitude, were <u>Tom
Sawyer</u>, <u>Huckleberry Finn</u>, <u>Little Women</u>, <u>Heidi</u>, and <u>Treasure
Island</u>.   Among later stories treating of racial problems, <u>Call
Me Charlie</u> and <u>Steppin and Family</u> were mentioned. [4]

Caroline Shrodes' doctoral dissertation at the Univer-
sity of California in 1950, a 344-page document, was entitled
"Bibliotherapy: a theoretical and clinical experimental study. "
It explored the theory and practice of bibliotherapy and pre-

sented a definitive case history and briefer studies to illustrate and corroborate the theory.

Favazza, in 1966-67, studied what happens to reading patterns in patients who have psychiatric disorders, as compared to patients who have primarily organic medical diseases. His results led him to conclude that it would be worthwhile to inquire about shifts in reading patterns among persons with psychiatric illnesses such as schizophrenia or depression.

In 1967 R. H. Alexander, a professional librarian with a background in psychology and psychotherapy, attempted to measure attitudinal changes in patients after a program of reading and discussion of literature selected with reference to the psychiatric category, namely chronic schizophrenia. Her study showed that with the application of bibliotherapy, chronic schizophrenic patients under drug therapy can learn to perform tasks hitherto considered beyond their ability. [5]

Research in the behavioral sciences (psychology, social psychology, sociology and anthropology) has resulted in the accumulation of enough knowledge about the course of human development that practitioners of bibliotherapy can help individuals to anticipate problems and crises, and in many cases eliminate them before they occur.

A related group of studies focuses upon bibliotherapy and its relationship to mental health. Darling[6] presented a global overview of mental hygiene books; and elsewhere, analyses are made in terms of the social psychology of children's reading material, [7] the validation of mental hygiene literature, [8] and the content of mental hygiene books. [9]

Hannah, in 1955, described experiments in the use of books carried out at the Naval Hospital in Portsmouth, Virginia, to aid patients in their rehabilitation. [10] The first issue of the Association of Hospital and Institution Libraries Quarterly (Fall 1960) announced a regular page devoted to the reporting of research in the field of bibliotherapy. A perusal of the quarterly issues since that date should give a summary of at least the most important studies and experiments. The contributions of research in bibliotherapy to language arts programs was surveyed in 1950 by D. H. Russell and Caroline Shrodes in School Review. [11]

Elizabeth Pomeroy described the results of a study of

the reading interests of 1, 538 individual patients from 62 Veterans' Administration facilities in April, 1937.   The individual
case reports completed by libraries in cooperation with clinical directors and chief medical officers showed the similarities and differences in reading interests of the neuropsychiatric
and general medical and surgical patients.   The author states:
"... The study has confirmed the belief that supervised reading has its definite and industrial therapeutic role in the hospital program. "[12]

Janis Berry was involved in a group reading experiment at Cleveland Psychiatric Institute for two years. [13]
Seventeen chronic schizophrenics for whom intensive therapy
of all kinds was planned were the subjects.   The reading
period was for two hours once a week.   The results of each
session were reported at a meeting of all the therapists the
next day.

Biographies showing great success in life despite great
difficulties evoked the most response.   Jim Piersall's biography Fear Strikes Out, on mental illness, was most popular;
Irving Stone's Love is Eternal, which includes Lincoln's three
bouts with depression, was rated second in popularity.   One
patient with a record of two hospitalizations who had become
an alcoholic would not speak or participate for four months,
then offered to give a book talk.   He chose his own book, a
biography.   He was released soon after, was not hospitalized
again.   The program, unfortunately, was later abandoned for
lack of money and trained personnel.

Despite some confusion and limitations, there is sufficient evidence to support the claim that carefully selected
reading for the right subjects can have and does have therapeutic value.

Recommendations:

1.   Individual librarians, public and specialized, who do not
     realize the possibilities of bibliotherapy need to acquaint
     themselves with some of the literature in the field, at
     least that which deals with the basic principles.

2.   Schools of library science must take a more active in-
     terest in the training of bibliotherapists, offering courses,
     seminars, workshops, and clinical field experience in
     bibliotherapy.   A course taught by Louis A. Rongione at

Villanova University in the fall of 1970 was very well received and occasioned sufficient response for it to be given again in the 1972 spring semester. A follow-up course to include clinical experience was also planned.

3. State library associations should join the American Library Association in promoting study of and interest in the practice of bibliotherapy. State libraries should sponsor local workshops either independently or in cooperation with accredited library schools in their respective states, preferably, of course, as cooperative projects.

4. General hospitals, mental and correctional institutions, as well as schools, not now including bibliotherapy in their library and counseling programs should investigate the possible benefits of making use of people trained in bibliotherapy and biblio-counseling.

5. More research of the truly scientific type is desperately needed in the following areas:
   a. A study of the concomitant benefits that seem so often to accompany bibliotherapy but are not the direct result of the therapy itself.
   b. Studies of the effects of various types of books upon various types of individuals under scientifically controlled conditions.

6. There should be established a research center for bibliotherapy at one of the country's great universities, funded by a foundation grant, the federal government (Department of Health, Education and Welfare), private philanthropy, and/or other possible sources.

7. A National General Bibliotherapy Association, including or in cooperation with the already existing National Association for Poetry Therapy, should be established to bring together all those interested in the art and science of bibliotherapy to share experiences and techniques; to hold an annual conference, sponsor workshops, focus national interest on bibliotherapy as a growing force. Such a group would strive to gain members among general physicians, psychiatrists, neurologists, psychologists, librarians, nurses, administrators of institutions, counselors in schools and various types of institutions, social workers, etc. While the American Library Association has had a bibliotherapy committee, it does not draw from the other professions which need to work together to publicize and

use bibliotherapy.

8. Standards for training of bibliotherapists should be set
   and the courses that are set up should consistently prepare bibliotherapists to meet these standards. The
   standards should be reviewed from time to time and adjusted as new facts emerge from research or new demands arise from changing social conditions.

9. Research need not be confined to hospitals but could be
   carried on in schools, social agencies, correctional institutions, anywhere bibliotherapy can be carried
   out.

There is no doubt that bibliotherapy as such is matur-
ing. It is no longer just anecdotal reporting; investigations
and studies are being conducted on a sounder scientific basis
by librarians, physicians, and members of other disciplines.
There is, admittedly, still far too little research, but the
field is broad and challenging, and in the decade of the six-
ties the field of application broadened.

We can expect to see a greater use of audio-visual
aids in conjunction with, or independently of, books, magazines, and other library materials traditionally used in bibliotherapy practice. A more inclusive name, such as media-
therapy, seems to be inevitable as this trend grows.

One very interesting project using films and discussion was carried out at Kings Park State Hospital, Kings
Park, New York, where a group of severely regressed adults
showed marked improvement over a control group. The project was conducted with LSCA Title IV-A funds. Particulars
of this experiment can be secured by writing Miss Grace
Lyons, Librarian, Kings Park State Hospital, Kings Park,
New York, 11754. [14]

The medical profession, especially in the 20th century, has increasingly accepted the concept that the state of
mind and the state of the emotions are vital factors in causing and in curing physical illnesses. As this concept continues to grow, bibliotherapy or media-therapy will occupy an
increasingly important place in treatment procedures.

Notes

1. Gilsen, Preston, and Al-Salman, Janie. "Bibliotherapy in Oklahoma. " Oklahoma Librarian, v. 22, July 1972,

2. Zaccaria, Joseph S. , and Moses, Harold A. Facilitating Human Development Through Reading. Stipes Publishing Co. , c1968, p. 27-28.

3. Delaney, Sadie P. "Time's Telling. " Wilson Library Bulletin, v. 29, Feb. 1955, p. 461-63.

4. Smith, Nila B. "The Personal and Social Values of Reading. " Elementary English, v. 25, Dec. 1948, p. 490-500.

5. Alexander, R. H. , and Biggie, S. E. "Bibliotherapy with Chronic Schizophrenics: The Therapeutic Function of the Psychiatric Librarian in a State Mental Hospital. " Journal of Rehabilitation, v. 33, Nov. -Dec. 1967, p. 26-27, 42.

6. Darling, Richard L. "Mental Hygiene and Books. " Wilson Library Bulletin, v. 32, Dec. 1957, p. 293-296.

7. Lind, Katherine N. "The Social Psychiatry of Children's Reading. " American Journal of Sociology, v. 41, Jan. 1936, p. 454-69.

8. Townsend, A. "Books as Therapy. " The Reading Teacher, v. 17, Nov. 1963, p. 121-126.

9. Tyson, R. "The Content of Mental Hygiene Literature. " Journal of Clinical Psychology. v. 5, April 1949, p. 109-113.

10. Hannah, R. G. "Navy Bibliotherapy; Library Programs." Library Journal, v. 80, May 15, 1955, p. 1171-73.

11. Russell, D. H. , and Shrodes, C. "Contributions of Research in Bibliotherapy to the Language Arts Program. " School Review, v. 58, Sept. -Oct. 1950, p. 335-42.

12. Pomeroy, Elizabeth. "Bibliotherapy--A Study in Results of Hospital Library Service. " Medical Bulletin of the

Veterans' Administration, v. 13, April 1937, p. 360-364.

13. Berry, Janis. "Bibliotherapy." Catholic Library World, v. 39, October 1967, p. 123-24.

14. Letter to author from Eleanor A. Ferguson, New York State Library, Division of Library Development.

CHAPTER 16

CASE STUDIES

A leading and successful Boston business man who before he was stricken commuted from his suburban home and
served his town in official positions, became mired in a bog
of mental exhaustion. After fifteen years in hospitals he
made a marvelous recovery and is now enjoying a normal
life at home and in a constantly widening field of interests.
What happened to him is happening to many today.

For fifteen years he was exiled from his home. A
long period of treatment with skilled nursing, supervised exercise, wholesome occupations and guided reading kept him
in good physical condition and held in check his chronic depression. After he had spent eleven years in the institution,
the doctors decided to try electric shock treatment, and it
wrought a miracle. Overwork, mental exhaustion, work and
anxiety caused his breakdown. Entrance into town politics
had caused intense strain. He was Chairman of the Planning
Board, had a business loss in a firm he had invested in, and
as a result had an inferiority complex. His reading and the
book reviews he wrote for the McLean Hospital paper were
potent factors in his recovery, according to his own statement. [1]

Mrs. Pearl G. Elliott, in a talk before the Illinois
Library Association in 1958, described a number of cases in
which reading aided in recovery. In one case,

> a sullen boy from an underprivileged home refused
> any reading material and read only comic books.
> One day he did take a book, and on the librarian's
> next visit he met her, face aglow. He loved that
> book and wanted another.

> A very withdrawn little girl never chattered with
> her roommates nor did she read. The other girls
> had been reading a book that contained a recipe,

and now they wanted a book with more recipes--a cookbook. Then the quiet child beckoned to the librarian. 'I'd like one too,' she said, 'but I'd rather have one about sewing.'

She was given The Hundred Dresses by Eleanor Estes, and that book seemed to bring her out of her dream world into the activity of her ward. [2]

Clara Lucioli, in an article entitled "Out of Isolation," relates an interesting case: [3]

> For 20 years, from her 76th to 96th birthday, we fed, promoted and enlarged the reading interests of a homebound lady who maintained a small apartment in a residential hotel. When family members tried to move her from the city her main reason for refusal was the homebound library service. After a fall and broken hip hospitalized her, the family disposed of her belongings and enrolled her in a fine nursing home. The librarian, who was called upon to help clear out the personal library, visited the patient in the hospital and was satisfied her mind was as keen as ever.
>
> When the few remaining contents of the apartment and its bewildered owner were settled in one tiny room, the adjustment was a traumatic experience for the old lady. She was frightened and unhappy but the continuation of the library service in the new setting was a link and gradually more and more of the old interests were salvaged. The day came when the librarian could return many of her personal books on lace making and patterns and the most skeptical of staff were convinced that here was a woman of imagination, skill, and exceptional interests. Who could deny the therapeutic value of books used in this instance as a bridge between the old and the new, making the pathway into the new smoother and less disturbing?

Hilda Limper of the Cincinnati and Hamilton County (Ohio) Public Library, who worked with exceptional children, says that the most dramatic evidence she has had came one day when a boy whose face was drawn with pain from a severe burn was brought in for the story hour. As he lost himself in the trials of Shawneen and the Gander she could literally see the lines on his face relax, and it seemed certain that for a time at least he had respite from his pain.

Charles Carner, in Today's Health, [4] reports the case of Robert A., whose feeling of hostility towards a domineering father was a contributing factor to his illness. Dr. J. Watson Wilson, consulting psychologist, first prescribed two books--Victory Over Fear by John Dollard, and Through Children's Eyes by Blanche Weill. He instructed the patient to read these several times and suggested another appointment whenever the patient wished. The patient returned nine months later, much improved. He admitted the reading had helped, but he didn't know just how. In later meetings the following books were prescribed:

> Fink - Release from Nervous Tension
> Levy and Monroe - Happy Family
> Kraines and Thetford - Managing your Mind
> Tead - Art of Leadership
> Starch - How to Develop your Executive Abilities
> Hepner - Psychology Applied to Life and Work
> English and Pearson - Emotional Problems of Living

The last book was Peace of Soul by Bishop Fulton Sheen, because the patient wanted a book with a Catholic point of view. A final conference was arranged with a different psychologist, Charles D. Flory. He reported that Robert A. was well adjusted and highly competent. His personality was almost the exact opposite of what had existed a few years before. This patient was, of course, young, highly intelligent, had a good education, and was willing to cooperate and profit from his reading.

Katherine Keneally, discussing the "Therapeutic Value of Books," reports the following case as an example of the successful use of bibliotherapy by Dr. Thomas V. Moore of the Child Center of Catholic University of America. [5]

> A 16 year old girl was coming to the clinic because she was having epileptic seizures. At one interview she stated, 'I am sixteen now and I won't go to school any longer. I am going to leave home and live by myself.' She was determined to leave home because of a quarrel between her father and grandmother. When, in a violent temper, the father ordered her grandmother to leave the house, the girl, who loved her grandmother, decided to

leave home if her father carried out his threat.

After talking the problem over with Dr. Moore the
girl promised to delay her departure from home for
two weeks and took home Land Spell by Carroll to
read.   In a few days Dr. Moore received a letter
in which his young patient said that since she had
read the book she saw what he meant.   She must
have an education in order to go out and face the
world.   She had gone to school for a week and could
truthfully say she had never had a better time. She
felt that her father really loved her and did not
want her to leave.   In summarizing the case Dr.
Moore said, 'In these acute adolescent crises a delay of a few weeks is often all that is needed to tide
over the present difficulty and lay the foundations of
a therapeutic procedure which will modify the whole
personality. '

G. O. Ireland related the following case of a patient
who had a fairly good background. [6]   His attendance at school
had been irregular, and he seemed to have been backward.
He was large for his age and evidently sensitive about it,
which may have accounted for his delay in finishing school.
He had no particular interests.   He was somewhat religious.
He was fairly sociable and liked boys and girls equally well.
He had been married but because of an unfortunate marital
experience had separated from his wife.   At one time the patient smoked to excess but had given this up since he was
discharged from the army.

When this patient was admitted to the institution he was
confused, mumbling and self-accusatory.   He had evidently
developed a psychosis during his stay in a general hospital
after an appendectomy.   He was generally inaccessible, but
at other times was willing to talk.   He showed marked delusional and religious tendencies and had ideas of self-abase-
ment, believing that he had committed some horrible sin. He
became confused and gradually sank into a stupor.   About
three weeks after his admission he seemed well enough to be
taking some notice of his surroundings, and a copy of Popular
Mechanics was brought to him after he had been asked if he
would care to write home and had refused the suggestion.
His attention was temporarily aroused and when he was left
alone he gradually grew sufficiently interested to turn the
pages and read.   After some time he asked if he might not
have writing material, and then wrote a fairly coherent letter

home. After that time he showed more interest, performed
his occupational therapy assignment and visited the library
fairly regularly. He was put on parole and given a regular
occupational therapy assignment, assisting in one of the diet
kitchens.

The following brief cases were reported by Sadie P.
Delaney, a member of the therapy team in the Antabuse Clinic
of Tuskegee, Alabama:[7]

> M. G. ... Limited educational background. Pre-
> viously used the library, reading all magazines.
> His periods of alcoholism interrupted his reading
> and interest. During antabuse treatment he read
> stories from Saturday Evening Post and Collier's
> magazines, and the books, You Can Stop Drinking,
> by H. M. Sherman; Other Side of the Bottle, by
> Dwight Anderson; Spirit of St. Louis, by Charles
> Lindbergh. He gave a creditable review of the
> Collier's magazine article on Adlai Stevenson's
> world tour and made a weekly news report
> and reviewed the books he had read at Antabuse
> Clinic. At the Thursday Evening Press Club he
> was News Reporter. Prior to his antabuse treat-
> ment his memory was somewhat impaired. He is
> now assigned to the library for periods assisting
> with exhibits and newspaper and magazine racks.
> He is chairman of the Alcoholics Anonymous Asso-
> ciation organization on Ward T at the hospital.
>
> J. S. ... Limited background. This patient did
> not use the library prior to antabuse treatment. He
> showed no signs of interest in the first Bibliotherapy
> Hour. Later he began to comment on what others
> reviewed. Soon he presented various original
> drawings. He said he would 'let these take the place
> of book reviews. ' When he came to the library he
> later discovered First Book of Negroes, by Langston
> Hughes. He expressed a desire to read this book
> and to draw pictures from it. He gave a very good
> review of the book at Bibliotherapy Hour at the
> Antabuse Clinic and exhibited his pictures. He re-
> ceived much praise from his comrades. He finally
> contributed newspaper article reviews. This praise
> for accomplishment seemed to aid his feeling of
> well-being. He is at present on trial visit.

E. N. ... This patient had limited background but
became interested in <u>Natural History</u> and <u>Nature</u>
magazines.   He was especially interested in the
chimpanzee.   He reviewed two magazine articles on
Christine, the famous chimpanzee, and gave a
lengthy discourse on Cheetah of movie fame.   This
led him to other reading.   He often vied for first
place on the Bibliotherapy Hour.   He is now on trial
visit.

A. G. ... This patient had a good educational background, and before antabuse he read <u>Other Side of
the Bottle</u>, by Dwight Anderson, and <u>You Can Stop
Drinking,</u> by Harold M. Sherman.   He expressed a
desire to keep the latter book and finally purchased
a copy through the mail. He gave an excellent review
in the Antabuse Clinic Bibliotherapy Hour, and his
comments on the reading of other patients were
splendid.   During an emotional upset, he requested
religious material and refused any other reading.
On advice from his ward psychiatrist, this material
was not given him.   His psychotic behavior caused
him to be removed from the group.   He was later
discharged from another service.   He has returned
to the hospital and attends the library.   He is a
constant reader of other books, and so far has re-
frained from alcohol.

E. M. ... This patient had a limited background.
During some of the first Bibliotherapy Hours in the
Antabuse Clinic he reported on crime stories from
magazines and articles on crime from newspapers.
His comrades refused to listen to him.   The librarian suggested <u>National Geographic</u> magazine.
The articles on people in other countries interested
him and awakened his memory of personal experiences with people in other countries.   He received
much applause for his weekly contributions.   He
appears less nervous and now has his freedom of
the grounds.

G. P. ... Limited background.   This patient at first
refused to participate in the Bibliotherapy Hour of
the Antabuse Clinic.   Later he read <u>Travel</u> magazine and reviewed articles from it.   His reviews
were enthusiastically received.   His attitude has
changed from apparent seclusiveness and he is more

sociable. He has obtained freedom of the grounds.

J. W. ... This patient had an exceptional background, and used the library over a period of years
reading classic literature exclusively. His interest
was curbed by alcohol indulgence. During his period
in the Antabuse Clinic he reviewed articles from
Reader's Digest, Biography of Winston Churchill
and History of San Francisco. He requested the
book Red Jacket, by Arthur C. Parker, but on finding accounts of Indians drinking said, "I don't want
to read about anyone drinking." He gave a scholarly
review on History of Leather and spent much time
in reference books for his material. He is a genius
in leathercraft at Occupational Therapy. He attends
the Thursday Evening Library Press Club and is
sergeant-at-arms in this club.

Ann Matthews tells of several cases when she served
as adult services librarian of the Jackson Public Library,
Jackson, Michigan, providing library service to local hospitals:[8]

How does the patient's library in your hospital function? If your volunteer group is efficient, then the
greater percentage of your patients are cared for
effectively.... What about the special needs of the
long-term patient in the general hospital? Is your
hospital forced to forget the unique problems of a
young patient, such as we served, who spent months
in traction following an accident? Her parents and
little brother were killed in a crash. When I first
called on this child she kept her eyes shielded from
the world. I left a book on her bedside table and,
later, when I passed her room, she tightly hugged
the familiar book to her breast, though she still hid
her face from the world. As the weeks passed, she
asked for old favorites she had read before. Books
helped her find security in a changing life in a
strange city. We librarians call this bibliotherapy.

Or consider the young man in traction who was hospitalized for over a year. His education had been
limited but his desire to read could not be satisfied
by the hospital's volunteer cart. He wanted to study
music, psychology and mathematics. He was considering correspondence schools and the library was

supplying information on such schools when an operation speeded up his release. He continued to
come into the library for his reading needs while
still on crutches and as yet unable to return to work.
He now reads technical books that would help him
on a new job. He could not return to the hard
physical labor he had followed before his accident.

In our hospital, an occupational therapist sat one
afternoon listening to a talking book with a mental
patient unable to focus her eyes following an operation. Our library supplied the record player and
long playing recordings. The patient is now released, and the city library joined the city hospital
in giving the disturbed patient the comprehensive
care needed.

I had visited this patient before her operation. She
was crying uncontrollably the first time I entered
her room. She had rejected the books on the volunteer cart in the ward room. Even in her deep
dejection her reading desires were specific. She
received no book from my cart that had not first
been read by a member of the library staff. This
patient needed the services of a trained librarian.
As I left her room upon that first of many visits,
she had thrown away her tear-soaked tissue and sat
up in bed to read.

Sofie Lazarsfeld reports on the use of fiction in psychotherapy in the following cases:[9]

A woman came to ask for help because her husband
was cruel to her. According to her version she
was without fault. Experience has taught me to
suspect those who put all the blame on others of
being responsible for the crime. One may by sure
that the person who says nothing of his own faults
but catalogues only those of his persecutor is responsible at least 50 per cent for the mess he is
in. And as my client painted her husband in dark-
est colors, the certainty grew in me that she had
contributed substantially to her marital troubles.
Yet her shortcomings remained obscure to me; she
seemed to be a decent sort, rather easy-going and
soft and not aggressive at all.

I started her readjustment in the usual way, but
found her strangely unreceptive, impregnably en-
closed in her own set ideas.   Finally I resorted to
the 'Fiction test. '

I asked her for books that had especially impressed
her.   Instantly, without reflection, she named three
books whose contents differed widely; but there was
a similarity in all three books, concealed but significant: the heroines, upon analysis, were all the
same.   Each got everything she wanted from the
hero without herself contributing anything.   It was
a formula: men have to give; the role of woman is
to receive.   Furthermore, all three authors had
painted this arrangement in the agreeable colors of
a normal, moral status.   Subsequent sessions with
my client verified my belief that this was her conception of a normal love-relationship.   She said
that she never had been conscious that this was her
fixed attitude, or that it was unusual or that it
should be questioned.   When the inequity of such a
love-relationship became explained to her, she saw
immediately that her conflicts originated from her
expectation of getting 100 per cent while contributing nothing.   She learned to give something to the
partnership and from there on her marriage proved
more successful.

This time my client was a young woman who had
been her mother's favorite to such a degree that a
strong neurotic bond had been established between
mother and daughter.   It dominated her life, long
after her mother's death.   She walked through life
as if everyone were under obligation to look upon
her as her mother had, namely as the center of the
world for whom nothing was good enough.   Any experience that fell short of this extravagant expectation became to her deep disappointment because
unconsciously her guiding goal was mother's approval and every act was gauged by whether or not it
would satisfy mother.   Of course, mother never
would be satisfied by the world's treatment of her
beloved child.

Such a style of life inevitably brought her continuous misery.   It endangered her marriage.   Intelli-

gent, and a logical thinker, she quickly grasped the
nature of her problem but this did not prevent her
from lapsing into the old pattern.

Her dreams showed that she was attacking her
problems, and I thought that fiction might accelerate
the process.   Therefore, without any apparent connection with the rest of our conversation, I asked
her one day whether she remembered Grimm's fairy
tale, "Fallada Oder die Gaensemagd. " She was a
European and I knew that she must have known this
fairy tale, like all the children there.   She could
not remember it offhand, but after a few suggestive
remarks, she suddenly came out with the very quotation I had hoped she would recall: 'Wenn das Eure
Frau Mutter wuesst, das Herze wuerd ihr brechen. '
('If your mother could see this, it would break her
heart. ')

In "Fallada or the Goose-maid, " a princess travels
to a distant land to marry a prince, upon a faithful
horse that her mother gives her to guard her from
harm.   But the princess is captured and is made to
be a goose-maid.   Her horse is killed, his head
nailed upon the wall.   When the princess in her
state of subjugation passes the horse's head, it
speaks to her, in the words of the quotation which
my client's memory singled out.   The close similarity of the story and my client's approach to life
is evident.   She articulated the quotation under
strong emotional stress and immediately showed the
symptom of real insight, that is, she drew conclu-
sions and applied her new understanding spontaneously to her own situation.

The following is by a patient in a Veterans' Administration hospital at East Orange, New Jersey.   Mr. Thomas
Ruggerello had suffered a disabling accident of such drastic
proportions as to render him incapable of walking or performing any task involving his fingers.   He tells how he was
bored with TV, restless and irritable.   The days seemed
endless, yet he dreaded the arrival of night.   Then the hospital librarian used a projector and a roll of microfilm to
throw the image of book pages on the ceiling.   To flash the
next page in view, he had only to raise his hand a fraction
and let it fall on a button placed near it.   He began reading

in earnest. Time began to fly, and he spent less and less time brooding. The world and life itself began to interest him more. Through reading in this manner he learned to play chess and bridge. He gained a reasonable knowledge of accounting and law. The stock market was no longer a mystery, nor was insurance or banking. To use his own words, "I crawled back through history and jetted into the future. I was exposed to physiological man, psychological man, and philosophical man. I ran the gamut of man's experience and received in the process an appetite for more."[10]

As his arms grew stronger he was able to hold a book and could even turn the pages with the heel of his hand. It took longer to turn a page than to read it, but he felt that the joy of reading was well worth the effort. Newspapers and magazines were a special problem, but in time Mr. Ruggerello developed a method for gripping and holding the flexible paper by flexing his own wrists so that the thumb pressed against the index finger with enough force to withstand the weight of the paper.

The methods for handling his reading problems were not developed easily or quickly. They evolved, one small stage after another, over many months and even years. The salve to ease the torture of this process was the immense joy and deep satisfaction he gained from reading. When he finally could use a wheelchair he started haunting the library. He was fascinated by it, and says, "Just as some enjoy the fresh smell of a new car or the feel of its paint so I enjoy the smell of books and the feel of one in my hand."[10]

A woman was about to undergo surgery and her anxious husband and daughter stood by her bed wondering what to say. She was an avid reader and indicated to the librarian who had stopped by that she wanted to keep the stack of books she had chosen on the previous visit of the book cart. To break the awkward silence the librarian told the patient of a book by Carl Jung, The Undiscovered Self. "I'd like to read that, " the woman said, smiling when the librarian turned to the family with the remark, "It's a pleasure to have such a discriminating reader. "

They spoke of books for a minute and the tension seemed lessened. Here is a case where a mere discussion of books and their presence served as bibliotherapy. That stack of books was something of a symbol, a conviction that all would go well and the patient would return and read again.

Patients now and then ask for a book as they are being
wheeled out of their rooms to surgery, according to Pearl G.
Elliott, and sometimes an unfinished book is carefully left
open on a bedside table to be finished when the ordeal is
over--a symbol perhaps of the continuity of life. [11]

In St. Louis some years ago the public library cooperated with a neighboring public school by organizing a
special summer reading club for a group of children who had
done failing work in school because of various behavior problems.   Boy-crazy girls were led to read stories of wholesome
boy-girl relationships.   A girl who suffered from an inferiority complex due to a hare-lip was given stories of people
who had successfully adjusted themselves to various handicaps.
An orphan who had developed the defense mechanism of bel-
ligerency and sulleness to combat a feeling of "not belonging"
read of an orphan who did not go around with a chip on his
shoulder.   There were many other cases.   So successful was
this experiment in bibliotherapy that the children became
regular users of the library, and even after they had "graduated" from the children's library they continued to return to
visit their friend, the librarian.

Books may serve as a bridge between the world of
sickness, bewilderment and despair, and the world of nor-
malcy.   E. P. Moody, then a librarian in the Hospital and
Judd Fund Division of the Cleveland Public Library, relates
the case of a Polish girl, Anna, who was confined to a hospital because of a hip injury. [12]   However, she lay for months
on her bed, thin, quiet, and expressionless.   When he, as
the librarian, visited her each week she always shook her
head when a book was offered, even though some books were
in Polish.

Finally another patient left a book on her table and
Anna read it.   It was about pioneers who came to America
from Europe and the hardships they suffered.   The librarian,
noticing this, took her more books on the same subject, such
as My Antonia, O Pioneers, and Death Comes for the Arch-
bishop.

Anna asked what Nisei meant.   Was it a term of dis-
paragement like "Nigger," or "Polack."   Her intensity on
this question gave the librarian an inkling of her problem.
Anything Can Happen, by Helen and George Papashvily,
brought a smile from Anna the next time Mr. Moody came.
It was the first time she had shown any expression, and she

even discussed the humorous situations.

Anna then loosened up sufficiently to relate her own "greenhorn" experiences as a Polish immigrant at the age of seventeen and was able because of the Papashvily book to regard them for the first time as funny. The librarian discussed with her similar things that happen to Americans when they go to a strange country.

Anna then read in rapid succession Mama's Bank Account, Hyman Kaplan, and Sophie Halenczik, American. She liked them all and talked about them eagerly, revealing more hidden heartbreaks, bringing them out in the open to give her emotional release.

The next book prescribed by the librarian was one on Poland, with the many illustrations captioned in Polish. When a Polish priest visited her, Anna was delighted to be able to show him the book and talk about it. Her self-confidence had been built up to the point where, subsequent to her release from the hospital not long after this, she entered into a new life. A suitable job was found for her where she could live and work in the same place. Because of the permanence of her hip injury Anna was a shut-in. Books were taken to her each three weeks, both in English and Polish. She became happy, self-respecting and a living proof of the fact that "books can help; books have power; books can build a bridge."

The case of Anna is one in which medical personnel did no prescribing; there was no collaboration between doctor and librarian. The librarian had a problem case. With some initial help from another patient, he used bibliotherapy effectively with the non-medical or "art" technique.

Perrie Jones related the following cases in 1967:[13]

> A 20-year-old Marine wrote to Betty Smith about A Tree Grows in Brooklyn. 'I went through Hell in two years of combat overseas.... Here in sick bay I have read your Tree twice and am halfway through it again. Ever since the first time I struggled through knee-deep mud carrying a stretcher from which my buddy's life dripped away in precious blood and I was powerless to help him, I have felt hard and cynical against this world and sure that I was no longer capable of loving anything or anybody. I can't explain the emotional reaction that has now

taken place.... I only know that it happened. Your
story restored to me my faith.... I feel that maybe a fellow has a fighting chance in this world after
all.'

A frustrated, embittered man of 38, partially paralyzed and suffering from tuberculosis in the right
lung, had never been much of a reader. Hunting
and fishing were his loves. But when the librarian
gave him Terry McAdam's story of a paraplegic,
Very Much Alive, he did read it. 'This is the sort
of book all the aides and nurses should read, ' he
said. 'Then they would know how a fellow feels. I
loaned it to . . . .'

A severe accident resulted in paraplegia for a young
high school athlete. Despondent and discouraged,
he was taking no interest in his future. Then, with
the help of prismatic glasses he began to watch
television. Volunteers were found to read aloud to
him. A tutor directed his school work. A reading
table was devised so he could do his own reading.
He was graduated with his class.

A woman of 60 with cardiac complications read
A. C. Govan's Wings at My Window. Her comment
was, 'I liked the way the author built a new life for
herself and for her family--not because of a physical
handicap, but through it. '

'Books mean everything to me. ' Speaking was a
65-year-old ex-seaman, born in Sweden, whose stay
in a hospital was long drawn out. 'I can't understand people who don't read. Just see these two--
Bill Geagan's Nature I Loved, and Dan Cushman's
Stay Away Joe. ' With that he started to chuckle
over his memories of Joe.

Doctor's orders for a woman of 50 preparing for
heart surgery were: 'keep her occupied but quiet.'
She turned to reading about the out-of-doors and
natural history. 'These books give me a sense of
well being, ' she told the librarian. 'I feel so encouraged, so relaxed when I read of the small things
of nature. Peattie's A Cup of Sky is so warm and
gave me so much to hang on to, my surgery didn't
seem so terrifying. '

A Kentuckian of 51 with little schooling but a good
mind especially liked Janet Holt Giles's Hannah
Fowler, Clark McMeekin's The Kentucky Story,
and Jesse Stuart's Year of My Rebirth. Of the
last he said, 'I like this story because Jesse was
a mountain boy like me. We don't give up easy.
He licked this thing and I will, too. '

A 19-year-old with epilepsy profited from working
in the library as well as from his reading. He had
learned to use his seizures as an excuse for not
completing difficult assignments. Tense, ill at
ease, rigid, he found even casual conversation very
trying. At the hospital he continued his school
work but balked at the idea of reading a book--in
fact, boasted that he never had. After several
false starts he did finish one of Tunis's stories and
said he liked it. Then followed a series of easy-
to-read books and, although he did not develop into
an avid reader, he came to use the library quite
naturally. After surgery he seemed to be cured of
his seizures but the mannerisms, habits, and mental
blocks acquired during his illness remained. As
part of his rehabilitation therapy he was assigned
to work in the library two hours a day. The librarians were brought into the plan and asked to
help the patient overcome his fear of social situations, his tense way of talking to people, and his
tendency to give up on any task that was difficult
or boring. The doctors credited his reading and
his work in the library with speeding up his resocialization and final discharge. He had rejected
many ideas suggested by the psychologist or social
worker, yet when he encountered the same ideas on
the printed page he looked on them as a personal
discovery and eagerly tried them out. Every success increased his confidence. Two years later he
came back for more surgery and he was still reading: Fink's Release from Tension and For People
Under Pressure, Lennox's Science and Seizures,
Menninger's Human Mind.

An amputee of 42 met the librarian with 'It's about
time you got here. I haven't a darned thing to
read. The nurses brought me this (Alice Bretz's
I Begin Again). You can see how hard up I was--
to read a book by a woman. But say, that gal's

got guts! Maybe I can get used to being without a
leg. '

A man of 43 with arthritis asked, 'Can you get me
Adventures in Solitude by Ray Stannard Baker? I'm
getting ready for my seventh operation and I get
more help from that book than anything I have ever
read. '

A young woman of 21 with a farm background and
two years of high school lay on a rocking bed,
paralyzed as a result of poliomyelitis.   She was
apathetic, hostile, overwhelmed by her misfortune.
Gradually she became interested in fashion and home
magazines and tried the ceiling projector, using
books with photographs and cartoons.   It became a
game with her to operate the controls with her chin.
Then she read M. Daly's The Seventeenth Summer
on film and progressed slowly to simple biographies.
Then she tried a page-turner.   In no time she was
priding herself on her reading accomplishments.
Her attitude had changed completely.

A 30-year-old civil engineer who contracted tuberculosis was advised to change his occupation because
of his illness.   Through the library he developed an
interest in photography and with the cooperation of
the university, correspondence courses were arranged.   After 18 months he was discharged and
accepted an excellent position with an x-ray company.

Withdrawn patients, seemingly locked in their own
small world, can sometimes be reached through
books.   On a psychiatric ward a Lutheran minister
sat with head in hands.   All efforts to establish
contact with him so far had failed.   Knowing that he
probably had had a classical education, the librarian
picked Richard Halliburton's collegiate trek up and
down Mount Olympus from her much-too-meager
collection.   The pastor looked at it, broke into
tears, and poured out his story.   His only son, also
named Richard, also a classical scholar, had been
obliged to leave college and take a job with a section
gang to help pay his father's hospital expenses.   The
poor man's bottled-up feelings of disappointment,
guilt and frustration had unbalanced him.   After he

pulled himself together he took a simple Cape Cod story of homely wisdom called <u>Uncle William</u>, by Jennette Lee. That night he slept for the first time in a long while.

A big glowering lumberjack from the north woods plodded up and down the hospital corridor without a word to anyone. Everything in his new environment was strange to him, including the book cart. But a paperback Buffalo Bill story with a lurid cover caught his eye. It was something he had seen before. He stopped. For an instant he focused his attention on an object outside himself. He took the book and put it in his pocket. All rules of orthodox procedure went out the window. The book was neither cataloged nor charged to the borrower; the title and format were questionable. But this sick, confused man had found his first toe-hold for the long climb back.

Now and then poetry proves therapeutic. In Scandinavian hospitals books of poems are in great demand. In this country the writing as well as the reading of poetry in mental hospitals seems to bring marked relief to some patients. One--somewhat irritable and hard to interest, with tastes tending toward the morbid--was persuaded to read a book of verse. Following that he read most of the poetry in the library and then turned to writing it. Though he produced nothing of literary value, his efforts kept him occupied and changed the direction of his thinking. Another patient was unable to concentrate on anything for any length of time. He came to the library every day to read a short poem or two.

A discussion and reading hour on the theme of "Travel by Means of Poetry" captivated a farmer in the psychiatric ward. 'I've never been farther away from home than 50 miles, ' he said. 'I sure liked that one about the mountains. ' A hypomanic woman in the same group added, 'Just keep reading poetry. I'm so relaxed for the first time in days. '

For weeks an arthritic old woman refused even to look at the books on the cart, though she would take magazines. One day she spied a volume on gardening and needlework and from that time on she was

a steady customer.   When a reading group was
formed for patients on a metabolic balance study she
joined, attended regularly, and participated actively.
Several weeks later the librarian asked the group to
comment on the sessions and make suggestions.
This woman surprised everyone with a long statement extolling the library service and crediting it
with enlarging her world.

In another group a 24-year-old schizophrenic sometimes took his turn reading aloud but read poorly
and was ill at ease.   One day, at someone else's
request, the group read "A Psychologist Helps a
Youngster, " by T. S. Krawiec from The Wonderful
World of Books.   The article deals with help available to poor readers. In the ensuing discussion where
everybody opened up, the patient was able for the
first time to talk freely about his difficulties, admitting he had been afraid of reading since he was
in the lower grades.   As a result, word study became a regular part of the reading period and more
emphasis was placed on improving the reading of the
individual.

An eight-year-old who had sobbed out her grief over
the loss of a gangrenous foot wiped her eyes and
said briskly, 'But I can read if you'll get me a good
book!'   A wailing five-year-old responded to the im-
mortal Peter Rabbit.   He had to stop crying to hear
the story, and at the end he was relaxed enough to
sleep.

One ward of girls recovering from rheumatic fever
became tremendously enthusiastic over cookbooks.
They spent long afternoons discussing baking and
roasting and jelly-making among themselves and with
everybody on the staff.   Books on etiquette and 'how
to act with boys' were also popular, as was the
sizable collection of 'guides to dating. '

A 14-year-old boy who suffered from epileptic seizures had never read an entire book or visited a library until he came to the hospital, although he had
attended school for several years.   The hospital librarian and the teacher cooperated in steering him
through Meadowcroft's Benjamin Franklin, d'Aulaire's
Benjamin Franklin, Smith's William Bradford--Pil-

grim Boy, Foster's George Washington, Graham's
Christopher Columbus, Will James's Cowboy in the
Making, LeSueur's Little Brother of the Wilderness,
and others. His most exciting experience was discovering the encyclopedia. Obviously books had become part of his life.

One final incident. A very sick little girl of twelve
found what she needed in Just Plain Maggie, by
Lorraine Beim. She would not be parted from
Maggie, her new and true friend. Her last words
to the librarian as she went to surgery were,
'Please, don't take Maggie.'

In an article in Library Journal Sadie P. Delaney discussed five mental cases, a surgical case, and one general
ward case, arising out of her experience as librarian of the
Veterans' Administration Hospital at Tuskegee, Alabama:[14]

Surgical case. "This patient was obliged to lie in one
position for long periods and had the use of only one arm.
He was very discouraged about his condition and became a
chronic complainer. He was finally persuaded, by the librarian, to read books. He soon became interested in such
books as Ask Me Another, by Spafford and Esty, and Five
Thousand New Answers to Questions, by Haskin. Soon he
took delight in encouraging other patients who visited him.
He read all current magazines and The Negro in Our History,
by Woodson. He was gratified at being so popular and became optimistic and cheerful. He was given a book review
and is now among the best informed patients on his ward. He
is greatly improved and cooperative."

Mental case. "This man was uncommunicative; was
almost mute. It was difficult to have him respond, even to
questioning. He sat and stared blankly, dully. He was
brought to the library with the Bibliotherapy group each day.
He was given books of poetry to read. Later he began copying poems. Daily, poems were selected from his copies for
circulation to bed patients. He was given selected editorials
and essays to read at each Library Press Club meeting. This
gave him a chance to talk. Also he would read aloud to other
patients. Gradually, by reading aloud, he has become com-
municative for periods and it is felt that with continued treatment he may become normal."

Mental case. "This patient was deteriorated. He was

at last brought to the library with the Bibliotherapy group.
It was found that he had previously had some training in art.
He was given drawing ink and books with photographs of
artists.   He became calm and subdued and not only made re-
productions but steadily improved them greatly.   He improved
daily in drawing and reading.   He requested information on
all he was copying.   Later he was given oils and painted
pictures of Sir Galahad and Pushkin and Lord Byron.   He
prepared for an art exhibit held in the library annually. "

Mental case.   "This patient was paroled to the library.
He had a fair educational background.   An effort was made
to aid him in view of his weakness.   He became interested
in the clipping service and collected valuable articles on many
subjects.   He read extensively and attended the library daily.
After ground parole he continued his interest.   He read
Habits that Handicap, by Towns; He Can Who Thinks He Can
and Everybody Ahead, by Marden, along with biographies of
men who have succeeded.   He began to gain the confidence of
his associates.   He assisted his daughter in the preparation
of her valedictory for graduation, with material he read in
the library.   He improved rapidly and was discharged.   It
was reported that he has become a community leader and has
adjusted himself satisfactorily. "

Mental case.   "This patient was paroled to the library;
he was found to have had a splendid educational background,
but was apathetic and discouraged at first.   He soon began to
take interest in the library.   He improved gradually and became a zealous reader.   Finally he asked to be given some
library training.   He assisted in library desk work.   This
gave him great pride in his accomplishments.   His ward surgeon noticed his rapid improvement.   He participated in the
Library Debate Club, also the Press Club.   His interest in
books seemed to lead him to a new world.   Home difficulties
arose but his interest in books seemed to fortify him.   He
has been giving his entire day at the library and is an asset.
He is composed, interested in his personal appearance and
hopes to secure enough training to become an assistant in
some library. "

Mental case.   "This patient because of family difficulties had become bitter toward life and anti-socially inclined.   He had been a practicing physician.   He was given
parole to the library.   The librarian interested him in reading.   He first read A Fortune to Share and Let's Start Over
Again, by Young.   He used these books at the Library Press

Club meetings.   He soon found great interest in reading and
requested each time to review his books to the patient group.
He is so influential with the patients that he serves in an
official capacity with them.   He is now accountable and makes
excellent talks in the library to patient groups in their library
meetings, and in Saturday Debates, assisting in the selection
of reference material.   His entire personality has changed.
He sent book lists and reviews to his family and through this
interest a family adjustment has been brought about.   This
serves to extend new ways to him for his future.   He is
allowed time daily to study and soon hopes to be given trial
furlough to make plans to resume his practice. "

General Ward case.   "Wheel-chair case.   This patient
was a bed patient for a long period and then progressed to a
wheel chair.   His chronic condition made him despondent at
first.   He became interested in reading and read on the average of a book a day and kept abreast through many newspapers and magazines.   He soon began to give reviews of his
books to his ward mates and recommended to them the books
he had read.   This gave him such prestige with his associates
that he lost sight of his condition.   Although it seems that he
will always be incapacitated, he looks forward to being a
bookshop owner when discharged. "

"Thus the library has proven a factor in the Medical
Service of hospitals and is classed as an effective therapeutic
measure in the rehabilitation of all types of patients. "[14]

Eugene X was given a two-and-a-half-year treatment at
the Adelphi University Reading and Study Center.   He had been
institutionalized at age 7-1/2 at a state hospital at the request
of his parents.   The diagnosis was schizophrenia (childhood
type), and his behavior was marked by outbursts of violence
toward his younger sister.   He was the oldest of three children in a chaotic household with a history of mental illness in
the family.   The mother was often incapacitated by a series
of illnesses. [15]

After one year at the hospital Eugene was released,
with evident improvement in his behavior.   He was assigned
to the third grade in his neighborhood school.   At 7 he had
been tested on the Wechsler Intelligence Scale and his scores
fell within the dull normal limits.   He was functionally a non-
reader, although he had memorized some easy pre-primers
and was able to recognize certain words on sight.   Remedial
help was then started at the Center twice a week in 50-minute

sessions. At first he was taught with another child of like
reading difficulty, but he resented this child and was upset
and threatening.

Eugene seemed to fear involvement with words since
words might possibly convey his distortedly hostile feelings
and so become dangerous tools. He was now diagnosed as a
child having an "intense-passive-aggressive personality trait
disorder with a possible underlay of schizophrenia." There
was also a suggestion of organic impairment. He communicated with difficulty, had a blank look on his face, alternating
with stares at the therapist. Responses were monosyllabic,
and he often rocked in his chair. There was also frequent
flatulation.

He was taken off the paired instruction, put on soli-
tary. He could not retain words, made impulsive guesses
or blocked when asked to perform. Letters and symbols
seemed too loaded with emotional content for him to be able
to handle them properly. He needed to be reclaimed quickly
before withdrawal became a fixed pattern of response. Special indulgences and favors were necessary. He craved candy
and he chose stories to have read to him. Sometimes he
played with clay and building blocks. This routine was maintained until his anxiety decreased and he was able to gain
greater physical control. He began to anticipate events, contribute ideas, and become more involved in learning activities.
Simple matching picture word games were used and other
means of building up a minimal sight vocabulary. Oral reading was done informally with simple materials. He then progressed to pre-primers, then phonic elements. His progress
was rather uneven and slow but the change in his attitude was
dramatic. He would come charging into the room exclaim-
ing, "I'm here," and his face lost most of its previous fore-
boding stiffness. He was encouraged to finger-point at words
while reading. Words were written with a magic marker,
brushing glue and sugar coating on for a raised effect.

After one year another child was paired with Eugene
and was accepted, although at first Eugene was somewhat
cautious and fearful. They were taught individually but brought
together for other activities. Real growth was shown when
Eugene realized he could be successful even under competitive
circumstances. He began to block less and retain more. His
reading performance reflected an emerging sense of self
esteem. After 2-1/2 years of this instruction Eugene could
read with fluency and ease at the second grade level. A

continuing program was planned, including recreational reading.

Tested again for I. Q. at age 11 Eugene showed a gain of 22 points on the verbal scale, 20 points on performance, and 23 points on the full scale over his 7-year rating. He was not psychotic at the time his treatment ended and the case was recorded in print in 1965. He appeared to be making an adequate adjustment to his situation at home and at school. There was, in fact, marked improvement all around.

Notes

1. Kimball, Frank W. "Hope for Tired Minds." Hygeia, v. 24, December 1946, p. 906-907, 946.

2. Elliott, Pearl. "Bibliotherapy: Patients in Hospital and Sanitarium Situations." Illinois Libraries, v. 41, June 1959, p. 477-482.

3. Lucioli, Clara E. "Out of Isolation; The Patients' Library." Library Journal, v. 92, April 1, 1967, p. 1421-23.

4. Hannigan, Margaret. "Bibliotherapy: Its Part in Library Service." The Bookmark, v. 15, March 1956, p. 133.

5. Keneally, Katherine G. "Therapeutic Value of Books." In: Henne, F. and others. Youth, Communication, and Libraries, American Library Association, 1949, p. 74-75.

6. Ireland, G. O. "Bibliotherapy as an Aid in Treating Mental Cases." The Modern Hospital, v. XXXIV, June 1930, p. 91.

7. Delaney, Sadie P. "Bibliotherapy for Patients in Antabuse Clinic." Hospital Book Guide, v. 16, October 1955, p. 141-42.

8. Matthews, Ann. "Bibliotherapy Gives a New Lease on Life." Hospital Management, v. 95, January 1963, p. 56-57.

9. Lazarsfeld, Sofie. "The Use of Fiction in Psychotherapy." American Journal of Psychotherapy, v. 3, Jan-

uary 1949, p. 26-33.

10. Ruggerello, Thomas J. "The Feel of a Book." Wilson
     Library Bulletin, v. 35, January 1961, p. 38.

11. Elliott, Pearl G. "Bibliotherapy: Patients in Hospital
     and Sanitarium Situations." Illinois Libraries, v. 41,
     June 1959, p. 477-482.

12. Moody, E. P. "Books Bring Hope." Library Journal,
     v. 77, March 1, 1952, p. 387-392.

13. Jones, Perrie. "Hospital Library Service Makes a
     Difference." Minnesota Libraries, v. XXII, Winter
     1967, p. 91-94.

14. Delaney, Sadie P. "The Place of Bibliotherapy in a
     Hospital." Library Journal, v. 63, April 15, 1938,
     p. 307-308.

15. Aaronson, Shirley. "Changes in I. Q. and Reading Per-
     formance in a Disturbed Child." The Reading
     Teacher, v. 19, November 1965, p. 91-94.

APPENDIX A

BIBLIOGRAPHIES AND REVIEWS

Beatty, W. K. "A Historical Review of Bibliotherapy, " Library Trends, 11:106-117, October 1962.
One of the most comprehensive and current histories of bibliotherapy available. Highly documented with a 79-item bibliography.

Creglow, E. R. "Therapeutic Value of Properly Selected Reading Matter; with Bibliography, " Medical Bulletin of the Veterans Administration, 7:1086-1089, November 1931.
The author cites studies showing the effects of mental stress on the body, and patients' reasons for reading or using the library in a mental hospital to illustrate that "the right kind of book may be applied to a mental illness just as a definite drug is applied to some bodily need. " Bibliography on the relation of books and the mentally ill.

Dolan, Rosemary, (comp.). Bibliotherapy in Hospitals, 1900-1957. Medical and General Reference Library, Department of Medicine and Surgery, Veterans Administration, Washington 25, D. C. , 1957.
An extensive annotated bibliography of books and articles pertaining to the application of bibliotherapy in many types of hospital situations.

Dolan, Rosemary, (comp.). Bibliotherapy in Hospitals: An Annotated Bibliography, 1900-1961. Medical and General Reference Library, Department of Medicine and Surgery, Veterans Administration, Washington, D. C. , July 1962.
Essentially an updating of the earlier bibliography, Bibliotherapy in Hospitals, 1900-1957, with the addition of 67 items.

Kent, M. L. "The Psychological Effects of Reading; a Bib-

378 Bibliotherapy

liography, " Hospital Book Guide, 13:65-67, June 1952.
An annotated bibliography of articles and reviews on
bibliotherapy and hospital library work.

Kinney, M. M. "Bibliotherapy and the Librarian, " Special
Libraries, 37:175-180, July/August 1946.
An analysis of the relationship of bibliotherapy to the
librarian. Stresses the need for specialized training
in applied psychology, knowledge of conducting and
interpreting surveys, and establishment of standards,
if libraries are to practice real bibliotherapy. Bibliography included.

Laux, P. J. Bibliotherapy, The Public Librarian and "The
Worried Reader", (with an annotated bibliography).
Madison: University of Wisconsin Library School, 1952.
Review of aims and possibilities of bibliotherapy.
Particularly valuable for annotated bibliography on
bibliotherapy.

Peltier, M. and H. T. Yast. "Hospital Library Service--A
Selected Bibliography, " American Library Association
Bulletin, 55:347-349, April 1961.
A useful annotated bibliography of recent books and
articles dealing with hospital, medical, nursing
school, and patients' libraries.

Russell, D. H. and C. Shrodes. "Contributions of Research
in Bibliotherapy to the Language Arts Program I, "
School Review, 58:335-342, September 1950.
A brief description of and orientation to the field of
bibliotherapy. Includes a 73-item bibliography including much research.

Russell, D. H. and C. Shrodes. "Contributions of Research
in Bibliotherapy to the Language Arts Program II, "
School Review, 58:411-420, October 1950.
An extensive discussion of research cited in the
lengthy bibliography of the previous article by these
authors, "Contributions of Research in Bibliotherapy
to the Language Arts Program I, " School Review, 58:
335-342, September 1950. Suggestions for librarians
and teacher.

Schneck, J. M. , M. D. "A Bibliography on Bibliotherapy and
Hospital Library Activities, " Bulletin of the Medical
Library Association, 33:341-356, July 1945.

Bibliography of 350 items dealing with bibliotherapy.

Schneck, J. M., M. D. "Bibliotherapy and Hospital Library
   Activities for Neuropsychiatric patients; A Review of
   the Literature with Comments on Trends, " Psychiatry,
   8:207-228, May 1945.
      A review of the literature on bibliotherapy and hos-
      pital library activities for neuropsychiatric patients
      in which the material is divided into sections, and
      critically evaluated. Trends are indicated and sug-
      gestions are made in regard to future practice.

Schneck, J. M., M. D. "Bibliotherapy in Neuropsychiatry, "
   (In: Dunton, W. R., Jr., M. D., and Licht, Sidney,
   M. D., eds. Occupational Therapy, Principles and
   Practice. Springfield, Illinois: Thomas, 1950, pp. 197-
   223.)
      A historical review and discussion of author's own
      use of bibliotherapy as psychotherapy. 74 items
      bibliography.

Tews, R. M. (ed.). Library Trends. Urbana, Illinois:
   University of Illinois Graduate School of Library Service,
   Vol. 11, Number 2, October 1962.
      This entire issue is devoted to the topic of "Biblio-
      therapy. " Excellent articles by authorities in the
      field discuss the subject from many angles.

Young, P. "Rx Book and Bandages, " Catholic Library World,
   26:124-125, January 1955.
      A short annotated bibliography. Non-technical and
      useful for the newcomer to the field.

BIBLIOTHERAPY: GENERAL LITERATURE

Agnes Lucile, Sister. "Bibliotherapy: A Counseling Technique, " Catholic Library World, 18:147-149, February
   1947.
      The author discusses the technique to be followed in
      using books for counseling purposes. A valuable in-
      troduction to the use of books for therapy.

Burkett, R. R. "The Patient Approach, " Wilson Library
   Bulletin, 25:437-439, February 1951.
      Outlines the qualifications and qualities required of a
      hospital librarian in order to provide good bibliotherapy.

Coville, W. J. "Bibliotherapy: Some Practical Considera-
    tions, " Hospital Progress, 41:138, April 1960; 20, May
    1960.
        Defines bibliotherapy and traces its history and
        growth to the present, pointing out the increasing
        interest in this technique since 1961. States that
        the fact that 84% of the literature on bibliotherapy
        has been written by nonmedical authors and 62%
        appeared in non-library journals clearly indicates
        that the field of application is broadening. The author
        stresses the individuality of each patient's emotional
        status and thus of his reading needs. Points out the
        necessity for close cooperation between all profes-
        sions dealing with the patient, to assure the most
        valid assessment of needs.

Craigie, A. L. "Cheering Stimulus of Poetry in Veterans
    Bureau Hospitals, " Modern Hospital, 33:85-88, Novem-
    ber 1929.
        A discussion of the place of poetry in a Veteran's
        Hospital library. All types except free verse seemed
        to be enjoyed.

Dane, C. "Psychology in the Library, " Assistant Librarian,
    48:20-23, February 1955.
        Certain conclusions of two American authors (Gilbert
        Highet in The Art of Teaching, 1951, and W. H.
        Sheldon in Varieties of Temperament, 1942) regard-
        ing the relationship between physique and personality
        traits are applied to the choice of books for library
        users. Sheldon identified three main types although
        many people do not conform, and it is necessary for
        the librarian to recognize these types when choosing
        books for readers. The psychological motivations of
        the writing and reading of science-fiction are briefly
        considered. Bibliotherapy, although the cause of
        much controversy, is regarded as being of use for
        the normal as well as for the abnormal.

Darrin, R. (ed.). "Library as a Therapeutic Experience,"
    Medical Library Association Bulletin, 47:305-311, July
    1959.
        An overview of bibliotherapy procedures and tech-
        niques in the hospital. Discusses orientation of pa-
        tients to the library; ward libraries and reading
        rooms; reading aloud to groups; discussion groups;
        employment of patients in the library; special pa-

tients with language difficulties and physical handicaps; reader's guidance; and the use of volunteers in
a library.

DeLisle, M. M. (Sister M. Isabel). "You, the Nurse, and
I, the Hospital Librarian, " Catholic Library World, 13:
208-213, April 1942.
Written for the nurse, who often serves as an intermediary between patient and library. The suggestions are excellent for anyone striving towards
"good" bibliotherapy.

Dunkel, B. "Bibliotherapy and the Nurse, " Nursing World,
125:146-147, April 1951.
A hospital librarian presents bibliotherapy to nurses.
This excellent article is an admirable introduction
for all to the aims and goals of hospital library work
and bibliotherapy.

Elliott, P. G. "Bibliotherapy: Patients in Hospital and Sanitarium Situations, " Illinois Libraries, 41:477-482, June
1959.
Suggests techniques and cites cases in which children
were helped through books in a hospital setting.

Folz, Carolyn. "Pied Piper of the Modern Library, " Library Occurrent, 11:39-44, April/June 1933.
An excellent review of the values of hospital library
service managed through extension from the public
library. Specific references to titles; some recommendations are dated, although others are sound.

Hirsch, M. C. "Bibliotherapy; Some Aspects and Values and
Need for Research, " American Library Association
Hospital Book Guide, 17:111-115, June 1956.
Report of the seminar held at the VA Hospital,
Downey, Illinois, on February 2, 1956. The article
is in the form of questions put to Dr. Hirsch, followed by his candid answers. He distinguishes
sharply between merely keeping patients "busy" reading, and bibliotherapy. He suggests that librarians
be charged with the responsibility of administering
bibliotherapy with the prescription of the doctor in
charge. Nurses and aides are not equipped for this
work. Bibliotherapy must be individual not group
treatment and must be directed toward adjustment of
a specific mental or emotional condition. Dr. Hirsch

points out the difficulties inherent in attempting scientific research in the field, since there are so many
uncontrollable variables which may affect the results.
He suggests questionnaires to patients and case
studies as the most promising approach.

Hirsch, L., M. D.   "The Function of the Hospital Librarian:
    Service to Patients--Bibliotherapy, " Hospital Book Guide,
    13:95-102, October 1952.
        A psychiatrist discusses the types of personalities
    met in hospitals, and considers the value and utility
    of bibliotherapy.

Huntting, I.   "The Role of the Occupational Therapist as Re-
    lated to Bibliotherapy, " Library Trends, 11:207-216,
    October 1962.
        A discussion of the many ways in which occupational
    therapists and librarians or bibliotherapists augment
    and assist each other. A historical relationship of
    cooperation is shown and both groups are challenged
    to further professionalize their fields through addi-
    tional training and research.

Jackson, E. P.   "Bibliotherapy and Reading Guidance: A
    Tentative Approach to Theory, " Library Trends, 11:
    118-126, October 1962.
        A consideration in depth of the psychological bases
    of bibliotherapy. The author supports the interper-
    sonal theory of Harry Stack Sullivan as a promising
    context in which to consider the role of reading. She
    concludes that more research into the reading inter-
    ests of specific types of individuals is essential, and
    suggests greater emphasis on the role of biblio-
    therapy in librarianship at library schools.   Good
    bibliography.

Kinney, M. M.   "The Bibliotherapy Program: Requirements
    for Training, " Library Trends, 11:127-135, October
    1962.
        The author defines the scope and aims of biblio-
    therapy and discusses in detail the personal, educa-
    tion, psychological and philosophical qualifications
    viewed as essential for librarians entering this spe-
    cial field.   Schools of library science are urged to
    develop more suitable curricula to provide the train-
    ing needed by professional bibliotherapists.

Levine, M. , M. D. Psychotherapy in Medical Practice. New
    York: Macmillan, 1946. pp. 107-108: Bibliotherapy.
        The author suggests the use of bibliotherapy in gen-
        eral medical practice.

Lundeen, A. "Books and Rehabilitation, " Illinois Libraries,
    40:403-405, May 1958.
        A discussion of the broad field of rehabilitation,
        physical, mental, correctional, old age, and child-
        ren's homes. Discusses means of obtaining books
        and suggests ways for expanding and making library
        services more effective.

Moody, M. T. "Bibliotherapy: Modern Concept in General
    Hospitals and Other Institutions, " Library Trends, 11:
    147-158, October 1962.
        A survey of concepts and practices in the use of
        bibliotherapy in general hospitals; correctional insti-
        tutions; schools for mentally retarded; mental insti-
        tutions; children's hospitals; and T. B. sanatoriums.
        A useful overview with a 17 item bibliography.

Shrodes, C. "The Dynamics of Reading: Implications for
    Bibliotherapy, " Etc. , 18:21-33, 1961.
        A penetrating discussion of the psychological bases
        of bibliotherapy. Emphasizes identity, catharsis,
        and insight as major operant elements. Suggests a
        few cautions in the use of bibliotherapy.

Strode, J. Social Insight Through Short Stories. New York:
    Harper & Bros. , 1946.
        Designed for the adult reader, this book contains
        stories which are intended to increase awareness and
        understanding of human values and relationships.

Webb, C. G. , M. D. "The Prescription of Literature, "
    American Journal of Surgery, 12:155-163, April 1931.
        Discusses the physician's responsibility for prescrib-
        ing reading matter for the patient's mind as well as
        taking care of his sick body. Evaluation of literature
        appropriate to various states of illness with emphasis
        on individual need.

BIBLIOTHERAPY: RESEARCH

Bailey, M. "Candle of Understanding, " Education, 76:515-

521, May 1956.
  The author suggests that some writers have created
  confusion concerning the meaning and use of bibliotherapy. She pleads for simplicity and suggests two
  classroom methods: (1) incidental, when the child is
  left to seek and select books to meet his own needs;
  and (2) direct, when books are suggested or group
  discussion of specific books are utilized. She submits that the method is less important than the end
  result which is to relieve the child's insecurity
  whether it concerns relations with peers, family relatives, failures, physical factors, or economic problems.

Bottschalk, L. A. , M. D.   "Bibliotherapy as an Adjuvant in
  Psychotherapy, " American Journal of Psychiatry, 104:
  632-637, April 1948.
  Prescribed reading is shown as a useful tool in psychotherapy through case histories.   An excellent bibliography, although dated.

Clarke, E. K. , M. D.   "Books for the Convalescent, " Library Journal, 62:893-895, December 1, 1937.
  Seven guides to consider in recommending books for
  convalescents are discussed by Dr. Clarke, Director
  of the Psychiatric Division of the University of
  Rochester School of Medicine.   His remarks are based
  on personal experiences and observations as to the
  types of books which will "help create an emotional
  attitude of optimism" in the sick person and thus
  combat patient depression.

Delaney, S. P.   "Bibliotherapy in a Hospital, " Opportunity,
  February 1938.
  No bibliography is given as this is an article describing case histories in one Negro mental hospital.
  It is not related to the school or to normal emotional
  problems.   It describes specific programs for mentally ill people and how reading has helped these patients.   No list of criteria is given.

Ireland, G. O. , M. D.   "Bibliotherapy as an Aid in Treating
  Mental Cases, " Modern Hospital, 34:87-91, June 1930.
  A neuropsychiatrist in a Veterans hospital views
  bibliotherapy as a positive therapeutic measure and
  cites examples and case histories to illustrate.

BIBLIOTHERAPY: CHILDREN AND YOUTH

Bander, E. J. and F. W. Bander. "A Novel Approach to
  Juvenile Delinquency, " National Probation and Parole
  Association Journal, 1:25-30, July 1955.
    The authors discuss the role of fiction as a resource
    for social workers dealing with juvenile delinquents.
    They suggest and analyze a number of titles and in-
    dicate how they apply to each of several categories
    of problems. These include selections dealing with
    economic backgrounds, religious settings, problems
    of the broken home, racial relations, parental
    neglect, sexual immorality, etc. The authors chal-
    lenge the social worker to acquaint himself with at
    least the literature discussed so that he might sug-
    gest appropriate titles to parents and delinquents.

Beecher, W. "What to Use Instead of Moral Indignation, "
  Clearing House, 16:195-197, December 1941.
    In denouncing corporal punishment and humiliation as
    educational techniques, the author cites a hypothetical
    case of theft in the classroom in which the offender,
    rather than being punished, was helped to gain the
    acceptance which he sought by wrong behavior,
    through help in reading.

Bradley, C. and E. S. Boxquet. "Users of Books for Psychotherapy with Children, " American Journal of Ortho-
  psychiatry, 6:23-31, January 1936.
    The author, a psychiatrist, acknowledges that in
    dealing with problem children, selected reading ma-
    terial has proved to be a valuable adjunct to psy-
    chiatric treatment. In discussing the therapeutic uses
    of books he lists the following major values: (1)
    overcoming resistance; (2) developing interests; (3)
    providing informal schooling where the child is un-
    able to attend regular classes; and (4) supervised
    activity. A selected and categorized booklist is in-
    cluded.

Burton, D. "Books to Meet Students' Personal Needs, "
  English Journal, 36:469-473, November 1947.
    This article provides suggestions for dealing with
    emotional problems of students at the high school
    level. Ideas may also be adapted for use at other
    levels.

Clift, N. "My Topsies!" NEA Journal, April 1943.
Discusses the writing of autobiographies by problem
ninth grade students. Reading these aloud in the
classroom had a bibliotherapeutic effect and served
to close the chasm between problem children, teachers, and peers. Useful technique for junior and high
school levels.

Darling, R. L. "Mental Hygiene and Books; Bibliotherapy
as Used with Children and Adolescents, " Wilson Library
Bulletin, 32:293-296, December 1956.
Concerned with the use of books to help solve emotional problems of the emotionally disturbed by bringing a similar experience through books. Therapeutic
effect is explained in terms of identification, catharsis, and insight.

Dolch, E. T. "Books for the Hospitalized Child, " American
Journal of Nursing, 61:66-68, December 1961.
The author points out that books are as much a
source of information, entertainment, and security
for the pre-school child as the adult. She submits
that there is hardly a more effective way of gaining
the confidence of and relieving the physical and emotional discomfort of the hospitalized child than reading a charming or exciting picture book to him. She
discusses the psychology of the confined child and
indicates what types of books are best suited to meet
children's needs. General developmental characteristics of children are reviewed briefly and stressed
as essential considerations in book selection.

Emeruwa, L. "Bibliotherapy Via the Library Club, " School
Activities, 29:145, Jan. 1958.
The author defines the role of the junior high school
"Library Club" in helping children: (1) read better;
(2) develop good reading habits; and (3) solve personal problems. She suggests that the program be
the joint responsibility of the literature teacher,
guidance counselor, and librarian. "Directed" reading is seen as the best method of helping youngsters
develop emotional maturity.

Limper, H. K. "Public Library at Work with Children in
Hospitals and Institutions, " American Library Associa-
tion Bulletin, 55:329-331, April 1961.
"Words not only affect us temporarily, they change

us, they socialize or unsocialize us.... The child is
allowed to gird himself for the battle of life in a
small circle of light cast by his reading lamp or
candle. " The author, a special education teacher,
discusses children's needs and cites cases and books
used in dealing with exceptional children.

McGuinnes, A. E. "Reading Guidance in the Junior High
School, " Wilson Library Bulletin, 28:682-685, April
1954.
A librarian discusses the wide variety of reading
needs which must be met. The disabled and indifferent reader; the average reader of impoverished
background; the average but disinterested reader; the
high I. Q. advanced reader with narrow interests; the
good reader unable to differentiate the mediocre from
the excellent. She makes many suggestions of titles
to match personality and problem types and recommends humor and surprise as valuable means of
achieving the confidence of adolescents.

Mary Doloretta, Sister. "A Primary Teacher's View of Bibliotherapy, " Catholic School Journal, 54:39-41, February 1954.
The author defines bibliotherapy in the classroom as
"Guiding children away from bad principles and habits
and leading them on to adopt sound moral principles
of conduct through the correct and timely use of
books. " She states that this occurs in two ways:
(1) by identification; and (2) by seeing general principles of mind which the child can apply to his own
life. Three phases are distinguished: (1) establishment of rapport; (2) careful book selection; (3) following up and reinforcing behavioral adjustments.
She points out that the primary child has need of
material, emotional, and spiritual security, and in
attempting to satisfy them may become a behavior
problem. Major problems revolve around selfishness, fear, and anger. The teacher, by providing
or reading carefully chosen selections and stimulating
discussion, can solve many such problems. A useful list of classified titles is included.

Mary Jerome, Sister. "Retarded Children Can Enjoy Reading, " Catholic School Journal, 59:34-36, February 1959.
The basic needs of retarded children are in no way
different from those of normal children. All children,

bright or dull, dream of being safe, comfortable,
wise and of making achievements worthy of admira-
tion.   The retarded child frequently feels insecure,
and threatened!   He needs help in learning to read
and in the selection of reading material which will
provide reinforcement for feelings of self-respect and
self-confidence.   The author lists a number of series
which she feels appropriate.   She submits that with
the help of bibliotherapy, retarded children can
achieve their maximum potential.

Panken, J.   "Psychotherapeutic Value of Books in the Treatment and Prevention of Juvenile Delinquency," American
Journal of Psychotherapy, 1:71-86, January 1947.
This article gives the psychological reasons behind
juvenile delinquency.   It concludes that juveniles
helped by books show a low percentage of recidivism.
As the juveniles read prescribed books, they tend to
identify themselves with the upright hero and to lose
their bad traits.   This article lists the faults of bibliotherapy and tells of the types of children that cannot be helped or that require a specific type of help.
The article relates case histories.

Rivlin, H.   Educating for Adjustment.   New York: Appleton,
1936.
A general mental hygiene point of view.   Indicates
how the principles of mental hygiene can be applied
effectively in the classroom through the teacher's
attitude, school activities, and procedures without
involving her in the responsibilities and duties of the
trained psychiatrist.   Implications for bibliotherapy.

Steinmetz, N.   "Books and the Discipline Problem Boy,"
Library Journal, 55:814-815, October 15, 1930.
The author recounts successful experiences with bibliotherapy as worked with a special school for discipline problem boys.   She cites several cases in
which boys were assisted in making acceptable behavioral adjustments through reading specific books.
Two essentials noted were: (1) knowledge of the individual children; and (2) knowledge of many books.
By-products of the library program involved acceptance of responsibility for care of books, and development of school spirit.

BIBLIOTHERAPY IN GENERAL MEDICAL PRACTICE

Baatz, W. H. "Patients Library Services and Bibliotherapy," Wilson Library Bulletin, 35:378-379, January 1961.
A discussion of the many ways in which bibliotherapy may be applied in the hospital. Through professional library service, attempts are now being made to divert the patient from escape literature to books which will give him insight into his economic, social, vocational, and personal problems, particularly as they relate to his illness.

Hyatt, R. "Book Service in a General Hospital," Library Journal, 65:684-687, September 1, 1940.
Excellent and practical suggestions for relating books to hospital patients. Again this is from the standpoint of public library cooperation with local hospitals to provide service to patients.

Levine, M. Psychotherapy in Medical Practice. New York: Macmillan Co., 1942.
Recognizes bibliotherapy as an appropriate method of psychotherapy for use by general practitioners in suitable cases. Briefly discusses uses of this technique and lists a number of books felt to be appropriate for certain cases.

McFarland, J. H. "A Method of Bibliotherapy," American Journal of Occupational Therapy, 6:66-73, 95, March-April 1952.
This is a report on a method of bibliotherapy based upon a psychology of structure as "merchandising." Books, magazines, newspapers are structural objects. This means that they have certain psychological effects, which continue in different sizes, shapes, and colors. These arrangements have varying influences on patients. The author describes and illustrates with photographs an extensive array of techniques for presenting books to patients in ways which, though indirect, nevertheless elicit positive responses.

Mereness, D. "Bibliotherapy: Its Use in Nursing Therapy," Library Trends, 11:199-206, October 1962.
The author discusses the general reluctance of nurses to accept and apply the concept of bibliotherapy. She decries the lack of communication between nurses

and hospital librarians, and, although she recognizes
some of the basic reasons such as differences in
preparation, and varying roles in patient care, she
suggests that these need not be barriers. The author
feels that nurses generally need to recognize their
position as members of the therapeutic team and to
strive for mutual respect and cooperation in relations
with librarians. By this means, patient care can be
immeasurably improved.

Ruggerello, T. J. "The Feel of a Book, " Wilson Library
Bulletin, 35:380, January 1961.
The personal account of the rehabilitating effect of
reading by a man who had suffered a disabling accident which left him incapable of walking or of any
task involving the use of his fingers.

BIBLIOTHERAPY WITH THE MENTALLY ILL

Allen, E. B. , M. D. "Books Help Neuropsychiatric Patients,"
Library Journal, 71:1671-1675, December 1, 1946.
A psychiatrist describes his own "bibliotherapeutic
laboratory" and a few ways in which a science of
bibliotherapy may eventually develop. His remarks,
addressed to librarians, demonstrate attitudes and
approaches to use with mental patients, and stress
the idea that discrimination rather than prohibition
be the guide for selecting reading materials.

Brower, D. "Bibliotherapy, " (In: Brower, D. and L. E.
Abt, eds. Progress in Clinical Psychology II. New
York: Grune and Stratton, 1956, pp. 212-215)
The author deals with the effect that bibliotherapy
has on the mentally ill. He makes the point that the
value of the method depends on the type and degree
of mental illness found in the subject. The author
lists the areas in which the therapy is useful and also
the cases in which it is definitely harmful.

Bursinger, B. C. and S. Kenyon. "Neuropsychiatric Hospital Library, " Library Journal, 79:2153-2155, November 15, 1954.
In addition to the usual ward and book cart visits,
the librarians of a large VA psychiatric hospital
sponsor a book club, simple quizzes, a group therapy
session, slides and film strips.

Condell, L.   "Story Hour in a Neuropsychiatric Hospital;
      With List of Picture Books Used, " Library Journal,
      70:805-807, September 15, 1945.
          Describes successes in a neuropsychiatric hospital
      in getting withdrawn patients to focus their attention
      on something outside themselves through a weekly
      "story hour. " The project, supervised by librarians
      and carried on by an experienced volunteer, is seen
      as a valuable therapeutic technique with long term
      patients on an infirmary ward.

Delaney, S. P.   "Library Activities at Tuskegee, " Medical
      Bulletin of the Veterans Administration, 17:163-169,
      October 1940.
          Numerous library-sponsored projects in a mental
      hospital contribute to patient improvement.   Pro-
      grams, clubs, clipping service, discussion groups,
      etc. are discussed by a librarian who knows first-
      hand how Tuskegee patients have responded to them.

Ely, V.   "The Right Book for the Right Patient, " Wilson
      Library Bulletin, 29: 453-458, February 1955.
          The librarian of a Public Health Service neuropsy-
      chiatric hospital discusses the great part the library
      plays in rehabilitating the mentally-disturbed patients.

Flock, M.   "Use of Fiction or Drama in Psychotherapy and
      Social Education, " American Library Association Hos-
      pital and Institution Book Guide, 1:57-64, December
      1958.
          The author points out that while non-fiction has been
      used extensively in psychotherapy, therapists have
      tended to shy away from fiction. He suggests that
      this is due to the fact that fiction books have not
      been sufficiently analyzed, tagged, and worked up to
      be utilized as a specific for various conditions. This,
      he submits, needs to be done. Some major contri-
      butions to be achieved through the use of fiction are:
      (1) identification; (2) new experiences, (3) reactiva-
      tion of dormant ideas; (4) breaking down of resistance
      ("entering one's past by the back door"); (5) a cata-
      lyst in speeding up the process of therapy. The
      author warns that haphazard and unguided reading of
      fiction may be harmful. The article concludes with
      several illustrative cases in which the therapeutic
      use of fiction was successful.

Gagnon, S., M.D. "Is Reading Therapy?" Diseases of the
    Nervous System, 3:206-212, July 1942.
        An analysis is made of the reading of mental patients
        comparing them with public library readers. It
        shows an emphasis on fiction. No conclusions are
        drawn as to reading preference of mental case types.
        Quotations from patients regarding the hospital li-
        brary and its service indicate favorable attitudes
        toward bibliotherapy.

Hirsch, Lore, M.D. "Bibliotherapy with Neuropsychiatric Pa-
    tients, " (Individual and group therapy), Hospital Book
    Guide, 17:87-93, May; 111-117, June 1956.
        Many psychiatric patients prefer to discuss their
        reading rather than themselves. The therapist needs
        to be fairly well read in order to meet the patient
        comfortably. Dr. Hirsch does not ordinarily recom-
        mend specific books for therapeutic reading.

BIBLIOTHERAPY IN THE CORRECTIONAL INSTITUTION

American Library Association. Objectives and Standards for
    Libraries in Correctional Institutions. Chicago: Ameri-
    can Library Association, 1962. In: Association of Hos-
    pital and Institution Libraries Quarterly, Spring 1962,
    pp. 9-19.
        A comprehensive guide to the prison official and li-
        brarian who are striving to build a meaningful pro-
        gram. Clearly states the library's responsibility in
        the total rehabilitative process.

Barnes, H. E. and N. K. Teeters. New Horizons in Crim-
    inology, 3rd ed. Englewood-Cliffs, New Jersey: Pren-
    tice-Hall, Inc., 1959, pp. 194-195, 517-521.
        Discusses pernicious effects of crime comics upon
        children. Cites several research sources on the sub-
        ject. Cites many examples of literary contributions
        made by prison inmates provided with opportunities
        to read and write.

Floch, M. "Bibliotherapy and the Library, " The Bookmark,
    18:57-59, December 1958.
        The clinical psychologist of the Detroit House of Cor-
        rection, Plymouth, Michigan, discusses the impact
        and potential of specific books upon drug addicts. He
        points out that psychotherapy is basically nothing else

but personal influence exerted by one person on
another, and that books are substitutes for people.
The author envisions the day when correctional institutions will become genuine educational institutions in
which the librarian will play a key role by analyzing
and cataloging books for prescription by therapists.
An inspiring forward look.

Floch, M. and G. Casey. "The Library Goes to Prison, "
American Library Association Bulletin, 49:126-218,
March 1955.
Discusses the program of the Extension Department
of the Detroit Public Library in connection with the
Detroit House of Correction. The author points out
that most prisoners have an extraordinary interest
in themselves and their own mental processes ...
probably because they have been in the toils of various
social agencies since they were children. Inmates
are quoted: "We know that somewhere we have taken
a wrong turn, and we want books to help us understand where and why. " "Books can sometimes change
a man's life, especially his way of thinking. My incarceration and reading good books here have done
this for me. I have plans for a much better and
more wholesome life. " Good insight into value of
prison libraries.

Gray, W. "Reform Through Reading, " Library Journal, 85:
502-503, February 1, 1960.
The author describes a highly successful program of
adult education carried on at an Oklahoma penal institution. The format was similar to the "Great
Books Discussion Clubs. " The culmination of several
years' efforts on the part of the Oklahoma City Libraries was a public discussion group demonstration
by eight inmates. The author observed real rehabilitation. Of the participants he says, "They had
learned to stretch mentally with a good book and
found it as comfortable as stretching upon arising in
the morning. " Also observed was an improvement in
the general reading tastes and interests throughout
the institution.

SELECTED BOOKS FOR USE IN BIBLIOTHERAPY

American Association of Home Economics. Committee on

Home Economics in Education Through Libraries (comp.).
Books of Fiction Dealing With Home and Family Living.
Washington: American Association of Home Economics,
1948.
Useful for all ages--elementary and high school stu-
dents and adults.

Baker, L. "The Written Troubles of the Handicapped. " New
York State Education, 41:203-205, 1953.
Bibliotherapy is of proven value in the resolution of
problems of the handicapped, but reading material
should be selected with discrimination to help both
the patient and those around him. Books about specific illness should be recommended with discretion.

Broderick, D. M. "The Opportunities That Books Offer, "
Junior Libraries, 6:13-23, December 15, 1959.
An excellent annotated bibliography of literature suit-
able for hospitalized and handicapped children.

Cohoe, E. "Bibliotherapy for Handicapped Children. " N. E. A.
Journal, 49:34-36, May 1960.
Carefully chosen books are used with the handicapped
child to help him improve his attitude toward his handicap and to accept objectively the attitudes of others toward him. Undersized or oversized children as well as
those with speech defects, or unattractive facial features
may receive as much profit from guided reading as do
those with disabilities, such as deafness, blindness, or
a crippling condition. The author suggests that the alert
teacher will keep abreast of reviews of children's books
and accumulate a list of suitable stories. She includes
in the article a list of 12 annotations of fiction books and
two of biography, all of which deal with overcoming some
form of handicap. Grade levels range from 3 through 9.

Rein, D. M. S. Weir Mitchell as a Psychiatric Novelist.
New York: International Universities, 1952.
The fiction writings of the great neurologist were
analyzed for psychiatric content. Excellent background reading for gaining insight into types of mental disorders and possible reading suggestions for
patients.

Spangler, M. V. (ed.). A Basic Book Collection for Junior
High Schools. 3rd ed. Chicago: American Library
Association, 1960.

Compiled with assistance of consultants representing ALA; ASCD; NCTE; Department of Classroom Teachers of NEA; and National Science Teachers Association.

All of the foregoing items are taken from: Farrow, Vern L. "Bibliotherapy: An Annotated Bibliography, " Vol. XIX, No. 234, May, 1963 of Curriculum Bulletin published by the School of Education, University of Oregon, Eugene, Oregon, edited by Hugh B. Wood.   Copies of the complete biography can be obtained from Oregon ASCD, Box 421, Salem, Oregon for $3. 30.   This is an excellent annotated bibliography grouped by topics, 33 pages, but of course includes no items beyond 1963.

APPENDIX B

OTHER BIBLIOGRAPHIES

Bibliotherapy in Hospitals--An Annotated Bibliography 1900-1961. Medical and General Reference Library. Department of Medicine and Surgery. Veterans' Administration, Washington, D. C. , 1961.

Busby, D. R. , comp. "New Horizons. Readable Books about the Physically Handicapped Adults and Young People. 1953-1956. " Hospital Book Guide, 17:188-192, November 1956.

Crowley, Linda. Bibliotherapy: An Annotated Booklist for Use in a Program of Bibliotherapy in the Elementary School. Master's thesis, Oregon School of Education, Eugene, Oregon, 1965.

DeLisle, M. M. (Sister M. Isabel). Analysis of Some of the Problems of Book Selection for the Catholic Hospital Library, with a Classified and Annotated Bibliography. Master's thesis, Catholic University of America, 1950. 126p.
    A valuable contribution to both bibliotherapy and hospital library administration. The author's presentation of the qualities and qualifications necessary for a good hospital librarian is excellent.

Farrow, Vern L. Bibliotherapy: An Annotated Bibliography. University of Oregon School of Education, Eugene, Oregon, 1963.

Flandorf, Vera S. "Books to Help Children Adjust to a Hospital Situation. An 89-item bibliography with a one-sentence annotation for each. " Reprinted from Hospital Book Guide, February, 1956 issue, in The Bookmark, New York State Library, March 1957, p. 140-143.

Grannis, Florence. Books for Mental Health--A Bibliography

for Bibliotherapy. Master's thesis, University of Southern California, 1957.

Hendrix, Margaret M.   Fiction Books that Deal with Children's Problems.   Oregon State Library, Salem, Oregon,
1970.

International Reading Association.   Bibliotherapy: An Annotated Bibliography.   International Reading Association
Annotated Bibliography Series no. 16.

Johrden, J. A.   Bibliotherapy for Children: A Selective,
Annotated Bibliography, 1950-1962.   Master's thesis,
Catholic University of America, 1964, 34p.

Junier, Artemisia Jones.   A Subject Index to the Literature
of Bibliotherapy, 1900-1958.   Master's thesis, Atlanta
University, 1959.

Kraus, Eileen, comp.   "Bibliotherapy for Beginners in Hospital Library Work."   AHIL Quarterly, 2:10-12, Winter,
1962.   A short, annotated reading list prepared by the
Chief Librarian, Veterans' Administration Hospital,
Montrose, New York.

Macrum, A. M.   "Hospital Libraries for Patients--A Bibliography."   Library Journal, 58:78-81, January 15, 1933.
Bibliography of 187 references with a few annotations;
includes both bibliotherapy and hospital library administration.

Miles, N. M., comp.   "Professional Reading for Library
Staff and Volunteers in Hospital and Institution Libraries."
Hospital and Institution Book Guide, 2:146-149, March,
1960.
A short annotated bibliography.   Books which did not
recognize the value of reading as therapy were excluded.   Miss Miles, a professional librarian, serves
as a hospital library volunteer, and the list is somewhat oriented toward volunteers.

Nieman, D. E.   "Reading Aids for the Handicapped."   Rehabilitation Literature, 20:330-334, November 1959.
A selective, annotated list of reading aids for the
handicapped.

Selected List of Periodicals that Publish Articles Concerning

the Handicapped.   National Easter Seal Society for
Crippled Children and Adults, 1972.

Selection of Recent Books about Handicapped Persons.   A
    Checklist of Popular Fiction and Biography in the Li-
    brary, Rev. ed.   National Society for Crippled Children
    and Adults, Chicago, Ill. , 1970, 20p.

Smithson, H. E.   Bibliotherapy Reference Guide.   Detroit:
    We, The Handicapped, Inc. , 1956, 75p.
        An annotated bibliography of books dealing with
        physical disability, fictional and non-fictional, classi-
        fied by disability.   (Reviewed in Physical Therapy
        Review, 37:765, November, 1957)

Stein, E. A.   Bibliotherapy; a Discussion of the Literature
    and an Annotated Bibliography for the Librarian.
    Master's thesis.   Western Reserve University, 1950,
    53p.   Contains 109 references from 1950-1949.

We Call it Bibliotherapy.   An Annotated Bibliography on Bib-
    liotherapy and the Adult Hospitalized Patient, 1900-1966.
    Medical and General Reference Library, Department of
    Medicine and Surgery, Veterans' Administration, Wash-
    ington, D. C. , 1967.

Young, Paula. "Rx Book and Bandages. "   Catholic Library
    World, 26:124-125, January 1955.
        A short annotated bibliography for the newcomer to
        the field.

A recent and very fine bibliography is contained in the Fall
1973 issue of News Notes of California Libraries, pages 380-
422.   It is divided into two sections, one compiled in 1972,
one issued in 1973, and is classified by subject: e. g. Adolescence, Alcoholism, Amorality, Anger, etc.   One-line descriptions summarize the content.   These bibliographies were
prepared under an LSCA grant (1972) for use in bibliotherapy
sessions at Agnews State Hospital for the Mentally Ill.   After
the closing of the hospital to the mentally ill in June, 1972,
the bibliotherapy program was transferred to the community
of San Jose, California, and administered by the Santa Clara
County Library.   The bibliographies in question were prepared by Clara Lack, librarian-bibliotherapist, and Bruce
Bettencourt, bibliotherapist, Santa Clara County Free Library.

Adelphi University Reading and
Study Center 373
Aged, bibliotherapy with 254-
255
Agnews State Hospital, San Jose,
Ca. 239
Group therapy in 47-49
Two-year program of biblio-
therapy 281
Alcoholism, treatment by bib-
liotherapy 20
Alexander, Ross H. 46-47, 347
Allen, Dr. E. B. 31
Al-Salman, Janie 339-340, 344
Alston, Dr. Edwin F. 35
American Association of Retired
Persons (AARP) 144
American Heritage Discussion
Group 43
American Library Association
Meeting in Chicago, 1912
25, 120
Preconference program on
bibliotherapy, 1964 284
Promoting interest in biblio-
therapy 349
American Psychiatric Association
42, 306
American Society of Group Psy-
chotherapy and Psycho-
drama 306
Anne Arundel County Library
(Maryland) 305
Antabuse Clinic, Tuskegee, Ala-
bama 125-127
Antabuse Clinic Bibliotherapy
Hour 357, 358
Aphasia, bibliotherapy for 55-
56
Army libraries, First World
War 25
"Art" of bibliotherapy, require-
ments for 10

Art therapy 191-192, 342
Audio-visual materials, use in
bibliotherapy 145-146
Aureon Institute (New York
City) 306

Ball, Dr. Ralph 23
Balow, Bruce 159
Berry, Janis 348
Bettencourt, Bruce 239
Bibliocounseling see Biblio-
therapy
Bibliographies 24, 25, 61-63,
64-91, 132-133, 134-139,
174-177, 177-179, 215-
224, 257-279, 353-398
Biblioprophylaxis 9
Bibliotherapists, advertisement
for 19
Do's and don'ts for 101-105
Duties of 295-296
Personal qualifications for
281-283, 286-287
Training for 243, 283-286,
288-289
Bibliotherapy Committee, Ameri-
can Library Association
18-19, 21, 24
Bigaj, James J. 203
Binger, Dr. Karl 334
Blackshear, Orilla T. 20,
225-227
Blake, Joseph 180
Blanton, Dr. Smiley 306
Bledsoe, E. P. 29
Blind, bibliotherapy with 246-
247
Bogard, Dr. Howard M. 36
Book reports see Telling
about books
Book selection for bibliotherapy,
principles of 14, 188-190
Brain-damaged patients 51-